NATURAL SCIENCES IN AMERICA

NATURAL SCIENCES IN AMERICA

Advisory Editor
KEIR B. STERLING

THE

ANTELOPE AND DEER

OF

AMERICA.

BY

JOHN DEAN CATON

ARNO PRESS
A New York Times Company
New York, N. Y. • 1974

Reprint Edition 1974 by Arno Press Inc.

Reprinted from a copy in the Pennsylvania
  State Library

NATURAL SCIENCES IN AMERICA
ISBN for complete set: 0-405-05700-8
See last pages of this volume for titles.

Manufactured in the United States of America

————◆————

Library of Congress Cataloging in Publication Data

Caton, John Dean, 1812-1895.
    The antelope and deer of America.

    (Natural sciences in America)
    Reprint of the 1877 ed. published by Hurd and
Houghton, New York.
    1. Deer--North America. 2. Pronghorn antelope.
3. Mammals--North America. I. Title. II. Series.
QL737.U55C35 1974   599'.7357   73-17806
ISBN 0-405-05723-7

THE

ANTELOPE AND DEER

OF

AMERICA.

Yours truly

J D Caton

THE

ANTELOPE AND DEER

OF

AMERICA.

A COMPREHENSIVE SCIENTIFIC TREATISE UPON THE NATURAL
HISTORY, INCLUDING THE CHARACTERISTICS, HABITS,
AFFINITIES, AND CAPACITY FOR DOMES-
TICATION OF THE

ANTILOCAPRA AND CERVIDÆ OF NORTH AMERICA.

BY

JOHN DEAN CATON, LL.D.

NEW YORK:
PUBLISHED BY HURD AND HOUGHTON.
BOSTON: H. O. HOUGHTON AND COMPANY.
Cambridge: The Riverside Press.
1877.

RIVERSIDE, CAMBRIDGE:
PRINTED BY H. O. HOUGHTON AND COMPANY.

PREFACE.

THE natural history of those animals, the pursuit of which has always been with me a favorite recreation, has occupied my leisure for many years. He who would enjoy the full measure of field sports must have a good knowledge of the natural history of the objects of his pursuit, and the more complete that knowledge the more complete will be his enjoyment.

For many years I have kept in domestication the American Antelope and all of the American deer of which I treat, except the Moose and the two species of Caribou or American Reindeer. This has given me opportunities for making observations of them, which I could not make in their wild state, and a habit of noting my observations has accumulated a vast amount of facts which those quite competent to judge deemed of scientific value, and so was I induced to attempt to put them in a form which would make them available to others. This I undertook some years since, but soon discovered that I should never complete the work to my own satisfaction, for new observations constantly demanded additions or changes in what I had thought finished, and so might I continue for years to come. I have, however, taken the advice of a scientific friend to no longer delay in the vain hope of attaining completeness, conscious that much remains to be discovered relating to the objects of my study, and that many of my conclusions may require modifications.

I make no attempt to exhaust the natural history of even the few animals of which I treat, but content myself with a mere monograph of them, leaving their osteology and anatomy almost entirely for other and more competent hands, invading their province only so far as was necessary to give completeness to the externals of the animals studied. In a utilitarian view the branch which I have examined may be of the most interest, but for strictly scientific research the others are not less important, for all must be exhausted before the natural history of an animal is understood.

If I have been more minute in describing the characteristics of my animals than those who have gone before me, it is because it has been possible for me to do so, by limiting my inquiries to a few species, while others have embraced in their investigations the whole or a large portion of the animal kingdom, and could give to each species but a very limited space, and so must confine themselves to a few facts deemed the most important, necessarily omitting others, which when properly understood may prove of the greatest scientific value. Without facts we can have no scientific knowledge, and the more facts we have the better are we qualified to form correct conclusions. My aim has been to carefully observe facts and to accurately state them, and so truly exhibit nature and her workings. If I have stated many facts which others have not observed or deemed worthy of note, I have omitted many observations for fear of prolixity.

It is not to be denied that zoölogy, especially when treating of the larger animals, man alone excepted, has been the subject of less careful study than many if not most of the other natural sciences. From the great extent of the field it is impossible for any one man to originally explore the whole, or any considerable part of it, except in the most general way, and so it has been impossible for any of our great naturalists to descend to that minuteness in their investigations which characterizes the students of some other branches of science. Let us admire the painstaking archæologist who overlooks nothing which can throw a ray of light upon the subject of his inquiry. A chip from a flint implement; an impress upon a piece of pottery; a hole in a pebble; a scratch on a fragment of bone, — all are noticed, recorded, pondered, and compared with others brought perhaps from a distant part of the world, until that which was dark and unmeaning now becomes light and instructive. So it is that by patience and perseverance the student learns how to observe those letters of antiquity, and to comprehend their value and significance, and to combine them into words and sentences and discourses, while others who have not thus trained themselves, can see nothing but chips and fragments and scratches.

The geologist, too, is patiently learning the language of the rocks and the drift, written long ages ago, which can alone be interpreted by comparing fact with fact, each of which, when well authenticated, is a new word in this new language, in which nature tells the story of what once was and the changes she has wrought in bringing her works to their present state. So must the lessons of all the sciences be studied before they can meet the demand for knowledge made by the advancing standard set up by the inquiring mind of this our day, which we may well anticipate, will be greatly elevated in the immediate future.

If zoölogy is among the oldest of the natural sciences it is among the lowest in its standard of fullness and exact observations, and yet without these we can never hope to arrive at correct conclusions. In this work, by confining myself to a few objects, I have thought it possible to go beyond my predecessors in the accumulation of facts, hoping that others may take up other divisions of the subject and treat them so thoroughly as to leave nothing to be desired, till at last the whole subject will be so wrought in detail that the generalizer will find in his hands abundant material for his part of the work. His great want now is well attested facts. These I have attempted to give without adornment as to the animals treated of. In preparing my illustrations, I have tried to make them true to nature, regardless of the question whether they were ornamental pictures or not. In the full figures I have as far as possible drawn from photographs, taken when the animals were standing at ease, believing that in this way I could give a truer idea of them than if they were made to assume striking and unusual attitudes, which might be more attractive to the eye. If my animals differ in position and appear less elegant in form than the same animals are generally represented in books and in paintings, I can only say that mine are as near to nature as I could represent them, without any attempt to improve upon what nature has actually done, for so I thought I could be most truthful and most instructive.

I must here acknowledge my indebtedness to many friends for encouragement and assistance in the preparation of this work, some of whose names will be found in the text.

OTTAWA, ILL., *March,* 1877.

CONTENTS.

ILLUSTRATIONS.

———

THE ANTELOPE OF AMERICA.

CLASSIFICATION.

ACCORDING to the arrangement of Cuvier the Eighth Order of Mammalia is the

RUMINANTIA

These are all distinguished by two peculiar and invariable characteristics : —

First. They have no incisors in the upper jaw, and

Second. They all re-masticate their food.

Other peculiarities, not observed in the other orders of the mammalia, are found in a part of the Ruminantia; by which these may be separated into divisions or classes; to some of which, naturalists have already given appropriate and convenient names; but as we study them and better understand their peculiarities, we feel constrained to make changes in these classifications by enlargement, diminution, or transposition.

This order may, with propriety, be separated into two important groups : —

First. Those which have horns or their equivalent, antlers ; and

Second. Those which are without these appendages.

The first of these may be represented by the ox, the antelope, the goat, the sheep, the elk, and the like ; while the second embraces the camel, the llama, the musks, some of the chevrotians, etc.

As we study them still more we feel constrained to further classify the first group into divisions, as follows : —

First. Those which have hollow horns, all of which are epidermal emanations ; and

2

Second. Those which have solid horns, or more properly, antlers, which are osseous in their structure and are provided with a *periosteum.*

Still we find such important differences among those which compose each of these divisions, that we are not satisfied till we further subdivide them into classes : the first division of this group into

1. Those which have hollow and persistent horns ; and

2. Those which have hollow and deciduous horns.

All the hollow horned ruminants have persistent horns, and so are of the first class; except the American antelope (*Antilocapra Americana*) which has a hollow·horn, which is shed and reproduced annually, and so is the sole representative of the second class. Then, again, those which have solid horns or antlers also require a further classification : —

1. Those which have solid and deciduous antlers, which embraces all the solid horned ruminants except

2. The giraffe, or camelopard, which alone has a persistent solid horn.

EIGHTH ORDER.

SECOND GROUP OF THE EIGHTH ORDER.	FIRST GROUP OF THE EIGHTH ORDER.			
	Second Division of the First Group of the Eighth Order.		First Division of the First Group of the Eighth Order.	
	Second Class of the Second Division of the First Group of the Eighth Order.	The First Class of the Second Division of the First Group of the Eighth Order.	Second Class of the First Division of the First Group of the Eighth Order.	First Class of the First Division of the First Group of the Eighth Order.
Camel and Llama, Musks, etc.	Giraffe.	Elk, Reindeer, etc.	Prong Buck, or American Antelope.	Ox, Goat, Sheep, Antelope, etc.

If, however, we look to the feet as a means of classifying the ruminants, we should be obliged to make important changes in this arrangement, for we find that those which have hollow persistent horns, and those which have solid deciduous horns, or antlers, as well as the musks, which have no horns — all have feet alike, with four hoofs or toes to each foot, two in front, which are active and useful, and two small posterior hoofs quite above the others, which seem to be comparatively useless. Then we find the camel and the llama have feet quite different from the others; while the American antelope, which alone has the hollow deciduous horn, and the giraffe, which alone has the solid persistent horn, have but two toes to each foot, being entirely deprived of the small posterior hoofs, yet having the cloven anterior hoofs, like the ox and the stag.

We may go further into the anatomical structures of the different Ruminantia, and find it convenient to change and interchange these classifications, till at last we despair of arranging them into groups, divisions, and classes entirely satisfactory.

When we descend from these general classifications, and proceed to the formation of genera, species, and varieties, the naturalist meets with difficulties in the expression of general laws whose application will lead him at all times to satisfactory results. Hence it is that we often find students of nature disagreeing as to the generic or specific disposition to be made of certain individuals; sometimes because of the development of previously unobserved characteristics, and sometimes because of the greater or less importance attached to certain or peculiar indicia.

To meet these many disagreements, and to make certain that which would be otherwise uncertain, the student of zoölogy is driven to the use of synonyms which in some cases are almost as numerous as the authors who have treated originally of the different subjects.

It is manifest, then, that I cannot hope to agree either in my generic or specific assignments, with all who have gone before me, for they do not agree among themselves; but, beyond this, the discovery of new facts will sometimes compel me to make new assignments, or to disregard old ones, in obedience to well recognized and established laws.

I shall first treat of the Prong Buck or American Antelope, which, in the arrangement suggested, fills, so far as is now known, the Second Class of the First Division, of the First Group of the Eighth Order, or Ruminantia. This animal possesses extraordinary characteristics, some of which were not supposed to exist in the animal economy, previous to its discovery,

or even for half a century later, and when discovered and announced, were discredited, as being at variance with what were
considered well established zoölogical laws.   These peculiarities
will be fully considered as we proceed.

Adult Antelope.

Kid Antelope.

ANTILOCAPRA AMERICANA, Ord.

American Antelope : Prong Buck.

Antilocapra Americana. . . . . Ord., Jour. de Phys., 80, 1818.
J. E. Gray, Knowsley Menag-
erie, 1850.
Aud. & Bach., N. Am. Quad.,
II. 193, 1851, pl. lxxvii.
Baird, U. S. Pat. Off. Agrl.
Rep., 1852, pl.
Baird, Pacific R. R. Rep.,
VIII. 666, 1857.
Harlan, Fauna, 250.

Antilope Americana. . . . . . Ord., Guth. Geog., 1815.
Harlan, F. Am., 250, 1825.
Doughty, Cab. N. H., 49, 1833.
Maximilian, Reise in das innere
Nord-Am., I. 403, 1839.

Antilope. . . . . Lewis & Clark, Expedition
by Paul Allen, I. 94 et seq.
1804.

Antilope furcifer. . . . . . . Ham. Smith, Lin. Trans., XIII.
28, 1822.
Desmarest, Mamm., II. 479,
1822.
Richardson, F. B. A., II. 261.
Fig. 1829.
Giebel, Zoölogie; Säugt., 305,
1855.

Antilope (Dicranoceros) furcifer. Ham. Smith, Griff. Cuv., V.
323.
Wagner, Sup., IV. 403.

Antilocapra furcifer. . . . . . Desmarest, Mamm., II. 479.
Antilope palmata. . . . . . . Smith, Trans. Linn. S. Lond.,
XIII., 28, Fig.
Ibid., Griff. Cuv., IV. 323.
Desmarest, Mamm., II. 479.
Wagner, Schreb. Säugt., V., I.,
1250.
Ogilby, Pr. Zoöl. Soc. Lond.,
IV. 124, 1836.

Antilope (Dicranoceros) palmata.   HAM. SMITH, Griff. Cuv., V.
                                      323, 1827.
Antilope anteflexa. . . . . . .   GRAY, Pr. Zoöl. Soc. Lond.
Cervius hamatus. . . . . . .   BLAINVILLE, Bull. Soc. Philo-
                                      mat., 73, 1816.
Dicranoceros furcifer. . . . .   SUNDEVALL., Kong. Sv.Vetensk-
                                      Handl., 1844.
                                      IBID. Horns. Archv. Skand,
                                      Beit., II. 268, 1850.
Dicranoceros Americanus . . .   TURNER, Pr. Zoöl. Soc. Lond.,
                                      XVIII. 174, 1850.
Teuthlalmacame. . . . . . .   HERNANDEZ, Nov. Hisp., 324,
                                      325, pl. 1651. (Richardson.)
Cabree. . . . .   GOSS, Journ., 49, 111.
                                      CANADIAN VOYAGERS. (Rich-
                                      ardson.)
Cervus bifurcatus. . . . . . .   RAFINESQUE. (Richardson.)
Apistochickoshish. . . . . . .   UMFREVILLE, Hud. Bay, 165,
                                      1790. (Richardson.)
Prong-horn Antelope. . . . . .   SMITH, Griff. An. Kingd., IV.
                                      170. Fig.
                                      GODMAN, Nat. Hist., II. 321.
                                      Fig.
                                      BAIRD, Pacific R. R. Rep., VIII.
                                      666.
Prong-buck. . . . .   BARTLETT, Pr. Zoöl. Soc. Lond.,
                                      1865.
                                      CATON, Trans. Ott. Acad. Nat.
                                      Sci., 8, 1868.

SIZE less than Virginia deer ; form robust ; body short ; neck short,
flexible, and erect ; head large and elevated.   Horns hollow and deciduous, with a short, triangular, anterior process about midway their length,
compressed laterally below the snag and round above.   Horns situate
on the super-orbital arches.   Tail short ; legs rather short, slim, and
straight.   Hoofs bifid, small, pointed, convex on top, and concave on
sides.

No cutaneous gland or tuft of hairs on outside of hind leg or inside of
hock.   No lachrymal sinus or gland below the eye.   Mucous membrane
very black ; lips covered with short, white hairs, with a black, dividing,
naked line in front of upper lip, extending from the mouth to, and surrounding both nostrils.   Face brownish black, with sometimes reddish
hairs upon it.   Top of head above the eyes white ; cheeks and under
side of head white.   Ears white, with dark line around the edges, — most
pronounced on front edges ; a brown black patch under each ear.   Horns

black, with yellowish white tips. Top and sides of neck, the back and upper half of sides, russet yellow; below this, white, except usually three bands of russet yellow, beneath the neck. White extending up from the inguinal region involving the posteriors, uniting with a white patch on the rump. Tail white, with a few tawny hairs on top. There is an interdigital gland on each foot, a cutaneous gland under each ear, another over each prominence of the *ischium*, another behind each hock, and one on the back, at the anterior edge of the white patch; in all eleven.

While the description already given of this interesting animal may enable the naturalist to distinguish it from all other quadrupeds, it by no means explains its natural history, nor does it give even a synopsis of it. To do this, we must descend to greater particularities.

HABITAT.

The native range of the Prong Buck is comparatively limited. It is not only confined to North America, but to the temperate region of the western part of this portion of the continent.

We have no account or evidence that the Prong Buck was ever an inhabitant east of the Mississippi River, and it only reached that river in the higher latitudes. It is now found only west of the Missouri River. Westward, it originally inhabited all the region to the Pacific Ocean, within the present limits of the United States, except the wooded districts and high mountain ranges. It was very abundant in California, twenty-five years ago. My information is full that they were equally numerous throughout all the valleys and open country of that State. They were by no means uncommon in the open portions of Oregon. They are very scarce, if any exist in that State now; and California is at this time almost entirely deserted by them. Their native range extends from the tropics to the fifty-fourth degree of north latitude. Within the described limits, they do not invade the timbered country, or the high naked mountains. Their favorite haunts are the naked plains or barren rolling country. If they endure scattering trees in a park-like region, or scanty shrubs, forests possess such terrors for them that these animals avoid them at any sacrifice.

They appear to endure the presence of civilization in the eastern and southern districts of the range better than in the northern and western; although a quarter of a century ago they were more abundant in the open country on the Pacific coast than in any other locality, — a region which they have now quite deserted.

ITS DISCOVERY.

This animal differs, in many important particulars, from all other ruminants. It has been long known to the hunters and trappers, but the scientific world is indebted to Lewis and Clark for the first accurate information concerning it; not from the description of it which they give, for they do not pretend to describe it, and only speak of a few of its peculiar habits; but rather from the specimen which they brought with them. They sometimes speak of it under the name of goat. Richardson's description is the most satisfactory up to his time. Audubon and Bachman add valuable information, especially of its habits; while later still, Baird has given us a description which is remarkable for its scientific accuracy, especially when we consider the means at his command. These gentlemen all labored under some very important errors, and were not aware, or could not believe in the existence of those anomalous characteristics which widely distinguish this animal from all other ruminants, and entitle it to a separate place in natural history.

These marks or peculiarities will be considered in their proper places.

SIZE.

This animal is not so large as the Virginia deer, and is more compactly built. A fair, average adult male, as he stands naturally on the ground, will measure, from the end of the nose to the end of the tail, four feet ten inches to five feet. Height at shoulder, two feet ten inches; at hip, three feet one inch; length of fore-leg, one foot six inches; and of hind leg one foot ten inches.

THE HEAD.

The head is short, and rather broad and deep from the upper to the lower side. The face is rather concave. The muzzle is fuller than on the deer. The upper lip is covered with hair except a narrow line in the middle, which is naked, and extends up so as to embrace the nostrils, which are large.

The Eye.

The eye is larger than that of any other quadruped of its size. By a careful comparison of the living eye with the taxidermist's scale, to enable me to order artificial eyes of the proper size for mounting specimens, I found it necessary to select the next to the largest. Indeed the eye is very nearly the size of that of the elephant, and much larger than that of the horse or the ox. Those who examine only the dead subject would most likely be deceived in the largeness of the eye. The eye is black — intensely black — so that it is impossible to distinguish the pupil from the iris or its surrounding. No white part is ever visible, unless the eye is turned to one side ; but all that is seen is one uniform brilliant black. But for all this, the expression is soft, gentle, and winning. In this respect, it is the rival of the true antelope gazelle.

I had one of these in my grounds, which came from Asia, and at the same time several of the Prong Bucks, including a male one year old that was not much larger than the female gazelle, which was fully adult. In size, the eye of the Prong Buck was larger than that of the gazelle, which, however, was considerably larger than that of the common deer, more than four times her size. In color and expression, the eyes of the two were as nearly alike as possible — both very black, but, as stated, of a mild, soft, and affectionate expression.

The eye-winkers are long, coarse, and stiff, more on the upper than the lower eyelid, but not very abundant on either.

The Ear.

The ear always stands erect when the animal is standing at ease. When it becomes excited, the ears are projected forward to catch the least sound, which imparts a look of animation to the animal.

The ear is five inches long, and three inches broad at the widest part, and terminates in a pretty sharp point, and is covered with hair inside and out.

The Horns.

As the horns of the American Antelope constitute one of its most remarkable characteristics, and one which strikingly distinguishes it from all other ruminants, it is proper that we should examine them with considerable care.

The first allusion which I find to the deciduous character of the horns of this antelope is in the letter-press of Audubon and Bachman,[1] where they say, " It was supposed by the hunters of Fort Union that the Prong-horned Antelope dropped its horns ; but as no person had ever shot or killed one without these ornamental and useful appendages, we managed to prove the contrary

[1] *Quadrupeds of America*, vol. ii., p. 198.

to the men at the fort by knocking off the bony part of the horn and showing the hard spongy membrane beneath, well attached to the skull, and perfectly immovable."

The hunters were right, and the scientists were wrong; but we see how near Mr. Audubon came to discovering the truth, and had he been a little more patient in his investigations, and a little less wedded to preconceived opinions, he would have had the honor of this important discovery. But that was reserved to others.

Some years later, on the 10th of April, 1828, Dr. C. A. Canfield, of Monterey, California, in a paper which he sent to Professor Baird of the Smithsonian Institute, communicated many new and interesting facts concerning the physiology and habits of this animal; and, among others, the surprising announcement that although it has a hollow horn, like the ox, yet this horn is cast off and renewed annually. This statement by Dr. Canfield was considered by Professor Baird so contradictory to all zoölogical laws, which had been considered well established by observed facts, that he did not venture to publish it, till the same fact was further attested by Mr. Bartlett, superintendent of the gardens of the Zoölogical Society of London, who, in 1855, repeated the fact in a paper published in the Proceedings of that society. In the February following, the paper which Dr. Canfield, eight years before, had furnished the Smithsonian Institute, containing the first well attested account of the interesting fact, was published in the Proceedings of that society.

At the time I gave an account of Mr. Bartlett's observation, in a paper which I read before the Ottawa Academy of Natural Sciences in 1868, and which was published by that society, I was not aware that the same fact had been previously communicated by Dr. Canfield to Professor Baird, else I should have taken pleasure in mentioning it.

This animal has a deciduous hollow horn, which envelopes a persistent core, which is a process of the skull like the core of the persistent horns of other ruminants. This shell is true horn, and, as we shall presently see, has the same general system of growth as other horns, although it is cast annually like the antlers of the deer, and so reveals to us an intermediate link between those ruminants which have persistent and those which have deciduous corneous appendages. Only the lower part of this horn is hollow, the core extending up scarcely half its length. When the horn is matured, the portion above the core is round and well polished, and is black, except that the top is frequently of a white or dull yellowish shade. The lower part, which is hollow, is flat, thinnest anteriorly, is striated and rough, with more or less hairs on the surface till they are worn off. No annular ridges, as is usually observed on the hollow horns of other ruminants, are observed. These ridges result from the growth of the horn being principally at the base, while, as we shall see, the growth of the horn of this animal commences at the top and proceeds downward to the base. Whoever will carefully study the process of the growth of this horn will readily understand why it is striated in structure instead of annular.

The older the animal is the earlier in the season does the horn mature, and the sooner it is cast off, in obedience to a universal law which governs the growth and shedding of the antlers of the deer, although there are occasional exceptions, as to the time of the shedding in individual cases in some of the species of deer, and possibly more extended observations would show exceptions in this animal. The aged specimens usually cast their horns in October, while the kid carries his first horns till January. Indeed on late kids the horns are but slightly developed the first year, and are frequently carried over and grow on to maturity the next year, when they become larger than when they mature the first season, and are cast earlier.

The horn of this animal is situated just above the eye, directly upon the super-orbital arch; it rises nearly in a vertical position, or at an angle of about one hundred degrees to the face, so far as the core extends, when soon commences a posterior curvature, growing shorter towards the point, where it much resembles that on the chamois. The horn of the female cannot be detected on the kid, on the yearling it can easily be felt; later I have found them half an inch long, and less than that in diameter at the base, and it is only on the fully adult female that the horn appears above the hair. I have never met one more than one inch long, but others have found them three inches long. The female is less cornuted than the females of hollow horned animals which are persistent, while, with one exception, females of those species which have deciduous corneous members are entirely unprovided with these weapons. When looking for something intermediate between these two great families of ruminants, this feature may be referred to at least as a make-weight in the argument.

I will first describe the superficial occurrences which are manifest during the growth and the shedding of the horn of the antelope and will then proceed to examine more minutely the origin and process of that growth.

Although, as before shown, both male and female antelopes have horns, we can only distinctly detect even the rudiments of the horns on the male at the time of its birth. It then may be felt as a slight protuberance on the skull. This rapidly increases in size, and when about four months old the horn breaks through the skin, and a horny knob appears. At this time it is not firmly set upon the core, which as yet is but rudimentary, and the little horn may be moved about appreciably. After this the core grows pretty rapidly, and soon fixes the horn more firmly in its position. On an early kid, in my grounds, this little horn matured and was cast off on the second day of January, when I found it quite thrown off the core, and suspended by a slight fibre on one side, and so I saved it. The next day I found the other horn in the same condition, which I likewise saved. At this time the horn was fully one inch long.

The new horn had already commenced its growth, and the tip was already hardened into perfect horn, and was extended appreciably above the core, which at that time was less than nine lines long. The new horns grew very rapidly through the winter, so that in six weeks the cores had more than doubled in length, and the horns were extended more than an inch above the cores, and the hardened, perfected horns had extended down to near the top of the cores.

But this process is better observed on the adult males. This law seems to govern the times of shedding the horns of the antelope, — the older the animal, the earlier the horn matures, and the sooner it is cast. On old bucks the horn is shed in October, while on the early kids it is shed in January, and still later on later kids, or else it is carried over till the next year. A late kid in my grounds on the first of December, the horn was not more than a quarter of an inch above the skin. It grew slowly all winter, and till the time of its death in May following.

Let us observe the horn of the adult male antelope, which is shed in October. If we make our examination so soon as the horn is cast off, we can readily understand the process by which it is removed. By looking into the cavity of the cast-off horn, we shall see that it extends but about half way its length, or a little way above the prong; and we shall also see that it contains a large number of coarse lightish-colored hairs, all of which are firmly attached to the horn, and many of them, towards the lower part, passing quite through it. We see the core of the horn is covered with a thick vascular skin, which is pretty well covered with the same kind of hairs as those seen in the cavity of the horn. We now appreciate that these hairs grew from the skin, and more or less penetrated the shell or horn, and when this was removed some were torn from the skin and others from the horn.

We observe, further, that the new horn had commenced its growth a considerable time before the old one was cast, for the new horn was extended several inches above the top of the core, nearly in a vertical direction, though with a slightly posterior inclination. The top of this, for nearly half an inch, is already hardened into perfect horn. Below this it is softer, and a little way down it has lost the horny texture, but is a pretty firm and somewhat flexible mass down to the core and around it, at the upper part of which, however, it has rather the appearance of thick, massive skin, of a high temperature, showing great activity in the blood-vessels permeating it. As we pass lower down, the skin is thinner, and shows less excitement or activity. Upon this skin enveloping the core, we find the hairs already described.

This was the condition of the new development when the old horn was cast off. It shows that the new horn had already made considerable upward growth from the top of the core, which only extended up into the old horn a little above the snag, or about half its length ; all above this, of the old horn, was solid, and was not intersected by the hairs as it was below.

Now it is perfectly manifest that as the new horn was extended in length above the core, it must have carried with it the old horn which it detached from the core, and tearing out the hairs, the roots of which were in the skin, and many of which extended into or through the old horn. Until these were mostly torn asunder, or were withdrawn from the canals by which they had penetrated the shell, they served to prevent it from being easily lost ; but finally, when these were all or nearly all severed, it fell off, as a favorable position occurred, or some slight violence assisted the removal. I have never observed the animal to assist this process by rubbing its horns against convenient objects, but my opportunities have not been such as to authorize the statement that they do not sometimes do so.

When the old horn was cast off, the new one, as we have already seen, had made a considerable growth above the core, which was already tipped with perfected horn, and a section below it was more or less hardened, or partially converted into horn. This intervening section gradually moved down the horn, constantly invading the soft skin below, and followed above with perfected horn. All this time the horn was growing in length above the core, and assuming that posterior curvature near its upper part which so much resembles the curvature of the horn of the chamois. After the horn is perfected down to the top of the core, it ceases to increase in length, while the apparently converting process steadily progresses downward along or around the core. The core being laterally compressed, the horn assumes that form, not, however, conforming precisely to the shape of the core, but extending considerably in front of it, where it is thinner than the posterior part.

At the upper extremity of the wide, flattened part the snag or prong is thrown out, which consists of little more than an abrupt termination of the wide part, with an elevated anterior point.

By the latter part of winter, on the adult, the horn has attained about this stage of growth. From this it presses on, hardening in its downward growth till the latter part of summer, or the commencement of the rut, by which time the growth is perfected down to the base, and is a complete weapon for warfare, and it so continues during the rut, and until the growth of the new horn is commenced and loosens the old one from its core, and raises it from its seat, as has been described.

But science is by no means satisfied with these superficial observations. It is exceedingly interesting to watch the progress from day to day; to observe how the old horn is thrown off and the new one grows on to perfection; but we desire to know *how* it is that the soft warm skin, everywhere permeated with blood-vessels, in a very high state of activity, appears in so short a time to be converted into the black, hard shell, as perfect horn as grows upon the buffalo or the antelope, which takes a lifetime to perfect it. In this investigation I am indebted to the able assistance of Professor Lester Curtis of Chicago, whose superior instruments and skill with the microscope, readily solved what appears to the superficial observer so exceptional, and I may add so wonderful. We found, however, that this growth is not so exceptional after all. It is like the growth of the horns of other ruminants, like that of the hoofs and claws of animals, and of the nails on the human subject. And it is only because of its rapid progress, and that we can see more of it than we can of the growth of these, that it seems to us so strange. We see' horn invading skin, or skin apparently converted to horn, as we have never seen it before; hence it is that even the general reader feels a greater interest to know how this takes place, while he has felt no interest to inquire how his nails grow because he sees nothing in their growth which is exceptional, no evidence that the skin is converted into nail. We shall, however, find something anonymous besides the rapid growth.

First, it is necessary to inquire what is this core over which this horn grows and forms a shell, and what is this covering which envelopes it, and which appears before our eyes to be converted into horn so rapidly ?

The core itself is a proper bone, a part of the skull itself, elevated at its upper part into the form observed, and is persistent through the life of the animal, as any other internal bone. The first covering of this bone, like that of all other bones, is a *periosteum*, traversed by arteries, which throw off great numbers of branches which penetrate the bone through canals, thus affording to it nourishment, and contributing to its growth. Immediately upon the periosteum reposes the skin without the interposition of any muscular tissue. This consists, first, of a layer of *subcutaneous cellular tissue*, if that may be called a part of the skin ; second, of *derma*, or corium ; and third, *epidermis*. All these together constitute the skin which immediately overlays the periosteum. The naked eye is incapable of individualizing these separate parts composing the skin, and so it appears as if the whole were converted into horn, which appears to take its place over the periosteum ; but, by the aid of the microscope, these different parts are plainly revealed, and we readily determine to which the growth of the horn is due, and the exact mode of that growth.

The illustrations show the epidermis and the outer section of the skin which overlays the periosteum. Fig. 1 under a power of 60 diameters, and Fig. 2 magnified 296 times. These we shall the better understand as we proceed.

The lightish-colored hairs previously described, which rather sparsely cover the skin which envelopes the core before the horn is formed, and on the lower part of the horn when its growth is completed, passing quite through it, and showing themselves on the outside, have their roots in the inner part of the skin tissue next the periosteum.

It will be observed, on examining Fig. 1, that the outer part of the skin *b*, presents an irregular corrugated appearance, occasioned by protuberances and depressions, called *papillæ*, varying considerably in height and depth. With this uneven surface terminate those blood-vessels of the skin which carry the red blood in sufficient quantities to produce a stain. Upon this uneven surface rests the epidermis, or the outside coating of the

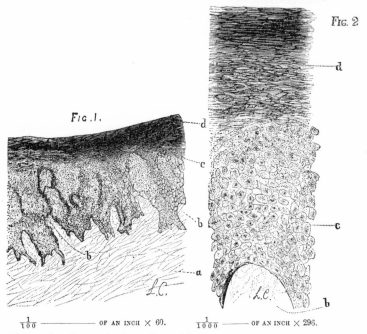

$\frac{1}{100}$ ——————— OF AN INCH × 60. $\frac{1}{1000}$ ——————— OF AN INCH × 296.

Thin section of a growing horn of an antelope, cut perpendicular to the surface.

FIG. 1 shows the general structure under a low power. FIG. 2, more highly magnified, shows the cell structure. The letters refer to the same parts in each figure.

a. The connective tissue continuous with the periosteum of the core of the horn.

b. The papillæ, *very large and irregular.*

c. The cell growth upon the papillæ.

d. The outer portion, seen to be made up of the flattened and desiccated cells of the layer beneath, already converted into horn.

skin. If this appears to want uniformity of structure, a critical examination shows that this results from a change of form of the cells of which it is composed, which become flattened and consolidated by compression, and by evaporation, or by becoming dried up. Thus is the epidermis converted into true horn. Chemically, the constituents of epidermis and of horn are nearly identical. The true horn at *d* is but the flattened and dried up cells which were formed upon the papillæ *b*, and were pushed up by new cell formations beneath them, till they reach their final form and destination in the horn. The entire epidermis seems to be composed of these minute cells, far too minute to be detected, or even their existence suspected, by an examination with the naked eye.

The source of this horn, then, is the epidermis. This alone undergoes a change, and is converted into horn, while the great body of the skin beneath remains substantially unchanged.

Let me be more particular, and endeavor to explain how this horn growth proceeds — how this change takes place.

As before intimated, immediately upon this uneven surface — the papillæ, — the derma cells are always being formed with more or less rapidity, as the exigencies of the demand may require. The new cells formed being always at the bottom, are ever pushing up their predecessors to supply the demand above, produced either by the ordinary waste at the surface of the skin, or the extraordinary demand of a growing horn. At the same place, and among the structural cells, pigment cells are formed in which the coloring matter is generated and carried up, for they accompany the former in their progress. At first these cells are nearly spherical, with nuclei in their centres. As they are pushed up by new formations beneath, they assume irregular forms, and finally they become flattened out, till at last they become exceedingly thin, with correspondingly expanded surfaces. These flattened and desiccated cells become very much compacted together and hard, and thus is the horn built up. So we see that the horn is but the hardened and thickened outer epidermis. The exact progress of this growth may not be stated in its minute detail with absolute certainty. It is very clear, however, that the outer portion of the epidermis becomes consolidated into horn, which cleaves off from the softer portion within, always leaving a stratum of epidermis covering the corium. The outer hardened shell, or true horn, seems to be lifted off or separated by the increased cell growth so as to leave a line of demarcation between the perfected horn and the epidermis beneath, though the nutrient vessels still maintain their integrity, as is the case with the persistent horn of other ruminants, until they are severed by the final catastrophe which loosens the horn from the core, and throws it off.

As the solidification or conversion of this outer portion of the epidermis into horn progresses downwards along the core, the unsolidified portion remains beneath it, comparatively inactive, and undergoes little change till the period arrives in the succeeding

3

year when the formation of new cells upon the papillæ increases to a degree commensurate with the demand.

This increased activity first commences at the upper part of the core, where the new horn commences its growth. Here the demand is greater than ever occurs lower down on the core; here an increased flow of blood stimulates to a more rapid formation of cells, which are successively forced up, flattened, and arranged, sufficient to form a considerable part of the cylindrical portion of the horn before any great activity is observed below, and these act with sufficient force to lift the horn from its seat, tear asunder the hairs which connected it with the skin, and finally cast it off. An active circulation is still kept up through this newly-formed cylinder, which is still somewhat soft and flexible, and quite warm, which, however, gradually dries up and hardens into the perfect horn, at the upper part first, and progressing downward.

Now the peculiarity about this is, not that the epidermis is the source of the horn, or is converted into horn, but that a very limited section should be stimulated to extraordinary activity till its work is accomplished, and then subsides into a comparatively dormant state; and then another portion wakens to the same vigorous action, to be again succeeded by another active section still lower down; this state of activity commencing at the top of the core and gradually passing along down it, followed by the perfected horn, and the quiet condition of the epidermis lining its cavity; and that this extraordinary phenomenon should occur annually. The horn from the epidermis was to be expected, for the cells when forced to the surface of the cuticle on our own skin even, are always of a horny texture, and in that condition are worn away by friction, or are thrown off, with greater or less rapidity, and are succeeded by those beneath, which are brought to the surface to be thrown or worn off in their turn; but in the ordinary cuticle this process is regular and continuous, while this is spasmodic, or rather periodic.

The horn of the ox grows from the cuticle as well as this, but it is of slow and regular growth, and is pushed up from its base, while this horn grows from the top downward, taking up or converting in its progress the epidermis all the way down the core. While the growth of this horn is undoubtedly on the same principle as the growth of all other horns, here is an important modification of the process rendered necessary by the deciduous character of this horn. Its growth must be characterized by extraordinary energy, when it is to be accomplished in a few months' time, while in all other cases the whole life of the animal is devoted to the growth of the horn, which is regular and approximately uniform, though slower in advanced life than earlier.

The only exceptional feature observed about the source of this cell growth, which manifests such extraordinary activity at times, is the very unusual size and great irregularity of the papillæ, from which the cells originate and receive their nourishment. It is at this precise point we are to look for this wonderful phenomenon, having no parallel in the animal economy. Nature has provided something in these papillæ which produces it, and if we knew better how to look for this something, or perhaps would more critically compare these papillæ with those of other portions of skin, the peculiarity might be detected which produces this remarkable result, if we may not attribute it to the increased size of the papillæ.

THE TAIL.

The tail of the Prong Buck bears no resemblance to that of any of the smaller species of deer, but remotely approaches to that of wapiti. It is very short, not more than three inches in length, and is covered with coarse hairs which are a little shorter on the under side than on the upper. It is nearly round, and maintains its size to near the end, where it terminates with a blunt point. It is usually carried closely depressed for so short a member, and is never seen erected to a vertical position. When the animal is excited or animated the tail may be seen raised to a horizontal position or a little above it, but that is all the change in its position observed under any circumstances. It is useless as a weapon for defense against the attacks of flies and mosquitoes; from which, however, it does not suffer nearly so much as the deer, probably because of the odor with which it always surrounds itself.

THE FOOT.

The feet of the Prong Buck are bifurcous, considerably smaller than those of the deer, slim and sharply pointed, strongly convex on top, having the outer edges slightly concave. In general they resemble the feet of the antelope gazelle, though the latter are considerably longer and more pointed, the points inclined to cross, or one to overlap the other. I may remark here, once for all, that the habits of all these animals have a decided influence on the form and the size of the foot, for which allowance must be made in all our comparisons. From more constant use, often in rough and stony ground, the foot of the wild animal, by continual abrasion, is reduced in size and changed in form, as compared with those that are kept in parks where they range but little, and then generally on the soft grass.

There is an entire want of even the rudiment of the posterior accessary hoofs found on nearly all other ruminants, situate above the useful hoofs. The leg or rather foot, where in other ruminants these accessary hoofs are attached, is as clean and smooth on the Prong Buck as on the horse, and even more so, for there is no appearance of that tuft of longer hair which is observed on nearly all horses at this place.

The color of the hoof is black throughout.

THE GLANDS.

The remarkable system of cutaneous glands found on this animal is a striking characteristic. In the specific description of the Prong Buck, the location of each of these glands — eleven in number — is given. These secrete a substance of a waxy consistence, of a saffron color and of a pungent odor, some more copious than others.

Sir John Richardson was the first to notice any of these glands. He says: " There is a dark, blackish brown spot at the angle of each jaw which exudes a strong hercin odor." [1] Although Richardson does not seem to have made any study of the glands, nor does he even mention them by name, the passage quoted points directly to those found below the ears.

Dr. Canfield seems to have been the first who bestowed any serious study upon the glands of this animal. He says, " The strong and peculiar odor* comes principally from the ischiadic glands." This observation was made on the living animal, while Richardson, from the dead subject, ascribed it to the subauricular glands. If I agree with Dr. Canfield, that the hip glands are the most effective in the emission of this odor, it is because the substance secreted is more pungent, for it is less in quantity than that secreted by the glands on the head. The single gland on the back is large, but not so active on the subjects I have examined as some of the others ; but in fact each does its part in tainting the atmosphere which surrounds the animal. If the glands between the toes do not contribute much to the odor we observe in the atmosphere, they are sufficiently active to taint

[1] *Fauna Boreala Americana* p. 267.

the ground at every step. To me, and I think to most persons, this is not agreeable, and yet it is not so unpleasant as to make it disagreeable to be near to or to examine the animal. It is quite different from that of the male goat, and I think less offensive. This odor is scarcely noticeable in the fawn of a few months old; is very perceptible when it is a year old, and seems to grow stronger with age, until the animal becomes three years old. This odor is not entirely due to the secretion of the glands proper, but partly arises from the oily secretions of the skin, as may be observed by rubbing the fingers upon the skin, at the roots of the hair on the sides and back.

The activity of these glands is not confined to the rutting season, but the odor may be observed at all seasons, though it may be more marked during the rut. Nor is it confined to the male, for the female emits the odor as well, though I think it not so strong; I have no facts which warrant me in saying that the flesh is ever tainted by those glands. I have eaten it frequently and at different seasons of the year without observing anything of the kind; nor have I been able to learn anything from the hunters to warrant such a conclusion. We may well suppose that glands confined to the skin would be less likely to taint the flesh, than those more intimately connected with the flesh or the circulation.

After Canfield, Bartlett next mentions the glands of this animal, but he does not seem to have studied them closely. This was reserved to Dr. Murie, to whom we are indebted for the first careful examination and description of them. He describes them all and gives their correct location, although in his summary he omits the large gland on the back. As he only had the dead subject to deal with, he could of course form no accurate opinion of the relative activity of the different glands.

GENITALS.

The genitals of this animal are much like those of the antelope proper. The scrotum, however, is smaller than that of almost any other ruminant of its size, and is not a twentieth part the size of that of the goat. It is slightly pendent, though less so even than that of the common deer. The theca extends up the abdomen about four inches on the adult. It has not any prepuce.

THE COAT.

Dr. Murie pronounces the hair of the antelope to be like the wool of the sheep. He says : " From a review of the foregoing anatomy and externals of the Prong Buck, if I were asked by a single term to denote what the animal is, I should be obliged to Germanize the English phraseology and name it, giraffe-hoofed, sheep-haired, deer-headed, goat-glanded antelope, — an expression, however rugged, yet explicit enough to baffle those who are skeptical of gradational forms." I shall not stop to discuss the characteristics stated, but will merely observe that I have been unable to detect the resemblance which the hairs of the Prong Buck bear to the wool of the sheep. They are coarser than the hairs of any of the deer ; they are hollow, with a larger internal cavity, are comparatively non-elastic, and exceedingly fragile. When bent short, they break down and never straighten again. They terminate in exceedingly sharp points, and although crinkled are not wavy, like wool. They have no more felting properties than dry brush-wood. The hair is largest a small distance above the root, thence it tapers very gradually for a short space, and then more rapidly to the sharp point. It is very brittle and easily broken off below the point and above the middle. The large internal cavity is filled with a light, spongy pith, and the whole is so fragile as to be readily crushed.

The lower half of the hair is covered with an oleaginous substance which gives it flexibility and endurance.

Other naturalists have failed to observe the fine under-fur, found to a greater or less extent on all of the deer, which certainly also exists on the Prong Buck as well, and in considerable quantities during the winter and spring. Pluck a lock of hair from the side of the mounted specimen in my collection, by grasping it near the roots, and sufficient fur will come with it to hold the hairs together when suspended by a very few. This fur is white, fine, and long, not crinkled, but curved into large, irregular convolutions.

This fur, like the fur on the deer, is not pointed, as is the hair, but is of a uniform size its whole length, and terminates abruptly.

In winter costume, the hair on the body is from an inch and a half to two inches in length. On the white patch on the rump, it is from two and a half to three inches in length. The mane is four inches long. On the legs and face the hair is short, quite solid, and without the under fur. On the belly it is not so dense as above, but finer and softer, and has the fur beneath.

Color.

The color of this animal is quite uniform on different individuals, though a difference in the depth of the shades may be observed. On the female, the colored portions are not of so deep a shade as on the male, and on the whole the marks are not so pronounced, although the white is quite as immaculate.

At birth, the young have substantially the same markings as the adult, though the dark shades deepen somewhat as they grow older. Not the least appearance of those spots is observed on the fawns, which so beautifully ornament the young of the smaller deer.

In a large majority of cases, downward from a line drawn between the outer base of the horns, the face is a dark brown or dull black. Two inches forward from this line the dark portion is narrowest, and is scarcely two and one half inches wide, while it is nearly four inches broad lower down. While this dark color embraces the nostrils, it is separated from them by a white stripe along the upper lip, which in front is seven lines broad, widening posteriorly, till at the angle of the mouth it is more than an inch broad. Here it unites with the white, which embraces the chin and most of the lower jaw, and extends along the cheek to the eye, the upper portion shaded with red. One inch below the eye, and involving the posterior portion of the cheek, is an irregular dark brown patch, from two to three inches in diameter. This is most conspicuous on the male. This mark is surrounded by the tawny yellow of the back, except between it and the lower part of the ear, where is a white patch two and one half inches long and one and one half inches broad. There is a dark circle around the eyes. Above the black on the face, to the ears, is white. The ears are white on both sides, but much less pronounced on the outside. The edges of the ears are black, considerably less so on the back edge than on the top and front. The eyelashes are of an intense black. So we may say the whole head is white, except the face, the spots beneath the ears, a circle around the eyes, the eyelashes, and the edges of the ears; though sometimes the russet yellow marks the back part of the cheeks. The long, coarse, stiff, erect hairs of the mane are very black at the outer ends; lower down they are rufous brown shading to white.

The prevailing color of the body is a dull rufous yellow. This covers the neck, except the mane and the lower portion of it. It covers the back and sides half way down, the shoulders and hips, except the white patch on the rump. This conspicuous white mark commences at the anterior end of the sacrum and widens to the extent of eight or ten inches, passes down around the tail, and unites with the white below, between the legs. In many specimens, this white patch is divided by a slight line of yellowish hair extending down the back and along the upper side of the tail. Frequently on the male the color over the spine is appreciably deeper than on either side. The tail, the lower part of the sides, the belly, the inguinal region, the legs, and the under side of the neck are white, except that the white under the neck is broken by three bands of the yellowish color above, which are broader at their base on either side of the neck, and become quite narrow, and are sometimes broken by the white under the neck. This appearance of the different colors on the neck shows the white in pointed sections on the lower sides of it, the points projecting into the colored portions above. The white on the front of the legs is not as clear as on other parts, and is tinged with a russet or brown shade.

On many specimens a shaded line may be observed from a point between the fore legs, extending back to the *umbilicus.*

The portions covered by the different colors, or the dividing lines between the colors, are somewhat variant on different individuals; but they always preserve their distinct characteristics. The white is perhaps most immaculate on the rump, but is very pure everywhere, except about the head and on the legs, where it is a little more dingy.

The hairs from the colored portion of the animal, when examined singly, are at their lower extremities white, turning to a dull bluish shade higher up; then they become yellowish-tawny, and at the tips black. The ends of the white hairs frequently become soiled, so that their purity is obscured, but the soiling rarely penetrates to a great depth, and by opening them their beauty is manifest.

As stated, all the cuticle not covered with hair — about the anus, the eyes, and the mouth, — as well as mucous membrane, is very black, while the healthy skin under the hair is of a salmon color. These colors remain after the death of the animal, although, if a patch of hair be removed from the living animal, the epidermis thus exposed very soon becomes black.

THE SKIN.

Notwithstanding Sir John Richardson informs us that the skin of this antelope is of no value as an article of trade, and although I learn that at the present day it is not prized by the traders, I must say that I have several skins of this animal tanned by the Indians, which are remarkable for their whiteness, softness, elasticity, and tenacity. In all these respects, except in strength, they are superior to the skin of the deer, in which respect the latter may have a slight preference. I have no doubt it is a very excellent article for wash-leather, rivaling the skin of the chamois for this purpose. I cannot be mistaken in the identity of the skins which I have, for enough of the hair remains around the edges and on the tail to fix their identity beyond dispute. I have had the skins tanned with the hair on for robes. Although pliant and warm, the hair is so fragile that they are of little value for this purpose.

VENISON.

Although Richardson informs us that the Indians will only eat the flesh of the antelope when other meat fails them, I know of no one who has tasted it that has failed to find it a delicate and choice morsel, which is much relished by the invalid. At Cheyenne and Laramie, travelers by the Pacific road enjoy their antelope chops very much, many preferring it to the flesh of the deer and the buffalo, — all of which are there provided in abundance. It is dark colored, fine grained and very tender, with an agreeable flavor. It is not as nutritious as the flesh of the deer, and especially of the elk. If used as a constant diet one soon cloys of it and desires no more. After almost living upon it for two weeks, I quite forgot how much I enjoyed it at first, and agreed with Richardson's Indians, and rejoiced at the change to the flesh of the deer and the buffalo. This meat, however, needs to be well ·dressed with butter to develop its prime excellences and fine flavor, even at the first, for broiled without accessaries it is rather dry. If butter is not at hand then fat pork or bear's grease will do very well as a substitute, but something softer than tallow is quite necessary to its full enjoyment.

ALIMENT.

Antilocapra Americana is not only a vegetarian, but is strictly an herbaceous feeder, avoiding arboreous food if left to his own choice, although probably if driven by dire necessity he might take tree food, but this is only inference. My observations on this point have been careful and continuous with excellent opportunities. I have often spent hours watching them when feeding. I have frequently tried them, with twigs and leaves when these were young and tender, as well as when quite matured, of every tree and shrub within my reach, including the hazel, several kinds of oak, the hickory, the sugar-maple. the ash, and the mulberry, but could never induce them to taste of any, though the deer seized them greedily. In winter I have seen them pick up the dried oak leaves from the ground possibly for the tannin they contained, and as a substitute for some grass found in their native range, but was not found in my grounds, but I never saw them touch the green leaf of a tree.

The dried and frosted leaves were not taken for the nutriment they contained, for they practically contained none ; and the blue grass was abundant and accessible, so that they did not want for food. I have observed them once or twice in winter time to pick the fine short parasitic lichens from the young live trees, but never the coarser mosses.

They would eat apples sparingly. but I never knew them to take acorns, wild plums, grapes, or cherries. They are fond of all the kinds of grain which I have ever offered them. In winter they will pick the leaves and heads of timothy hay and of clover, and fine clover rowen they take quite freely, but prefer to scrape away the snow for the grass when that is possible. Perennial grasses suit them best. In my grounds they preferred the blue grass ; but sometimes cropped the white clover. I never saw them touch the weeds of which the deer are so very fond. Bread and cake they took gratefully if it was fresh and good, but if stale they rejected it. Altogether, they are dainty feeders and very select in the choice of their food. In a wild state they no doubt live principally on the various kinds of buffalo grass, but probably find many other kinds of herbaceous food with' which we are not acquainted.

They are fond of common salt, and should have it always by them when in parks ; and if soda be mixed with it, no doubt it would be better for them, for their native plains generally abound with crude or sulphate of sodium, and long use may make this better for them, than in the form of the chloride. At least it is worth the trial by those who have pet antelopes.

HABIT.

The most interesting features of the habits of this animal, will be developed when we come to treat of its domestication. In its wild state it is very timid and shy, avoiding its enemies with as much intelligence as the deer, except that it is more liable to be betrayed into danger by its curiosity. In fleetness, it excels all other quadrupeds of our continent; but as might be expected from this, it is short-winded and so cannot maintain its wonderful speed for a great length of time.

As has been stated, it seeks treeless plains, ravines, and rolling foot-hills, avoiding the high mountains and heavily timbered regions, though at times it may be found in park-like countries where trees are sparse.

They are exceptionally gregarious in their habits. Dr. Canfield says: " From the first of September to the first of March antelopes meet in bands, the bucks, does, and kids all together. At the end of that time the does separate themselves from the band one by one, to drop their kids ; they produce two at a birth. After a little time the does collect together with their young, probably for mutual protection against coyotes; the old bucks in the mean time go off alone, each by himself or at most two together, leaving the young bucks and young does together in small bands.

" The old bucks now for a month or two wander a great deal, and are seen in the timber-lands, and in other places where they never go at any other season of the year, evidently ' tired of the world ' and fleeing from society. After two or three months, the young bucks and does join the old does and their kids, and finally by the first of September, all are together once more in bands of hundreds or thousands. Any particular band of antelopes does not leave the locality where they grow up, and never range more than a few miles in different directions."

The conduct of Mr. Cipperly's tame antelope, which I mention in another place as the only instance of which I have heard of their breeding in domestication, shows that the habit of the sexes separating during the latter part of the period of gestation, is quite as much attributable to the inclination of the male as of the female. I quote from a letter to me by Hon. L. B. Crooker, who kindly investigated their habits for me, which shows this, as well as illustrates several other characteristics : " In the spring, while the female was with young, the male seemed to lose his affection for her, and repeatedly went away, escaping when it could ; and in one instance was caught several miles away. The female never escaped or went away without the male. They were often allowed to roam about the farm (200 acres) at will, and often strayed away to the neighbors, who would dog them home ; and the antelopes seemed to enjoy it, and would act in a playful manner, apparently exulting in their superior speed, and tantalizing the dog by stopping, etc. They were affectionate and tame to those with whom they were familiar. During the rutting season, the buck was intensely cross and wicked to every one who came near." The account given by Dr. Canfield shows us that they have strong local attachments, which, however, have been broken up by the advance of civilization, not only at the place where his observations were made more than twenty-five years ago, but in a large portion of the country where they were formerly so abundant. Probably in Canfield's time they were more abundant in California than anywhere else; and yet, a quarter of a century later, scarcely any were there to be found. If they now appear to be less gregarious than he describes, it may be because of their diminished numbers every where ; and if they wander now more than then, it is probably because they are more frequently disturbed.

Of their combative disposition, I am not enabled to speak from personal observation. The three years' old buck I had in my grounds never manifested the least disposition in that direction, but I did not have him during the rut. Mr. Crooker's letter shows that Mr. Cipperly's manifested as belligerent a disposition during the rut as any of the deer, and it is only then that any of them are disposed to fight among themselves or to make war on others.

If the accounts of hunters may be relied upon, the mother does not lack courage in defense of her young, as it is said she attacks the coyote successfully with both feet and head. Her superior agility, no doubt, is of great service in such an encounter. It is said she conceals her young with great sagacity, till they are old enough to flee with her from their enemies.

As to the belligerent disposition of the bucks during the rut, I quote from Audubon and Bachman : [1] " The rutting season of this species commences in September ; the bucks run for about six weeks, and during this period fight with great courage, and even a degree of ferocity. When a male sees another approach-

[1] Vol. ii., p. 197.

ing, or accidentally comes upon one of his rivals, both parties run at each other with their heads lowered and their eyes flashing angrily, and while they strike with their horns they wheel and bound with prodigious activity and rapidity, giving and receiving severe wounds, sometimes, like fencers, getting within each other's 'points,' and each hooking his antagonist with the recurved branches of his horns, which bend considerably inward and downward."

For myself, I have never seen them in battle, nor have I seen any one who had seen them fight under such circumstances as enabled him to give me a clear idea of their mode of battle, so we may take the description quoted as accurate. In this connection, and for the purpose of comparing this habit of our animal with the African antelope, I may refer to what Sparrman, who, more than a century ago studied the various species of that animal in his native range, says: "The last mentioned antelope (*Antilope oryx*), according to the accounts given me by several persons at the Cape, falls upon its knees when it goes to butt any one." [1] He ascribes the same habit to the gnu. Although this is the only author I find who speaks of the mode of fighting of the true antelope, it is quite probable that this is a generic characteristic, and if so, it shows how widely they differ in this regard from our animal.

The rutting season occurs when the horn on the fully adult has about perfected its growth, and before it has been loosened by the new growth, and so is best adapted as a weapon. As its growth is not completed until July or August, and it is cast off in October or November, on the old specimens, and is loosened some time before it drops off, we see that the fighting season must be limited to the rutting season. Indeed, I have a mounted specimen which was killed in the latter part of July, from which I had no difficulty in removing the horn, for the purpose of examining the core and the cavity of the horn. I confess to a lack of that information on the subject which will enable me to say how long the horn continues a perfect weapon, and as that must measure the time during which the males are inclined to wage war on each other, I cannot say how long that continues; but, as the principal cause of hostility must be rivalry in love, it may be safe to assume that it is limited to the rutting season.

Dr. Canfield, speaking of a domesticated American Antelope which he had in his grounds, says, " He was the most salacious

---

[1] Sparrman's *Voyages*, vol. ii., p. 132, also *Ibid.*, p. 222.

animal I have ever seen. When three months old, he commenced to leap upon the other pet antelopes, the dogs, young calves, sheep, goats, and even people sitting down or bent over to pick up anything from the ground ; and as he grew older the more salacious he became. He always raised himself on his hind feet, and then walked up behind the animal that he wished to leap on, and without sustaining himself at all by his belly or fore-legs, he commenced walking around, directing the erected penis only by movements of the body, poised on the hind feet, until, having introduced the penis, he instantly gave one convulsive or spasmodic thrust, clasping spasmodically the female with the fore-legs, which he had before held up in the air without touching her. He would in this way go at anything held up to him.''

From this exhibition of passion, we may well suppose that fierce battles must occur among the males during the period of its sway. A young male which I raised till he was four months old, when in perfect health he met a violent death, never attracted attention by such exhibitions as described by Dr. Canfield ; but the ordinary rutting season of the animal had hardly commenced when he was killed, so that I am unable to say whether the conduct of the one observed by the doctor was exceptional or not, though I am inclined to think that it was, at least to some extent. The traits described strongly suggest the disposition of the goat.

Our antelope has the faculty of weeping when in affliction. I first observed this in a specimen which had been taken wild when adult, and still retained all his natural fear of man. I had placed him in a close cage in the evening, intending to familiarize him with my presence, and divest him of his fears when he saw me by convincing him that I would not hurt him. When I approached him the next morning, he seemed struck with terror, and made frantic efforts to break out, which he soon found was impossible. His great black eye glistened in affright. I spoke softly and kindly, while he stood trembling, as I introduced my hand and placed it on his shoulder. Despair now seemed to possess him, and he dropped on to his knees, bowed his head to the ground, and burst into a copious flood of tears, which coursed down his cheeks and wet the floor ! My sensibilities were touched ; my sympathies were awakened, and I liberated him from that cage as quickly as I could tear the slats from one of the sides. Whether he appreciated this or not I cannot say, but his great fear seemed to leave him as soon as he was liberated; he ran but a little way, and not at full speed, when he stopped and began to pick the grass.

Whenever this animal is excited in play, by fright or by rage, the hair of the white patch on the rump rises up and assumes a more or less curved radial position, from a central point on each side of the vertebræ, as we sometimes see two radial points on the human head. From these points the hairs point in every direction, only they are as nearly erect as their curved radial position will permit. It is impossible to give a just idea of this appearance by words, nor could I help the matter much by a drawing. It is not the position of the hairs alone which we admire, but their immaculate whiteness completes the beauty of the display. How much the flashing of the great black eyes augments one's sense of admiration, the observer may himself be at a loss to determine. As we shall hereafter see, under similar excitement, the corresponding white patch on the rump of the elk is elevated, but the hairs do not assume the radial position of the others. Nor is this uniform in degree on the antelope. On some specimens which I have observed, this curved and radial position of the hairs was almost entirely wanting, and the hairs were simply elevated to vertical positions as observed on the elk under similar circumstances.

Notwithstanding its astonishing fleetness, the Prong Buck cannot, or rather I should say does not know how to leap over high obstructions like animals which inhabit wooded countries. This is well illustrated by Captain Bonneville's account of the manner in which the Shoshokoe Indians on the Upper Lewis River capture the antelope, as given in Irving's "Bonneville," pp. 259, 260. I quote: "Sometimes the diggers aspire to nobler game, and succeed in entrapping the antelope, the fleetest animal of the prairies. The process by which this is effected is somewhat singular. When the snow has disappeared, says Captain Bonneville, and the ground becomes soft, the women go into the thickest fields of wormwood, and pulling it up in great quantities construct with it a hedge, about three feet high, inclosing about a hundred acres. A single opening is left for the admission of the game. This done, the women conceal themselves behind the wormwood, and wait patiently for the coming of the antelope, which sometimes enter this spacious trap in considerable numbers. As soon as they are in, the women give the signal, and the men hasten to play their part. But one of them enters the pen at a time, and after chasing the terrified animals round the inclosure, is relieved by one of his companions. In this way the hunters take their turns, relieving each other, and keeping up a continued pursuit by relays without fatigue to themselves. The poor antelopes, in the end, are so worried down that the whole party of men enter and despatch them with clubs, not one escaping which has entered the inclosure. The most curious circumstance in this chase is, that an animal so fleet and agile as the antelope, and straining for its life, should range round and round this fated inclosure without attempting to overleap the low barrier which surrounds it. Such, however, is said to be the fact, and such their only mode of hunting the antelope."

When I received a three-year old buck, lately captured on the plains, and sent me, I feared he would scale the eight feet paling fence which incloses the parks, for I had seen the female which I had had before make most astonishing horizontal leaps across ravines in the park, without an apparent effort, which she might just as well have walked across.

Although I had observed this buck, whilst confined in the yard, when frightened by a person going in, dash against the palings not three feet from the ground, in his efforts to break through the fence, without attempting to leap over it, yet it never occurred to me that he could not make high vertical leaps, till I met the statement above quoted. Subsequent observation of the conduct of these animals in my grounds convinced me that this statement might well be true, and that the Prong Buck may be restrained by a fence which would be sufficient to confine our domestic sheep.

In speaking of Mr. Cipperly's antelopes, Mr. Crooker says, " A four foot fence was ample to confine them."

This inability to leap over high objects may no doubt be attributable to the fact that they live upon the plains, where they rarely meet with such obstructions, and so they and their ancestors for untold generations have had no occasion to overleap high obstructions, and thus from disuse they do not know how to do so, and never attempt it when they do meet them.

If the antelope on the plains desires to cross the railroad track, when alarmed by the cars, as is sometimes the case, he will strain every muscle to outrun the train and cross ahead of it, as if he suspected a purpose to cut him off from crossing; and thus many an exciting race has been witnessed between muscle and steam. The same disposition is manifested by the bison, or the buffalo, as we call him; and if either is beaten in the race, he will turn away to the plains in apparent disgust, but will never cross the track immediately behind the train.

Were our antelope compelled to live in a forest, no doubt, in a few generations, they would learn to make as surprising leaps vertically as we now see them make horizontally. Then it would be a very difficult matter to restrain them by inclosures. A Virginia deer, in attempting to jump a fence when frightened, will strike against the palings from six to seven feet high, if on level ground, and yet he cannot compare in speed or in horizontal leaps with the Prong Buck.

DOMESTICATION.

Under this head I shall find it convenient to further explain the habits of this animal, but under different circumstances, or in different conditions of life. Hitherto we have only considered its habits in the wild state, where our observations have necessarily been very much circumscribed. In that limited degree of domestication to which it has been subjected, we shall observe many traits or characteristics, undeveloped or not discovered in his wild state, manifesting a degree of intelligence not otherwise suspected.

Considerable numbers of the young are found every year by hunters and travelers passing over the plains where they roam. If very young, these are taken without difficulty by simply picking them up, while those of a few days old will lead a considerable chase before they are captured. These latter are not so likely to live as the former. Like the fawn of the deer, if taken very young, they will attach themselves to their captors in a short time, and attempt to follow them as they would their mothers.

From necessity, these young kids are fed upon the milk of the cow, or preferably of the goat, if to be obtained. Very soon they commence to eat grass, and to ruminate. Experience shows that but a small percentage of these are raised. Dr. Canfield experimented extensively in this direction at Montera, where the wild ones were very abundant all about him. He says they are first attacked with diarrhœa. "If they escape this, they live a long time, one, two, or three months, growing slowly ; but at the end of that time all the female kids, and almost all the male ones, become diseased, having scrofulous inflammation of the joints, get a cough, become lame and poor, and finally die after lingering some weeks. I never yet have known a female ante-

4

lope to be raised artificially ; the males are more hardy, and with care nearly all can be raised."

Better success has attended the effort to rear the young antelope on this side the mountains. The first antelope I ever had was a female, sent me by a friend when she was a year old. She had followed a wagon into Kansas, from the distant plains, where she had been caught the year before and raised on cow's milk. Thence she was sent me by express, in a rough cage, five hundred miles. She was badly bruised in the rough journey, the hair being torn from her sides in places as large as my two hands, so that I feared she could not recover from these bruises. However, so soon as I turned her loose in the park she moved off with agility to the rich pasture before her ; but she could not wait long to satisfy her appetite, before she exercised her muscles in a race among the trees and over the lawn, which, I thought, resembled more the flight of a great bird than the running of a quadruped. Very soon the new fine hairs appeared upon the black naked skin, and rapidly grew to the length of the others. During the six months I had her, I never discovered any symptoms of sickness or lameness. She was at last found dead in the grounds, with blood in the mouth, evidently from an internal injury. She probably came near an elk, and received a fatal blow from its fore foot. She was always sprightly and playful, and always followed me in my walks and drives in the park.

In July, I purchased a male kid at Cheyenne, and brought him home on condensed milk. The distance is nearly a thousand miles, and occupied two days. He arrived in apparently perfect health, and so continued till October, when he met a violent death. He was always sprightly and playful. He was kept about the house, and ranged through the flower garden and about the lawns at will. Of all the pets I ever had, none was ever so much prized by all the household as he. I have had many others since, but all have died after a few months, of disease, many of them breaking out in sores. I have observed none to be troubled with diarrhœa, and rarely a decided lameness, but rather a stupid languor seemed to oppress them. Most of those I have had were one or two years old when obtained, had been raised in Kansas, where the wild ones were found, and reached my grounds in apparent health, and so continued for a month or two, and would then sicken, and after one, two, or three months would die, much emaciated. The females appeared quite as healthy, and survived quite as long, and in some instances longer, than the males. Several of my friends have been more successful than I have in their attempts to rear this animal. Probably my grounds are peculiarly unfavorable for him, being almost entirely forest, though mostly open and devoid of under-bushes. There are but a few acres devoid of trees. These were most affected by the antelope. My information is that in Kansas, and in fact in all other places this side of the mountains where they are found in a wild state, those which survive for a month or so are tolerably healthy, and if they escape accidents, may be expected to live for several years at least. It is manifest that experiments have shown that, from some unknown cause, there is more hope of rearing this animal on this side of the Rocky Moun-tains than on the Pacific Coast, where, in a wild state, they were once the most prosperous.

The Prong Buck is very easily tamed, and soon loses all fear of man, seeks his society, and enjoys his company. When taken young, and brought up by hand, they become at once attached to the one that feeds them. I raised one thus, which was taken charge of by a little girl, and nothing delighted it so much as to have a play and a romp with her; and in watching them to-gether, it was easy to persuade one's self that the little pet showed not only observation and intelligence, but even reflection. He assumed he had as much right in the kitchen as any of the do-mestics; and if he found the doors open, he enjoyed a visit to the parlor, and especially a siesta on the lounge in the library.

When I turned the wild buck loose, as before stated, I was agreeably surprised to observe that he made no attempt to es-cape, and did not even dash away, as if greatly alarmed. After a few leaps, he trotted away two or three hundred yards, and then commenced grazing upon the blue grass. For a few days, he would not allow me to approach him.

Whenever I walked in the park the younger one, which had been brought up by hand and was very tame, the moment he saw me, no matter how far away, would rush up to me with the greatest delight, and rub his head against me in a most affection-ate manner, and receive the gratuity, which he always expected, with great satisfaction; and would follow me constantly where-ever I went, gamboling around in much the same way as is observed in a young dog. Scarcely a week elapsed before I ob-served the older one, which was so wild in close confinement, following me at a distance. Each day he ventured nearer and nearer, till I observed he would not keep more than twenty or thirty feet in the rear, and would so follow me for an hour or more, if my walk should continue that long. I now began to notice him, and throw him corn, which he took with great apparent relish, nor was it long before he would venture to take corn from my hand, though with timidity, and he never became so entirely divested of fear as was the younger one. I know of no member of the *Cervus* family, when taken wild at three years of age, that will ever become so tame as did this Prong Buck in a few months.

I may quote some remarks of Dr. Canfield, in the paper above referred to, upon a young antelope which he had raised in domestication. He says: " He used to follow the ranch dogs, and in the night, if they chased coyotes, he would run after coyotes also, always ahead of the dogs, for nothing could outrun him."

But this antelope would not only hunt coyotes in the night with the ranch dogs, but he was fond of hunting other game in the daytime with the doctor, and so followed him on his hunting excursions; and on one occasion when twelve miles from home they became separated, when the antelope went home alone, where his master found him on his return.

Dr. Canfield tells us that he had another antelope at the same time which never became so tame as the first, and after the death of the first became uneasy, and finally deserted the ranch and relapsed to the wild state; but the wild ones " abounded everywhere in all the plains and valleys of the western slope down to the Pacific Ocean."

There is evidently a wide difference among individuals, in their adaptability to domestication, in sagacity and intelligence. Generally, however, it readily becomes attached to one who shows it kindness, and it would be unsafe to assert that long continued domestication would not develop those traits in as great a degree as they are ordinarily found in that great friend of the human race, the dog.

In intelligence, too, and reflective powers, they are exceptional. The young specimen of which I have spoken, was allowed to follow me from one park to another, and even out of the parks into the fields and meadows. He frequently followed me into the park where the elk or wapiti were kept. These would chase him away, when he would look to me for protection, which could not always be made effectual, for they would watch for opportunities to make dashes at him, when he would escape to the outside of the band of elk, but when he saw me approach the gate to pass out, he would dash up almost like a flash to go out with me. These visits to the Elk Park soon became disagreeable to him, so that when he saw me approach the gate leading into it, he would get before me, put his head against my legs and try to push me back or retard my progress as much as possible, and seemed to beg of me in every way in which he could convey his wishes not to go in there. I would frequently yield to his remonstrances and turn away in another direction, when he would manifest his satisfaction by gamboling about in the greatest delight. When he was allowed to follow me out of the park into the fields and meadows, he would scour away as if to try his speed, but in a few minutes would go to hunting about for some choice tufts of grass, and would sometimes get two or three hundred yards away, but he always kept a close eye upon me, and when he saw me going towards the park gate, though it was far away, would gradually lessen the distance, but so soon as I reached the gate, he would rush up at full speed and perhaps prance around as if very happy, or rub his head affectionately against me. Who will blame me if I loved the little pet and enjoyed his company in my walks, and really mourned his loss when he died? He was not singular in his traits of intelligence and marks of affection. Before that, the female, already spoken of, exhibited the same disposition, though I think in a less remarkable degree, probably because I was not so well acquainted with the habits of the animal, and did not so well know how to develop these peculiar characteristics.

They seem to be much more nearly allied to the antelope than to the deer family. I never observed one to show the least fondness for the society of a deer, but the young buck I have spoken of and the female gazelle from Asia, showed some inclination to associate together. Both showed the same disposition to follow me in my walks, though the gazelle would follow no one else, and was easily diverted from my companionship, by any choice spot for grazing she might meet with. If, for instance, she followed me into the North or East Park, she would often desert me before my return, and I would be obliged to leave her behind : and this at last cost the poor thing her life, for I once left her in the East Park, when some dogs broke in and killed her. I found her the next day in the corner by the gate, cruelly bitten and quite dead. I had less fear of dogs in the Elk Park, for if ever the elk see them there, they have no time to hunt anything but the place at which they came in. If ever I allowed this gazelle to follow me out of the park, she would never return with me voluntarily but would immediately start off, exploring in her own way. This gazelle and the young antelope would follow me together, not only in my walks, but also when I drove, or rode on horseback in the parks. She disliked a visit to the elk as he did, though she did not resort to as intelligent means to tell me so. When both were following me, especially when I was riding, they would race together at top speed, all around me and sometimes two hundred yards away, as if ambitious to exhibit their agility, and would seem to enjoy the gambol together, as much as would two young dogs, though I never saw them play thus together except when following, and the gazelle showed less inclination to the sport than the Prong Buck, perhaps because she was older.

After very extensive inquiries on this subject, I heard of a single instance of this animal breeding in domestication. Mr. Stephen Cipperly, in Bureau County, Illinois, has a pair which are in no way confined, but allowed the range of the neighborhood, and frequently visit the neighbors, several miles away, and seem to enjoy the sport if they can get dogs to chase them home. The female of this pair, when she was two years old in 1876, dropped one kid, which, however, was still-born, or at least dead when it was found. It can no longer be said that our antelope will in no case breed in domestication, but certainly it must be but rarely expected. We should have expected this to occur in the country where they flourish in a wild state, and it is certainly remarkable that it has occurred so far away, and in a region so unfavorable to their well-being.

The reason of the sterility of these animals in domestication is not very apparent. There is certainly no want of ardor on the part of the male, and the female is not without an inclination to breed, but from some unknown cause their union is not fertile. That their reproductive powers should be impaired by domestication, we should expect, in obedience to a very general law governing a very large majority of wild animals and birds, when reduced to domestication; but this may be largely accounted for by the disinclination to breed, manifested to a greater or less degree by both sexes. Such can scarcely be said to be the case with our antelope, yet it is undoubtedly true that its general health and vigor is more impaired than is generally the case with wild animals when domesticated or confined. Until the one taken adult sickened and died after a few months' confinement in the park, which is so large that the confinement, one would think, could scarcely be felt, I had imagined that the constitutional vigor might have been impaired when young, by having been nourished by cows' milk ; but such was certainly not the case in this instance. If in my grounds they fail to find some kind of food which their well-being requires, such could not have been the case where Dr. Canfield tried his experiments. Altogether it is manifest that further observations must be made, and further experiments tried, than I have been able to make or learn, before we arrive at a satisfactory comprehension of this branch of our subject.

I believe, however, that with time and care all the difficulties which now present themselves to the complete domestication of this interesting animal may be overcome, and that without these they will soon be known only as an extinct race. They would require at first to be kept in large inclosures on their native plains, with a keeper to show himself among them daily, who would introduce them gradually to new food, such as the various kinds of cereals, with a careful observation as to how they could bear it. Even then, some might sicken and die, but others no doubt would be capable of bearing it, and the small restraint and partial change of food would leave some of them capable of re-production. In that way the more feeble would be weeded out, but the more robust would rear a race, which, by degrees, might be restricted in their range, and live upon different food, and gradually be transferred to new conditions of life and ultimately become capable of enduring complete and permanent domestica-tion. It may be that not more than one per cent. would be found capable of enduring the least restraint and change of food, but if any could be found which could retain their full vitality and vigor and reproductive powers, even with the limited re-straint and change of condition suggested, the experiment might not prove a total failure. At any rate, I think there is little hope of their permanent domestication, by suddenly transferring them to the east of the Mississippi River, where they never roamed wild. We may keep them for a short time, but they will not prosper, and will soon sicken and die. We may have little hope that any individual will undertake this project; but may we not anticipate that the laudable enterprise which our government, especially of late years, has shown in the promotion of scientific researches, which has produced such rich results, and from which abundant practical benefits may be surely anticipated, will prompt it to undertake to reduce this and many other of the wild animals peculiar to this country, to complete domestication, and thus add largely to our useful agricultural products? We have an abundance of territory well adapted to this purpose, now laying waste, and a limited appropriation, to be expended under the direction of the Smithsonian Institute, for instance, whose expenditure of the funds committed to its charge has been characterized by the soundest judgment and the highest integrity, might promise success. What would we not give could we resuscitate some of those animals which were formerly abundant on our continent, but have recently become extinct? The danger, if not the probability is, that our successors in the not distant future will make the same reflection in reference to the bison and the prong buck, if not the moose and the wapiti.

THE CHASE.

The chase of the Prong Buck affords an exciting pastime to the sportsman, and has sometimes proved a profitable employment to the hunter. He who would study how to pursue the antelope with success must learn the character of the ground which that animal frequents, his capabilities for escape, and the infirmities which beset him. His strength and his weaknesses must be well understood and considered.

We have already seen that he inhabits the treeless plains and rolling foot-hills. To call these, naked plains and hills would frequently be a misdescription. Often they are so, covered only with a light coat of bunch or buffalo grass, so that an antelope may be seen at a great distance, although sometimes the color of the country so corresponds with the color of the animal as to make it very difficult to distinguish him even at a moderate distance, though no object may intervene to obstruct the view. A good field-glass is an excellent thing for the antelope hunter always to have by him. But they frequent grounds more or less densely covered with the cacti, the wild sage, and the grease bush. These sometimes attain the height of four or five feet, and afford excellent covert for the animal.

A correct knowledge of their sense of sight, of smell, and of hearing is necessary for the success of the hunter, for these should often control his course.

Notwithstanding the large, prominent eye, which is of a brilliant black color, the sight of the antelope is not reliable. He cannot readily identify unfamiliar objects if they are not in full view nor in motion. He cannot readily tell a horse from a buffalo, or a man from a bush, if they are perfectly still, unless they are quite near. Their sense of smell is very sensitive and discriminating. Their sense of hearing is also very acute, though not as much so as of many of the deer family. They are naturally very timid and shy when their fears become aroused, but they are not as suspicious as most of the deer. They have a curiosity which is very remarkable, and which prompts them to examine every strange object which they see. This completely overpowers their caution, and often leads them into danger and to destruction. The hunter must remember they are exceedingly fleet of foot, far outstripping all other animals of the plains. Audubon says, " They pass along, up or down hills or along the level plains with the same apparent ease, while so rapidly do their legs perform their graceful movements in propelling their bodies over the ground, that, like the spokes of a fast turning wheel, we can hardly see them, but instead observe a gauzy or film-like appearance where they should be visible." Colonel Redfield once told me that he saw a frightened flock of antelopes flee to a very steep and high mound of rather loose scoria, near the Yellowstone River, which they seemed to go up almost like rockets, the detached material rolling down behind them like a line of smoke. Some of them lost their footing on the almost vertical side and fell back to the bottom, but the instant they reached that they flew back like the rebound of a ball, without any appreciable pause.

I have seen them in my grounds make prodigious horizontal leaps across a ravine or depression in the ground from a standing position or a leisurely walk when there was no obstruction to impede their walking across it if they had chosen so to do. These leaps seemed to require scarcely more effort than the walk. It was a horizontal bound so light and elastic that it seemed like a fleeting shadow, when the gentle walk would be instantly resumed with no more animation or excitement than if they had walked across the space. Still, as has been already explained, they are unable to make vertical leaps. I think it safe to say they cannot overleap an obstruction a yard in height. As before stated, when considering the habits of this animal, it is incapable of sustaining its astonishing speed for any great length of time. It will soon seek some eminence, if to be found, stop, take breath, and look around for the object which alarmed it.

Another fact should not be forgotten. This animal is remarkably tenacious of life, or if this does not express the exact truth, he can sustain himself for a length of time with such severe wounds as would prostrate almost any other animal. With a broken leg he will flee almost as rapidly as if uninjured, and the hunters insist he will maintain the chase nearly as far. They insist he will carry off more lead than any other animal of his size. I was once on a hunt in the Sierra Madre Mountain, near the Laramie Plains, when it was a standing joke in camp, that one of the party, a distinguished judicial officer of Wyoming, who was an excellent sportsman as well as a good judge, had shot fourteen balls into a buck antelope, and only so crippled him, that by throwing away his gun in despair of killing his game in that way, he was enabled to overtake him on foot and knock him on the head with his hatchet. While undoubtedly the antelope must fall to the shot if hit in a vital part, he can carry severe wounds, and frequently escapes unless these reach some part upon which life or locomotion immediately depend.

All of these characteristics should be constantly borne in mind by the sportsman or the hunter if he would pursue the American antelope with success.

Our antelope was an essential article of food among the aborigines inhabiting the country which it frequented before the introduction of fire-arms among them. They had various modes of capturing it, chief among which was with the bow and arrow. This mode involved the necessity of their getting a very close range. This could only be done by some kind of artifice, or by the most skillful and cautious stalking, always remembering its defective eyesight, its acute senses of hearing and smelling, as well as its inordinate curiosity. The latter infirmity — for such it often proves to the animal — was taken advantage of by the savage, who, approaching the game as nearly as he safely could from behind the sage bushes or other concealing object, exhibiting in irregular motion a piece of the tanned skin of the animal colored red or white, or some other attractive object, would attract the game. When the attention of the antelope is attracted by such an object alternately appearing and disappearing, its curiosity becomes excited, and an interesting struggle commences between that and its timidity, and it will approach cautiously, then retreat a little, then prance around, drawing towards the object gradually till it is finally brought within bow-shot. Then it was that the Indian would let fly his arrow from his concealment, or spring to his feet, the arrow to the string, and the bow partly drawn, and strike his victim before his fleetness could carry him beyond reach.

In stalking this animal the Indians show great dexterity now, though we may well assume not equal to that of their ancestors, who knew not the use of fire-arms. This feat is extremely difficult though not impossible in the naked plains, where neither sage-bush or ant-hill is found to conceal the approach, but only the short, sparse grass is found. When this or the former mode is resolved upon, the first step of the hunter who sees his game in the far distance is by describing a wide circle, if need be, to obtain a position to the leeward of the game, so that the odor with which he taints the air may not betray him. Thus, if upon the naked plain, while yet a long distance off, he must get down upon the ground and crawl as close to it as possible, always when moving keeping his eye upon every one of the band, and the instant one of them turns his head towards him stop every movement, no matter what his position may be, till the animal turns away or again goes to feeding. If none of the animals smell him or hear him, or see him move, he may steal upon them and secure a prize. No matter if they do see him, unless they see some motion the chances are that no one of them will recognize him or suspect that the object is anything harmful. They will not notice that they have never before seen an object there on the naked plain. If they see the least motion their fears are instantly aroused, and they dash away like the wind to a safe distance, when they will usually stop and turn round to see what it was that alarmed them. If the hunter still remains perfectly quiet their alarm will not usually subside entirely for some time, but they will soon renew their retreat, though perhaps not at full speed, and if they even go to feeding not far away they are apt to keep a vigilant watch of the object so that it is hardly possible to approach them again.

Stalking among the sage brush is of course much less difficult, for there the hunter has cover, behind which he may conceal his approach. Still, when he deems it necessary to get a view of the game, he must raise his head above the brush as little as possible, and so slowly and cautiously that if one of the animals happens to be looking in that direction he will not observe it. Of course it is presumed he will already have taken advantage of the wind which would help to prevent the hearing of any slight noise he might accidentally make, for if the sense of hearing of this animal is not as acute as that of the moose, it is so sensitive as to require the extremest care to prevent his becoming alarmed in that way.

Formerly the Indians were aware of the fact that our antelope will not leap over even moderate obstructions, and took advantage of it, as was shown under another head. Even small prairies, nearly surrounded by woods, with but a narrow door to the open country, have become slaughter-pens for the timid antelope, when they have been bordered by dense under-brush. Their only thought seems to be to escape by the same opening they came in at. If prevented in this they seem to have no other resource. In their fright their wits seem to forsake them, and they become confused and distracted.

As illustrating this characteristic of the animal, I will quote from "Adventures of James C. Adams" (pp. 46, 47). With several men he had surrounded a drove of about fifty antelopes in an open prairie of high grass, when he says : "And upon closing in, the animals, seeing too late that they were surrounded, became bewildered, and, huddling together, wheeled and tramped around in utter amazement, apparently not knowing what to do or where to go.

" In the mean while, taking care to keep our bodies concealed in the long grass, we had continued to approach, and being now within sixty yards of the panic-stricken animals, I rose upon my feet, took deliberate aim, and fired into their midst. Sykesey and Tuolumne followed the example, and the Indians discharged their arrows. I reloaded as quickly as possible and fired a second shot, then, dropping the rifle, pulled my revolver in my right and my bowie-knife in my left hand, and rushed into the thick of the herd, which continued wheeling and tramping around in a circle, seeing themselves surrounded on all sides, and too much alarmed to fly. At the same time my comrades rushed forward, and we were soon all mixed up together, myself, the Indians, and the antelopes. Having discharged the shots of my pistol I began plying my knife, and as the Indians used theirs we wounded several that escaped our fire-arms. In the midst of the excitement a buck broke away from the herd and was immediately followed by all that were able to get away, some dragging lamed limbs after them. As, however, six dead and five wounded lay before us, there was no use pursuing the flying band, and they were allowed to escape, although we might easily have procured a dozen more."

As we shall hereafter see, this description answers almost exactly to the conduct of the barren-ground caribou under similar circumstances.

They have often been killed by the hunter, who has ridden upon them on horseback when they were asleep and alone. If the instant the animal starts the horseman will stop he is almost sure of a shot. Under these circumstances the antelope will make but a few bounds before he will stop and look around to see what has alarmed him, when he may be taken at short range. The white tent of the hunter on the plains or in the ravines so attracts the curiosity of the Prong Buck that he will go quite up to it for a close inspection of it if he sees no one about it or in the neighborhood, and many a one who has been laying in camp from indisposition or for rest has thus secured antelope chops for supper as a surprise to his wearied comrade, who may have been unfortunate during the day, and when wending his weary way back sadly thought of an empty larder near the camp fire.

I have seen accounts of coursing the antelope with greyhounds, but my information is not sufficient to enable me to speak advisedly on the subject, never having participated in the sport myself, nor conversed with one who has done so. I can imagine no finer game for this sport than the Prong Buck. A practically limitless plain, smooth and level, with no impediments to obstruct the view or the chase, presents the fittest ground for such sport. With an animal so fleet that he would leave the hounds far in the rear for the first few miles, yet always in sight so as to stimulate the dogs in the pursuit, whose better wind would soon tell, they would, before many miles were passed over, run into the quarry.

After they obtained horses, and before they procured fire-arms, the aborigines pursued the antelope on horseback. Under date of August 14, 1805, Lewis and Clark gave an account of a hunt on the pass of the Rocky Mountains, between the head waters of the Missouri River and Lewis River. They say: " The chief game of the Shoshonees, therefore, is the antelope, which, when pursued, retreats to the open plains, where the horses have full room for the chase. But such is its extraordinary fleetness and wind, that a single horse has no possible chance of outrunning it, or tiring it down; and the hunters are therefore obliged to resort to stratagem.

" About twenty Indians, mounted on fine horses, and armed with bows and arrows, left the camp. In a short time they descried a herd of ten antelopes; they immediately separated into little squads of two or three, and formed a scattered circle round the herd for five or six miles, keeping at a wary distance so as not to alarm them till they were perfectly inclosed, and usually selecting some commanding eminence as a stand. Having gained their positions, a small party rode towards the herd, and with wonderful dexterity the huntsman preserved his seat as he ran at full speed over the hills, and down the steep ravines, and along the borders of the precipices. They were soon outstripped by the antelopes, which, on gaining the other extremity of the circle, were driven back and pursued by the fresh hunters. They turned and flew rather than ran in another direction; but there, too, they found new enemies. In this way they were alternately pushed backwards and forwards, till at length, notwithstanding the skill of the hunters, they all escaped; and the party, after running for two hours, returned without having caught anything, and their horses foaming with sweat. This chase, the greater part of which was seen from the camp, formed a beautiful scene; but to the hunters is exceedingly laborious, and so unproductive, even when they are able to worry the animal down and shoot him, that forty or fifty hunters will sometimes be engaged for half a day without obtaining more than two or three antelopes."

That the antelope can frequently, on favorable grounds, be run into with the horse, is established beyond dispute. I have met several gentlemen who have done it, or seen it done; and I once had a three years' old male antelope which had been thus captured. The marks of the cords with which his legs had been tied were still very plainly to be seen, and are even still distinct on the mounted specimen in my collection. To do this requires a horse of great *bottom*, or endurance, for, in any event, he must be left far behind for the first few miles; but the great speed of the antelope soon tells upon him, and when he begins to falter, if still pressed, and not allowed to stop and take breath, he fails very rapidly, and almost complete exhaustion ensues. It may be that the antelopes thus captured have been exceptionably slow, or short-winded, and that even with a majority it is not practicable to capture them in this manner. It is very certain, however, that it has sometimes been done.

The antelope, when pursued on the plains, is inclined to run in a circle, and thus may be taken advantage of by the horseman keeping well within the circle, and as if attempting to head off the chase, which is sure to provoke the animal to make every effort to avoid this result, which brings his course more in the circular form. In this condition the game must soon succumb, in consequence of the greater distance he has to run.

HIS PLACE.

The position in natural history which should be assigned our antelope has already occupied the attention of zoölogists. If Pallas made it but a species of the antelope, later naturalists have agreed to assign to it a separate classification, and have adopted the name given it by Ord in 1818, *Antilocapra Americana*, or American Goat-Antelope. Sir John Richardson says : " The term *Americana* is objectionable as a specific name, where more than one species of the same genus exists in that country." Subsequent investigations have shown that this objection was altogether without foundation, for there is but one species of the genus.

A careful study of specimens from every part of its range shows that there are not even varieties of the species. All are as near alike as possible. There is now no pretense for placing *Capra Americana* with our animal, for it is well settled that it is a true goat.

Dr. Murie, to whom we are first indebted for the osteological description of this animal, seems inclined to go farther, and assign it " a new or a fourth section among ruminants. In regard to the second premise, its place, judging from the totality of structure (excluding the brain not examined), it appears to me that the proposal to rank the Cabrit as a family *per se* (*Antilocapridæ*), merits attention. Notwithstanding what has been said of transitional forms, the present career of biological inquiry has not yet arrived at the stage when limited divisions can be dispensed with, although lines of demarcation are broken apace. Provisionally, therefore, and for aught I can say to the contrary, the single genus and species, *Antilocapra Americana*, may preside as the type of a family. Still I am far from the opinion that it will long remain in solitary grandeur, for I am convinced that its more aberrant features are but bridges, the further connecting end of which temporarily hazy to us, from our temporary, circumscribed view."

I have already, in another place, quoted a passage from this author bearing directly on this branch of our subject; but, as it will be remembered, it is hardly necessary to repeat it here. The comparison he there makes between this animal and the sheep, the giraffe, the deer, the goat, and the antelope, is for the purpose of showing that, in some respects, he partakes of certain characteristics supposed to be peculiar to each of these animals.

We have already seen that to compare the hair of our animal to that of the sheep is a strained expression, while the other parallels are not without reasonable warrant. I cannot help remarking, however, that it seems to me that the learned doctor, in seeking for intermediate grades in the characteristics of our animal, has quite overlooked that which is the most striking of all; and that is the horn. If he combines characteristics resembling peculiarities of several different genera of ruminants, his horn seems to be constructed upon an intermediate plan between the hollow-horned ruminants, of which there are several genera, and the solid-horned ruminants which may all be embraced in the genus Cervus, if we are inclined not to multiply classifications too freely. The former have hollow horns, which are dermal emanations with osseous cores, which in fact are processes of the skull. So has this; but all other hollow horns are persistent, while this is deciduous. This latter characteristic, has been hitherto supposed to be peculiar to the Cervidæ, all of which have solid horns purely of osseous structure. The only thing in common which these two classes of head appendages have, is that they may be considered ornamental, and serve as weapons of warfare; to which, however, we may add that they appear more generally on the male than on the female. They are provided for both the male and female of our antelope. On no other animal do we find a hollow horn which is branched or bifurcated, while this is a characteristic of nearly all solid horns. This hollow horn alone is branched, not so distinctly, by any means, as is usual with the solid horns, but still there is the rudiment of a branch, at least, which has been recognized by all naturalists as a prong. If, then, we are in search of a bridge to span the wide space between the hollow-horned and the solid-horned ruminants, we find it in this animal and in this animal alone.

Besides the horns, it more resembles the hollow-horned than the solid-horned ruminants, and most of all, the antelope. Its genital organs are very nearly like those of the true antelope; and in my grounds it showed a disposition to associate with the antelope gazelle, while it was never known to pay the least attention to either the angora or the common goat, any more than to the deer, the sheep, or the cows. In only two characteristics can I find it resembles the goat. One is, that it constantly emits an odor, which, however, is mostly confined to the male in the goat, while it is common to both sexes in our antelope. Then, again, the lachrymal sinus is wanting in both the Prong Buck and the goat; so it is wanting in many other hollow-horned ruminants, as the sheep and the ox, while it is present in the true antelope, and, I believe, in all the deer family. In all other respects it differs from the goat, except in those things which are common to all ruminants. In their food, especially, they are widely apart, though both are strictly vegetarians; so are all ruminants. The goat is the most promiscuous consumer in this order of quadrupeds; while no one is more delicate and select in its food than the Prong Buck. The goat affects rough and rocky grounds, and climbs with ease and safety dangerous cliffs and difficult passes, while the habit of our antelope is exactly the reverse. I must say that I think if his natural history had been well understood, he would never have been charged with a near kinship to the goat, and *Capra* would not have been a part of his name. Surely a more appropriate name could have been found, — one clearly expressive of the striking peculiarities of this extraordinary animal. But it is now too late to change it. It is far better to adhere to a bad name by which it is now known to the scientific world, than to attempt to introduce him by a new name, no matter how much more appropriate.

In its osteology, Dr. Theodore Gill, a gentleman eminently qualified for the investigation, excludes it from all the classifications of the hollow-horned ruminants, and distinctly places it among those which have solid deciduous antlers; while, as we have seen, Dr. Murie finds in its anatomy elements peculiar to each of these classifications. Like the deer, the female has four active mammæ, while the goat has but two. In common with the hollow-horned ruminants, it has the gall bladder, which is wanting in all the Cervidæ.

5

THE DEER OF AMERICA.

To the First Class of the Second Division of the First Group of
Ruminants I have assigned the Cervidæ. On this continent they
are more widely distributed, and more numerous than either of
the other members of the group, while in some other parts of
the world they are excelled in numbers by those assigned to the
First Class of the First Division.

There are native of North America, eight distinct and well
defined species of the Genus Cervus, namely : —

1. CERVUS ALCES.
Moose Deer.

2. CERVUS CANADENSIS.
Wapiti Deer. American Elk.

3. CERVUS TARANDUS.
Woodland Caribou. Reindeer.

4. CERVUS MACROTIS.
Mule Deer.

5. CERVUS COLUMBIANUS.
Columbia Black-tailed Deer.

6. CERVUS VIRGINIANUS.
Common or Virginia Deer.

7. CERVUS TARANDUS ARCTICA.
Barren-ground Caribou. Reindeer.

8. CERVUS ACAPULCENSIS.
Acapulco Deer.

There may be and probably are, several other distinct species
in Mexico and Central America, but I am not sufficiently informed to speak of them with assurance ; so I leave them as
proper subjects for future investigation, and confine myself to
those of which I can speak with some confidence.

It will be observed that I retain the reindeer in this genus,
following Cuvier, for instance, rather than go with Hamilton

Smith and others, who place them in a separate genus — *Rangi-fer*, — for which I fail to find sufficient warrant. I confess I do not sympathize with that disposition, which seeks to multiply genera and species on slight distinctions, as the presence or absence of canine teeth, or the female being provided with antlers or not, as constituting a generic difference. Of the first, third, and seventh species of which I treat, I do not speak from that careful personal study of great numbers of living specimens, which I could desire, and am obliged to depend to a large extent upon information derived from the observations of others. Of the others I am enabled to speak with assured confidence from personal observations of live specimens in my own grounds, where I could study them with the greatest care through a course of years, and from hunting them in the wild state.

It will be observed that in my list of species I have omitted *Cervus leucurus* and *Cervus Mexicanus.* I do this because I find them to be simply *Cervus Virginianus*, with scarcely sufficient distinctive characteristics to entitle them to the rank of separate varieties. When I come to treat of this species, I shall give my reasons in full for writing *Cervus leucurus* and *Cervus Mexicanus* out of the list of species of the American Deer.

Naturalists disagree, and perhaps ever will, as to what diversity shall be required to distinguish varieties, species, genera, orders, etc. From the nature of the subject it may be impossible to lay down a general rule by which even its author would in all cases be able to place some particular specimen which might occasionally be selected.

Nor is it of the first importance that all should exactly agree on this point. At least it is more important that we get all the facts relating to a particular subject; and then our disagreements about names, although inconvenient, may not be of vital importance. I may, however, say, that at least before we can declare a species as distinct from a variety, we must find distinctive characteristics constant and uniform in every individual of the proposed species, and wanting in every other individual of the same genus, which characteristics should not be attributable to factitious circumstances or local causes, as aliment, climate, altitude, and the like, which at most should only be allowed to mark varieties of the same species. Still we are liable to meet with difficulties, which may only be removed, if at all, by long and careful observation and study, which may enable us to determine upon the thousand points of divergence or similitude which may be manifested under a great variety of circumstances.

Male Moose.

CERVUS ALCES, Linn.

Moose Deer.

Cervus Alces. . . . . HARLAN, Fauna Am., 229, 1825.
GODMAN, Am. Nat. Hist., II. 279.
GRIFFITH, An. King., IV. 72, Fig.
RICHARDSON, Fauna Boreali Americana, 232, 1829.
DE KAY, N. Y. Zoöl., 15, 1842, Fig.
AUD. & BACH., Quad. N. Am., II. 179, Fig.

Cervus orignal. . . . (Dierville) Reichenbach, Vollst., Naturg. Säugt., III. Wiederkauer, 10, 1845, Figs. [Baird.]

Cervus lobatus. . . . AGASSIZ, Pr. Bost. Soc. N. H., II. 188, 1846.

Alces Americanus. . . JARDINE, Nat. Lib., III. 125, 1835. [Baird.]
BAIRD, U. S. Pat. Off. Agr., for 1851, 112, 1852.
BAIRD, Pacific R. R. Rep., VIII. 631.

Alces machlis. . . . . OGILBY, Pr. Zool. Soc. Lond., IV. 135, 1836.

Alces malchis. . . . . GRAY, Knows. Menag., 67, 1850.
GRAY, Pr. Zoöl. Soc. Lond., XVIII. 224, 1850.

Alces muswa. . . . . RICHARDSON, Zoöl. of Herald, Foss. Mamm., 101, 1852.

Elan, Stag, or Aptaptou. DE MONTS, Nova Francia, 250, 1604.
Eslan ou orignat. . . SAGARD-THEODAT, Canada, 749, 1636.
Alce Alces. . . . . . GILPIN, Mamm. N. S., 119, 1871.
American Black Elk. . GRIFFITH, Cuv., IV. 72.
Moose. . . . . . . UMFREVILLE, Huds. Bay, 1790.
HERRIOT'S TRAV., Fig. 1807.
BAIRD, Pacific R. R. Rep., VIII. 631, 1857.

Moose Deer. . . . . PENNANT, Arct. Zoöl., I. 17, Fig., 1784.
WARDEN, U. S., I. 328.
GODMAN, Nat. Hist., II. 274.
AUD. & BACH., Quad. N. Am., II. 179.
RICHARDSON, F. B. A., 232.
DUDLEY, Phil. Trans., No. 368, 165, 1721.

Orignal. . . . . . . LA HONTAN, Voy., 72, 1703.
CHARLEVOIX, Nouv. France, V. 185, 1744.
DENY, Descr. de l'Amer., I. 27.
DU PRATZ, Louis., I. 301.
FRENCH CANADIANS. [Rich. F. B. A., 231.]

The Elk. . . . . . .   GRIFFITH, Cuv., V. 303.
The Moose. . . . . .   HARDY, F. L. in Ac., 45, Fig., 1869.

Largest of all the deer family and most ungainly in form.   Head long
and narrow.   Eyes small and sunken.   Nose long and flexible and covered with hairs, except a spot between the nostrils.   Ears very long and
coarse.   Antlers large and spreading; broadly palmated with numerous
sharp points.   Neck short and stout and nearly horizontal; higher at
the wethers than at the hips.   Body short and round.   Legs long and
stout; fore legs the longest.   Accessory hoofs large and loosely attached.
No metatarsal gland.   Tarsal gland inside the hock present but small,

J.MANZ–CHICAGO.

Female Moose.

and covered with black reversed hair.   Hair long, coarse, and rather
brittle; longest about the neck; color variant from black to brown and
yellowish gray.   Antlers wanting on the female, which is smaller than
the male and lighter colored in winter.

GENERAL REMARKS.

I have never attempted the domestication of this species, and
have seen but few live specimens, and then under circumstances
not favorable to a careful study of the animal.   Hence my ex-
aminations have been principally confined to mounted specimens

and skins ; therefore, I am vastly more indebted to the trust-
worthy observations of others, than to my own original observations. Fortunately the Moose has been treated of by several
naturalists of great ability ; each of whom has added something
to the general stock of knowledge, to which I may be able to
make but slight additions. That there is much yet to learn, may
not be questioned, and I much regret the want of opportunities
for studying this animal under domestication, for in this way
alone, do I deem it possible to attain anything like a thorough
knowledge of any member of this interesting family of ruminants.
I hope it may be my good fortune to do this at some future time,
but if I should not, then I trust some other person, better qualified to observe facts and to draw correct conclusions through careful and patient observations, will feel sufficient interest in the
subject to incur the expense and take the time to make proper
investigations, and in the interests of science to make them
known.

HABITAT.

The habitat of this, the grandest of our native ruminants, with
perhaps one exception, originally extended from about forty-
three to seventy degrees north latitude, occupying the entire
breadth of the continent. He was seen as far south as the Ohio
River, and has been met with as far north as the mouth of
Mackenzie River ; though I think they should be regarded as
having been visitors rather than settled residents in both these
localities. In portions of the territory which I have assigned
them he was rarely if ever found, because of the absence of the
conditions required by his habits ; but wherever these conditions
did exist, he occupied the country in numbers proportioned to
the favorable character of them. Everywhere these conditions
have been impaired, and in places destroyed, by the presence of
the white man ; and in proportion as this has obtained has he
disappeared altogether, or greatly diminished in number. Indeed,
this may be said of most of our wild animals. They could stand
the Indians, and could multiply and prosper in their presence.
The rude weapons of the natives seemed not to have any abiding
or fatal terror for the Moose, while the weapons and modes of destruction adopted by the white man have either destroyed them,
or driven them to the most secluded places attainable. When
Hennepin and Lasalle first visited Illinois, two hundred years
ago, the bison abounded in prodigious numbers, although the

whole country was occupied by Indian tribes, who to a great extent lived upon them. For the next hundred years but few white men visited the country, and scarcely any settled in it; and yet in that time nearly all the bison had crossed the Mississippi River; and after the most diligent research, I cannot learn that one has been seen in Illinois for the last eighty-five or ninety years. The last bison were observed in Illinois between 1780 and 1790.

If the range of the Moose is more inaccessible than that of the bison, and so he has been enabled to protect himself better when partially surrounded by civilization, his habitat has been constantly more and more circumscribed, as civilization has advanced upon him, till now he is only found in considerable numbers in Northern Alaska. Whimpon, who explored the Yukon River in 1867, found the moose very abundant in 65° and 66° north latitude, and about 146° west longitude. He says: " This part of the river abounds in Moose. At this season (June) the mosquitoes in the woods are a terrible scourge, and even the Moose cannot stand them. He plunges into the water and wades or swims, as the case may be, often making for the islands. This is, therefore, a favorite part of the Yukon for the Indian hunter. The Moose are scarce at Nuclukayeth, and never known as low as Nulato. They must, however, be abundant on the smaller rivers, as, for example, the Newicargut, where the meat obtained was nearly all of this animal." Nulato is in west longitude 159° and within less than two degrees of the Pacific Coast, and but little south of Behring Strait.

Some are met with every year in Montana, where they are sometimes called by the hunters *Tree Toppers*, and are represented as being much taller than the average of the species; though this I much doubt, presuming the size has been exaggerated by hunters desiring to sell me live specimens at exorbitant prices. They are said to be found in considerable numbers in the Dominion north of Montana, whence they are now rapidly disappearing.

It is impossible to say how abundant they are in the extreme northern part of the continent, but it is probable they are not much diminished, for there they were never in great numbers, and probably never remained through the arctic winter. A few still remain in the extreme northeastern parts of the United States. In Nova Scotia and New Brunswick a few are taken each year, but it requires the most skillful hunters, with patient perseverance and hardy endurance to insure success in hunting them. But they are noble game, and worthy the ambition of the true sportsman. They have probably entirely ceased their visits to Newfoundland ; but in Labrador many still remain, though gradually retreating thence towards the more secluded and inaccessible portions of the country. From Upper Canada all are gone, and but very few remain in Lower Canada, where, fifty years since, they were quite abundant. What are left have retreated to the great, dense forests of the north.

ALIMENT.

Their principal food is arboreous, though they take for variety some of the grasses and mosses freely ; and, when necessity demands, will live on almost any sort of vegetation found in their range. In winter, when all herbaceous vegetation is deeply buried in the snow, they depend entirely on the trees and shrubs.

Their favorite haunts, especially in summer, are in the neighborhood of rivers, lakes, and marshy or swampy grounds, where the grasses which flourish are long and coarse. In winter, they are more inclined to resort to higher ground, but generally where dense forests and almost impenetrable thickets prevail. Their long legs, and short, thick necks, incapacitate them to gather the low grasses upon which most other vegetarian quadrupeds may freely feed, so that they can only conveniently feed upon the upper portions of the taller grasses. The deep snow in the regions in which they live conceals them in winter, when they are obliged to depend on the forests for sustenance. This necessity, of itself, is sufficient to form habits and tastes inclining them to this class of food. So it is that we generally find the habits of animals spring from constraint or necessity, which conforms them physically to the conditions in which they live.

Exceptionally, among ruminants, the Moose feeds upon evergreens, as well as upon deciduous trees and shrubs.

THE CHASE.

Even before the introduction of firearms among them the aborigines were successful in their capture, and even depended largely upon the flesh of the Moose for their support. To accomplish this, great ingenuity and perseverance were often exercised, while at other times, as in the water or on the crusted snow, it was not a difficult undertaking, and even now these conditions render them an easy prey to the hunter.

Under other conditions the keen senses of smell and hearing make it difficult to approach the Moose, and the sagacity with which he eludes his enemies and the endurance with which he flees from them makes his pursuit even with firearms a difficult and laborious affair.

FORM AND SIZE.

In form the Moose is an ungainly animal ; short body, a very short tail and neck with a prodigiously long, ugly head, with a projecting nose or upper lip, which give the animal a revolting look. He has enormous ears, short spreading palmated antlers, and very long legs, to which he is indebted for his great height, which some authors have stated has sometimes exceeded eight feet. It is safe to say, without the fear of exaggerating, that they sometimes attain a height of six feet at the wethers, or even more in extreme cases.

The average weight of the adult male Moose may be given as seven hundred pounds, while I think the statement well authenticated that specimens of twice that weight have been killed.

The male Moose, and sometimes the female as well, is furnished with a pendulous appendage under the throat. This may vary in length from four to ten inches on different individuals. It is covered with long coarse black hairs. Its diameter outside the hairs is about one fourth its length. This by some has been supposed to be of a glandular structure, but on examination it is found to be simply dermal, without any muscular tissue. The one I dissected was five inches long, without the hairs, and half an inch in diameter ; simply a round piece of skin of uniform bigness its whole length, thickly set with the coarse hairs all around. These occupy a descending position all the way. They are quite firm, elastic, and enduring, like those of the mane of the horse, and probably are not shed with the rest of the coat, spring and fall. This *bell*, as it is called by the hunters, is not found on the young male, and disappears when the animal gets old and his vigor and vitality are on the decline, so that it is in general confined to the male Moose in the prime of life, although as stated it is in rare instances found on the females. I will suggest, without the authority of positive information, that these females would, upon examination, be found to be exceptionally vigorous.

I am not prepared to offer any conjecture as to the purposes of this appendage, — which after all seems to be transitory, — in the economy of the animal. There is no gland or tuft of hair on the outside of the hind leg, but on the inside of the back is a small gland covered with a tuft of black hair occupying a horizontal position.

THE COAT.

The summer coat of the Moose is of soft, fine, firm hair, while the winter coat, which is at first short, fine, and glossy, as the season advances becomes coarse, open, and spory, non-elastic and rather fragile, though never as much so as those on several of the other species. During the winter the Moose has an abundant undercoat of fur.

The early winter coat on the Moose when in the prime of life may be said in general to be black. Toward spring it fades very considerably, more on the aged than on the younger specimens. When the Moose has passed his prime, he loses that glossy brilliancy which once distinguished him, and the color degenerates to a dirty gray, especially in old age.

HABITS.

The rutting season of the Moose, at least in the lower latitudes, commences in September, although the females do not reciprocate till October ; and during the interval the bucks are almost beside themselves with passion and are avoided by the females. At the proper time the female seeks a companion, when they retire to some secluded spot and spend the honeymoon together, quite contented in each other's society unless disturbed by some intruder. They are more strictly monogamic in their habits than any other of our deer, or indeed most other quadrupeds.

In this respect it resembles the roe deer (*Capreolas dorcas*) of Europe, although it is not as constant in its conjugal relations as the roe deer. These continue constant through life, manifesting throughout the year the same affection for each other, both parents devoting themselves with equal fidelity to the charge of their young, while the constancy of the Moose is limited to a single season and during the rut. Still this is a great improvement on the beastly habit of our elk, wapiti, which goes to the other extreme, as we shall hereafter see.

Male Elk or Wapiti, in early winter coat.

CERVUS CANADENSIS, Erxleben.

American Elk. Wapiti Deer.

Cervus Canadensis. . . . . DESMAREST, Mamm., II. 433, 1822.
HARLAN, Fauna Amer., 236, 1825.
MAX VON WIED, Reise, II. 24, 1839.
SCHREBER, Säugt., V. 990.
GODMAN, II. 294.
GRAY, Pr. Zoöl. Soc. Lond., 1850,
226.
GIEBEL, Säugt., 1855, 348.
BAIRD, Pacific R. R. Rep., VIII. 638.

Cervus Elaphus Canadensis. . ERXLEBEN, Syst., 305, 1777.
BODDAERT, Elenchus Anim., 135,
1784.

Cervus (Elaphus) Canadensis. SMITH, Griff. Cuv., IV. 96.
Cervus major. . . . . . . ORD., Guth. Geog., 292, 1815.
DESMAREST, Mamm., II. 432.

Cervus occidentalis. . . . . HAM. SMITH, Griff. Cuv., IV. 101,
1827.

Cervus strongyloceros. . . . RICHARDSON, F. B. A., 251, 1829.
SCHREBER, Säug.
SUNDEVALL, K. Vetenskaps Akad.
Hand. for 1844.

Cervus Wapiti. . . . . BARTON, Am. Phil. Trans., VI. 70.
LEACH, Jour. de Phys., LXXXV. 67.

American Elk. . . . . . . BEWICK, Quad., 112.
Elaphus Canadensis. . . . . DE KAY, N. Y. Zoöl., I. 118.
AUD. & BACH., II. 83.
BAIRD, U. S. Pat. Off. Rep. Agr.
for 1851, 116.

Alces Americanus. . . . . JEFFERSON, Notes on Virginia, 77.
Elk. . . . . LEWIS & CLARK, June 18, 1804.
Expedition, by Paul Allen, I. 19,
et seq.
AMERICAN FRONTIERSMEN AND
HUNTERS.
E. H. SMITH, Med. Rep., II. 157,
1805.

Le Wapiti. . . . . F. CUVIER, Hist. Nat. des Mamm.,
Liv. 20, 1820.
ST. HIL. & CUV., Hist. Mammif., IV.
1819, Fig.

Red Deer.	Umfreville, Huds. Bay, 163, 1790.
	Hudson Bay Traders (Richardson).
Stag.	Pennant, Arct. Zoöl., I. 27.
	Ibid., Hist. Quad., No. 45.
The Wapiti.	Smith, Griffith's An. King., IV. 96.
Wapiti.	Barton, Med. and Phys. Journ., III. 36.
	Warden, U. S., I. 241.
Wewaskiss.	Hearne, Journ., 360.

Larger than any known deer except *Cervus alces.* Head slim and finely formed. Muffle partly naked. Eyes medium size and moderately prominent. Antlers solid, cylindrical, with many anterior tines, large, expanding, retreating, deciduous. Ears large and coarse. Lachrymal sinus large and naked. Neck rather short and elevated. Body round and rather short, hips sloping. Tail very short. Legs well formed and stout, but not fleshy. Metatarsal gland high up. Tarsal gland wanting. Body yellowish brown. Belly black. Neck brown to black. Legs chestnut brown. Rump and buttock white. Hoofs tawny brown. Antlers only on the males. Interdigital glands wanting on all the feet.

GENERAL REMARKS.

For more than fifteen years I have kept our Elk in domestication. In all I have had more than one hundred individuals, all of which, except twelve, were dropped in my grounds. I have had as many as fifty-four at one time, and now have between forty and fifty; and have devoted much time to their study. I have hunted and studied them in their wild state, and I have corresponded and conversed very extensively with those who have observed their habits in their native range. I must claim, therefore, that I have had excellent facilities for learning their natural history, and if I have not profited by these it is because I am incapable of doing so.

HABITAT.

But few quadrupeds in our country have occupied a wider range than the American Elk. He was found in every part of the present United States and in northern Mexico; and was abundant in both Upper and Lower Canada, and in Labrador. In the interior, he was found as far north as the fifty-sixth or fifty-seventh degree of north latitude; but I cannot find any evidence that he ever went so far north on either coast.

Our Elk preferred the woodlands or the mountains, and only inhabited the prairies in limited numbers. Like the bison they

Female Elk or Wapiti, in early winter coat

Young Elk or Wapiti.

fled before the approach of civilization and sought safety in seclusion, as much as possible, though they remained in mountainous
regions and in deep forests, long after the bison had been driven
away by the occasional presence of the white man. Indeed, they
followed the bison reluctantly, and braved the danger from their
new enemies with a certain degree of resolution. They were
found in diminished numbers on our prairies, long after the bison
had crossed the Mississippi River for safety. Indeed, not until
the white settlers began to locate on the borders of the groves,
did they finally depart. The last account I get of their presence
in northern Illinois was in the year 1820, or thereabouts. In
1818 they were not observed east of the Illinois River, and but
few were then found on the western bank of that stream. An old
settler of high respectability assures me that he saw their tracks
in the forest north of Peoria in 1829, but did not see the animals.

In the Canadas, as also in New Brunswick, Nova Scotia, and
in the northeastern parts of the United States, where their range
lapped over on that of the moose, the fear of the white man's
weapons has long since driven them all away, although their
larger relatives still linger there in diminished numbers, no doubt
because they can evade pursuit more readily in the deep snows
which there prevail than the Wapiti were able to do. Mr. J. M.
La Moine of Quebec, informs me that he can find no account of
Wapiti having been met with in Lower Canada in the last one
hundred and fifty years, though their fossil antlers are occasionally found there. Mr. H. Y. Hind, in his account of "Explorations of Labrador," says that they remained in the seclusion of
that peninsula till a much later period.

Till comparatively recent times they were found in northern
Iowa ; and in 1877 I saw several accounts of them having been
killed in the northern part of the lower peninsula of Michigan,
also in Minnesota. So, too, in the southwest, in Arkansas and
Texas, they still linger where they can find protection in the
dense thickets. In California, where they were once exceedingly
abundant, they are now rarely seen, although they maintained
their ground for some years after the miners had invaded that
territory. In Oregon and Washington territories, they have
been driven back by the white settlements, it is true, but still
they are there though in diminished numbers ; and the same
may be said of British Columbia.

From necessity they no longer abandon a country on the first
appearance of the white settlers, for now scarcely any place is left

for them to flee to, where they will not hear the report of the
hunter's, or the miner's, or the herdsman's rifle. They are now
sometimes met with not far west of the Missouri River in secluded
places, along the borders of the streams, coming down from the
far off mountains, as well as along the broken foot-hills of the
Rocky Mountains ; and high up, on the main ranges, the Elk are
still to be found, sometimes singly, and sometimes in considerable
bands. In 1870, Dr. Hayden's party killed one, on the head-
waters of the east fork of the Yellowstone, at an altitude of
more than ten thousand feet above the sea. They will no doubt
continue to maintain themselves in the more secluded parts of
the country, where this, among the noblest of our game animals,
will occasionally reward the hardy hunter, who shall with great
energy and toil seek him in his retreat.

They have been observed quite lately on the Lower Yellowstone River in greater numbers than in any other place of which
I have any account. Lieut. L. B. Carpenter, U. S. A., informs
me that he has seen them there in immense droves containing
perhaps thousands. I have never heard of so large congregations
of the Wapiti in any other place at any time.

FORM AND SIZE.

In size the Elk is only less than the moose, but in this regard
they vary very much, when adult, as well as in form. The
southern Elk attain the largest size, which is exceptional among
the deer. The first male Elk I ever had was sent me from the
south, and he was the largest I ever owned. When he arrived,
he was three years old and weighed six hundred and fifty
pounds after having been four days on steamboat and cars. In
September, after he was five years old, some reckless or vicious
person shot and broke one of his hind legs, when I was obliged
to kill him. He was very fat, and the butcher who dressed him,
estimated that he would weigh nine hundred pounds live weight.
He stood over sixteen hands high, at the withers. As the Elk
grows till he is eight or nine years old, had the Elk we are writing about lived his full age I think he would have attained to
the weight of ten or eleven hundred pounds. I shall always regret the loss of such an opportunity to ascertain, approximately,
the greatest weight which the Elk will attain. I have had does
that would not weigh over three hundred and fifty pounds at full
maturity, and were scarcely more than three and a half feet

6

high. All these small specimens are now eliminated from my herd, while the impress of that first large buck is very percep-tible on my stock. I think six hundred pounds will exceed the average live weight of the full grown buck.

The Elk is taller and shorter in proportion to his weight, than either the ox or the horse. It is to be regretted that I neglected to take the measurements of the large specimen of which I have spoken; but the truth is, I did not understand the importance of the subject then as I do now, nor did I then feel the scientific in-terest in it which I now feel. Our Elk has a small, well-formed head, which is very broad between the eyes, which are rather prominent and brilliant. The nose is small and naked. The lachrymal opening is large, and is situate immediately below the inner corner of the eye, and is surrounded by a naked border.

It has a large, coarse ear. The antlers are cylindrical, with anterior tines, which are long, slender, and graceful. The neck is rather short. The body is round. It has a very short tail. The legs are long, clean, and flat. The fore legs are straight, the hind legs rather crooked. The feet are small.

The shades of color differ considerably on different individuals. In general it may be said that the head is a chestnut brown; neck dark brown; sides, back, and thighs, yellowish gray; under the belly black; legs, clove brown. On the rump is a white patch which extends down on either side of the tail and unites with the white below between the legs. The lower part of the white patch has a black border on either side.

The metatarsal gland is present, but is overgrown with hairs; the tarsal gland is entirely wanting, in which it differs from all the other species of this genus, in this country, though there are some in Europe and in India, in which this gland is also want-ing.

The Elk has a very thick skin, which affords a great protection against violence. He minds but little a blow from a club, or a whip, or a stone. It takes a hard thrust even with a hay-fork, to make him mind it much unless a very vulnerable point is reached, as close back of the fore leg.

The hairs of the summer coat and of the early winter coat are short and pretty solid, but as the season advances, on the body, thighs, and neck the hairs grow longer, and in diameter and the cavity within, are much enlarged; they become crinkled and more fragile, but never as brittle as on some of the other species. In winter, a heavy undercoat of fur is always present.

The flesh is fine flavored, but differs from all other venison. It is more nutritious than any other meat of which I have knowledge. A hungry laboring man is satisfied with about half the amount which would be required of beef. This nutritious quality of the flesh of the Elk is first alluded to by Lewis and Clark, and is fully confirmed by my observations.

FOOD AND HABITS.

This animal is the most promiscuous consumer of all the deer. All the grasses and most of the weeds within his reach are taken freely, and the leaves and twigs of all the deciduous trees are alike enjoyed. A considerable proportion of his daily food he desires to be arboreous, yet if deprived of it he will keep in good condition on herbaceous food alone.

In winter, he will take the coarsest food; even that which the ox and the horse reject, he eats freely.

They are gregarious in their habits both in a wild and domestic state, although they do not keep in close clusters like sheep, or gather generally in large droves like the bison. They are more separated in summer than in winter. During the rutting season, the monarch of the herd drives off the other bucks, and gathers the does into a band, which he appropriates to himself as much as possible. The other bucks hover around in his vicinity, generally keeping together, and annoying the chief by their unwelcome presence, and occasionally stealing away a part of his harem, for the does will slip away from his tyrannical rule whenever they get a chance. He is grossly ungallant in his selfishness, driving a doe from any choice bit she may find, with as little ceremony or affection as he would a buck. He has evidently no idea of love or affection, and is only pleased to act the tyrant and seek his own gratification, perfectly regardless of the feelings of others. Still there are degrees in this regard among different individuals.

The mother, however, has a strong affection for her young, and will defend it with great energy. Their greatest antipathy is dogs, and if one gets into the park, they harry him with a terrible ferocity. The does show this disposition to the greatest extent; but the bucks generally join in the chase, and the whole herd go tearing away at a rattling pace through the brush or across the open space, uttering their fierce squeal in a way that might frighten a lion. If the unfortunate cur is overtaken before

he can make his escape, a single blow from the fore foot of the
leading doe crushes him down, and he is trampled to death in a
trice.   If they see a dog through the fence, their combativeness
is at once aroused, and they will rush toward him and strike the
fence terrible blows.   The dog generally leaves at their first
bidding.

Sometimes the bucks are vicious and dangerous during the rutting season, but a very wicked one is a rare exception ; still all
at that time are more courageous than at other seasons, and it is
prudent to avoid any contest and leave him the path if you meet
one in the park.   In the wild state, their timidity prevents them
from attacking man, and they expend their courage or viciousness
on their own species.

In hot weather they are inclined to stand in the pools of water
in the bed of the creek, and the males wallow in the mud like
the hog, so that they are often seen well smeared with.the adhe-
sive soil, and present a disgusting appearance.

The Elk is not entirely voiceless, yet it never utters a sound,
except under strong provocation, generally of alarm or defiance.
Either expression is on a very high, sharp key, often uttered with
great force.   During the rut, the master buck is often heard in
loud defiance, which serves as a warning to the younger males to
keep clear of him.

I shall have more to say when we come to compare the different species of the deer, and consider them more in detail.

Male Woodland Caribou.

CERVUS TARANDUS, Linn.

Woodland Caribou.

Cervus tarandus. . . . . . HARLAN, Fauna Am., 232, 1825.
GODMAN, Am. Nat. H., II. 283.
SABINE, Supp. Perr. 1st Voy., cxc.
RICHARDSON, App. to Perr. 2d Voy.,
326.
ROSS, Perr. 3d Voy.

Cervus tarandus caribou. . . KERR, Linn. 297, 1792.

Cervus hastalis. . . . . . AGASSIZ, Pr. Bost. Soc. N. Hist., II.
188, 1846.

The Caribou. . . . . . . HARDY, For. Lf. in Acad., 120.
GILPIN, Mamm. of Nova, 55.

Caribou, ou, Asne sauvage. . SAGARD THEODAT, Canada, 751, 1636.
LA HONTAN, t. i., 77, 1703.
CHARLEVOIX, Nouv. France, t. v.,
190.

Carre boeuf, or Caribou. . . FRENCH CANADIANS (Richardson).

Tarantus caribou. . . . . AUD. & BACH., Quad. N. Am., III.,
III. 1853, Fig.
BAIRD, Pacific R. R. Rep., 633, 1857.

Rangifer tarandus. . . . . DE KAY, N. Y. Zoöl., 121, 1825.

Rangifer hestalis. . . . . BAIRD, U. S. Pat. Off. Rep. Agr. for
1851, 108, 1852.

Tarandus rangifer. . . . . OGILBY, Pr. Zoöl. Soc. Lond., IV.
134, 1836.
J. E. Gray, Pr. Zoöl. Soc. Lond.,
XVIII. 225, 1850.

Rein-deer, or Rain-deer. . . DRAGE, Voygs., I. 25.
DOBBS, Huds. Bay, 19, 22.
PENNANT, Arct. Zoöl., I., 22.
CARTWRIGHT, Labdr., 91, 133.

The Reindeer, or Caribou. . RICHARDSON, F. B. A., 238.

In size less than wapiti. In color lighter than any of the other deer. Face, neck, and belly approaching white, and lighter on the back than on the sides, a shade darker anteriorly than further back. Tail white with a dark tinge on the upper side. Legs dark chestnut-brown. Upper lip or muffle covered with short silver-gray hair. Nose and ears have a chestnut shade. A white band surrounds the top of each hoof. Hoofs, very broad, flat, and short. Inner lines straight, outer convex. Accessory hoofs very large, broad, and flat, and subject to muscular control. Hoofs all black, metarsal gland wanting. Tarsal gland large. Interdigital glands present in hind feet only. Antlers of male curved, long and slender, with branches more or less palmated and very irregular in form. Antlers on female smaller and less palmated.

GENERAL REMARKS.

My opportunities for a personal study of this species have been limited, nor have extensive inquiries among those most familiar with this deer resulted as satisfactorily as I had hoped. For the present, I must say that a broad field is left for future observations, before our information will approach completeness.

The range of this species is confined to the northern regions of America, Europe, and Asia. It has crossed the great drainage of the lakes and the St. Lawrence, only on the lower course of that river, and on Lake Superior. It is still found in New Brunswick and Nova Scotia, and possibly in Maine, but is becoming annually more and more scarce. It resides in great numbers in Newfoundland, where it has been little disturbed by white settlements, and whence it is said frequently to cross on the ice to the continent.

If it was ever abundant south of Lake Superior, where it was found when the copper and iron mines first invited extensive settlements there, the fact is not well attested, and I cannot learn that any have been met with south of that lake within the last twenty years or more. In the woodland districts of Labrador they have always been at home, extending as far north as Hudson's Bay.

From Lake Superior they extended west to the Pacific coast, and west of the Barren Grounds, their range extends north to the limits of the continent. In the northern parts of Montana and Washington territories, and in British Columbia, they are claimed to be larger than on the Atlantic coast. If they are larger in size on the Pacific slope than in more easterly regions their numbers are not so great. As they affect wooded countries almost exclusively, existence of forests in the far northwest may explain their presence there; still we must remember that the isothermal line trends rapidly to the northwest of the one hundredth meridian. In portions of the Selkirk settlement, and west of Hudson's Bay these deer were formerly very abundant. Sir John Richardson says : " Mr. Hutchins mentions that he has

Female Woodland Caribou.

Young Woodland Caribou.

seen eighty carcasses of this kind of deer, brought into York Factory in one day and many others were refused, for the want of salt to preserve them. These were killed when in the act of crossing Hayes River, and the natives continued to destroy them, for the sake of the skins, long after they had stored up more meat than they required." The half century which has intervened since Richardson's observations, has greatly diminished the number of these Reindeer, in nearly all the countries where they were formerly quite abundant. We have no evidence that they were ever abundant in the neighborhood of Montreal and Quebec, though a few wanderers found their way to those parts of the Canadas after they had been settled by the whites ; but many years have now elapsed since any have been heard of there. They still maintain their ground in Nova Scotia and New Brunswick, where they show more persistence in remaining in the vicinity of the settlements of the white man than in any other portion of their original habitat.

The Reindeer branch of the deer family present extraordinary peculiarities in their cornute appendages. The most striking is the fact that the females have antlers, though of less size than those of the males. Then, again, we are struck with the extraordinary variety, or want of uniformity in the forms of the antlers, no two, even from the same animal, being alike, usually differing as much from each other as those taken from different animals. Still there are certain peculiarities about them which enable the most careless observer to recognize them at a glance, with as much confidence as he can the antler of the wapiti. The beam of the antler is usually very long in proportion to its thickness, and is always more or less angular instead of round. On the adult male, the antler is always more or less branching, and some of these branches are usually palmated. The upper branches have usually posterior projection, while the lower, that is, the brow and the bez tines, are anterior. These latter are usually much longer either on one or both antlers in proportion, than the upper posterior projections, though frequently one or the other of these is but rudimentary, or even entirely wanting. With very rare, if any exceptions, the brow tines on one of the antlers is broadly palmated, descending between the eyes, the compression being lateral. Like the elk, the brow tine usually projects from the antler immediately above the burr, which is very small.

The old males shed their antlers usually before Christmas, but the young males carry them later ; the yearlings till spring, and the females later still, and until after they have dropped their young.

When I come to treat of the antlers of the deer as a distinct subject, and compare each with the other, I shall compare the antlers of the European reindeer with our own, when it will appear that the European are appreciably less palmated than the American; still I agree with those who find no specific difference between the reindeer of Europe and our Woodland Caribou.

The forms of the feet and hind legs enable them to travel over the deep snows better than any other ruminant of their size. The foot itself is very broad and thin, and the same is true of the accessory or hind hoof, which on this animal seems to serve a real purpose.   In traveling through the snows, or soft marshy ground, the Caribou throws his hind feet forward, so as to bring the leg into something of a horizontal position, spreads wide his claws, and broad accessory hoofs, and thus presents an extraordinary bearing surface to sustain him on the yielding ground, and so he is enabled to shuffle along with great rapidity, where any other large quadruped would mire in a bog, or become absolutely snow-bound.   The Reindeer alone leaves in his track the marks of all four of his hoofs belonging to each hind foot, and specimens show the effects of attrition on these secondary hoofs, and prove that they serve a useful purpose in the economy of the animal.

The white band around the lower part of each leg, extending up so as to embrace the hind hoofs, and even slightly above them, is an interesting mark.   Its regularity and uniformity at once distinguishes it from the erratic and irregular white observed about the feet of the Virginia deer, and very rarely on the wapiti deer, while it is entirely wanting about the feet of all the other Cervidæ, so far as my investigations enable me to speak. The dress of this animal is admirably adapted to the rigors of the climate in which he winters.   The hairs are long and spongy, containing a large amount of confined air.   As the season advances, they grow in diameter so that they become very dense, even to the degree of forcing them to a certain extent into an erect position.   Underneath is a dense coat of fur, like that of the American elk.   The hairs are crinkled, and terminate with a sharp point, being coarser in full winter costume than those found on most of the other members of this family.

The skin is thin, and makes soft, pliable leather, and is highly prized by the natives for clothing, and, when properly tanned with the hair on, makes a suit almost impervious to the cold.

This deer is fond of arboreous food, grasses, and aquatic plants, but its great resource is lichens. It frequents marshy and swampy grounds more than any other of the deer family; for which, as we have seen, it is admirably adapted, and where it is well protected from pursuit. In the winter it resorts to the dense forests on higher ground.

As an article of food, its flesh is not highly prized. Indeed, it is deemed inferior to any other venison, although, when in good condition, it is both palatable and nourishing.

It has been sometimes domesticated in this country, but I have heard of no attempt to train it to the harness, as is done with its congener in the north of Europe.

I presume no systematic effort has been made to rear a race of domesticated Reindeer in this ountry. To do this, probably the same difficulties would have to be overcome that are met with in the domestication of other deer, and it would require an effort with many generations before habits of domestication would become established and hereditary. Still, in proper localities, time and judicious perseverance would no doubt accomplish the task; when they would become a valuable addition in the north to our domesticated animals. Sir John Richardson says: " Contrary to the practice of the Barren-ground Caribou, the Woodland variety travels to the south in the spring." But if this be a general rule, it must admit of exceptions; for it is established beyond all question that many at least pass the entire year in Newfoundland, and on the continent, near the southern limits of their range. Indeed, so far as I can learn, observations are still wanting to inform us fully of the habits of this animal. It may be found that it is rather more restless than strictly migratory, moving in various directions at all seasons. We shall discuss the subject further when we come to comparisons.

Mule Deer.

CERVUS MACROTIS, Say.

Mule Deer.

Cervus macrotis.	SAY, Long's Expd., II. 254.
	HARLAN, Fauna, 243.
	SABINE, Frank. Journ., 667.
	GODMAN, Nat. Hist., II. 204.
	WAGNER, Supp. Schreb., IV. 371.
	PUCHERAN, Mon. Cerf. Archiv. du Mus., VI. 369.
	PEALE, Phila. Ad. Sci., I., II.
	RICHARDSON, F. B. A., 254.
	BAIRD, Pacific R. R. Surv., 656.
	AUD. & BACH., Quad. N. Am., II. 206.
	GRIFFITHS, An. Kingd., V. No. 794.
Cervus (Cariacus), macrotis.	GRAY, Knows. Menag. Ung., 67.
	GRAY, Pr. Zoöl. Soc. Lond., XVIII. 239.
Cervus auritus.	WARDEN, Hist. U. S., 640 [Richardson].
Cerf mulet.	DESMAREST, Mamm., 443.
Black-tailed Deer.	LEWIS & CLARK, Exped., by Paul Allen, I. 95, 220, 242, 462.
	GODMAN, Nat. Hist., II. 305.
	RICHARDSON, F. B. A., 254.
Black-tailed, or Mule Deer.	JAMES, Long's Exped., II. 276.
	GASS, Journal, 55.
	LEWIS & CLARK, Exped., by Paul Allen, II. 410.
Great Eared Deer.	GRIFFITH, An. Kingd., IV. 133; V. 794.
Mule Deer.	LEWIS & CLARK, Exped., by Paul Allen, I. 301, 303, 311, 315, 324; II. 211, 515, 526, 530.
	WARDEN, U. S. I., 245.
	AUD. & BACH., Quad. N. Am., II. 206.
	BAIRD, Pacific R. R. Rep., VIII. 656.

Larger than the common deer, and coarser built. Color dark gray. Antlers, only on the male. They are once or twice and sometimes thrice bifurcated. Ears long, broad, thick, and clumsy, well covered with hair on both sides. Tail, short, small, round, white, terminating with a tuft of long black hairs ; naked on the under side. Metatarsal gland very large and long. Tarsal gland, present. Hoofs black. No white hairs about the feet or the metatarsal gland. A white section opposite and below the tail.

GENERAL REMARKS.

This deer was first discovered by Lewis and Clark on the 18th of September, 1804, in north latitude 42° on the Missouri River, and called by them *Black-tailed* Deer. By this name they often mention it, until the 31st day of May, 1805, when Captain Clark, in enumerating the animals found on the Columbia River below the falls, calls it the *Mule* Deer. And by that name they ever after speak of it, except in one instance they again call it the Black-tailed Deer. On the 30th of August, 1806, near where they first saw this deer in 1804, they procured a specimen to bring home and called it the *Mule Deer*. This is the last mention they make of it. The excessive development of the ears well justified them in the name which they gave it. In the Rocky Mountain region where the true black-tailed deer is not found, it is still known among the hunters and settlers as the black-tailed deer. On the Pacific coast, where the true black-tailed deer is known, this is called by its true name, the Mule Deer, by which designation it is also recognized by naturalists.

The original range of this deer has not been very much restricted since he was first discovered, though he has been driven back from the Missouri River, and has deserted other limited localities, where the miners or settlers have driven him away. Its most natural home is a mountainous region, but it is found on the great plains hundreds of miles east of them, and it may not be improbable that many ever live there that never see a mountain. On the great plains it most affects the borders of the streams where the ground is broken and arboreous food can be found.

West of the Rocky Mountains this deer is met with almost everywhere, though much more abundantly in some places than others. In the Coast Range of northern California they are almost entirely replaced by the Columbia black-tailed deer, while in the Coast Range of southern California scarcely any other deer is met with. Here, however, a very distinct variety of this deer occurs, differing in important particulars from those found east of the Sierras, as will be more particularly explained hereafter. In all of Oregon, in Washington Territory, and in British Columbia, this deer is met with, though much less abundant than the true black-tailed deer, or even the Virginia deer. This deer occupies about thirty degrees of latitude, from Cape St. Lucas on the south into British Columbia on the north.

If their numbers are diminished by the intrusion of the white man, they still maintain their ground with more pertinacity than the elk. They have the same defect of vision as have the other members of the *cervus* family, which however is in a measure compensated by an acute sense of smell and of hearing. At the present time at least they are wary and not to be taken by the inexperienced hunter. At their best speed they do not get over the ground fast. They do not run, in a proper sense, but when in haste they bound along, all the feet striking and leaving the ground at once. For a few minutes they may make pretty rapid progress in this mode, but it soon seems to fatigue them. Once when sitting on a crag on the Rocky Mountains, nearly ten thousand feet above the sea, with a glass, I watched one which had been started by a companion, while he bounded through a valley a thousand feet below me. Though he was in view for less than half a mile, he showed evident fatigue before he passed out of sight. The labor of such a mode of progress, as compared with the long graceful leaps of the common deer when at full speed, must be apparent to any one who has carefully observed the two.

Their legs are much larger and coarser than those of the Virginia deer, and so in their every motion they are less agile and graceful. In their entire form they are awkward and ungainly. Their great uncouth ears, so disproportioned to every other part of the animal, are the most ugly feature about them, and in fact give tone to the whole figure and tend to dispel any admiration which might otherwise be excited.

In color, this deer for its summer dress has a pale, dull yellow. As this is shed in the latter part of summer, it is replaced by a very fine short black coat as it appears in places denuded of the summer coat as seen partially through it. It retains the black but for a few days. Almost immediately it begins to turn gray, so that before the summer coat is fairly shed the black is mostly gone. As the hairs of the winter coat grow longer they grow larger and so become more dense, while they also become lighter in color as the season advances. The front border of the ear is black. Generally, though not by any means universally, black stripes descend from the inner sides of the eyes and unite an inch and six lines below, and from the eyes extend up towards the antlers, presenting in the forehead of the deer what the hunters call the *horse-shoe.* A black or dark brown spot also is seen below each side of the mouth, growing lighter in color as it passes around back of the chin, sometimes uniting there and sometimes not. The brisket, and the belly back of the fore legs are black, growing lighter towards the umbilicus; thence backward a lighter shade prevails, till at the inguinal region it is a dull white; passing up between the hind legs it becomes quite white, widening out towards the tail so as to involve all the buttock, where the white portion is from six to eight inches broad, presenting a very conspicuous appearance when the animal is viewed from behind. Unlike the white patch on the elk, the antelope, and the big horn, this white portion does not extend up the rump above the tail more than about an inch, but spreads out from the root of the tail each way to the breadth of three inches and then descends, widening and then contracting to the inside of the hams; so that at the top the white is six inches broad, lower down it is eight inches, and then contracts to four inches between the legs. Below the knees and elbows the legs are of a dark cinnamon color.

He subsists upon the same sort of vegetation as that on which the other deer of the temperate regions feed. He seems unable to masticate freely hard substances, such as dried corn or hard shelled nuts, which the others have no difficulty in grinding to pieces.

J. MANZ-CHIC.

Black-tailed Deer.

CERVUS COLUMBIANUS, Rich.

Black-tailed Deer.

Cervus macrotis, var. Columbianus.	Richardson, F. B. A., 257.
Cervus Columbianus.	Baird, Pacific R. R. Rep., 659.
Cervus Lewisii.	Peale, Mamm. and Birds U. S. Ex. Ex., 39.
Cervus (Cariacus) Lewisii. . . .	J. E. Gray, Pr. Zoöl. Soc. Lond., XVIII. 239.
Cervus Cariacus punctulatus. . .	Gray, Knows. Menag., 67.
Cervus Richardsonii.	Aud. & Bach., III. 27.
Columbia Black-tailed Deer. . . .	Aud. & Bach., III. 27.
Black-tailed Fallow Deer. . . .	Lewis & Clark, Exped., by Paul Allen, II. 209, 210, 211, 27.
Black-tailed Deer.	Baird, Pacific R. R. Rep., VIII. 659.

Less in size than the mule deer. Short body and short legs. Ears large but less in size than those of the mule deer. Eyes large and brilliant. Tail short and round. One fourth of the circumference of the tail on the under side is white; the balance is a tawny dull black. The black is of the deepest shade on the lower part. Metatarsal gland between the tarsus and the middle of the leg, is intermediate in size between those on the mule deer and those on the Virginia deer. Tarsal gland much the same in size and form as on those two species, and of a shade lighter color than the surrounding coat; color of body a tawny gray, with white on back part of belly and inguinal region, extending to root of tail. The face is gray with darker forehead. Under the head white. Legs generally of a uniform dark cinnamon color, not a white hair to be found upon them below the hock. Antlers once or twice bifurcated. Gait like that of the mule deer. Is found on the Pacific coast of the United States and British Columbia only; having the most limited range of all the deer found in the United States, and perhaps on this continent.

GENERAL REMARKS.

This interesting species of deer was first discovered by Lewis and Clark, near the mouth of the Columbia River. They first mention it under date of the 19th of November, 1805. They say : " This, like all those we have seen on this coast, are much

7

darker than those of our common deer. Their bodies, too, are deeper, their legs shorter, and their eyes larger. The branches of the horns are similar, but the upper part of the tail is black from the root to the end, and they do not leap, but jump like a sheep frightened."

In their general description of the fauna observed during their expedition (vol. ii., p. 209), they enumerate the Cervidæ thus : " The common red deer, the black-tailed fallow deer, the mule deer, and the elk." They hunted it for the larder, but did not admire its flesh, pronouncing it dry and hard. From this we may infer that the deer were then in bad condition, for subsequent observations prove that the venison is of good quality. It is a cautious and wary animal in the forest, which it much affects, requiring all the skill and caution of the practiced hunter to secure success in its pursuit. The most extraordinary fact in connection with this deer is the extremely narrow limits of its range, which is within a narrow belt along the Pacific coast of America, in the temperate zone. In many parts of this district it is the most abundant deer to be met with. Why it has never wandered beyond these bounds, it is hard to say. It has never even reached the base of the Rocky Mountains, except possibly in the extreme northern part of its range. The mountain barriers could not restrain it ; for it ranges high up on the Sierra Nevada, and is found at the eastern slope of that range. If the deserts at the south would deter it from an eastern migration, the valleys of the streams heading in the Rocky Mountains, and emptying into the Columbia River, invited it to follow their banks, and would have led it to the summit of the range, and to practicable passes. The mule deer, which associates with it on the coast, although less enterprising than our common deer, the elk, or the moose, has occupied the entire range of the Rocky Mountains, and all the habitable parts of the desert country west of it, and also extends its range far down the plains which lie eastward, and formerly reached the Missouri River as far down as the Big Sioux, if not the mouth of the Platte. In my grounds they have endured the change of climate, food, and habit better than the mule deer, if there be any difference, so that they were not deterred from extending their range further eastward by the rigors of the season any more than their larger neighbors. Still some conditions exist which I am unable to point out, which seem to confine them to that circumscribed country, beyond which it is impossible for them to pass. An imaginary line which becomes quite as impassable as a Chinese wall to an entire species of animals who have full physical power to traverse it, but do not, while all others pass it unhesitatingly, is certainly a curious and an interesting fact, well calculated to stimulate the naturalist to seek for the cause, which has hitherto eluded all inquiries.

In its own home, this animal seems to be healthy, vigorous, and prolific, the females generally producing two and sometimes three at a birth.

The bifurcated antler and the bounding gait observed in the mule deer, are found also to be characteristics of this deer, but they are strictly confined to these two species; nor is it easy to conceive why this laborious and fatiguing gait has not in the course of time given place to the more easy and enduring running pace of the Virginia deer, which inhabits the same country.

Both these deer know how to gallop, and do so when not excited and at a moderate speed; but when alarmed and seeking to make a rapid flight, they strike into the nervous bound, which although rapid at first, can be endured but for a short time, and is particularly laborious on broken ground.

CERVUS VIRGINIANUS, Pennant.

Common Deer.

Cervus Virginianus. . . . . Boddaert, Elenchus Animalium, I. 136, 1784.

Zimmermann, Penn. Arkt. Zoöl., 31, 1789.

Gmelin, Syst. Nat., I. 179, 1788.

Kerr, Linn., 299, 1792.

Shaw, Gen. Zoöl., II. 284.

Schreber, Säugt, V. 1836.

Desmarest, Mamm. II. 424.

Harlan, Fauna Am., 238.

Doughty, Cab. Nat. Hist., I. 3.

Godman, Am. Nat. Hist., II. 306.

De Kay, N. Y. Zoöl., 113.

Wagner, Supp. Schreb., IV. 373

Aud. & Bach., N. Am. Quad., II. 220; III. 168.

Baird, Pacific R. R. Rep., VIII. 643.

Cervus (Cariacus) Virginianus. J. E. Gray, Knows. Menag., 66, 1850.

Cervus dama Americana. . . Erxleben, Syst., 312, 1777.

Cervus leucurus. . . . . . Douglas, Zoöl. Jour. IV., 330.

Richardson, Fauna B. A., 25.

Wagner, Supp. Schreb., IV. 375.

Aud. & Bach., N. Am. Quad., III. 773.

Pucheran, Mon. du Cerf, Archiv. du Mus., VI. 322.

Baird, Pacific R. R. Rep., VIII. 629.

Cervus Mexicanus. . . . . . Gmelin, Syst. Nat., I. 179, 1788.

Wagner, Supp. Schreb., Säugt., IV. 378.

Giebel, Säugt. 1855, 340.

Baird, Pacific R. R. Rep., 653.

Virginian Deer. . . . . . . Pennant, Syn., 51.

Shaw, Genl. Zoöl., II. 284.

About the size of the Columbia deer, with longer legs and longer body; head lean and slim; nose pointed and naked; eyes large and lustrous; ear small and trim; antlers have a spreading posterior projection, and then curve anteriorly with posterior tines; neck long and slender; body long for its size; tail long and lanceolate in form; legs straight and long.

Lachrymal sinus covered with a fold of skin; tarsal gland present; metatarsal gland small, and below the middle of the leg, naked, and surrounded by white hairs; outside of these there is usually a band of dark brown hairs, which are surrounded by long reversed hairs of the color of the leg.

Two annual pelages. Summer coat, from bay red to buff yellow; winter coat, a leaden gray, greatly variant. Deciduous antlers, and confined to the males.

Common Deer.

GENERAL REMARKS.

This deer has the widest range of any member of the family in any part of the world. Its range is from the Atlantic to the Pacific, extending into Canada and British Columbia on the north, and penetrating far into Mexico on the south. It may be found to-day, in every State and Territory of the United States. It inhabits alike the dense woodlands and the open prairies, the high mountains and the lowest valleys, the arid plains and the marshy swamps.

As we **might** well expect from its wide distribution and varied

range, we find several more or less distinctly marked varieties of
this species, all of which have well defined indicia which determine their specific identity. This branch of our subject will be
considered in another place.

From its wide distribution and great numbers it is quite familiar to nearly all Americans, and is almost the only one known to
most of them.

In form and action it is the most graceful of all, and has been
more frequently domesticated than any other, yet rarely have
persistent attempts been made to reduce it to complete and permanent domestication. When young it is a pretty pet around
the premises, but in a few years it becomes dangerous, and so is
generally got rid of. In its markings it is less stable than either
of the other species. In shades of color there are wide differences
among individuals in the same neighborhood, while fugitive markings are frequently observed, which are present only for a single year, and some individuals have permanent markings which
are wanting on others. In summer pelage a large majority are
of a bay red, but with a great diversity in shade, while others of
the same herd will be of a light buff yellow ; between these extremes almost every shade may be seen.

In a given neighborhood there is a great difference in the size
of individuals, but there is a permanent difference in size in different localities ; the smallest being found in the southern part
of the range, bordering the Gulf of Mexico and in Northern
Mexico, the westerly ones being the smallest of all, where they
have been classed by naturalists as a separate species, under the
name of *Cervus Mexicanus*. In their northern range and in the
mountainous regions of the west, the white portions cover a
larger surface of the body than in other regions, where they have
been ranked by many naturalists as a separate species under the
name of *Cervus lacurus*. By hunters these have been called
the long-tailed, or white-tailed deer, the latter name having
been used by Lewis and Clark, while in truth their tails are no
longer than those found in other regions. From the larger extent of white frequently if not generally found on them, we
might possibly be justified in assigning them the distinction of a
variety, though this peculiarity is by no means universal, for
many individuals cannot be distinguished from those found in
Illinois or Wisconsin. I have one specimen from northwestern
Minnesota, with all the legs entirely white, to several inches
above the hocks and knees, with occasionally a tawny hair in-

terspersed among the white. The white on the belly, too, extends up the sides further than is usually observed. This is exceptional, though not very uncommon in the northwest, but I have never seen it in their middle or southern-range. I have never found any black on the tails or faces of the northern variety, while it is very common on more southern and eastern varieties. This accords with a law, which however is not universal, by which we are led to expect more white on the same species of quadrupeds or birds, which are permanently located, in the north than in the south.

The antlers of the Virginia deer are peculiar and easily recognized. The curvature described is more abrupt than on any other species, while the posterior projection of the tines from the beam is peculiar to this deer, except that it is sometimes observed on exceptional antlers of the mule deer and the Columbia deer, as will be more particularly described in the appropriate place.

I have closely studied this interesting animal for many years, both in domestication and in its wild state; and the notes of my observations upon it would fill a volume, but I think I can better present such of the facts as I can find space to insert, under the different branches of my subject, where I propose to compare the different species. Perhaps I should make this monograph fuller, as I am strongly tempted to do, but I fear I should not know where to stop, and so might compel myself to too much repetition hereafter, when I shall necessarily have to go over many of his leading characteristics, to show where they agree with or differ from the other species.

Barren-ground Caribou, Male.

Barren-ground Caribou, Female.

RANGIFER GROENLANDICUS, Baird.

Barren-ground Caribou.

Rangifer Groenlandicus. . . .	Baird, Pacific R. R. Rep., VIII. 634.
Cervus tarandus Groenlandicus.	Kerr, Linn., 297.
Cervus tarandus, var. α, Arctica. ·	Richardson, F. B. A., 241.
Common Deer.	Hearne, Journey, 200.
Barren-ground Caribou. . . .	Richardson, F. B. A., 241.
Tarandus arcticus.	Baird, U. S. Pat. Off. Rep. Agr. for 1851, 105.

This animal is of the reindeer type, but is much smaller than *C. taran-dus*, and indeed is smaller than any of the deer which we have hitherto described. Antlers much longer and more slender than those of the woodland caribou. The tines are very erratic in form, some of which are palmated. In color it strongly resembles the larger species of rein-deer, though it is of appreciably lighter color. In the specimen before me the legs, instead of the brown color of the other species, are white with a brown shade on the anterior side, extending half way down. In-stead of a white section around the top of each hoof, the whole foot is white to some distance above the accessory hoofs, where the brown hairs in front begin to invade the white. Metatarsal gland absent. Tarsal gland present.

GENERAL REMARKS.

I confess to feeling a very great interest in this little reindeer, and exceedingly regret the want of an opportunity to study it in its arctic home, or even to inspect a living specimen; my own observations have been confined to mounted specimens, to skins, feet, and legs in my collection. From these I can understand sufficient for a simple monograph of the animal, but for all else necessarily I am indebted to the observations of others, both printed, written, and oral. Fortunately, I have met with some very intelligent gentlemen who have spent years of their lives where they abound, and whose observations are of the greatest value. The specific place to which this animal is entitled in nat-ural history, has not been definitely settled by naturalists. Sir John Richardson very strongly intimates that it is his opinion that it is a distinct species from the woodland caribou, yet he does not say so directly. While he treats these two species in separate articles, yet he introduces both under the specific name of the Lapland.reindeer, *Cervus tarandus*, the smaller variety he designates *arctica*, and the larger, *sylvestris*, so that he is far from asserting a specific difference. Audubon and Bachman, with very limited opportunities for judging, incline to the opinion of specific identity, and Baird leaves the question undecided. After much study and reflection I am of opinion that they are distinct species.

The range of this deer extends from the Atlantic Ocean on the east, to Mackenzie's River or the Rocky Mountains on the west. Beyond this it is replaced by the woodland caribou. On the north it extends its range beyond the continent and visits the islands of the Arctic Ocean. Richardson fixes their southern limits on the east, at Churchill in north latitude 59° on Hudson's Bay, but Mr. McTavish, of the Hudson's Bay Company, informs me that they are found still further south on the peninsula of Labrador. Westward of this point they do not come so far south; so that the line of their southern limits from the Atlantic pursues a course north of west. This may be accounted for by the fact, that the temperature is much colder on the eastern coast than in the same latitudes in the interior and on the western coast. Captain Hall found them north and east of Hudson's Bay, and nearly all arctic explorers have found them on the islands of the Arctic Sea, where they serve to supplement the supply of sea food to the Esquimaux. They are very abundant on the peninsula east of Hudson's Bay, where from necessity their migratory range is very circumscribed. Its habits are more arctic than any other ruminant of this continent except the musk-ox, which affects the same frigid temperature, but is even less widely distributed and far less numerous.

The statement of Dr. King, as quoted by Baird, for the purpose of showing a specific difference between the barren-ground and the woodland caribou is this: "that the barren-ground species is peculiar not only in the form of its liver but in not possessing a receptacle for bile." This implies certainly that Dr. King had found on examination that the woodland caribou has the gall bladder attached to the liver. This certainly is not so, for the gall bladder is wanting in the woodland caribou as well as in all of the other members of the deer family, a fact long since observed and attested by several naturalists and often confirmed by critical examination. Notwithstanding there are many strong similitudes between our two kinds of caribou, there are numerous well authenticated differences, which when well considered not only justify but compel us to class them as distinct species.

The difference in size, if this were the only distinction, would be entitled to but little weight in the consideration of this question, especially when we remember that we often find animals of the same species occupying high latitudes, smaller in size than those of warmer countries. The reverse, however, we find generally the case with our Cervidæ. Our common deer are the smallest in Texas and Mexico, where, simply on account of their diminutive size, without any other well established and universal distinction, they have been classed as a distinct species, *Cervus Mexicanus.* The mule deer in Lower California are even more diminutive in size, and their antlers have been reduced to a single spike. We may find little difference in the size of the moose, which we may ascribe to a difference in the latitude of their habitat. In the valley of the Mississippi the weight of evidence is that the southern Elk are the largest; but I do not learn that this is so on the Pacific slope, or even in the Rocky Mountains. I repeat, however, that I should not consider the difference in size, which is fully one half, sufficient of itself to establish a specific difference.

The proportionate difference in the size of their antlers is still greater, and I think possesses more significance. While the size of this animal is only half that of the woodland caribou, its antlers are fully twice as large. This proportionate difference of four to one is entitled to weight in this inquiry. Buffon and some others have concluded that the size of the antlers depend largely upon the amount and quality of the food supplied the deer. This position is not absolutely refuted in this instance, for the supply of food to the Barren-ground Caribou is really unlimited, and is of the most nutritious quality, but the same is true also in that portion of Labrador occupied by the larger species. Hind assures us that he there found the beds of reindeer moss three feet deep, affording comfortable walking over vast fields of erratic rocks, which were almost impassable where the moss had been burned off, and yet not a word is said about an excessive development of the antlers of the deer. If the great abundance and excellent quality of the food supplied the northern deer, has stimulated to this excessive growth of the antlers, it would certainly be not unreasonable to expect that it would have equally promoted an increase of the body of the animal, for all admit that the size of all animals largely depends on the quantity and the quality of the food with which they are supplied. This is much better established than that the size of antlers is dependent on the same cause. The question is, why are the larger antlers grown on the smaller animal? Is it due to accidental or factitious causes or to a specific difference? I perceive no cause which could have produced this great development of the antlers, which would not also have produced an equal development of the whole animal.

In habits, too, they differ very considerably. The larger species are much less gregarious than the smaller. I do not know, however, that I should make very much out of this, for it may be accounted for by their greater numbers. The woodland caribou are nowhere so abundant as the others, and are seldom found in large bands; two or three, or a dozen at most, being found together, except in the interior of Newfoundland, where their numbers are much greater, and there they are found in larger herds than on any part of the continent, as far as I can learn, except to the west of Hudson's Bay, where Richardson informs us that large numbers assemble together and move in bodies. Cormack, to whom we are indebted for the first reliable information of the habits of this deer in the interior of Newfoundland, tells us that they migrate in search of food in single file, in herds of from twenty to two hundred each, and so the whole country is cut up in every direction with their paths. We have no account that the northern species travel in this order, and they assemble in bands of thousands.

We may, perhaps, attach more weight to the difference in their habits of migration. The northern species are strictly migratory, traversing in their migrations some ten degrees of latitude or more from the Arctic Ocean, south, excepting where confined by physical barriers, as in Labrador. The woodland caribou are migratory too, but to a less extent, or rather the habit is less universal. In Newfoundland, their migrations are necessarily limited in extent. On the continent, they are at liberty to go to the Arctic Sea, but they stop short of the sixtieth degree of north latitude, and probably but a small proportion reach that. The migrations of many, if not of a large proportion, are probably from one part of some pretty large district adapted to their wants to another part, as may be prompted by circumstances, either the disturbed condition of the country, or the exigencies of food supply. Those living in Nova Scotia and New Brunswick probably rarely leave those provinces, while they may frequently pass from one favorite haunt to another. They are very restless animals, almost constantly on the move, and, indeed, this is the disposition which promotes habits of migration.

The summary of all the evidence I can gather on the subject is, that the woodland caribou are migratory in their habits, but to a much less extent than the northern species, even where there are no physical obstructions to limit their migrations.

The most singular feature of this habit is thus stated by Sir John Richardson ("Fauna Boreali Americana," p. 250), who says: "Contrary to the practice of the Barren-ground Caribou, the woodland variety travels to the southward in the spring. They cross the Nelson and Severn rivers in numerous herds in the month of May, and pass the summer on the low marshy shores of James Bay, and return to the northward, and at the same time retire more inland in the month of September." Here, then, we find the woodland caribou migrating to the northward, on the west coast of Hudson's Bay, and west of it as high as 55° to 57° of north latitude, which is within one degree of Churchill, which is near the southern limit of the range of the Barren-ground Caribou in that longitude as given by Richardson, though I have authentic evidence that they sometimes come considerably farther south in exceptional seasons. Mr. McTavish assures me, that in the winter of 1856, the Barren-ground Caribou came in great numbers down the Mississague River to Lake Huron, about thirty-six miles below the Bruce Mine. This was in about 47° north latitude, and the extreme southern point of the range of the woodland caribou. This, we may admit, was very exceptional, but we may, I think, safely assume, for all the evidence clearly establishes the facts to this extent, that the northern range of the southern species, and the southern range of the northern species overlap each other, for at least a degree, and sometimes very much more, not only in Labrador, but also west of Hudson's Bay. As we go still further west, even to the Coppermine and Mackenzie rivers, which is the western limit of the range of the Barren-ground Caribou, the southern line of their range trends more to the northward, and so does the northern range of the woodland caribou, and as the latter travel north in the fall, at the same time that the smaller species return from the arctic regions with their young, they must there, sometimes, meet on common ground during the rutting season, at least the latter part of it. This season, with individuals, continues for months after it has passed with most of them, with the species in my grounds, and it is no doubt so with all the species. Much of the southern or winter range of the Barren-ground Caribou is south of the barren grounds, or intersects their southern parts, so that there the woodland caribou finds the forest which is indispensable to his contentment, and to those forests the Barren-ground Caribou resort during the winter season. Richardson says: " Except in the rutting season, the bulk of the males and females live separately; the former retire deeper into the woods in the winter, whilst herds of the pregnant class stay on the skirts of the barren grounds and proceed to the coast very early in the spring."

Now, from all this it is impossible to avoid the conclusion that the two species occasionally, yes, frequently, meet on this common ground, at times when the sexes are drawn to each other, and yet there is no evidence that there has been any intermingling of the species. Each maintains its individualities as distinctly as when first discovered, and no doubt as they have existed for ages. This could only have occurred from sexual aversion, which does not exist between varieties of the same species, but only where there are specific differences. Take a white or albino deer of any species, and there is no sexual or social aversion between it and the other members of the species, and the same is true of all other animals. By some means all seem to look beyond the exceptional appearance of the individual and recognize their fellow at a glance. This aversion is not absolute and universal, no doubt, for we sometimes see individuals of different species, and even of different genera, contract a fondness for each other, even to the extent of sexual intercourse; but when this is entirely voluntary, it is very exceptional. This more frequently occurs among animals in domestication or in semi-domestication than in the wild state, but even there it may sometimes occur when a mate of the same species cannot be found. Such union between individuals of different species, when it does take place, may most likely be fertile, and the hybrids may possess the powers of reproduction, and may transmit that capacity to their posterity, as we shall see, when we come to treat of *hybridity*, but this is not conclusive of the specific identity of the original parents.

But for this general sexual aversion between individuals of different species, no mere imaginary line could have kept these two kinds of reindeer separate, to say nothing of how they originally separated with no physical barrier between them. According to a universal law of selection the larger males of the woodland caribou would have driven off the males of the smaller species, whenever they did meet on the common ground, and would have left their impress upon their progeny, which being larger and stronger than the pure bloods would soon have usurped the entire paternity of the race and all distinction would long since have been obliterated. It is no answer to this to refer me to different varieties of the same species occupying different and distant localities, and which vary in size, for instance, as much as these do, as the Virginia deer or the mule deer. Those species are not migratory, so that they remain substantially in the same locality for many generations, if not driven away by violence, so that climate, aliment, and other accidental conditions may in time produce a hereditary impress upon those occupying the particular locality where the particular causes exist. This is not possible with migratory animals, where as in this case nothing but an imaginary line separates the territory occupied by each, and where even that line is frequently if not annually overstepped by individuals. Even without the habit, mentioned by Richardson, of the southern species migrating north and the northern species south in the fall, the habit of migration would in time have brought them together, when the larger males of the south would have become the progenitors of the entire race, and the broad distinctions, now so conspicuous and so constant, would have been lost. If not migratory, then we might accept the explanation suggested by their different localities as a sufficient reason for the differences observed.

Why, then, do these two members of this great family live upon contiguous and even overlapping territories and continue so completely separated, with no visible cause to keep them apart? It must be because of inherent constitutional, specific differences. It is evident that their well-beings require different conditions of life arising from organic differences which are permanent and inflexible : one cannot live and prosper where the other must live in order to prosper.

We learn of the differences which have been pointed out, as it were, by accident, for their habitat is so remote and inaccessible that the Barren-ground Caribous have been rarely visited by competent naturalists, and I have no doubt that when they shall be carefully studied and thoroughly understood by competent observers, still broader distinctions between the two species will be found to exist, which will remove every doubt which may be still entertained as to their specific differences. For myself, I do not believe it possible for simple varieties of the same species with migratory habits to occupy contiguous territories, and still maintain differences so pronounced and so constant as we find between these two kinds of reindeer. When the comparative anatomist shall have taken the subject in hand and carefully studied both, he will probably find many similitudes not yet noted; so too he will probably find differences not yet imagined.

We have many facts stated which will subsequently appear in the different divisions of this work, and especially "The Chase," which tend strongly to show that the eye of the Barren-ground Caribou is duller than that of any of the other deer, and that this defect is not compensated by so sensitive a smell as is possessed by the others. They moreover show that it is a most witless animal, easily dazed and confused by danger or fright, without stratagem or the capacity to evade its enemies. It seems more likely to run into danger than to avoid it, although the way of escape may be plainly open before it. In all this it is the very reverse of the woodland caribou, except that the latter has an unreliable vision, although not to the extent of the former. Even the moose is hardly more fertile in resources to elude pursuit, or escape from danger than the woodland caribou, and it is a proud triumph for the sportsman who takes one.

Of the endurance of the smaller species, I am not sufficiently advised to speak understandingly, but from the accounts given of their capture I am led to the conclusion that they are prostrated by a wound which most other deer would survive for a considerable time.

They have a foolish curiosity fully equal to that of our antelope, of which hunters know how to take advantage, and by which the animal is often beguiled to destruction.

The young have been often caught and tamed, and like the other deer they soon lose all fear of man and become interesting pets, but when they have been removed from their native boreal regions they have soon perished.

CERVUS ACAPULCENSIS, Caton.

Acapulco Deer.

SMALLEST of all the North American deer. Head broad and full. Eye prominent and bright. Ear small and thin, covered with very short, fine hair, black outside and white inside. Nostrils large. Nose naked and moist. Neck slim, tapering, and elevated. Body short, round, and compact. Legs short and slim. Accessory hoofs small. Tail short, bushy, and rather flat. Antlers small and short, and flattened towards upper part, and notched at end, with small basal snags; beams are triangular near base. Pedicels high and far apart. Metatarsal gland wanting. Tarsal gland present. Face black. Under the head and throat white, but proportionally less than on common deer. Neck, back, and sides, dark chestnut brown; darkest on top of neck and back. Brisket nearly black. Belly, inguinal region up to the tail, and under side of that member, white.

GENERAL REMARKS.

After diligent search, I find but one mention of this deer by which I am enabled to recognize it. This occurs in a sentence in Audubon and Bachman's " Quadrupeds of North America " (vol. ii. p. 200), when treating of our antelope. I will quote the sentence entire : " The Antelope has no lachrymal pits under the eyes, as have Deer and Elks, nor has it any gland on the hind leg, so curious a feature in many of those animals of the deer tribe, which drop their horns annually, and only wanting (so far as our knowledge extends) in the 'Cervus Richardsonii, which we consider in consequence as approaching the genus Antelope, and in a small deer from Yucatan and Mexico, of which we had a living specimen for some time in our possession."

I cannot forbear correcting some of the important errors expressed in this single sentence. Of all authors which I have consulted, here alone Cervus Columbianus is given the name of Cervus Richardsonii. Instead of being destitute of the metatarsal gland, it is the most conspicuous on him of any of the deer family, except the mule deer, and the learned authors should have known that that gland is wanting both on the moose and on the caribou. They did not consider this gland of sufficient importance to require particular study, but merely considered it a *curious* feature ; yet for its supposed absence they make an antelope of

8

a deer. The real value of the sentence is in the last two lines, in which the author says he had in his possession a small deer from Yucatan (?) and Mexico, in which this gland was wanting, by which we are enabled to recognize it with as much certainty as if he had given the most elaborate description. In our deer this gland is wanting also, which distinguishes it from all of the smaller deer in this country.

This exceedingly beautiful animal first attracted my attention in Woodward's Gardens in San Francisco, where I found one female. The next day I learned that Governor Latham had received a specimen by the steamship *Republic*, and hastened to his country residence at Menlo Park, where I had the good fortune to meet the Governor, who had the deer still in the cage, which he at once told me to consider my own. Here I had an opportunity to study her with all the leisure and care I desired. I then turned her loose in his park to recruit, and examined the rest of his herd of deer. I found he had six species: the wapiti, the mule deer, the Columbia black-tailed deer, the Virginia deer (called in the West the white-tailed or long-tailed deer), this same Acapulco or South Mexican or Central American Deer (some of which the keeper told me came from Panama, and some from Southern Mexico), and one buck from the Island of Ceylon. Here was a rare opportunity for study which I enjoyed. The keeper took me to the remains of an Acapulco buck, the first ever introduced to the park, which had lately died of old age, as he said, and was now *dried* up, but was still susceptible of examination, at least in some important particulars. There was no mistaking its identity with the specimen just presented to me. I secured the skin of the outside of one hind leg for microscopic examination for the metatarsal gland, the antlers, and a part of the skull attached, which are shown in the illustration. These antlers differ so widely from any others with which I have ever met or seen described or illustrated, that, if typical, they declare a distinct species, were there not abundant other specific differences to attest the same truth. Under the proper head these will be fully described, when they can be compared with the antlers of the other species of deer.

This deer is decidedly darker in color than the common deer, with some important differences in the location of the white and the dark portions, which will be particularly explained in the proper place.

Mr. Woodward presented me with one female of this species,

which was ill in his gardens, and died soon after I received her, and two Ceylon does. The first was of a much darker color than the one presented by Governor Latham, which survived, which has always been perfectly healthy. Of all the deer I ever had, she shows the greatest tendency to fatten. She remains in fine order when shedding the winter coat in the spring, when most of the other species of deer become very poor. She even suckles two hybrid fawns almost as big as herself, and still remains in fine order. I never procured a male of this species till 1876, three years after she was turned into my grounds. He was a very small specimen, two years old. I do not think they noticed each other before September, when I occasionally saw them together, or rather the buck seemed inclined to seek her society, but she showed herself quite a virago, and would dash after him as if she desired above all things to give him a good beating. This, however, she was much more inclined to do when I was around than when she did not see me. If this was a pretense of modesty on her part, it was the merest affectation, for, as I shall hereafter explain under the head of *Hybridity*, I fear she has become thoroughly debauched, by breeding to bucks of another species, and that she will still favor them instead of the male of her own species, which she seems so much inclined to punish. However, I have lately seen him several times turn upon her, as if inclined to defend himself from her vicious attack, and I hope he will soon be able to tame the termagant. It is evident she will find him a very different subject to deal with from the great awkward Mule buck, which she tyrannizes over so wickedly.

In 1873, at the same time that I procured the Acapulco doe, I procured a buck and two does of a size scarcely larger than the former, in form and color, and indeed in most characteristics resembling her very much. The buck was presented to me by Governor Latham, who informed me that he purchased it from the deck of a ship just arrived from the Island of Ceylon, whence, he was informed, the deer was brought, so that I can no longer doubt as to the place of its nativity. The does are undoubtedly from the same place. Their close similarity to the Acapulco deer will induce me to compare them when we discuss the different branches of our subject. For the present, I will only say that they are nearly the same in size, color, and form. Antlers about the same size, but differing in form. Both are very courageous, and combative with other deer. Both are robust, good feeders, and fatten easily, and bare giving suck remarkably well, though the

Ceylon does do not keep in as good condition while raising their fawns as does the Acapulco doe. The Ceylon deer is of a shade the lightest color. The most important distinction is that the metatarsal gland is present in the Ceylon deer, while it is wanting in the Acapulco deer. Although the Ceylon buck and the Acapulco doe were brought from California together in a cage, and seemed much attached to each other when turned in the park, the doe refused to breed to him at the proper season, although there was no buck there of her own species. This Ceylon deer is probably the same deer which Sir Samuel W. Baker designates as the *Red Deer* of Ceylon, although I can find no vestige of the canine teeth.

We shall learn more of these beautiful little deer hereafter.

COMPARISONS.

HAVING given a description of each of the species of our deer with their characteristics more or less minute, we may find it profitable to enter into more detail under different headings, by which we may the more completely understand each, and by comparison perceive their similitudes and their differences. If in doing this we find it necessary or convenient to repeat something which has already been said, we may find a recompense for it by having the same facts presented in different lights and in different connections, and thus the better appreciate their importance and fix them the more permanently in the memory. Indeed much of the value of our investigations must consist in comparing the observed facts relating to each species, with those of all the others, and to do this we must classify them and bring them into as close juxtaposition as practicable.

FORM AND SIZE.

It may be proper that we commence the comparison of the different species of deer of which I treat by examining their respective physical configurations and sizes. In pursuing the plan hitherto adopted I will commence with the largest, — the Moose.

Our Moose is not only the largest of the American deer, but it is the largest living representative of the family as yet discovered in any part of the world. In comparatively recent times a much larger species existed in Ireland, whose fossil remains have been found complete and are now exhibited as interesting relics of former times, but our Moose considerably exceeds in size the same species in Europe, the Scandinavian elk; whether he has there degenerated in size, may be an open question, but I think the weight of evidence shows that he was formerly of a larger size than he is now, although individual specimens still are sometimes met with as large as the average of our Moose.

This animal is the most ungainly in form of all the deer tribe. Its long head and short neck, its long legs and short body, its lack of symmetry in almost every line, leave no room for admiration, while its small sunken eye, with its sinister expression, compels the observer to turn away with an unpleasant sensation. Still its structure in many respects seems to adapt it to meet the exigencies of the life which it is obliged to lead. Its long and powerful legs enable it to force its way through snows and thickets which it often encounters in winter, and to wade and swim in the water, to which its summer habits lead it. Its fore legs are considerably longer than its hind legs, which makes it much taller before than behind, while its short horizontal neck seems to magnify this deformity.

They vary much in weight as well as in height. The largest specimens attain a weight of more than twelve hundred pounds, and are six and one half feet tall anteriorly, though the average weight and height are much less than this. The female is considerably smaller than the male.

The next in size is our Elk, the Wapiti Deer. One is not struck with the beauty of this animal when it is listlessly standing in some retired shade quietly ruminating, but when awakened by excitement it seems to change its form : animation and expression pervade every feature of the animal, and we are at once charmed by a beauty and a symmetry which before were entirely wanting. Though considerably smaller than our moose, it is scarcely less in size than the European elk. There is no member of the family in which a greater diversity of size is met with than in the adult Wapiti, both male and female. This is especially true of the length of their legs. Some having very short, and others very long legs. The maximum live weight of this deer exceeds one thousand pounds, and in height the largest exceeds sixteen hands, or five feet and four inches. I had one which was fully that height, and when he was killed at five years old he was estimated to weigh nine hundred pounds, which I think was not too much, as at three years old he weighed six hundred and fifty pounds without antlers. I have had adult females of less than four hundred pounds' weight.

The Woodland Caribou ranges next in size. It has shorter legs and is not so high in proportion to weight as those above named. Among them, too, is a very considerable difference in size. Four hundred pounds is the largest weight I find specified for this animal, though I think it probable this weight is sometimes exceeded.

This animal approaches nearer in form and proportions to our domestic ox than any other deer, though the American variety is less so than the Lapland reindeer. This is shown more clearly by a reference to the illustrations than could be done by any verbal explanations.

The next in size to the woodland caribou comes the Mule Deer of the Rocky Mountains and the West. This animal rarely attains a live weight exceeding two hundred and fifty pounds, though individuals have been killed exceeding this; still the average is much less. Its head and neck are well proportioned, though its enormous ears greatly disfigure it; its body is long and well poised; its legs are long, straight, and rather heavy. Its unsprightly action contributes more to its awkward appearance than any disproportion of its members.

There is a great difference in size among individuals of the species, depending much on the altitude of their habitat, those inhabiting the higher elevations being the largest. I have referred in another place to a remarkable variety of this species found by Mr. John Xantus, as I am informed by Professor Baird, one of the most reliable collectors for the Smithsonian Institute, who forwarded several specimens to Washington from Cape St. Lucas, in Lower California. With all the other indicia of the Mule Deer, they are very diminutive in size, and have spike antlers about six inches in length. This is one of the most remarkable modifications of a well-established species to be met with, which we must attribute to peculiar conditions of life; and yet I am not fully informed what these peculiar conditions are which produce this remarkable physical change. If mere size and peculiarity of antler were alone sufficient to establish a specific distinction, we should be justified in pronouncing these to be a distinct species. I have not been able to learn that this diminutive Mule Deer has been met with except in the lower part of the peninsula, and the extent of its habitat there is as yet uncertain. In connection with this deer, this fact should be remembered.

The average size of the Columbia Black-tailed Deer is but little greater than that of the common deer, and I have heard of no individuals having been met with as large as some of the latter species. Its limited range may explain its greater uniformity in size. It is probably rare to meet an individual whose live weight would reach one hundred and fifty pounds, while the average of adults would be considerably below that figure.

It has a broad head, with a large and brilliant eye. Its ears are large, but not so disproportioned as to attract attention. Its body is rather short and round. Its legs, too, are short and rather stout, but by no means clumsy. The position in which the tail is curved adds much to its appearance. This is only drooping instead of being closely depressed when at ease, as is the case with all the other deer.

Cervus Virginianus varies very much in size, even in the same latitude, though as a general rule they are larger at the north than in their southern range. About forty years ago I saw the carcass of one in the Chicago market, which I was credibly informed weighed two hundred pounds. Many years ago I killed one near the entrance to Deer Park, in Lasalle County, Illinois, which I mention elsewhere, which three stout men found a heavy lift to put into the end of the wagon, though it was so poor as to be unfit for the table. He must have weighed more than two hundred pounds. As he was leaping through the brush when I shot him, he looked like a large elk, though the excitement of the moment no doubt magnified him in my eyes. In the fall of 1876, I shot a buck in northeastern Wisconsin, which was judged by several experienced hunters to weigh nearly two hundred and fifty pounds. Four of our Indians came from camp but would not undertake to carry him in (not more than a third of a mile), although we were very anxious to have it done. They dressed him on the spot and made four loads of him. The chief Indian remarked that one might hunt a lifetime and not see such a deer as that, and I deem myself to have been exceedingly fortunate in having met two such deer and bagged them both with dead shots. Even a deer cannot travel after the bone of the neck is torn to pieces with a bullet, or the vertebra is severed at the top of the shoulder.

The largest Common Deer of which I have any authentic account was killed in Michigan, and weighed before he was dressed, two hundred and forty-six pounds. But such specimens are rarely met with. It is much more common to meet adults that will not exceed eighty pounds in weight, and the average weight may be set down at not more than one hundred pounds. The *guesses* of hunters often give much larger weights.

These deer differ very much in form and proportions. Some have long legs and long slim bodies, while others have short legs and short bodies. This has been so observable among those in my grounds, that I have sometimes been inclined to class them into varieties, transmitting these peculiarities to their offspring. Since, however, nearly all of those taken wild have disappeared, and

I have only the descendants from two does, both of which were medium in size and form, there is a great uniformity in their proportions among those which I now have.

Of all our deer this is decidedly the most beautiful in form as well as graceful in motion. Whether standing quietly on the bank of a streamlet, or bounding through the forest, it equally challenges our admiration. It is the very embodiment of graceful form and agile motion.

The Mexican Deer, which I find to be but a variety of *C. Virginianus*, although it has been often ranked as a distinct species (*C. Mexicanus*), is much smaller than his northern brother, and this, as we shall see elsewhere, constitutes his only claim to a specific distinction. This variety of the Common Deer, I find no account of north of Arizona, and very rarely north of Mexico. They are not uncommon in Texas, but east of Texas in the Gulf States, they approach much nearer in size to the common variety found in their northern range.

The next in size is the Barren-ground Caribou, or Arctic Reindeer. In form it resembles the larger species, but i s slimmer in proportion to its length, and its legs are a little longer in proportion to its weight. The illustration is from a photograph kindly furnished me by Mr. McTavish of the Hudson's Bay Company, whose kindness has been already mentioned. The largest specimens of this animal are found on the peninsula of Labrador, where they seem confined to a more southern range than those west of Hudson's Bay. A large specimen may weigh one hundred and fifty pounds, but the average is much less. Ordinarily the hunter can easily throw it on his back and carry it to camp.

The smallest of the North American deer which I have studied, is the Acapulco Deer. None of the specimens which I have had, weighed over about thirty or forty pounds. The male which died in Governor Latham's park, probably when in health would have weighed fifty pounds. The male which I now have, is not quite three years old and is the smallest I have seen and probably the youngest. I have seen a number in California, but none as large as the female in my grounds, the measurements of which I give : —

	Inches.
Length of head from between the ears to end of nose . .	10½
Space between the ears	4
Length of ear	4½
Width of ear	3

From end of nose to root of tail 44
Vertebræ of tail 3¼
Length of hairs beyond 2
Length of hoof on top 1
Length of hoof on bottom 2
Around both hoofs at top 3¼
Height at shoulder 24
Height at hips 26

That we may make the comparison I will here give the measurements by Lichtenstein, as quoted by Professor Baird, of a male *C. Mexicanus*, remembering that my measurements are of a large female : —

	Feet.	Inches.
Total length to root of tail	4	9
Length of tail		6
Head to between ears	1	
Horn from the burr to top of posterior point . . .		9½
Horn from the burr to top of anterior point . .	1	
Length of ears		5½
Height of body anteriorly	2	9
Height of body posteriorly	2	10

The length of the antlers of the Acapulco which died of old age, is seven inches ; they have no prongs proper, but are simply notched at top with small basal snags. From these measurements, we might conclude that the Acapulco deer was not more than half the size of the smallest variety of the Virginia deer, were it not for the fact that the Acapulco deer is shorter legged, and shorter bodied in proportion to its weight than the common deer; still the difference in weight must have been very considerable.

The discussion of other branches of our subject will necessarily involve, to a certain extent, allusions to the size and form of the different species as they come under review.

COAT AND COLOR.

When we carefully examine and well consider the coat, or covering of hair with which nature has provided the several species of deer, interesting peculiarities are revealed, some of which are common to all, while others are confined to species or varieties or even to individuals.

The first to be observed is that the coat on the body is cast off and replaced twice in each year,—a provision peculiar to the deer family in a state of nature, and almost as extraordinary as the deciduous character of their antlers. These coats are well adapted to the comfort of the animals during the different seasons when they prevail. They widely differ, both in structure and quantity. So soon as warm weather is established in the spring, as on most other quadrupeds, the heavy winter coat, by which they have been protected from the rigors of the season, becomes loosened and is thrown off; and is replaced by another coat of hairs of an entirely different texture. The new hairs spring from the same roots which nourished the old ones. As the new hairs shoot out they gradually loosen the old ones, which finally drop off. With some species, the process is quite gradual, and occupies a considerable time While with others, all seem to be loosened nearly at the same time. This is particularly so with our Elk (Wapiti), when the winter is being replaced by the summer pelage, while the change from the summer to the winter coat is very gradual. The winter coat is all detached so nearly together, that if the hairs were dropped off so soon as they are loosened, the animal would for a time appear almost naked, so short would be the new coat. But the inner coat of fur has during the winter become felted together, embracing and confining the long coarse hairs, so that they cover the animal as with a blanket, after a considerable portion have become loosened, thus allowing the young hairs to attain some length before their predecessors are gone. Indeed, this old coat does not in fact drop off, as in ordinary cases, but it is torn away in large patches, by contact with the shrubbery. There would be no difficulty in gathering many baskets full of this coat from the bushes in my grounds in the month of June. The large proportion of fur in this pelage would render it quite practicable to convert it into yarn and cloth, or into felted goods. When the old coat is gone the new one is very short and fine, and fairly glistens in the bright sunshine.

How this process progresses with the moose and the caribou, I am not fully informed, only that it occurs at the same time in the spring, when other quadrupeds discard their winter garb. From the fact that this occurs at a time when the deer are not in season for the hunter, but few observations have been made of them at this time. Careful observations can only be made when they are in semi-domestication or in confinement, where they can be studied the year round.

The other species in my grounds shed the winter coat gradually, much as is the case with the cow, so that the new coat has attained a considerable length before the whole of the winter coat is gone. On the Virginia deer, and especially on the Columbia deer, the young red coat showing through the thin remnant of the old one, gives the animal quite a curious appearance for a few days.

The hairs of the summer coat differ very materially from those of the winter coat. They are small in diameter, and as solid and straight as those of the cow. Coming from the same roots as the discarded coat, we may assume they are the same in number, but they are so much smaller in diameter that they present an open and loose appearance, admitting freely the summer air. With this coat there is no appreciable coat of underfur. This semiannual change of coat I have only been able to clearly demonstrate on the body and neck, while on the head, legs, and tail, I can only vouch for one change of garb, which seems to take place later in the spring, or in the summer. This is certainly so, on the tails of all the species in my grounds. There, the old hairs are gradually lost through the summer, and the new ones as gradually appear and grow, and only become conspicuous when the winter coat comes on in the fall. The black tuft on the tail of the mule deer is persistent.

The length of the summer coat on the moose, the caribou, and the wapiti is relatively much shorter than on the smaller species. On our elk it is less than one fourth the length of the winter coat when both are at the longest. On the mule, the Virginia, and the Columbia deer, it is about half the length; on the Acapulco deer, and the Ceylon deer, it is more than half the length of the winter coat, which as we shall see is very short.

On the ears of the Virginia deer and the smaller species, the summer coat is very thin and light, so that the blood-vessels show plainly through it, and the ear appears translucent when the sun shines into the front side of the ear and the observer stands behind it. The ears of the larger species are well covered with hairs during the summer, although light in comparison to the winter coat.

The hairs of the summer coat are without any crinkled or wavy appearance so characteristic of the winter coat of all the Cervidæ. Indeed, this coat seems well adapted to the transmission of heat and to promote the comfort of the animal during the heat of summer ; with this great disadvantage, however, that it affords slight protection against the flies and mosquitoes, which so frequently infest the native ranges of these animals. The summer coat is longest and most dense on the Columbia deer, and so affords the best protection against insects, though it may be too warm for comfort on a hot day.

The great objective point for the flies and mosquitoes, is the face, from the eyes to the nose. If there is a fly in the forest he will be sure to be found on the deer's face, which after a while seems to become quite insensible, for I have often observed them quite happy taking corn from my hand while the face was half covered with bloated mosquitoes. The insects, however, do not confine themselves to this favorite locality, but attack every vulnerable point where the hair is thin and short.

This summer coat is worn but three months or less. By August it begins to disappear, and by September is entirely replaced by a new garb. This at first is always fine and short, but the hairs grow rapidly in length and diameter, till by winter they form a dense mass, which bids defiance to the bleakest winds and the coldest storms.

For some years after I had commenced my observations I believed that our Elk had but one pelage during the year, and so was an exception to the general rule which governs this genus. One day in September, long after I had publicly announced this as a fact to a scientific body, I was startled to observe on the side of an Elk a slight difference in the color between the upper and the lower portions of the side, although the line of demarcation was not well defined. I at once suspected that I had fallen into an error. I continued my observations, long and anxiously scrutinizing every part of each individual in the band, which I could induce to come sufficiently near for the purpose. At last it became perfectly clear that I had been in error. The summer coats were disappearing and were being replaced by the new coats, but the new were in length and color so nearly like the old, and the process was so gradual that it had been hitherto overlooked, although it had often been the subject of examination. The truth is I had not known *how* to examine for it, for it had not occurred to me that the old and the new could be so nearly alike, and that the new hairs could spring up among the old ones so gradually, and be so well calculated to elude the scrutiny of the observer. After I learned how to examine and comprehended the mode of the change, the evidence of the truth rapidly accumulated, till finally the whole process appeared perfectly plain. I could see it now very distinctly, and was surprised that I had been so long blind with my open eyes. I could now see that some of the animals had already taken on almost the entire new suits, while others had hardly commenced to cast off the old ones, and yet the difference in color was no more than that observed between individuals at any season of the year.

On our Elk it will be observed that the change of coat in the fall is exactly the reverse of that in the spring ; while the former is so gradual as nearly to elude detection, it will be remembered that the winter coat is cast off in great patches, felted together so that large portions are carried dangling in tatters after the hairs have been actually detached, and present altogether a very extraordinary appearance. On this animal we see the two extremes of the process.

The particulars of this process in the Moose and the Caribou has not been carefully studied by any one, so far as I can learn. But few have had facilities for studying it, and these have taken no interest in the matter. Naturalists have deemed it of so little importance, that they have rarely even mentioned the two pelages, although the marked difference in color of the two coats on the Virginia deer, which has been much more studied than any of the other species, has been frequently spoken of.

The *red* and the *blue* coats have been constantly remarked by hunters, because the deer are always poor when in the red, and are only worth killing when in the blue. If I find occasional mention made of the summer and winter coats of the moose and the caribou, I lack the necessary facts to give a clear idea of the minute differences which they exhibit.

I have in my grounds all the species of which I treat, except the moose and the caribou, and have been enabled to study at leisure the living specimens, and so may speak with the utmost confidence of them.

In all, the change from the summer to the winter coat is gradual, the new displacing the old by dislodging the hairs promiscuously, till they become so thin that the new coat is seen through the old. This is not simultaneous over the whole animal, for the neck and shoulders may be clothed entirely with the new dress, while the old still prevails on the thighs and rump ; or the winter coat may have replaced the old on the back, while the belly still shows only the summer pelage. In some, the new coat attains a greater length than in others before the old disappears. For instance, on the Mule Deer, the winter coat is scarcely three lines long when it appears in place of the old ; it is very soft and fine, of a beautiful glossy black, although it undergoes an appreciable change every day, so that it very soon loses its fine luster, and shows the gray, which is its characteristic color during the winter. Were this change of garb to take place simultaneously over the whole animal, it would for a short time appear in a beautiful black suit ; but the change is usually so gradual, that a casual observer might not remember the black appearance at all, for the part of the new coat which had been exposed for a few days would have already assumed its grayish hue, and a part would still be covered by the old yellow summer coat. The finer the condition of the animal, the more intense and brilliant is this black, and the longer it resists the tendency to turn gray. I once had a farrow doe that was very fat, which retained the black till the yellow was all gone, so that for a few days she was as black as a bear, and specimens of the new coat, plucked from the loin, were not more than five or six lines long. An examination of these hairs showed that the black was confined to the upper part, while the lower was of a considerably lighter shade, but none of the annular rings of different shades had yet appeared.

So it is on all the species, to a greater or less extent. When the winter has replaced the summer garb, the hairs are short, fine, and soft ; but they rapidly grow in length and diameter, and undergo the changes of color peculiar to the species. At first, they lie down smoothly, but presently the diameter become so great, that they force each other up to a more vertical position, or at right angles to the skin. As the diameters increase, he cavities within enlarge and become filled with a very light pith, they become brittle, and lose their elasticity, so that the integrity of the walls is destroyed when sharply bent, and they remain in the given position. Towards spring these hairs become so tender near the outer ends that they are liable to be broken off by the animals rubbing against the trees. This is especially the case with the caribou, which by reason of the darker ends of the hairs becoming broken off, appears in almost a white garb towards spring. I have observed the same occurrence in many instances in the Virginia deer in my grounds. I have known a few instances in which the Virginia deer had bitten off, towards spring, almost the entire winter coat. I supposed this was caused by their being infected by vermin, but I was unable to verify this supposition.

On all the species, the hairs of the winter coat, except the short ones on the face and legs, are crinkled, and all are tipped with black, wherever the coat is colored, except on the caribou, where this law seems reversed. Even the very white hairs, which are always found sparsely scattered through the blackest Moose, are provided with a jet black tip, so fine, that the naked eye will scarcely discern it, though it may be from two to three lines in length. Below this is a tawny annular section of the same extent; below this, again, the hairs are as white as snow. All of the black hairs on the Moose have the russet or tawny section of two or three lines in extent, about four lines below the sharp, black points, and are white on their lower parts, for from one quarter to one eighth their length. The black hairs are more elastic than the white ones, and the lower white portions of the black hairs are more brittle than the black portions, so that the coloring matter seems to add to the strength and elasticity of the hairs.

On the Caribou, the hairs are much shorter than on the moose, but they are very dense and compact, forming a remarkably warm covering for winter ; and their skins are highly prized by the northern natives, who use them for garments. The hairs are more uniform in color throughout their length, than on any of the other species. As before stated, they are not like the others, tipped with black, while they are lighter near the body. On the Caribou, where the white generally prevails, the hairs are white the whole length, and where the dark color prevails, they are dark colored the whole length.

On our Elk the hairs are longer, and very abundant. They are exceedingly light, and excellent non-conductors of heat. They are more crinkled than on any of the others, and although less brittle than on the caribou, they are quite non-elastic. When used as robes, they are very warm and comfortable for covering. When used as a cushion, for riding, or in camp for a bed, the hairs break down under the pressure, and their beauty and even comfort are spoiled. The surface of the hairs appears very smooth, but under the microscope the appearance of minute scales is disclosed. In form, the hairs on Wapiti for one fourth of their outer length taper, terminating with an exceedingly fine point, more difficult to be seen than the point of a fine needle. Below this the diameter is nearly uniform till near the end, where they contract to the root, the neck of which is about one eighth the largest diameter of the hair, then the root swells out to double the size of the neck and terminates in a semi-spherical form. The length of the root is nearly twenty times its largest diameter.

On both the male moose and the elk a heavy mane is found under the neck. The hairs of this on our elk are eight inches long, but I have not found them so long on the moose, though others have. On the sides of the neck they are not so long, still they are very much longer than on any other part of the animal. The mule deer also has a distinct mane, but not so long as above, and it is on the top of the neck, and even extends along the back sometimes to the hips. This mane falls apart so as to hang over on either side along the top of the neck, and this parting of the hairs continues down the back for a considerable distance, and on one specimen I observed it reached the hips.

On some aged specimens in my grounds I have found this mane less conspicuous, and the parting on the top of the neck less or scarcely observable; but the darker line along the top of the neck and back I have found on all the individuals examined, whether in my grounds or in the Chicago market, where I have seen hundreds, or in the woods, though this mark is less pronounced on some than on others. On the rump, just above the white tail, where this dark stripe terminates, the black is deeper than it is further forward, especially on those where the dark line is the faintest.

The hairs on all the species continue to increase in length and diameter till January or even February, by which time, on the bodies of the elk and the mule deer, they have attained a length of two inches or more. On the foreheads they are an inch or more in length, which on the elk lie in wavy tufts, but on the mule deer they stand up loosely, and are fine and soft. On all the species the hairs on the face below the eyes are short and stout, and have a backward or lateral set, which must tend to admit the rains when the animals are feeding, but allows them to remain undisturbed by contact with the brush, or tall grass, or weeds, when running through them, and with the wind when facing it.

On the legs, also, the hairs are short, but are the longest on the mule deer. On different parts of the legs, the hairs point in various directions. Along the middle of the leg their direction is rather lateral and upwards, and near the foot downward. Those which cover the glands are described elsewhere.

On the Virginia deer, the Columbia, and the Acapulco deer, I do not find any appearance of a mane, either at the top or

9

bottom of the neck, although the hairs may sometimes be found a little longer on the neck than on the body.

I have sought on specimens of the Columbia deer in Washington Territory, in Oregon, and in California, for the tuft of long hairs near the umbilicus, described by Audubon, but I could never detect the least appearance of it. Sir John Richardson's figure of the mule deer represents that species as provided with a similar appendage, but this I can confidently assert is a misdescription, as well as the long bushy tail which he puts on the same animal. Indeed I have never found this tuft, which is universally found on the common bull, on a single individual of either of the deer family, and am very confident it is not an ordinary appendage to either one of them. This tuft on the bull marks the orifice of the theca, which on both the mule and the Columbia deer, is far back between the thighs, as is more particularly described in another place.

On the Moose in my collection, the upper lip or muzzle is covered with hairs, except in front, where there is a naked space shaped precisely like the cross section of an *H* railway rail, the head of which is exactly between the nostrils, and is one inch and ten lines wide; and from the top of the figure to the mouth, on which rests the foot of the rail, is one inch and six lines, and the thickness of the neck of the rail is three lines. This figure is surrounded with hairs not more than two lines in length, which radiate in every direction from the borders of the head of the figure, but below that point the hairs assume a descending position. These hairs on the upper lip are of a yellowish dun color dotted over with black spots, from each of which springs a stiff, tapering, black hair from three to six lines in length. For six inches above the naked space are found sparsely scattered similar hairs, from one to two inches in length. On this region, and above, the hairs assume an ascending direction, and grow lighter in color till a tawny brown is attained on the forehead; but on the cheeks and the under side of the head black prevails. This naked mark on the muzzle, and indeed this whole description, answers precisely to my observations on the Scandinavian elk, only the shades of color are generally lighter on the Moose.

On the Caribou alone, of all our deer, is the muzzle or upper lip entirely covered with short, stiff hairs, except a very narrow line along the lower edge of the lip. There is no naked line down the middle, as has been stated by some, but the coat is perfectly uniform entirely across. Between the nostrils, these hairs assume an ascending direction, and are of a light drab color, as far up as the middle of the nostrils; above this point they grow a little longer and become a chocolate brown for three inches, when they become of a lighter shade, but still the face is brown up to the antlers. Below, for say three inches, posterior to the light dun, or as far back as the angle of the mouth, it may be fairly called black. Back of that it fades out to a dirty yellowish white along the under side of the head. Around the eyes the brown is of a deeper shade than the rest. No long black hairs are found on the upper lip or nose of the Caribou, as observed on the moose, but in their place are a few white hairs, which show conspicuously on the dark ground. I found the same markings on the eastern reindeer's face.

The upper lip of our Elk is also covered with short hairs, except for seven lines in front and the space between the nostrils, which is naked, but a point of the coat above invades the upper part of this naked space. The dividing space in front, on the upper lip, for nine or ten lines above the mouth, is not entirely naked, but is dotted over with tufts of very fine short hairs, almost like fur. These tufts are less than a line in diameter, and over a line apart. These have something the appearance of the little tufts on many of the cacti family of plants, and constitute really a very distinguishing characteristic of the species. The hairs of the face are tawny in color, with a yellowish shade around the muzzle, but growing darker above, the under lip being lightest of all.

These three large species, of which we have just spoken, we see have the muzzle or upper lip either partially or entirely covered with hair; but on the smallest of the three it is alone entirely covered, while the next above in size is the least covered, and the largest is intermediate.

All of our species, inferior in size to those above considered, and which in other respects constitute a separate division of the Cervidæ, have the upper lip and the nose as far up as the upper part of the nostrils entirely naked, to about the same extent as the ox. This naked portion, when the animal is in health, is always moist and is cold to the touch, being the only part of the animal where an appreciable perspiration is observed. The form and relative extent of the naked portion is precisely alike in the mule deer, the Columbia deer, the Virginia deer and the Acapulco deer, and I may add the Ceylon deer; except that in the largest of these, the mule deer, the hairs above extend down between the nostrils for half an inch or more, terminating in a point at an angle of perhaps eighty degrees, while on all the others, the upper border of the naked portion passes directly across from one nostril to the other, at their upper extremities. This naked portion extends around the upper lip, to a point exactly below the centre of the nostril ; so that the posterior half of the nostril is only separated from the hair by an exceedingly narrow naked border, while all is naked around the anterior half. Always on all the species last named, the anterior point of the hair on the upper lip, where it meets the naked muffle under the nostril, is white. This white portion, although always present, varies much in extent. Posterior to this white spot, frequently occurs a black section extending back to the angle of the mouth, and from the mouth upward, embracing the posterior part of the nostril, and uniting on top with a similar black section from the other side, constituting a black band passing over the nose from the mouth on one side, to the mouth on the other. Not uncommonly, especially on the Virginia deer, this black section is not continuous, but is confined to a section back of the nostrils, thus not reaching the mouth. On the Virginia deer the hair above is separated from the naked muffle by a narrow white band, which on some is scarcely more than half a line wide, while on others it is fully three lines wide. This white border can generally be detected on the other species, scarcely larger than a thread, but is always the most conspicuous on the Virginia deer.

Back of this black section when it descends to the mouth, commencing at the angle of the mouth, occurs a white section the upper and posterior border of which is not well defined. On some specimens it is quite limited in extent, while on others it diffuses itself over the whole face, posterior to the black portion above described, which it sometimes compresses into very narrow limits on top, while on others the black occupies the whole face up to the eyes. Indeed this is nearly always the case on the Acapulco and Ceylon deer, though it never occurs on the mule deer and rarely on the Columbia deer, but happens very frequently on the Virginia deer. Thus it will be seen that the markings are on all alike till we come to the extent of the white portion posterior to the black band which passes over the nose just above the nostrils. Above that and even in that itself great irregularity is observed in the markings, only that there is always some white portion adjoining this black, though sometimes it may occupy but a small space just above the angle of the mouth.

On all these species also, just anterior to the angle of the mouth on the lower side, occurs another black section, which in a large majority of cases resolves itself into a black band embracing the lower jaw just behind the chin, though sometimes this band is broken on the under side, and sometimes it widens there, so as to cover the posterior part of the chin. I have studied this long and carefully to find some distinguishing characteristic as applicable to each species, but without very satisfactory results. The most I will venture to say is, that I am inclined to think that the black is not so deep and is rather less in extent on the mule deer than on the others, but on all the species it varies very much in individuals, both in extent and in depth of coloring. Its great value is that it is always found in each individual in all the species of this division of the family, while it is wanting on all the others. On all, the anterior part of the chin is always white, and so it is of a lighter shade on the elk and the caribou, but on the moose it is the blackest part of the head.

On the Moose, even when in his blackest dress, the forehead is a dark chestnut color, while the face is nearly black below the eyes, and the lower part near the muffle is reddish gray. The rest of the head is black.

On the Caribou the face and indeed the entire head is brown, with a reddish tinge, and is the darkest part of the animal, except the legs.

There is on all the species, except the moose and the caribou, a light colored band surrounding the eyes. This varies considerably in individuals, but it is always present in all; sometimes, indeed, it is hardly perceptible above the eye, while on others it is there the most conspicuous, but this variation is among the individuals and not among the species, unless it may be less pronounced on the smallest — the Acapulco deer, but the number of specimens of this which I have examined is too limited to enable me to affirm that it is so. Its entire absence on the moose and the caribou, and universal presence on all the others, is worthy of particular remark.

The face of the Elk is a uniform russet brown from the antlers to the end of the nose, except the white band which surrounds the eye.

There is no white under the head of our Elk, in which it resembles the other two large species, and differs from all the smaller species.

The forehead of the Mule and the Columbia deer is either

black or dark gray. Most commonly a black line extends from each eye to the base of each antler, and these lines extend down the face between the eyes, uniting at a point below the eyes, while a lighter shade prevails between these lines, which, however, is much darker than below. Below this, the nose or face is of a much lighter color; all this is to a degree reversed on the Virginia deer and the Acapulco deer. Their faces are blackest below the eyes, in many cases almost entirely black, while the forehead is not of so dark a color. In all these the under side of the head is always white, which extends back so as to cover the throat, and a very little below it, but not down the neck.

The colorings of the legs and about the feet show peculiarities worthy of study. On two of the species alone, white hairs are found about the hoofs. On the Caribou these white markings are constant and uniform. The bristles between the claws are white. This white extends up and completely surrounds both the lower and the accessory hoofs. On the posterior side, between the small and the large hoof, these white hairs are very stout and firm, partaking, like those between the toes, of the character of bristles, except that near the points they are stouter and less flexible. These peculiarities are found on all the feet at all ages and seasons, and on both sexes, and are peculiar to the Caribou.

In speaking of the white hairs around the hoof of the Caribou, Dr. Gilpin says: "The whole toe is enveloped in a beautiful fringe of coarse hair, curling down over the black hoof till it nearly covers it, passing between the toes to form a thick mop of coarse hair wrapping the sole and dew-claws in a warm cushion. On glittering ice or slippery slopes, how secure this ice-foot, with its keen, cutting edge; in soft snows, spreading the toes, it forms a soft cushion to hold up the deer upon its treacherous surface, as well as to shield it from the cold. We are immediately struck with an analogy most unexpected between the hairy feet of the deer and the feathered leg and claw of the falcon and great northern owl, and we are apt to speculate how the deer passing north has had his limbs thus clothed in hair, and has departed from the typical, slender, satin-skinned foot of his race."

Above the accessory hoofs on the Woodland Caribou, the color is variably of a clove brown for the winter dress; but in obedience to the general law, this dark color fades more or less as the winter advances.

The Barren-ground Caribou has a foot similarly provided with coarse stiff hairs, but the white is much more extended. Instead of being confined to a narrow band surrounding the hoofs, while the leg is of a nut-brown shade, the whole foot and leg are white, except a tawny brown stripe extending down the front of each leg, with white hairs interspersed, diminishing in extent as it proceeds downward, till it terminates in front of the accessory hoofs. At least this is the case with those in my collection, and I learn that mine are not peculiar in this regard. The difference in the color of the legs of the two species of reindeer, when placed side by side, is very striking. But this greater extent of white on the northern species is in harmony with a law already referred to.

In a great majority of cases, more or less white is found about the hoofs of the Virginia Deer, but rarely to the extent of that which is uniformly found about the foot of the Caribou, so that it must be considered a fugitive and not a permanent mark of the species. If present, this white is sure to be seen between the toes, and sometimes it is limited to that region. Usually this white mark extends in a narrow line up the front of the leg to opposite the accessory hoofs. The white also frequently shows itself around the upper part of the hoofs, perhaps only for a short distance, and sometimes, though rarely, quite around both. Sometimes these white markings appear on one or more of the feet, and sometimes on all. On some, no white ever appears around the feet. This white is very pure, not a colored hair being found intermixed with it. Above, the leg is of the rufous shade, varying very greatly in intensity, from the color prevailing on the body to almost pure white. I have in my collection a specimen, the legs of which are almost entirely of a yellowish white, only a line down the anterior edge of the leg has tawny red hairs intermixed with the white, imparting a sandy shade. The tuft over the metatarsal gland is a purer white than on the rest of the leg of this deer, but the difference is scarcely perceptible. I remark the exceptional feature, that the hairs composing the tuft over the tarsal gland are for their whole length a tawny yellow, contrasting strongly with the white, clothing the balance of the leg inside and outside. This specimen is from the Rocky Mountains, where it is called the white-tailed deer, or, further north, the long-tailed deer, or *Cervus leucurus* of some authors ; and yet the tail, although there is no black upon it, cannot be distinguished, either in length, form, or color, from many living specimens in my grounds. I have in another place assigned the reasons why we must class this with the Virginia deer, and it is scarcely entitled to the distinction of a variety, the only peculiarity being, that it has on the average more white on it than those native east of the Missouri River. This specimen has more white on it than any other which I have ever seen anywhere.

On one specimen only of the Wapiti deer have I found white hairs around the hoofs, and I have examined hundreds for them. This was a fine buck, sent from Laramie, on the Laramie plains, and probably killed in that neighborhood in January, 1875. I judge him to have been five years old. Around the hoofs on each foot was a band of pure white hairs. It extended quite around the upper part of the hoofs, and was about three lines broad, and was of the like dimensions on each foot.

We have seen in another place that white spots, or white hairs, frequently appear on the Elk, but they are fugitive, never appearing in the same form or place, if at all, the next year. It would be interesting to know if this was so on the Laramie elk.

On all the species, save the caribou and the Virginia deer, not a white hair has ever been detected around the hoofs, except the single elk just named; but if there be a distinction, the hairs around the hoofs are of a darker shade than those above, though I was disappointed not to find some white hairs there on the Acapulco deer and the Ceylon deer.

The legs of the female Wapiti are of a chestnut brown, and on the bucks they are brown black, fading out as the season progresses to the color of the females, but on the posterior edges on both, at all times, is the stripe of a much lighter and more yellow shade elsewhere described.

The leg of the Mule Deer, although quite dark in the early winter coat, fades out rapidly, so that by midwinter it is of quite a light color, and by spring, it is sometimes nearly white, but individuals differ very much in this regard. The same remark will apply to both the Virginia and the Columbia deer. On the Acapulco deer, the leg is of a darker color, and fades less during the winter, still it fades to a certain extent.

I have already spoken somewhat of the general color of the Moose. We have seen that the new winter coat on the young Moose is black, and so it is till he reaches his prime. Although, even before that, the intensity or brilliancy of the color may lose its lustre. Captain Hardy says: "The first two or three days of September over, and the Moose has worked off (from his antlers) the last ragged strip of the deciduous skin against his favorite rubbing-post." "His coat now lies close with a gloss reflecting the sun's rays, like that of a well-groomed horse. His prevailing color if in his prime is jet black, with beautiful golden brown legs and flanks pale fawn." [1]

Dr. Gilpin, in describing the color in September, of a male three years and four months old, says: " The color of this bull was in the highest summer coating of deep glossy black and short as a well-groomed horse. The muffle and forehead had a brownish yellow cast, the cheeks and neck dark black ; the ears were light fawn inside, a little darker outside ; the crest yellowish, mixed gray and white, and a yellow gray patch upon the croup. The inside of the buttock and all the legs both inside and outside were bright yellow fawn, the black of the body running down half way to the hocks and to the knees, and ending with an abrupt line in a point. There was also a black line running from each hock and each knee in front and widening to join the hoof. This line has heretofore escaped observers."

Audubon and Bachman, in closing their description of the color of the Moose, say : " The young animals, for the first winter, are of a reddish brown color ; individuals even of the same age often differ in color, some being darker than others, but there is always a striking difference between the summer and winter colors, the hairs in winter becoming darker ; as the Moose advances in age, the color continues to deepen, until it appears black ; thence it was named by Hamilton Smith, not inappropriately as regards color, ' the American Black Elk.' " Here are some errors that require correction. While the winter coat is darker than the summer coat the striking contrast is in September, when the winter coat first appears. From that time onward, it grows lighter continually. It is manifest, however, that they did not mistake the new winter coat for the summer coat, as very often occurs, but they clearly recognized the two pelages in each year, in the Moose, as occurs with all the other deer, which, however, has been rarely noticed or appreciated by those most familiar with the animal. How they fell into the error of stating that the color of the Moose deepens as it advances in age until it finally appears black, it is not easy to explain. All most familiar with the animal, agree that after the first year, the winter coat is blackest, and that after full maturity it sensibly grows lighter with advancing age. Captain Hardy says : " In old bulls of the American variety the coat is inclined to assume a grizzly hue."

Mr. Morrow writes me, quoting from a friend who often ac-

[1] *Forest Life in Acadie,* p. 66.

companies him in the chase of the Moose: " The younger animals are darkest. As winter advances the hair grows longer and gradually fades, becoming more gray." This fading out of the color to a sort of gray, with advancing age, is a fact so well recognized by all familiar with the animal, so far as I have been able to learn, that I do not deem it necessary to multiply quotations on the subject. That this is much more the case with some than with others, we may not question, any more than that individuals of all ages differ very appreciably in color, which is admitted by all. It is by far the darkest colored of all our deer, and it is probably the darkest of any known deer of any part of the world. It has always been recognized as much darker than the Swedish elk, with which, I am entirely satisfied by critical comparison, it is specifically identical.

As I have expressed the opinion so confidently, that the Moose has two pelages in the year, while admitting that I have not had the opportunity to personally verify this fact, and have not the direct evidence of any observer who has done so, it may be proper that I should group together some of the evidence which I think tends strongly to establish it.

Let us again recur to what Dr. Gilpin says of the coat in September of the three-year old male Moose: " The color of the bull was in the highest summer coating of deep glossy black and short as a well-groomed horse." Now this was at a time when the other species of deer have just discarded the summer coat and the new winter garb is just fairly developed. Had our author seen him a month earlier, I am very sure he would have found him less attractive, in a shabby fawn-colored summer dress, already preparing to give place to the one described.

At the time the Doctor wrote this description, his attention had not been called to this second pelage of the Moose, nor do I anywhere find a direct examination of the subject by any author, nor, so far as I know, have the hunters taken particular note of it. Hardy says: " His coat now lies close, with a gloss reflecting the sun's rays like that of a well-groomed horse." I find abundant evidence that the Moose has a new coat in the fall in many observations, like the above. Even without these, analogy tells us that such must be the case, and we should require the strongest evidence to dispute her teachings. The fact that the Moose is out of season and is never hunted when in the summer coat, — that then they are without their antlers, and seek the deepest seclusion, — explains how it is that they are rarely seen when in that unattractive summer suit. Naturalists, studying this animal, have not made this particular point a subject of inquiry, and so their attention has not been directed to the facts, even when seen, which would serve to elucidate it. We may see a thousand things without observing them, if we do not appreciate their importance. We see them and pass them by in forgetfulness, unless we see in them some significance. Even so accurate an observer and accomplished a naturalist as Dr. Gilpin, lived among the Moose, as we may say, for forty years, without his attention being directed to this particular branch of the subject.

In answer to my inquiries in reference to two pelages of the moose and the caribou, Mr. Robert Morrow, of Halifax, writes me : " They have a summer and a winter coat, but that they shed it more than once a year I cannot say. The Indians say no, but it is not probable that their attention has been drawn to the subject. Dr. Gilpin thinks, reasoning from analogy, that they partially shed their coat in the latter part of the summer, in which case the coat is shed spring and fall."

When I remember the difficulty I had to detect the shedding of the coat in the fall by the elk, and that after years of observation with the best opportunities, I was still of opinion that he had but one pelage in the year, I can appreciate how little reliance can be placed on the negative conclusions of even the Indians, who, as Mr. Morrow suggests, probably never thought of the subject. The observer who detected a clear and well-defined line between lighter and darker shades along the side of the caribou, saw the same thing, though more distinctly, that first led me to discover the change of coat at the end of summer on the elk.

The mule deer resembles the Moose most in the black color of the new winter coat, but it turns to gray much sooner than the black of the Moose fades to the grayish white, which it assumes during the winter or towards the spring. I again quote from Gilpin : " The winter coating (of the Moose) is formed of long hair so stiff as to stand bristly outward, and as each hair is lead colored at base, grayish-white in the middle, and black at top, the whole animal has a grayish appearance. The crest loses its yellowish wash, and the hair on the cheeks and neck is both darker and shaggier than on the body. There is still a yellowish brown wash on the muffer and forehead, and the ears are brownish fawn. The beautiful yellow fawn and black stripes of the legs disappear, and mixed gray cover them, hiding the abrupt lines of black and tan." Although our author was not aware that he was describing the same winter coat at two different periods of its growth, he has done so with marked clearness, and he would have appreciated this, if he had watched many individuals of most of the species day by day from the first appearance of the new winter coat, under the disappearing summer coat, through all the changes to the faded and worn out appearance of spring, and till it is finally cast off in its turn, — he would have appreciated that, like the garment of a man, it is most beautiful when it is first put on, and the longer it is worn the more faded and shabby it becomes.

Hardy says, the Moose sheds his winter coat about the middle of April. In September we find him with a fine, short, soft, glossy coat, as black as night. Can any rational man suppose that that is the same coat which he took on in the previous April, and which he had worn the whole summer? Has it been growing finer, shorter, softer, and acquiring a finer lustre all the summer? On all the others the summer coat continues to increase in length, and to lose its freshness during the summer, until, when it is thrown away, it has a dirty and ragged appearance, and all at once, in September, we find it changed to a rich and beautiful nuptial dress, the admiration of all who see him. No one ever mentions him in this dress in the summer time, and I imagine no one of sense will suppose he ever wears such a dress at that time, and to suppose that the same hairs which had been long and harsh, and dull of color, all at once become short, and soft, and brilliant, seems to me to bespeak an ignorance of the growth of the coats of quadrupeds. It seems to me impossible to account for this ornamental coat in the early fall, except on the conclusion that it is composed of new hairs, which have lately taken the place of others of a different color and quality just cast off.

Audubon and Bachman say: " But there is always a striking difference between the summer and winter colors, the hairs in winter becoming darker." Now this must be a recognition of the two distinct coats of summer and winter ; the former of which is certainly lighter than the latter, even after it has faded from its first brilliant hues. It would be an anomaly, indeed, for a sickly, pale coat to change to a brilliant black.

Both from analogy and attested facts, when their true import is properly considered, I think we are warranted in the conclusion that the Moose, with the others, has its two distinct pelages each year.

Of the individual hairs, Captain Hardy says: " The extremities only of the hairs are black ; towards the centre they become of a light ashy gray, and finally, towards the roots, dull white." With this description most authors substantially agree. My own examination, however, shows many exceptions to this, especially upon the neck, where I find many hairs black nearly their whole length, and quite a number snow-white, from one extremity to the other.

The coat of under fur, which is almost as abundant as on our elk, is of a uniform drab, and does not undergo the same changes of color which are observed with the long coarse hair, which alone are seen by the superficial observer.

While the head and the legs of the Woodland Caribou are always distinctly colored, in a large majority of individuals white predominates, especially on the neck, which is almost universally the whitest part of the animal. The long white mane of the old buck is a very striking characteristic. Hardy says, " The white mane reaching to over a foot in length in old males, which hangs pendant from the neck with a graceful curve to the front, is one of the most noticeable and ornamental attributes of the species." This description is undoubtedly of the late winter coat when the hairs have attained their full length. There is less uniformity in the colors of the bodies than of the head, neck, and legs. While the head and legs are tawny brown of varying intensity, and the neck white, on some much more pronounced than on others, the body is sometimes nearly all white, while others are a rich rufous brown on the back as well as the legs, and only the tail and rump are white above and the belly and inside of the legs are also white. Like all the others, the early winter coat, which replaces the summer coat in September, is of the deepest color, is finer, softer, and more brilliant than later, when the clove-brown shade which first prevailed has given place to the dirty white of midwinter.

Dr. Gilpin thus sums up the colorings of the Caribou: " In winter, soiled yellowish white ; neck, rump, tail, and under parts, pure white ; legs white inside, outside brown, with white fringes. In summer, neck, extending into fore-shoulder, rump and tail, under parts, and inside of legs pure white, all other parts clove-brown ; sometimes reddish and yellowish, with black patch on cheek and eye, with white fringe on hoofs."

The hairs when separately examined are found to be exceptional in color in this, that the tips are never black, and generally the hairs are darker beneath than at or near their outer ends, which is the exact reverse of what we observe on the other species.

The under coat of fur on the Caribou is very abundant, and is of the color of the hairs among which it is found. Of the coat and coloring of the Barren-ground Caribou, Sir John Richardson gives this description : " In the month of July the caribou sheds its winter covering and acquires a short smooth coat of hair, of a color composed of clove-brown mingled with deep reddish and yellowish browns ; the under surface of the neck and belly, and the inner sides of the extremities, remaining white in all seasons. The hair at first is fine and flexible, but as it lengthens it increases gradually in diameter at its roots, becoming at the same time white, soft, compressible and brittle, like the hair of the moose-deer. In the course of the winter, the thickness of the hairs at their roots becomes so great that they are exceedingly close and no longer lie down smoothly, but stand erect, and they are then so soft and tender below that the flexible and colored points are easily rubbed off and that the fur appears white, especially on the flanks. This occurs in a smaller degree on the back ; and on the under parts the hair, although it acquires length, remains more flexible and slender at its roots and is consequently not so subject to break. Towards the spring, when the deer are tormented by the larvæ of the gad-fly making their way through the skin, they rub themselves against stones and rocks, until all the colored tips of the hair are worn off and their fur appears to be of a soiled white color."

This certainly gives us a very clear account of the winter coat, from its first appearance till towards the spring, at least. It is very clear that it never occurred to our author to inquire whether the animal has two pelages, or but one during the year. That question evidently never engaged his attention, and he made no careful observations for the express purpose of elucidating it. Had he done so he would no doubt have settled it conclusively. As it is, I think further observations are required.

The new coat described is like the new winter coat of the other species, which usually comes on in September, upon the loss of the summer coat. It is " a short smooth coat of hair." If there are two pelages, the casting of the summer coat could hardly have occurred before August or September. But can it be that the winter coat is carried till July.

Our author says: "In May the females proceed towards the sea-coast. . . . . Soon after their arrival on the coast, the females drop their young; they commence their return to the south in September, and reach the vicinity of the woods towards the end of October, where they are joined by the males. . . . . Captain Perry saw deer on the Melville Peninsula, as late as the 23d of September, and the females with their fawns made their first appearance on the 23d of April." Now, although the period of yeaning is not necessarily identical with the time of shedding the winter coat, observation shows that it is intimately connected with it where the course of nature is unobstructed. If that is true of this animal, also, then the winter coat should be discarded in the month of May or June at the latest. Then we should have to put back the time when the summer coat is shed and the new winter coat taken till August or September or even October, which Dr. Richardson says is the time when the males join the females near the southern borders of the Barren Grounds. If, as Richardson says, this animal takes on his most attractive attire while he is still poor in flesh, while his antlers are in active growth, and three months before the season of love commences, we must indeed consider it very exceptional and very extraordinary. It seems to be a provision of nature, that the male should be made the most attractive to the female at this season. His antlers, which we may presume, according to caribou tastes are considered ornamental as well as useful, are perfected just previous to the commencement of the rutting season, and at the same time all the others wear their handsomest dress, and we pause before we accept the conclusion that this animal alone wears his best attire in deep seclusion, and quite beyond the notice of the other sex and before he is prompted to show himself to these this dress must be despoiled of its beauty and its attractiveness destroyed by two or three months' wear. This may all be so and this exceptional state of things produced by his high northern range and the short summers there, but I could not help making these reflections, which suggest the possibility that Richardson may have been mistaken in the date which he gives for the time when the most ornamental coat is taken on. I hope I have not been misled in making these suggestions by a desire to maintain a theory which I confess has somehow taken possession of me, that all of our deer must have two pelages in the year. I know that the maintenance of theories is the great bane to impartial investigation, and I try to guard against it, but a great number of harmonious facts all pointing in one direction, necessarily so arrange themselves as to suggest conclusions which soon crystallize into theories, and the danger is that when such conclusions have been thus reached, or such theories have been once formed, we are loth to see any thing which is not in harmony with them.

If Dr. Richardson is not mistaken in his dates, then I think it surely proved that this deer has but one pelage in the year and so is exceptional in this regard among our Cervidæ. Well, if they differ in this respect from all the others it may go a little way to show that they are a different species, which, however, I think abundantly proved in other ways.

I have elsewhere stated that the specimens in my collection show that the white embraces most of the legs as well as the body of this deer, while the legs of the larger species of reindeer are uniformly brown. As we have seen, the same thing occurs with the northern variety of the common deer, but it is hardly a make-weight in the determination of the question of specific identity or distinction.

We now come to those species which I have carefully studied in my own grounds and where I can depend on my own observations entirely.

The summer coat of the Wapiti deer is shorter and thicker than on the other species, and is of a dirty yellowish white color on the body, with a chestnut brown on the legs, neck, and head, and there is no appreciable difference between the males and females. When this coat first appears in June, upon the peeling off of the old winter dress, it is of a deeper shade and more glossy than is observed at any other season of the year, and so it is the most beautiful dress the animal ever wears. It is exceedingly short, fine, and soft, and fairly glistens in the bright spring sunshine. The contrast between this new spring dress, which may perhaps appear on a part of the animal while the balance is covered with the shaggy and tattered winter dress, hanging about in torn patches, some dangling a foot or two feet from the body, is indeed quite remarkable. The one seems emblematic of poverty and destitution, while the other looks like thrift and comfort. One appears like the fag-end of a hard winter, while the other suggests the freshness and the gayety of spring. This soft glossy lustre fades in a short time as the summer coat grows longer. During its height tatters of the old gar-ment often still hang to the animal. As the summer advances these short fine hairs grow longer and coarser, they lose their lustre and fade in color upon the body, while upon the head neck, and legs the color changes but little through the summer. With this summer coat the fur, which is so very abundant with the winter coat, does not appear.

In September this coat gives place to the winter dress, but as I have elsewhere observed, the change is so gradual as to require the closest scrutiny to detect it, although the new coat differs very materially from the old in some parts. This difference is greatest upon the necks and legs of the males, and upon the under sides of the bellies of all; still the change of dress and consequently of color is so gradual, that we may watch the herd day by day, and note the change of color, without being aware that it is due to a change of dress. We merely notice that these dark shades are growing deeper and deeper during the latter part of August and in September, and that upon the bodies of all a darker shade, which appears softer and more glossy, is creeping over the animal.

When the new winter coat is fairly established, a very marked difference in color is observed between the males and the females where the darker shades prevail. The neck, legs, and belly are a brownish black on the males, and the dark border on the lower part of the white posterior patch is a very intense black. At the same time, on the female, the head, neck, legs, and belly, are a chestnut brown. Under the belly it is the darkest — indeed, fairly black on all. We can hardly appreciate this, by observing the live animal, but when the animal is killed and turned on its back to be dressed, we are surprised that we had so much overlooked this darker shade of the belly, which now appears to be quite black.

The white patch on the rump commences at the top of the hip and extends back so as to embrace the tail; its outer border descends laterally in a circular form, so that when even with the seat of the tail, above that member, it nearly describes a semicircle; thence the outer border descends down the ham, gradually drawing inwardly, contracting the white section which, however, descends to unite with the lighter shades of the inguinal region. This white portion is bordered by an intensely black stripe, which commences on either side above the region of the tail and continues down to the posterior sides of the thighs, where it fades out and is lost. This black mark appears on animals of all ages and both sexes, but is the most brilliant on the male in the prime of life and in the fall of the year. The tawny yellow of the body of the Elk, as it appears in the fall, fades out to a sickly,

10

dirty white during the winter, but these shades of color differ very much in individuals, while it is dependent on neither age or sex. On the body the does are as dark as the bucks at all seasons. I have sometimes thought I could detect a darker shade on the adults than on the young animals, and the next time I would examine the herd with a view to this very point I would find myself obliged to abandon the distinctions. It is only on the dark portions, as the head, neck, belly, and legs, that the adult males are blacker than the females and the young in the early winter dress, but as before stated this distinction quite disappears by spring, except that on the mane of the adult, which may be nearly a foot in length, hanging from the lower side of the neck, for its whole length there is a black stripe two or more inches wide, about two inches from its lower border. These two inches of the lower ends of the hairs of this mane are a russet-brown, and such is the color also above the black stripe, passing quite over the neck to the black stripe on the other side. For a month before the shedding of the coat commences, this black stripe on either side of the mane becomes quite conspicuous, from the lighter shade to which the balance of the mane has faded. I have noticed that this prominent black mark is more conspicuous some seasons than others.

Audubon and Bachman have seen young elk, on which the white patch of the rump appeared to be wanting till they were one or two years old. I have constantly looked for such specimens, but have failed to find one on which this mark was not conspicuous, as far off as the colors of the animal could be distinguished, and I have been unable to detect any substantial difference in this regard between those of different ages.

Our Elk, this Wapiti deer, is the only American species on which this white patch above the tail distinctly appears, and is well defined; and the European stag or red deer (*C. elaphus*), is the only European species, so far as I know, in which it is distinctly defined as it is on the Wapiti, and on that it is less conspicuous and more variable. We have several other ruminants in which this distinguishing mark is equally conspicuous, notable among which are our antelope (*Antilocapra Americana*), already treated of, and our Rocky Mountain sheep, or the Big Horn (*Ovis montani*).

Of the fugitive white colorings or spots which frequently appear on the adult female Elk, I shall presently speak.'

I have already spoken of the deep black color in which the

winter dress of the Mule Deer first appears, which distinguishes it from all the other members of the family except the moose, but this dark shade is much less persistent than it is on the moose.

When this transient black disappears it is succeeded by a dark gray, constantly growing lighter. The black shade is most persistent along the top of the neck and the dorsal line, in which, however, individuals differ very much. Under the neck there is a dark line for the whole length, which is quite constant. This dark line deepens in color as it descends, till at the brisket it is a strong black occupying the whole space between the fore legs and along the under side of the body till within four inches of the thighs, when it grows lighter very fast, so that the inside of the thighs and the region between them is a light gray or soiled white. This white shade extends down to the gambrel joint, occupying the whole inside of the thighs, becoming more pronounced posteriorly to the seat of the tail. Commencing a little above the seat of the tail, extending downward about seven inches, is a white section. This is about three inches broad on each side of the tail, and from side to side is ten inches broad following the form of the animal. This is generally a pure white, but sometimes, like that on the tail, it has a slightly yellowish tinge. This is a very conspicuous mark when the animal is viewed posteriorly, and reminds one at once of the white patch on the croup of the elk, to which it makes a strong approach. This is not bordered with the deep black, as seen on the elk, in the region where it occurs on this deer.

The plain gray of the back sides and outsides of the thighs is without the tawny tinge which is observed on many of the other species, and is of a considerably lighter shade than under the belly, in this respect resembling the elk.

The individual hairs on this species when they have completed their growth, are less crinkled than on the elk. Two or three lines of the ends of the hairs, which are very sharp pointed, are jet black. Then, for two or three lines, they are a dull white; below this they are brown, shading down to a lighter color near the lower ends. Some are lighter throughout their lengths than others. The under fur is not so abundant as on the elk, still it is present in considerable quantities, and is of a uniform drab color.

In general, the color of the Columbia Deer most resembles that of the Virginia deer, but on individuals it is much less variable. All the specimens I have had in my grounds, which came from

Oregon and Washington Territory, were as near alike as possible. Nor have I been able to detect an appreciable difference in the color of these and those examined in California. The limited range occupied by this deer may account for this uniformity of color among the individuals.

The general color of the body in winter dress is a tawny gray, the red shade being much more distinct than is usually observed on the Virginia deer, and yet I have specimens of the latter in my grounds of precisely the same shade as the former. A hundred times have I studied them when both were eating from my hand, and could detect no difference in the shade of color, while perhaps another Virginia deer would be standing but a few feet away, so much lighter in color that one would suspect a different species.

There is a darker shade of color down the upper side of the neck, fading out along the back, but this mark is the most variable of any observed on the animal ; on some being scarcely distinguishable, while on others it is distinct and may be traced nearly to the hips.

On the under side of the neck is a dark line, which descending increases in depth till it becomes black on the brisket, with a lighter shade on either side as it joins the leg, which extends down the inside of the fore leg. Passing back from the brisket, the black melts away to a dark brown at the umbilicus, when it shades down anteriorly to a fawn color and then white, which involves all the inner part of the thighs, and passes up between them to the seat of the tail, which in another place will be particularly described. The tawny-gray color of the back and sides embraces, also, the outside of the thighs down nearly to the hocks, and also the fore-shoulder, well towards the knees. I have never seen the collar mark observed by Audubon and Bachman.

The individual hairs on this part of the animal are tipped with an intense black, then occurs an annular section of a tawny yellowish shade; then below that is brown, shading down to a drab, and nearly white on the lower part. The under coat of fur is present, but not very abundant, and is of a drab color.

I have already remarked that there is less uniformity in the color of both the winter and the summer coats of the Virginia Deer, than in either of the other species. Indeed, this may be said of nearly all the markings of this species, except only the ornamental dress of the fawns, which are wonderfully uniform in the shades of color.

In some specimens, as already shown, there is no appreciable difference in the color of the back, sides, outside of the thighs and neck, between the Virginia Deer and the Columbia black-tailed deer. But the rich russet shade of the Columbia deer is not common on the Virginia Deer. In general, there is a bluish shade observed on the Common Deer, which is so prevalent as to have given the winter coat the general appellation, as already shown, of the *blue*, among frontiersmen and hunters, who say the deer is in the *red* or the *blue*, as it may be in the summer or the winter coat. But the difference in the depth of this color is so very great, as well as the different shades of color, as to surprise one who will examine thirty or forty together. As the winter advances, all become appreciably of a lighter color.

On this deer, as on all the others of the smaller species, the white which universally prevails on the under side of the head, terminates with the throat, or just after it reaches the upper part of the neck. Thence the under side of the neck has no white, but is of the prevailing color of the rest of the neck, until we reach the lower extremity. There commences a black, or, on some specimens, a brown stripe, which is always constant, and extends along the brisket to a line even with the posterior part of the fore legs. On either side of this black stripe all is white, which extends down the inside of the fore-legs to the knees. All of the belly is also a very pure white, embracing also the inside of the thighs and hind legs to the hocks, and up to the tail. This is constant on all the Virginia Deer, but on no other species. This white of the belly widens all the way back from the fore legs to the umbilicus, when it involves all the under side of the animal. The white on the lower part of the legs varies much in extent on different individuals, as has been elsewhere stated. On some specimens there is a beautiful gray mark on the inner front side of the fore leg four or five inches long, and two inches wide at the upper end, and terminating in a point, below which it is separated from the white beyond by a tawny stripe extending from the body down to, and enveloping the lower leg.

The individual hairs are always intensely black at their extremities, with sharp points for perhaps two lines or more, then a lighter shade of about the same extent. Then again they become darker, but presently begin to grow lighter, till on the lower parts they are white or a light drab.

The under coat of fur is present with the winter coat, but not very abundant. It is irregularly and loosely curled around among the coarse hairs next the skin, and contributes largely to the warmth of the dress, which, like all the rest, constitutes a very warm covering, and enables the animal to endure the severest weather without complaint, if he can but get enough to eat. Indeed it is so complete a non-conductor of heat that snow, which he has left upon the leaves when he makes his bed, is not thawed in any appreciable degree but only compressed. This under coat of fur is not found with the summer coat, which consists of rather fine, firm, and elastic hairs. On some specimens this summer coat is of a light buff color, while on others it is of a bright mahogany bay or red, while others may show every intermediate shade between these two extremes.

We now come to the smallest of the North American deer, a description of which I have not been so fortunate as to anywhere meet, except by a single allusion elsewhere mentioned.

The color of the Acapulco Deer resembles much that of the Virginia and the black-tailed deer, though more the latter than the former. In its black face, however, it is more like the Virginia deer, and so of the white under the belly, a darker shade than either generally prevailing. On this deer, however, the white of the belly commences at a point in the middle just back of the fore legs. At this point it will be remembered that the white on the belly of the Virginia deer commences in a fork, being divided in front by the black stripe on the brisket. This feature, that the white on the belly of the one is divided in front and so forked, while on the other it commences in a single point anteriorly, being constant, is worthy of special attention. At the umbilicus the white has widened out till it involves the entire width of the belly, the inside of the thighs and extending up posteriorly to the seat of the tail, the color of which is described in the appropriate place. This small species, as well as the Ceylon deer, fades much less in color than do the larger species. In the spring, when the winter coat is cast off, it still preserves its darker shades, and the rufous tinge remains to the last, though faded very appreciably. The persistency of the deeper colorings is so great as to render the animals conspicuous, when promiscuously intermixed with a more numerous band of common deer.

The face of this deer is black, though not very intense, the black growing narrower and less intense below the ears and considerably lighter down the cheeks. The light band around the eyes is wanting in its upper half or above the eye, but is present below. The ear on the outside is black, and white on the inside, the hairs being long, fine, and soft, and slightly curled. Edge of the ear is black, which invades the inside on the lower anterior part. Below the opening of the ear it is surrounded by white which on the back side extends up nearly half the length of the ear. On the female is a small place of very black hair where the antler is situate on the male. On the Acapulco Deer the brisket is brown. The posterior part of the inside of the fore leg is white extending to the elbow. The white inside the hind leg is confined to the broad part, thence down the leg is fulvous yellow, lighter behind than below.

The strong resemblance of the Ceylon deer to this Acapulco deer, suggests the propriety of comparing them briefly.

The Ceylon deer is larger than the Acapulco, but the difference is not considerable. In form they are nearly alike, and in the general color of the winter coat there is not much difference, but in the summer dress the American species is decidedly darker and grayer than the other and has less of the red shade. In detail there is considerable difference in color or markings. The forehead of the Ceylon deer is marked much like those of the Mule deer and the Columbia deer. This is not observable on the female, nor is it seen on the male of the Acapulco deer. The faces of the Ceylon deer are grayer than those of the Acapulco deer, which are black. The ear is larger and has a denser coat of hair than the American species. Both are equally courageous and belligerent. The minor differences in color testify to no specific differences, and but for the presence of the metatarsal gland in the one and not in the other, and the difference in the antlers, I should not hesitate to pronounce them specifically identical.

ORNAMENTAL COAT.

We have no species of deer, in North America at least, where the adult is uniformly adorned with the beautiful spots of the fallow deer of Europe. All of our species are born with a coat more or less ornamented with spots, generally white on a colored ground. These white spots must be considered more or less ornamental. On the young of the moose and the caribou this ornamentation has nearly faded out, so much so that the spots are not observed on all the specimens, and indeed only upon a small portion of the young of the moose. But because I could not find them on the few which I have examined, it would be folly in me to say that they never occur and that those who claim to have seen them are mistaken. I do not know that any man has ever seen the spots on the adult Virginia deer except in my parks, certainly I never heard of them having been seen elsewhere. The affirmative testimony of one reliable observer who has seen them may be held as conclusive that they do sometimes occur, while the observations of many who have examined for them without success may equally convince us that in a majority of cases they cannot be detected. I presume that comparatively but few specimens have been examined on this point, and the casual observer, not looking for spots at all, would be very likely to overlook them when not very distinct. Again they may be evanescent, and observable but for a few days and so more likely to escape detection on those found in the woods, and we have no account of any having been born in domestication in this country, and Dr. Gilpin informs us that it is very difficult to raise them when taken young, by hand or even on the cow.

Of the ground color of the young Moose Dr. Gilpin says, "I have seen the young calves in June, when they could not have been ten days old ; they were a lovely fawn color." For myself I have only examined mounted specimens, which were of a redder shade than here described, approaching nearer to a light bay. But the doctor's observations of a living specimen are far the most reliable. This is a point on which the observations of hunters would be the least reliable, for they rarely meet with the young fawns, and when they do, even if they think to notice the color they rarely note it down at the time, and without this mere memory is of little worth. Only those who are in the habit of making notes of their observations *at the time* can appreciate their value. The very act of making the notes, systematizes and sharpens the observations and leads one to see many things which would otherwise have been overlooked. And he who, some time after, writes on a subject from memory, and then refers to his notes to verify his work, will be astonished at the number of errors he has to correct.

The ground color of the young Caribou I have had some difficulty in ascertaining satisfactorily. If it is given by any author I have overlooked it. That they are at least frequently ornamented with white spots is well established. The illustration of the young Caribou is from a drawing by Dr. Gilpin, which he kindly prepared for me, taken from life. This shows a line of seven spots along the flank and should be conclusive, but I may add the testimony of Captain Hardy ("Forest Life in Acadie,"

p. 127) : " The young deer (Caribou) are dappled on the side and flank with light sandy spots." Wherever I find the subject alluded to I find the spots mentioned, so we may conclude it is general if not universal. The Caribou is generally admitted to be among the oldest living representatives of the deer in this country. Their fossil remains have been found associated with the extinct mammals, which is certainly strong evidence of their ancient existence. It may be — and yet we cannot affirm that it is so — that this ornamentation of the young is fading out and becoming more rare or less distinct with time, but we must remember that the spots are more frequently found on the young Caribou than the moose, and yet the same amount of evidence is not produced of the great antiquity of the latter as of the former. The glandular system on the hind legs is the same in both, and this is constantly suggesting itself to me as connected with the antiquity of the races — that their ancestors long ages ago had the metatarsal gland, as we see it on all our other deer, except the smallest, and has in the course of time disappeared, whilst the tarsal gland, which is nearly dormant, alone remains, and that this too in the course of time will finally die out and disappear. I must admit that the want of facts in support of this suggestion leaves it scarcely worth the space it occupies ; but we all at times admit convictions, for the support of which the absolute proofs are inadequate, but then we may be permitted to state them as conjectures, honestly admitting the want of proof.

The young Elk or Wapiti is always provided with the spotted dress. The spots are large but not very profuse. They are of a dull white, on a yellowish tawny ground. These spots are found on the flanks, sides, and thighs, and a line on the neck. They are, not arranged with any definite system or order, but seem to be laid on rather carelessly and as if by accident. Neither the ground or the spots have that brilliancy which attracts admiration. Still the spots are no doubt ornamental and are always noticed with pleasure by the observer who looks at the Elk fawn for the first time. Half a dozen, by the sides of their dams, with high heads and their ears thrown forward and their eyes glistening, looking at the stranger, as if influenced partly by fear and partly by curiosity, form a pretty sight among the trees, which one, though not a naturalist, cannot but admire. If when he turns away he is unable to tell you the ground color of the fawn or the dam, he will be sure to tell you of the spots.

The young Elk which I had born in November, like those born in the spring, had the usual ornamental coat of his species. Unfortunately I was prevented from studying this specimen carefully, for I spent the succeeding winter abroad, and the keeper in charge, having caught and tied him to a post in order to put a ring in his nose, the youngster managed to break his own neck, and even the skin was neglected, and the stupid fellow could not tell whether he had lost his spots or not, or what sort of a coat he had at the beginning of March; so all that I can certainly say is that he commenced the winter in a summer dress, but as he was always reported lively and growing and in fine condition, I imagine that nature thickened up his summer garb, so that it kept him warm during the winter. We have all often seen how promptly nature responds to the demands of necessity in similar cases. The horse that runs in the fields and sleeps out in the storms during the winter, will then have more than twice the coat which he has when kept in the stable, though without grooming; and the horse which is constantly blanketed in the stable will have a much lighter coat than his mate, that stands beside him without the blanket. I have no doubt that my young Elk, under the favor of the same law, passed a comfortable winter although he wore a summer dress.

The fawn of the Mule Deer is well covered with white spots on a dirty yellowish ground. If they are smaller than on the young elk, it is only in proportion to the size of the animal. They too lack order in their arrangement. They occupy the same portion of the body as the other, but are more abundant on the neck. The white hairs constituting the spots generally disappear before the body of hairs constituting the ground are shed, so that this ornamentation disappears while the first coat is yet worn. In the mean time, however, this coat undergoes a gradual change of color, the yellowish shade assuming more of a mahogany hue. This in the fall is finally cast off and is replaced by the black, and then gray coat of the adult.

The Columbia Black-tailed Deer also produces a fawn which is more decidedly ornamented with the white spots than either of the others above mentioned. The ground coat is a bay red, the white has a cleaner appearance, the spots are smaller and more abundant and are more orderly in their arrangement. Now for the first time we can trace a line of spots along either side of the back and even up the neck. The disappearance of these spots progresses very much as in the case of the mule deer, but the ground coat after the disappearance of the spots undergoes so decided a change that at first I was inclined to think that an intermediate coat was supplied. But this is not the case. The first coat has grown long and looks rather rough, and has assumed a bright bay color, with nothing of the variegated appearance of the winter coat of the adult, but is like the universal summer coat. The ground color of this fawn is of a deeper or darker shade than that of any other of our fawns, except that of the Acapulco deer.

By far the most beautiful, is the ornamental coat of the fawn of the Virginia Deer. The spots are a pure white set in a bright bay red ground. The contrast is marked, and commands the admiration of all who see them. This is heightened by the exceedingly bright eye, erect attitude, elastic movement, and vivacious appearance of the little beauty.

Although a little out of place, I may as well describe the pace and motions of this fawn, in connection with his beautiful colorings, for each lends fascination to the other.

The highest perfection of graceful motion is seen in the fawn of but a month or two old, after it has commenced following its mother through the grounds. It is naturally very timid, and is alarmed at the sight of man, and when it sees its dam go boldly up to him and take food from his hand it manifests both apprehension and surprise, and sometimes something akin to displeasure. I have seen one standing a few rods away face me boldly and stamp his little foot, in a fierce and threatening way, as if he would say: " If you hurt my mother I will avenge the insult on the spot." Ordinarily it will stand with its head elevated to the utmost; its ears erect and projecting somewhat forward; its eye flashing, and raise one fore foot and suspend it for a few moments, and then trot off and around at a safe distance with a measured pace, which is not flight, and with a grace and elasticity which must be seen to be appreciated, for it quite defies verbal description. A foot is raised from the ground so quickly that you hardly see it, it seems poised in the air for an instant and is then so quietly and even tenderly dropped, and again so instantly raised that you are in doubt whether it even touched the ground, and, if it did, you are sure it would not crush the violet on which it fell. The bound, also, is exceedingly graceful and light. Indeed, the step of the fawn of the Virginia Deer is so light that it seems almost worthy the hyperbole of one refer-

ring to another subject when he said, " It was as light as the down
of a feather plucked from the wing of a moment." If, as it
grows up, it loses something of this lightness and elasticity of
step, it is only because of the increased size of the animal, which
enables one the more readily to individualize the graceful motions which, in the little fawn, seem blended together with a
charm like the blending of harmonious sounds.   There is a timid
caution expressed in every step, in the presence of the stranger,
which seems to fear the breaking of the smallest twig.   This can
only be seen in parks where they are subjected to semi-domestication.   It is destroyed by extreme fright of the wild deer
in the woods, and by close confinement in menageries.

This ornamental coat, with which the fawns are born, not only
corresponds in color with the summer coat of the adult, — only
the ground is a deeper red and is brighter, and the white spots
are wanting in the latter, — but it also corresponds in the structure of the hairs, which, as we have already seen, differ widely
from the hairs of the winter dress.   The latter are large, light,
and open or spongy, presenting large cavities filled with a pithy
substance and confined air, thus securing the maximum amount
of warmth, while the hairs of the former are small, hard, firm,
and elastic, much resembling in structure the hairs of the ox.
The fawn born in May sheds his ornamental coat in September,
about the time the adults change dresses, while later fawns carry
their first coat longer, but never more than the three or four
months assigned to young and old for the use of the summer
dress, if the animal is in health and fair condition.   The new
coat which succeeds the first is of the texture and the color of
the winter coat of the adult.   Now, for the first time, appears
the inner coat of fur, which is found in the winter coat of all the
species, but is wanting in the summer coat, probably of all.

Spots appear on about five per cent. of the adult Virginia
Deer in my grounds.   These spots appear with the winter coat, in
September, and continue visible from three to six weeks.   They
are not white, but simply a lighter shade than the ground color.
They are located in rows, on either side of the dorsal line, extending from the shoulders to the croup.   The lines of spots are
about four inches apart on the loins, are less separated at the
shoulders and posterior extremities.   There are sixteen of these
spots in each row from the shoulder to the hip, and five thence
posteriorly.   They are a little larger than a dime each.   The anterior ones are most distinct.   On some specimens but a few

of these spots are discernible from the shoulder back; on others they may be counted to the hips, and on others again the entire twenty-one.

On one specimen only, — an old doe which was raising a fawn, and was quite thin, as is always the case under such circumstances, — I observed these spots represented by tufts of the summer coat remaining, while all around the summer coat was entirely replaced by the new winter dress. It would be curious to know what was the condition of affairs beneath the cuticle under these spots which had retarded the growth of the new coat, and had served to retain the old, while all around was changed. Although I have but once observed this, when I could count all the spots thus shown, as it continued but a day or two, it may frequently have occurred without observation. I have on several others seen a part of the spots shown by tufts of the summer coat remaining.

These rows of spots on the back of the adults occupy the same positions as the rows on the back of the fawn, but are more regular in form and more detached. While the spots on the fawn are more distinct, from the contrast of colors, they are irregular in form and many of them confluent. I may make out the sixteen spots, for instance, on the fawn, between the shoulder and the hip, but I can as well make out twenty or more, for I must count several confluent or double spots to reduce them to the number to correspond with those on the adult. Again, on the neck of the fawn these lines of spots extend quite up to the ears, and are there even more brilliant than along the back, while I have never detected one on the neck of the adult. Still I cannot persuade myself but that there is some connection between these spots on the fawns and those on the adults, and the suggestion sometimes forces itself upon me that the Virginia Deer, at least, and, possibly, all the others, were once spotted like the fallow deer, and that this ornamentation has nearly died out on the adults, and may in time disappear on the fawns, as it has already nearly disappeared on the young of the moose and the caribou, and has even now much faded on the elk and the mule deer.

I believe these spots on the adult Virginia Deer have been entirely overlooked by naturalists till I mentioned them to Mr. Darwin, when he noticed them in " Descent of Man."

My opportunities for studying the ornamental coat of the Acapulco Deer have been limited. I have in my collection two fawns, produced out of season by a doe of this species in my grounds, from a Ceylon buck. As elsewhere shown, these species are nearly alike in size, and in many other respects resemble each other. These fawns were dead when found, and, as the weather was freezing cold, they probably did not live more than a single day.

The ground color is a deep mahogany bay. They are ornamented quite as profusely with white spots as are the fawns of the Virginia deer. The white is as pure as possible, and as the ground is darker than on the others, the contrast is greater. On either side of the neck and down the back these spots are arranged in regular lines, while on the sides below these lines, and on the thighs, the spots are irregularly disposed. In their arrangement they are like those on the Virginia fawn. Had these lived I think they would have been very beautiful.

The Ceylon fawns, a number of which I have raised, were quite as gay and beautiful as the Virginia fawns, and I presume the Acapulco fawns would have equaled either.

The markings on the heads of the fawns where the antlers will grow on the males, would seem to have some significance. These appear on the fawns of all the species in my grounds. On some these spots are blacker than on others, but on all they are of a darker shade than the surrounding coat, except on the mule deer, on which these spots are of a lighter color than the surroundings. These spots are more pronounced on the female fawns than on the males. On several of the species there are protuberances, or the skull is elevated under these spots.

When the winter coat first appears on the adult deer, it may with propriety be considered an ornamental dress. It is then short, fine, and glossy, with deeper colors than later in the season. This change of dress takes place in August or September, at the latest, while yet the weather is warm, and so it is not requisite that the new coat should be as heavy as during the rigors of the winter. This is the nuptial suit for all the species, and so it is fitting that it should be more beautiful and attractive than later when the sexes have become indifferent to each other, and so have no desire to attract or please.

Fugitive white spots often appear on the adults of several of the species. I have a large female elk, which was fully adult when I procured her, and was then nearly half white. All the legs were nearly white. And there were large white spots with well defined borders on various parts of the body. The next year the well defined white spots disappeared and the white was interspersed among the colored hairs, so that I had a light gray elk instead of a spotted elk. The year following that, the white hairs were very much diminished in number, but still were distinctly observable on several parts of the body and one leg. Since then, her coat has been undistinguishable from the other females of the herd. I have since several times observed on adult female elk, well defined spots of clear white hairs from one to four inches in diameter, but I have never found these to occur the second time on the same animal.

On the Virginia deer it is not uncommon to find a white hair scattered here and there in the coat, and I once had a doe on whose forehead, when a year old, a clear white spot appeared about half an inch in diameter. This was observed for two years and then disappeared, and never after was anything observed peculiar about the markings of this deer. Between these fugitive and transitory white spots observed on individual members of several species, and the perfect white coat and red eyes of the true albino, every imaginable gradation may be met with. I have mounted in my collection a Virginia doe about half the body of which is white, the balance is the normal color; the lines of junction of the two colors are well defined. While we are in the habit of calling such specimens albinos, they are probably not so in fact, but rather have exceptional markings which are present but a single year, or at most but a few years. These abnormal markings are far more abundant on *Cervus Columbianus* than on either of the other species. On an examination of a large lot of pelts of this deer in Portland, Oregon, I found a great many thus marked. I saw none that were pure white but some that were nearly so, others with but a little white upon them. I selected a skin for my collection, which I thought the most beautiful among those I examined, which I have now. The body is covered with a white ground. All over this are scattered numerous spots of different sizes and various colors. Most of them are either black or approaching the normal color of the animal.

I have met but one true albino deer; that was of the common species, in a park in the city of Philadelphia, many years ago. It was a good sized buck, as white as snow all over, and I have no doubt had red eyes, though I was not near enough to determine that question. I have heard of several others. That true albino Columbia deer are very common in Washington Territory, I cannot doubt. White deer are there so abundant in certain localities, that some have supposed they were a distinct species, and others have concluded that they are hybrids from some other species. On an island in Puget's Sound they are said to be very abundant and indeed to predominate. I have very little doubt that a critical examination would prove them to be the true Columbia deer, either true albinos or with the white markings unusually abundant. If albinos, their peculiarities may become hereditary, as we often see with the human species. I regret the want of opportunities to examine critically these interesting specimens, when there could be no difficulty in settling the matter definitely.

THE HEAD.

In the specific description of the Moose I have shown that its head is of enormous size, ungainly in form and quite devoid of beauty, according to our appreciation of beauty. Its great length in proportion to its width is magnified by the elongation of its upper lip or nose, which at last constitutes the most remarkable feature of this remarkable animal. It extends several inches beyond the lower jaw, over which it droops. It is flexible and actuated by powerful muscles ; is prehensile in its capacities, and is well adapted to the purpose of grasping branches of trees and bringing the boughs upon which it feeds within its reach. The nostrils are far apart, are very long and narrow, and capable of very great extension ; the posterior passages being very large, are designed to supply the lungs with a great amount of air, when required by hard exercise. The front of the muzzle is flat, as if cut square off, and is covered with short grayish hair, except a small space below each nostril, and a space about an inch and a half in diameter between the nostrils, with a narrow naked strip extending from this down to the mouth. This has been already particularly described.

This extraordinary feature — the elongation of the upper lip of the Moose — is scarcely apparent on the young calf, and during the first year is by no means remarkable, as will be observed by an inspection of the illustration of the young Moose. The eye is small, deep set, and has a sinister expression.

Next to that of the moose, the head of the Caribou is the least to be admired. In its proportions, the latter is the reverse of the former, for it is shorter in proportion to its thickness than any other of our deer. If we are not charmed with the proportions of the head of the Caribou, as compared with that of the moose we should consider it beautiful. The upper lip, or muffle of the

Caribou, is not extended remarkably beyond the lower, but it is round, heavy, and blunt, and is entirely covered with short gray hair. In this respect it differs from all our other species, but is precisely paralleled in the reindeer of Europe.

In striking contrast to the head of the moose is that of the Wapiti deer. It is symmetrical in form, with a very broad though flat forehead, and between the eyes, below which it is rather long and slender. It has a well developed eye, which has a pleasant expression, except when the animal is excited by anger or jealousy, when it has a wicked expression. This is much heightened especially in the male, in this condition, when he throws up his head with the face in a horizontal position, draws back his lips so as to show his front teeth, and grates his molars with a loud, harsh sound. This is not a pleasant smile but a horrid grin. It is so threatening that the observer is glad if he is separated from the brute by an impassable barrier. This is rarely observed in the male except during the rut, or the female when she has a young fawn to protect. The head of the elk is ornamented with the most beautiful antlers of all our deer, and is only disfigured by the coarse, awkward ears.

The head of the Mule Deer is well enough but for its disproportioned ear. The eye is of medium size, but lacks the animated expression of some of the other species. It has a sunken forehead with a small volume of brain. Below the eyes the face is larger and coarser than on any of the other deer, except the moose and the caribou.

The Columbia Deer has a fuller forehead, a slimmer face, and a larger and brighter eye than the mule deer. The ear, though large, does not seem to detract from its fine proportions.

The head of the Virginia Deer is more admired than that of any of the others except that of the wapiti. It has a sharp muzzle, rather narrow forehead, eyes rather small and of good expression. On the whole, the proportions of this head harmonize admirably, and it is carried in such a lofty, lordly way, upon a long, slender, and graceful neck, that it may always be looked upon with admiration.

The Acapulco Deer has a short but trim head. Its most marked feature is, its broad, full forehead with a very large brain cavity, and it certainly knows more than any of our other deer. A small, delicate ear does not disfigure it, while the eye is of good size and pleasant expression.

All of the deer show the lachrymal sinus, but it varies some-

11

what in position and much in extent. On all, it is below the inner corner of the eye. On the moose and caribou it is quite near the eye, and is covered with hair. Whether it is dilated in excitement, I have had no opportunity of observing. On the wapiti, we have already seen, the opening is located further be-- low the eye, is very large and has a naked border, which is concealed when in repose, though a portion below the corner of the eye extending to the orifice is naked. In excitement, the concealing hairs are thrown back, .the lips which were closed are widely parted, and the sinus is enormously expanded, which adds much to the threatening appearance of the enraged animal.

I cannot say that similar phenomena might not be observed with the moose and the caribou, with the same opportunities for observation, but to me these have not occurred.

In all the smaller species, this opening exists, but is smaller, or at least appears to be so, and I have never seen it exposed or dilated in excitement. In all, a sort of thin waxy secretion is exuded, though not profusely, and I have not observed any odor to emanate from it. We may assume that it serves some useful purpose in the economy of the animal, undoubtedly as connected with the eye, but as it is not embraced within the plan of this work, I have not carefully dissected the parts, and so cannot speak understandingly on the subject. I leave a broad field for the research of the comparative anatomist, which I have but rarely invaded. He will no doubt correct some of my conclusions.

I will close this branch of my subject by giving the measurements of the head of a large male Elk which I killed, five years old.

	Inches.
From top of head to end of nose	18
Between pedicels of antlers	3
Between the eyes	8
Between the eye and the pedicel	4
Between ear and pedicel	4
Length of nostril	$1\frac{1}{2}$
Between nostrils, lower	2
Between nostrils, upper	3
Length of mouth	5

The Ear.

The ears of the deer have been already incidentally or directly spoken of and described with more or less particularity, but many particulars remain to be noticed, which will enable us to compare those of the different species, from which I trust we shall derive much instruction.

In many respects the Moose and the Caribou most resemble each other, as for instance in their boreal habitat, their palmated antlers, their hairy muzzles, and in the shape of the foot; yet in their ears they present the two extremes. Of all the deer family the Moose shows the longest, the coarsest, and the ugliest ear, almost as broad as it is long, and nearly thick enough for a plowshare. On the other hand, the Caribou shows the least and the shortest ear relatively, of all the family, though by no means the finest or most delicate. While the Moose's ear may be fourteen or fifteen inches long, I have never seen the ear of a Caribou over four inches long.

On a male Moose in my collection, said by experts to be four years old, the ear is eleven inches long and seven inches broad. It rises from the head nearly two inches in a cylindrical form, before we reach the opening. It then varies but little in actual breadth for nearly half its height, and thence tapers to the end. It is thick and heavy in structure. On the outside it is covered with a dense coat of short, soft hair of a grayish brown shade. Inside the ear the hair is abundant, and is longer than on the outside. The front lower edge of the ear is black. The rest of the edge of the ear is a very dark brown.

The ear of the Caribou is erect and is much less subject to lateral motion than the larger ears; and yet I cannot say that the sense of hearing is at all impaired by the small ear, or that the large ear makes that of the Moose much more acute. In both the sense of hearing is very acute, as well as the sense of smell. When the hunter sends off the Caribou by the breaking of a single twig, he will regret that the scared animal was not a Moose; with the hope or belief that the latter could not have heard so small an alarm; but when on the other hand the Moose becomes alarmed by the least accidental touch of a rifle while the holder is passing a tree or a rock, and the Moose glides away and soon starts into his long swinging trot, the hunter regrets that Providence had not given the Moose a smaller or less acute ear.

The ear of the Caribou on the specimen in my collection, is

four inches long and five inches broad. It is situated behind the antlers one inch and four lines, and the ears are five inches apart. They are well clothed with hair on both sides. On the outside the hair is short and fine, of an ashy white color. On the inside, the hair is not so dense, is longer, somewhat curled, and of a lighter color. Of the positions in which the ear is carried in life, under different circumstances, I have had no opportunity for observing, nor have I any satisfactory information. From the small size of the ear, we may assume that it is carried erect, and is not so liable as the ears of others to change position under different circumstances.

On the reindeer of Europe the ear exactly corresponds in size and position with that of our caribou. I have never seen them when they were excited. When at rest ruminating, the ears stand quite erect, and are not often moved.

The ear of our Elk, or the Wapiti, is very large and coarse, and like that of *C. alces*, attracts attention by its unusual size. The maximum length of the ear of the adult Wapiti, is about nine inches, and its breadth seven inches, but there is an appreciable difference in the size of the ears, where there is not much difference in the height of the animal. The ear is thick and coarse, but is well supported, though it is not carried so erect ordinarily as the smaller ears of the same species ; and when the animal lies quietly ruminating the ears lop, as if their weight was a burden upon the supporting muscles ; but when excited or alarmed, they are projected forward more nearly to a horizontal position, as if to catch the least sound. When a hostile feeling pervades the animal, the position varies according to circumstances. If the alarm is threatening and he is doubtful of the attack, the position of the ear is depressed and set backward. When the attack is determined upon and commenced, the ear is projected forward even more than in the listening attitude. I have often been interested to observe these different attitudes, when separated by a secure fence from the wicked buck, during the rutting season. If merely giving notice to leave, he would approach with a deliberate, stately step, his ears laid back alongside his neck, his muzzle thrown up, so that the antlers were parallel with the back, the lips drawn back so as to present to view his front teeth, and a constant grating of the molars, which is a habit much affected by the male, whenever he feels cross or jealous. At such times the stranger, at least, always feels doubtful of the sufficiency of the fence which separates him from the threatening beast, and is inclined to retire and observe from a greater distance. If, however, an attack is resolved upon, he lowers his head so as to bring his face nearly level with the ground, with the nose nearly between the fore legs, the ears projected forward, and he comes against the fence with a fearful rush, which thoroughly tries its stability, and the fence is only enabled to withstand the strain, from the great number of the points of the antlers, distributing the force of the charge over so many different palings. But few can stand on the opposite side without flinching. This position of the ear is also particularly observed on the female when she sees a dog, which is her greatest antipathy. If on the opposite side of the fence, she will rush up, her ears straight forward, and strike fearful blows with her fore feet at the openings between the palings, in a vain effort to reach the object of her hate. Half a dozen or more enraged females beat a lively tattoo on such occasions, and the dog usually drops his tail and leaves without a second bidding.

Perhaps this characteristic position of the ear is most conspicuous when a stray dog finds a way into the park. As I was sitting at breakfast, one beautiful morning in August, the blinds of the bay-window which overlooks the South Park being open, I saw a flock of the common deer rush up the bank from the densely wooded ravine, their flags aloft and spread to the utmost. With astonishing leaps they ran towards the gate, where they were most likely to find protection. They were closely followed by a villainous cur, which gave a yelp of excitement at every leap. Barney, the keeper, had opened the gate from the North Park, to allow the elk to come down and show themselves to some guests, and there was the whole herd clustered around the gate, — the bucks, with their scarcely grown antlers still in the velvet, and probably a dozen females, with their young by their sides. The moment they heard the dog, the does projected their ears directly forward, stretched out their necks and started for that dog with an earnestness which proclaimed that they meant business, while the deer shot through their open ranks. The moment the cur comprehended the situation, he wheeled and ran as never cur ran before. It was the most exciting and laughable chase I ever saw. The pursuers gained on the pursued, but there was the sheltering thick shrubbery of the ravine close by, where was his only safety. The exultant cry of pursuit had been followed by the short quick yelp of despair which escaped the dog at every bound, while he would turn his head first to one side and then to the other, to watch the progress of the pursuit, the danger of which was becoming more and more imminent every moment, as the leading doe was already close upon him, and had commenced making desperate passes with her fore feet, any one of which, had it hit him, would have ended a worthless career. But this was in fact his salvation, since by striking too soon the elk lost ground, and just as he was about to receive the fatal blow, he gained the cover and shot into the thicket, where the advantage was all on his side, and thus he escaped; but I never heard of that dog having been seen in those grounds again. When the does returned, their ears were all thrown back in a threatening way, as if to challenge any other dog to invade their grounds. All this time, the bucks took no part in the affray, and manifested little interest in the result. They walked down the lawn, elevated their heads and looked earnestly if not wisely, — that was all. The chase began scarcely a hundred yards from where we sat, or rather stood, for in an instant all ran to the window to see the exciting sport, and so we had the best possible opportunity to observe the habits of the animal under such circumstances.

On another occasion, as I was studying the herd in the east park, a large pointer dog found a passage under the fence, and went ranging through the grounds in a characteristic way, when he espied some of the buck elks, which had strayed a little to one side, and started for them with great fierceness. Although their antlers were then hard, the suddenness of the onset frightened them at first, and they trotted in towards the herd, laying their ears back. The moment the does saw the dog they charged upon him with impetuosity, upon which that dog admitted that he had no further business in the park, and, aided by the shrubbery, he succeeded in effecting a safe retreat, which I did not regret. The whole herd of forty or fifty joined in the hunt, the bucks in the rear, but all with their ears forward, as if their only purpose was speed, without a hostile thought; but the noise they made as they crashed through the brushwood was like the rushing of many waters. As is always the case, on such occasions, the hair of the white patches on the rump became elevated like the bristles on the back of a boar at bay.

The Mule Deer (*Cervus macrotis*), has the largest ear of any of the species on either continent, in proportion to its size; hence its name.

The ear of the adult Mule Deer is eight inches in length,

whether measured on the outside, or from the opening on the inside. So it will be observed that the opening is at the very base of the ear, while, as we have seen, on the other large-eared species, the moose, the opening commences two inches above the head, or, for more than one sixth of its length, the ear is a closed cylinder. The ear is seven inches broad, is thick and massive. The outside of the ear is covered with a heavy coat of soft, gray hair. On the inside it is well filled with quite a dense mass of long hairs, mostly nearly white, though in the lower front part of the ear they are quite dark colored. Those hairs in the front part especially are inclined to curl.

When the animal is at ease the ear is quite erect and a little spreading, but when the animal is observing anything with interest the ears are projected forward, as if to catch the faintest sound. When running, the ears incline backward, perhaps from the pressure of the atmosphere, to which they expose so great a surface. The edge of the ear is black, which color is more distinct and is broader along the upper front edge.

The ear of *Cervus Columbianus*, the true Black-tailed Deer, is next in size to that of the mule deer, and when these and the Virginia deer are grouped together, the observer would pronounce the ear of the Columbia Deer to be in size about half way between that of the mule deer and of the Virginia deer, though a careful measurement shows that they are much nearer the latter than the former.

On the adult the ear is six and one half inches long, and at the widest part is six inches broad. The outside of the ear is covered with a shortish, tolerably dense coat of hair, of the prevailing color of the body. On the lower front, outside of the ear, is a patch of very light gray, nearly four inches long, pointed at the top and broad at the base. The hair on the inside of the ear is not so abundant as on the mule deer, but there is plenty of it, which is mostly white or very light drab. On the lower front side, and opposite the gray patch on the outside, is a tawny section three and a half inches long and an inch or more broad, pointed at both top and bottom. The edge of the ear is not black, as on the mule deer and the common deer. The ear is rather thick and heavy, but much less so than on the mule deer. The ear is carried more lazily than that of the mule deer, though never wholly drooping, but often partially so. When the animal is specially interested the ear is erect or projected forward. When cross and threatening, the ear is laid back close to the neck.

Not until we come to the Virginia Deer do we find anything to admire in the ear. His ear is of medium size, is well shaped, is thin and pliable, and is, perhaps, the most speaking feature about him. The coat on the outside is fine and soft, and is never heavy, while on the inside it is sparse and delicate.

Although the ear of the Common Deer is scarcely an inch shorter, and not more than an inch narrower than that on the black-tailed deer, yet the casual observer, when looking at them side by side, would believe the difference to be much greater. Even half an inch added to the length and breadth of an ear makes a greater appreciable difference than would be readily imagined. On the adult, the length of the ear varies from five and one half to six inches, whether measured on the outside or from the bottom of the opening on the inside, and is in width from four and one half inches to four inches and nine lines. On the outside, the ear is clad with a short, fine, thin coat of hair, nearly black. The ear is thin and delicate, as compared with the ears of the larger species. In summer dress, the arteries show plainly, and it is so nearly translucent, that when the sun strikes against the opposite side, the light shows through, giving it a pink shade. It is generally carried erect, a little spreading or inclined forward, though this position is not so observable as on the larger eared species. In a threatening attitude, the ear is thrown back, though not nearly so close to the neck as on the black-tailed deer. When running in fright, the ear is inclined forward.

On the Acapulco Deer, the ear is a little shorter and a little broader, and is almost as thin as parchment. On the outside, the hair is very short but thick set, of a darker color than on the other, and has a sort of lustre, particularly observable in the sunshine. In summer, it seems to be covered rather slightly with a sort of fine fuzz, rather than hair. It is rather restless, which is more indicative of the sensibilities of this animal than is manifested by any of the others. Both in anger and in play the ear is frequently thrown quite back upon its neck, and this is especially so when amusing itself in chasing some of the other deer, which may be twice as large as itself, around the park.

A mule buck, in my park, is very fond of following me in my walks through it, and if we accidentally meet this little Acapulco doe in our rambles, the chances are that she will try to cut him off from my protection, and run him at the top of his speed in some other direction. At such times she will make the rush with her ears lying flat to the neck, as if terribly in earnest, but after a turn or two, he generally manages to run up to me for protection, when she will stop a little way off, bring the ears to a vertical position, and look as if she would like to enjoy a hearty laugh at the alarm she had created in the great, cowardly brute, that is strong enough to toss her over the fence on his antlers.

The severe and long continued cold of the winter of 1875 was endured well by this tropical deer, and also by the Ceylon deer; but in the spring, I found the borders of the ears of all had been so frozen, that they were curled up in a sort of gathers all round the edges, but, with one exception, it was only on the very edges that the vitality seemed to be destroyed. This when it peeled off left the ear without perceptible change. I saw nothing of the kind on the ears of any of the Virginia deer, which are next in delicacy of structure. The longer these deer remain exposed to the cold winters of this latitude, the more dense becomes the winter coat on the ears, and even on the other parts as well.

The Antlers.

An examination of the antlers of the deer makes it first necessary that we inquire of their constituents, then of their system of nutrition, their mode of growth, their maturity, their decay and rejection, and finally of their uses.

An analysis of these antlers shows that they are composed of the same constituents as internal bones; that they are in fact true bones, though in the proportion of their constituents they differ slightly from ordinary bones. Healthy ordinary bone consists of about one third part of animal matter, or gelatine, and two thirds of earthy matter, about six sevenths of which is phosphate of lime and one seventh carbonate of lime with an appreciable trace of magnesia. The animal matter gives the bone elasticity and tenacity, the earthy matter hardness and rigidity.

The antlers of the deer consist of about thirty-nine parts of animal matter and sixty-one parts of earthy matter, of the same kind and proportions as is found in common bone. This is the mean of many results of analysis of antlers of different species of deer, by different processes, among which very little differences were found in results. This excess of animal matter seems necessary to give the antler elasticity and strength, and fit it for the purposes for which it is designed.

A critical examination shows that their system of nutrition and mode of growth are identical with those of internal bones, although the growth is much more rapid, and when completed other phenomena are noticed not observed in internal bones, which are required by the economy of the animal, which demands that they complete their growth, die, and be cast off annually. These modifications are entirely consistent with the general plan of osteal structure. During the period of growth of the antler it is provided with a *periosteum*, and with internal blood-vessels as well, though it has no medullary canal filled with marrow like the long internal bones.

As before intimated, the antlers of the deer are not persistent, like the other bones of the body, but they are grown from the beginning to maturity and then are cast away every year.

In most cases the matured antler is cast in the fall or winter, but in some cases they are retained till spring.

In those cases where the antler is dropped in the fall or winter, immediately the periosteum, which surrounds the pedicel or the process of the skull on which the antler grows, the edge of which was left naked and bleeding when the old antler was cast off, commences extending itself over the naked end of the bone which it surrounds, and which constituted the seat of the antler, and in a few days at most it has closed over it, and consists of a thick vascular naked covering with a black cuticle, and in this condition it remains, just fairly filling the concavity which is left by the lower convex end of the discarded antler. This vascular covering of the concave top of the pedicel, grows no more during the winter, but the blood circulates freely though moderately through it, maintaining about the same temperature as other portions of the skin of the animal which are clothed with hairs. While there are no hairs or fur observed on this black skin, a sort of scaly dandruff forms on it which the animal, if very tame, will allow to be gently rubbed or scraped off with the finger nail, and even seems to enjoy that operation. This remains in a quiet state till spring, when vegetation begins to shoot forth and a scanty supply is procured by the deer. Then those bucks which had carried their antlers through the winter, drop them, the oldest first. Then the top of the pedicel is immediately overgrown, as were those in which the antler had been discarded in the fall or winter. Then all commence rising up in a convex form, assuming first the appearance of a great blood-blister.

Now the antler commences a longitudinal growth, the top maintaining its convex form, while the beam attains at once its full diameter; and so it grows in length but never appreciably in thickness. When the beam has attained the height where it is to throw off a branch, it first becomes flattened at the end, and then the bifurcation takes place, and the two parts grow on *pari passu*, ever increasing in length but not in diameter, that which is to be the longest growing faster than the other, and so on to the completion of the external growth, so that all the parts shall be completed at about the same time. The burr of the antler is however an exception. It does not attain its full diameter at first, but is gradually enlarged during the growth of the antler, though it attains its full size before the growth of the antler is completed. When this growth is finished externally, the vascular covering, called the velvet, and which consists of the periosteum overlaid with a black thin skin covered with a short dense fur, is rubbed off by the animal against small trees or other convenient objects. At the time it is thus rubbed off this outer covering is quite tenacious and gorged with blood. I once saw a large elk in my grounds, soon after he had commenced this work of denudation. This velvet was stripped into long strings, which depended from various parts of the antlers, some reaching as low as his knees. These shreds looked like red cords ; the head, neck, and breast were covered with fresh blood, and the entire antlers appeared smeared with blood still moist. The animal appeared flushed and irritated, and soon rushed away to the thicket, and when I next saw him not a vestige of the blood or the shredded skin remained, but the antlers were clean and very white.

I had a very tame buck of the common species, with which I desired to try the effect of castration upon the immature antlers. I delayed the operation as long as I dared, and then, with the aid of some stout men, caught him, but he thrashed about at such a rate that in spite of us he hit his antlers against the ground and other objects, and to my surprise I observed the skin to peel off in long strings, scattering the blood with which it was fully charged in every direction. I saw at once that it was too late to execute my original purpose, and so I contented myself with a careful study of the antlers and their late covering, and in detaching portions still remaining. The surface of the antlers seemed hard and well matured, and the points hard and sharp, but I detected no interception of the blood-vessels around the burr, although that part of the antler had attained its full development more than a month before. There I could distinctly see the unobstructed arteries, some passing through holes and others through indentations in the burr. So was conclusively refuted the old notion that the growth of the burr destroys those blood-vessels by compression, and hence the velvet dies for want of nu-triment. This notion was the result of an ingenious guess with-out study and investigation. And so it is of many theories in natural history.

The evidence, derived from a very great multitude of observa-tions, made through a course of years, is conclusive that nature prompts the animal to denude its antlers of their covering, at a certain period of its growth, while yet the blood has as free access to that covering as it ever had.

While, as I have shown, this is a true bone, and is supplied its nourishment in substantially the same way as other bones are supplied, it is still an anomalous bone, and nature has provided means meet for these anomalies. It springs up rapidly, and, in a few months so far matures that it ceases to require nourish-ment for its enlargement, but only for its internal solidification, and does not, to any appreciable degree, undergo the changes of waste or absorption and renewal which take place with the inter-nal bones, but the equivalent of this is provided for by its entire removal so soon as it becomes inert, and then succeeds again its entire renewal. If the periosteum is destroyed on a portion of the internal bone, the part thus denuded is liable to die for want of the requisite nutriment and to be thrown off from the rest of the bone as foreign matter. In the antler, when the periosteum is entirely removed from the whole surface, it still lives for a time, and progresses with its internal growth, filling up the cav-ities of the cancellous tissue with great rapidity from the abun-dant supply of nutriment it receives through the beam from its very seat, till the work is done, and the antler becomes an inert mass, a foreign substance, and it is thrown off entire.

These are the peculiarities of this anomalous member. Now let us examine and we shall see how beautifully nature has pro-vided, in the system for nutrition, to meet these peculiarities, these extraordinary requirements. In doing this we shall be obliged to run a sort of parallel in the process of growth with the internal persistent bones, for so shall I be enabled to explain the most intelligibly the results of my investigations.

In both, the great source of nutriment, during active growth, is the arterial system of the periosteum. Within we find the Haversian system complete, with only such modifications as the exigencies which the peculiarities of this bone present. For instance, when it is matured it is comparatively a solid bone, with more or less branches, and there is an absence of the medullary canal, with its marrow, arteries, and nerves; but, as we shall see, we have their equivalents, and more, for the blood vessels traversing the interstices within are so expanded during the rapid growth of the antlers as to meet the anomalous demand for the elements of growth during that short but exciting period.

I will now explain briefly the system of blood-vessels provided to nourish the antler during its rapid growth. First, the external supply from the periosteum. These are an extension of a part of the arteries of the periosteum, which persistently covers the pedicel which forms the seat of the new antler. Second, a part of the arteries of the periosteum of the pedicel turn in and overspread the top of the pedicel at the articulation, and thence pass up through the interior of the new antler. And third, we find a number of arteries which pass up through the interior of the pedicel and into the growing antler. During the period of growth, many of all these three sets of arteries are of enormous size as compared with the blood-vessels with which internal bones are supplied.

Having thus briefly stated the system of blood-vessels provided for the growth of the new antler, let us now go back to where we left the top of the pedicel, — the concave seat of the antler overgrown with the thick vascular covering, which was an extension of the periosteum, which persistently surrounds the bony process of the skull, upon which the future antler is to be grown. Whether this has been accomplished months before, as when the antler was cast off early, or but a day or two before, as in the case of our elk, at the proper time when the active growth is to commence, in the blood-vessels passing up through the periosteum, the circulation becomes greatly accelerated, the temperature is greatly increased, the parts become exceedingly sensitive to the touch, and we have the appearance of a high state of inflammation, though in reality but a very active natural action. As before stated, the thick, massive periosteum is raised up from the bone beneath into a convex protuberance. Beneath, the space is occupied by a new system of blood-vessels, by far the greatest number shooting inward from the arteries in the periosteum, still others rising up through the bone below, the canals through which have suddenly become greatly enlarged by the absorption of the inner laminæ. As yet nothing like ossification has taken place, and if the part be now inspected it presents simply the appearance of coagulated blood, but, as might be expected, a closer examination discloses a regular and highly organized arterial and venous system, traversing a mass of soft and highly excited animal tissue.

Now commences the process of ossification. First around the border of the pedicel the osteal cells and the intercellular tissue receive deposits of the earthy particles, and thus the growth of the new bone is commenced at the external portion or the circumference at the seat of the antler. The process now goes on rapidly, by the formation of new intercellular tissue and osteal cells on the inner side of the membrane, which in turn receive their deposit of earthy matter, rapidly building up the outer wall and slowly filling up the interior with cancellous tissue. The cells of the cancellous tissue commence filling up with earthy matter, and arranging themselves into Haversian systems so soon as they themselves are formed, and so the lower circumference of the antler is first hardened into tolerably compact bone ; but it is at this very point that this process goes on the most slowly, else the sources of nutriment which rise up through the bony process of the skull, upon which alone the antler must depend for nutriment to finish its growth after the periosteum shall have been removed from its surface, would be cut off while there is much work to be done especially on young animals, after this greatest means of supply is gone. I was first made aware of this fact many years since, when I caught a young elk with his first antlers about two feet long, and finely branched near the ends. These antlers had been divested of their velvet for three months, and to all appearance entirely matured. Before putting him into the cage to be sent to the Central Park, New-York, where he played the sovereign for many years, I sawed off his antlers about two inches above the burrs. I was surprised to find the blood to flow quite freely, sufficient to stain the saw for the whole length used. In no other case have I sawed off the antlers from so young an animal, but very often from adults of the various species, from none of which did I find the blood to flow ; but in all cases, the blood-vessels and the color were plainly visible to the naked eye, for a greater or less area near the middle of the antler, until near the time when it would drop off.

But if Mr. George Kennan is not mistaken in what he saw, the blood circulates still more freely through the apparently matured antlers of the adult domesticated reindeer in Siberia. In " Tent Life in Siberia " (p. 186), he says : " To prevent the interference and knocking together of the deers' antlers when they should be harnessed in couples, one horn was relentlessly chopped off close to the head by a native armed with a heavy sword-like knife, leaving a red ghastly stump, from which the blood trickled in little streams over the animals' ears." If he had had the antlers sawed off instead of chopped off with a heavy knife, I should have liked it better and so probably would the deer, for if those antlers were as hard as ordinary deer's antlers, it must have been a very difficult as well as a very cruel task to chop them off with anything. The deer were perhaps castrated, though imperfectly, which would render the antler less dense with a more active arterial system than in perfect animals ; but certain it is that the antlers were well matured, for our author tells us just before that the deer were caught by throwing a lasso over the antlers of the deer, which made "tremendous leaps and frantic efforts to escape," to have borne which the antlers must have been pretty well matured, hard, and strong. This was in November, near the Arctic Circle, when on the full bucks, at least, the antlers must have been in their prime. However, making every allowance for inaccurate observations arising from want of appreciation of the importance of what he saw, we may safely conclude, that when the strong and pretty well matured antler was severed near the head, there was a discharge of blood at least sufficiently copious to drop down upon the ears. This is much more than I have ever observed.

But all antlers do not show equal solidity at the time they are dropped in the course of nature, and it is very uncommon to find one that is quite solid throughout. Usually towards the lower end and indeed for the greatest portion of it, and even extending into the tines, a part of the interior is more or less porous when the internal growth ceases, the antler dies and is thrown off. This internal growth is arrested before sufficient earthy matter has been deposited to fill up the interstices in the cancellous tissue and render the antler solid throughout. The result is that the antler, instead of being solid has an open interior of greater or less extent, which, however, is braced in every direction by thin plates of bone, leaving the antler lighter, more elastic, and perhaps as strong as if the solidification had extended thoughout. This arrest of the solidifying process, before all the pores had been filled up with earthy matter, results from the extreme solidification of a thin plate at the lower extremity of the antler, which is in actual contact with the pedicel, and through which the internal vessels had passed up into the antler, which had furnished the internal nourishment during the growth of the antler, and by which the hardening process within had been continued after the velvet had been rubbed off. The hardening of this lower extremity of the antler, so as to compress the vessels which pass through it and arrest the circulation through them, is the means by which the interior of the antler is left, to a greater or less extent, porous and light as above described, and which, as we can readily appreciate, is for the benefit of the animal.

The diameter of the antler is only enlarged during its growth by the elevation of ridges on the surface, so as to make channels or beds for the large arteries of the periosteum. These channels or grooves can be seen on the antlers of all the species, and show that the arteries were enormous for blood-vessels for a periosteum, which on internal bones are so minute that the naked eye cannot see them.

At the lower extremity of the antler, the enlargement continues, till the external growth of the antler is well advanced, forming what is called the burr, where, when the growth is completed, the bone quite surrounds some of the arteries, forming canals through which they pass, while others pass through deep indentations which protect them almost as effectually as do the canals.

This shows us that those naturalists who have attributed the death of the velvet to the compression at the burr, of the vessels leading into it, are mistaken. This burr, instead of compressing those vessels by its increased growth, is admirably designed to protect them from injury; and the protecting canals and indentations never do fill up by continued deposits of bone material, as occurs to the canals leading into the antler above. Hence it is that when the velvet is rubbed off or torn away, it is found gorged with blood thrown up by these unchecked arteries.

But there is another set of arteries, as we have seen, coming from the persistent periosteum on the pedicel below, which pass in at the articulation between the pedicel and the antler. These are numerous and so large that their canals may be readily detected with the naked eye. Let any one curious to examine this interesting subject, take the first deer's head with antlers, which he finds in the market, and carefully dissect away the skin below the burr, and he will, without the aid even of a pocket glass, find both these systems of canals through the burr, for the supply of the periosteum, and those passing into the articulation between the old and the new bone, for the internal supply of nutriment.

But this is not all. Copious as is the supply of blood which these great arteries are capable of furnishing, still it is inadequate for so rapid a growth ; so we find another set of blood-vessels, communicating directly between the persistent and the deciduous osseous formations. These pass up through the body of the pedicel into the antler, and together with those just described, perform the office of the medullary artery in the internal long bones, supplying it with nutriment internally, and communicating, as in the case of common bones, with the Haversian systems connected with the periosteum. Let us examine a cross section of the pedicel, just below the seat of the antler, when the antler is but half grown and the work is going on in its full vigor, and we find it open and spongy, apparently composed of pretty compact cancellous tissue towards the circumference, but with open canals near the middle. In the specimen now before me, which is cut across, one of these canals is nearly one line in diameter. This is the largest distinct canal for the passage of an artery through the pedicel which I have found, but when these canals are smaller, there are more of them, if examined at the same stage of growth. These canals afford abundant passage for the blood-vessels passing up through it into the new-growing antler.

Let us compare it with another, also on my table, on which the antler had become hard, and was nearly ready to be cast off. Now we find this pedicel, which a few months before was so porous, has become a compact bone throughout, with the cavities so far filled up as to collapse the blood-vessels and obstruct the appreciable passage of the red blood, though, of course, the lacunæ and the canaliculi are still preserved as necessary to its own continued vitality ; but all the visible canals are now filled up. Here, then, is an order of nature found nowhere else, because the necessities of the case nowhere else require it. We find a persistent bone, alternately compact and porous, alternating annually, simply because it is necessary to the performance of a peculiar function, nowhere else in the whole range of nature's works demanded.

When the time approaches for the new antler to commence its growth, the laminæ which had filled up the canals in the pedicel through which the nutriment to promote that new growth is to pass, are absorbed away and the canals are thus enlarged, and

12

the blood-vessels which had been compressed now swell out and become active conduits for the required nutriment for the new growth, and everything which had been for several months so dormant suddenly becomes the scene of intense activity. Then again, as this new growth approaches completion, and the necessity for this great supply of nutriment diminishes, a new deposit of earthy matter takes place, new laminæ are formed within these canals so lately opened by the absorption of the old, the blood-vessels are again gradually diminished, and finally practically closed, when their active functions are no longer required.

Thus we see how complete is the system, and how perfectly adapted is it for the anomalous requirements, to supply the nutriment, for the rapid growth of the deciduous antlers of the Cervidæ, and a perfect comprehension of this will enable us to understand the remarkable phases, under varied circumstances, which it will be necessary to explain before we complete our present subject.

A more particular description of the progress of this growth is now necessary, and we are the better prepared for this by the investigations already made.

As has been already said, the first structure is of the outer walls, or circumference of the antler forming a hollow cylinder, the cavity being in the form of an inverted cone. The specimen before me is a deer's antler less than half grown, and is six inches long and one inch in diameter. The ossified walls do not extend to the top, which consists of a mass of blood-vessels, the osseous wall at the upper end presenting a thin serrated edge, the cavity there being nearly one inch in diameter. Below this the wall gradually increases in thickness, and is composed of cancellous tissue, more dense towards the circumference; just above the burr, the cavity is nearly filled with this tissue, through which the blood-vessels pass, with a small open passage near the middle. The internal cavity does not entirely terminate at the seat of the antler, but continues down into the pedicel in the form of a canal, where it soon spreads out into many ramifications, whence come the tributaries transmitting the great flow of blood which passes through that channel for the nourishment of the rapidly growing antler.

The butt or lower end of the matured antler is more or less convex, corresponding to its concave seat at the top of the pedicel. This lower extremity of the antler, where the articulation occurs, is, as before intimated, exceedingly compact, corresponding, in that respect, to the articulate extremities of the internal bones.

The tips of the antlers, which are the last formed, are the first to become solidified quite through, and from these points the solidifying process goes on down through the branches and the beam, till the passages through the surface of the antler, which admitted the circulation from the periosteum, have become closed, soon after which the velvet is discarded. This circulation from the periosteum into the antler is first shut off at the upper extremities, and thence downwards, but the blood flows freely into this outer vascular covering all this time, for it is provided, though imperfectly, with a venous as well as an arterial system.

This velvet will never spontaneously disengage itself; but if it is not detached by violence, the blood-vessels which sustain it will soon close of themselves, not by mechanical compression at the burr, but in obedience to some law of nature not clearly understood. I think the most probable cause is the imperfection of the venous system of this periosteum, which is inadequate to return the blood as fast as it is thrown up by the arteries, now that the canals to the interior are closed, and so, after a longer or shorter struggle, this outer covering must die, if not previously torn away. It is rare that a portion of the velvet is thus retained, yet I have several specimens in my collection where it has died upon the antler, and presents the appearance of a thin sheet of gutta percha adhering to the antler with great tenacity, frequently resisting all subsequent attempts of the animal to remove it; but all the fur is worn off, and it is smoothly polished by subsequent friction. This rubbing process is not suspended so soon as the velvet is removed, but continued throughout the rutting season, when the upper part of the antler becomes finely polished, and the outer surfaces of the tubercles, which frequently appear on the lower part of the beam, are appreciably worn down. This process is carried on not only against the trunks of small trees, which are sometimes denuded of their bark for several feet, but also against the branches which are within reach. Indeed, the elk are often seen twisting their antlers among the extremities of the branches, and I once found a branch two inches in diameter which had been thus twisted off from a hickory tree, and which was divided into shreds for several inches at the end. It must have taken an incredible amount of hard work, and consumed much time in the accomplishment of the feat.

But we must return to the growth of the antler, and follow it to its completion and final rejection.

When deprived of its external supply of nutriment, by the removal of the periosteum, the outer portion has become thoroughly solidified, but the internal growth, except near the points, is still incomplete, and is composed of cancellous tissue. This is much more the case on young animals than on older ones. As we have already seen, this contingency has been already provided for, by the blood-vessels leading in through the lower extremity of the antler. Through these, earthy matter is carried up and deposited in the proper form of laminæ closing up the cells and pores, and obliterating the blood-vessels, both above and laterally. In the mean time, the arteries which passed up through the butt of the antler and supplied the interior, were becoming more and more compressed, as the lower part, and especially the articular plate, became more and more solidified, till finally they become entirely collapsed or cut off, and the circulation above arrested, and the work of filling up the inner cavities stopped before the interior of the antler had become completely solidified, leaving a portion of the interior still porous. The extent of this interior spongy part varies considerably in different specimens, not depending on a difference of the species. This closing up of the arteries, by the solidification of the articular plate, takes place much sooner on old animals than on the young ; still the canaliculi remain open for a considerable time, and maintain a certain amount of life in the antler. But even these at last succumb, or cease to transmit sufficient nutriment to maintain vitality, when the antler becomes an inert mass of bone, still so firmly attached to its seat that no available force can separate it from the pedicel at the articulation. If sufficient violence be used, the pedicel will be carried away with a part of the skull, or the antler will break off above the burr. However, organized matter cannot remain stationary. It must be either growing or decaying. So soon as the former process is finished the latter commences, at first very slowly, no doubt.

Nature has made proper provision for this, as is clearly disclosed by a careful study. Let us remember that there were three classes of arteries by which the antler was supplied during the period of its rapid growth. First, external, through the periosteum ; another, strictly internal, or those passing up through the pedicel into the growing antler, and again, those which branch off from the periosteum of the pedicel and pass through the articulation into the antler. The first have been destroyed by the closing of the surface canals through which they passed into the antler; the second have been cut off by the closing of the canals within the pedicel through which they passed into the antler; the third have been cut off by the consolidation of the lower extremity of the antler, which I have likened to the articular plate of internal bones. But remember, the canals through which these pass into the articulation have not been and never will be filled up, but within the articulation they retain their vitality, while above it they are practically destroyed. Now, these blood-vessels retaining their vitality within the articulation commence a new and important work which is assigned them — that is, the work of absorption. They pick up particles or rather groups of granules, of what I call the articular plate, and carry them away, and when a sufficient number of these particles have been thus removed, the antler becomes loosened from its seat, or at least the point of junction becomes weakened, and the antler drops off, or is more generally removed by some slight force before it has become completely loosened so as to drop off by its own gravity.

The moment the antler is thus removed the blood flows freely from the ruptured vessels which had passed into the articulation and done the work of absorption, but not a trace of blood can be found coming from the antler; the detached convex surface, which is of an immaculate whiteness, though rough like very coarse sand-paper, shows plainly where the particles had been removed by absorption.

Blood is frequently found on the end of the antler, which occurs when some force has been applied to the antler, when it is nearly ready to drop off, not sufficient to detach it entirely, but which partially separates it from the seat, and ruptures a part of the blood-vessels there, when the blood will insinuate itself wherever the separation has occurred and stain the end of the antler.

The fact that blood flows freely from vessels around the borders of the pedicel and not a particle from the antler, the moment the separation takes place, shows, what a more critical examination also proves, that at least some of the blood vessels passing into the articulation remain open and active up to the time of separation, while they are effectively closed by the solidification of the lower extremity of the antler.

I may give one or two examples to illustrate this. Early in April, while walking through the park, I met Dick, a very tame four-year old buck. One antler was standing, but the other was gone, and the seat was covered with fresh blood. As he was eating corn from one hand, with the other I seized the remaining antler. He immediately jumped back and severed the antler with a smart snap. He shook his head and ran away as if considerably hurt, while the blood flowed so freely from the exposed end of the pedicel that it ran down the side of his face and dropped to the ground. An inspection of the end of the antler, at the point of separation, showed not a trace of blood, but the rough convex surface was as undefiled and as white as it is possible to imagine. It was some minutes before he would so far forgive me as to come and take more corn from my hand. Then I saw the concave seat of the antler was filled with blood already beginning to coagulate, and the hemorrhage had nearly ceased.

The next fall, early in November, the same animal was following me through the grounds, begging for gratuities, while I wished to bestow my attentions more exclusively to a pet gazelle, and in my impatience at his persistent importunities, I kicked backward, just as he lowered his head, when I knocked off one of his antlers. The dislocation took place with a smart cracking noise and probably by the use of about the same force as on the former occasion, and precisely the same phenomena were observed. He carried the remaining antler but a day or two when it disappeared. On this occasion this was the first deer in the park to lose his antlers, while on the other he carried them the longest of any.

While the growing antler of the deer is but indifferently provided with a nervous system, yet the upper portion, above where the ossified wall has become established, is in a situation resembling a high state of inflammation, and like really inflamed parts is exceedingly sensitive. In the deer's antler the apparently inflammatory action or high temperature seems to subside so soon as the ossified wall becomes established, and the extreme sensibility in the outer covering disappears. There the antler may be handled, compressed, and even the velvet cut through, without manifestations of suffering, while above on the soft and yielding part, where the temperature is much higher than it is below, the least pressure or even touch seems to produce pain.

The antler of the deer sometimes though rarely becomes diseased, when the same phenomena occur as in diseased internal bones. The channels of the blood-vessels become large and the vessels become expanded, and even the whole diseased part of the antler becomes greatly enlarged by the separation of the laminæ by inflammatory deposits between them, presenting to the view a loose and porous appearance. When in this condition the diseased portion does not perfect its growth so as to dispense with the periosteum, at the time the healthy portion is prepared to do so, but even the portion of the velvet remaining on the diseased part retains a certain measure of vitality, from internal nutriment, when its proper supply is entirely cut off, by the destruction and removal of the velvet on the healthy portion below it. This is beautifully illustrated on the abnormal descending tine on the left antler from a Columbia deer shown in the illustration hereafter given. This black-tailed deer was killed on the dividing ridge which lies between Cottonwood Creek and Clear Creek, extending from Cottonwood station to Igo in Shasta County, California. It will be observed that a few inches of the outer extremity of the tine is greatly enlarged. At the time the deer was killed the velvet was remaining on this portion of the antler alone. All the rest was denuded and the surface well polished. After that remaining had become well dried, I peeled it off and found that the canals for the blood-vessels leading from the periosteum into the diseased bone had become so enlarged as to be perfectly distinct to the naked eye, indeed many of them were as large as a small pin. The visible mouths of these canals leading to the Haversian systems within are exceedingly numerous. Internally the cross section of the diseased part of the tine presents that loose spongy appearance so often seen in diseased bone.

When growing, the antler of the deer is quite pliant, and may be given almost any shape or direction, without apparent injury. Nothing is more common than to meet with antlers from all the species of this genus, taken from wild animals, with the beam or more frequently some of the tines occupying unnatural positions attributable to some force applied when in an immature state.

I have never known an instance where such injury to the antler has produced disease.

Once when taking a pair of black-tailed deer from a boat into the steamship in the Columbia River in a gale of wind, one of the antlers of the buck, which was a few inches long, got crushed down, and yet it did not appear to become diseased from the injury. It grew on in the form of an irregular mass, shed its velvet at about the same time as the uninjured antler, and was cast off about the same time, presenting no such appearance of disease as in the case first described. The next year the antler grown upon the same side was of, perfect form, showing that the pedicel had not been injured.

The Ceylon buck in my grounds arrived when his antlers were about half grown, and one of them was badly bruised and bent over, yet it grew on to maturity without showing any signs of disease, but without symmetry or definable form.

I have in my collection many specimens of deformed antlers, some of which I have illustrated. One without a beam on either antler but consisting only of snags or tines growing from the burr, others having apparently double or treble beams on the same antler. These deformities, I think, have arisen from injuries received in the early stage of the growth of the antlers. They would, I doubt not, have been shed at the proper time, and been succeeded by antlers of the proper form. Without injury there may be abnormal growths on the antlers. As where tines appear in unnatural positions or places, or where the beam is bifurcated with regular palms on each prong, as shown in the illustration of the antlers of the Scandinavian elk in Stockholm, but there are also unusual growths throughout the animal kingdom, for which it would often be difficult to assign a satisfactory cause.

The effect of emasculation upon the growth of the antlers of the Cervidæ is very marked, and has been the subject of long and careful observation. Although it has been long understood that this operation does produce some effect upon the growth of the antler, ideas have been very crude as to what that effect is. This I thought very remarkable, from the well known fact that castration has long been practiced by the Lapps upon their domesticated reindeer, and so its effect should be well understood by them, and opportunities for learning these effects by naturalists should have been abundant.

A careful investigation of the subject in Lapland, explained the matter very satisfactorily.

Early in July, when at Tromsö, in Norwegian Lapland, I visited a wealthy Lapp, named Anders Nilsen Heika, and carefully examined his large herd of reindeer, many of which were lying about within a few feet of me, and interviewed their owner for several hours as to their habits, treatment, etc. He was intelligent and candid, and seemed anxious to impart all the information possible. Many of my questions involved points which had never occurred to him before, and when this was the case, he frankly said so, that no undue weight might be given to his recollection or impression.

From him I learned that the male reindeer only are used for draft or burden. These are usually castrated when three years old. This is not done by amputation as with us, but by bruising and crushing the testicle with the teeth, without opening the scrotum and removing the member. This of necessity is but very imperfect castration, and while it may destroy the capacity for generation, it does not entirely remove desire, and moderates without destroying the spirits of the animal. Were the operation complete, it might leave the animal so dull and stupid as to impair, if it did not destroy, his usefulness.

It had never occurred to the Lapp, that this operation had any influence on the growth of the antlers, but he supposed they were cast off and renewed on the mutilated as on the perfect animal. On reflection, however, he remembered that many carried the velvet longer than usual, and that in a few instances the deer had carried their antlers through the winter, and it might be that the antlers were broken off near the head instead of being detached at the articulation as on the perfect animal.

My conclusion was, from all the information I could gather, that complete castration of the reindeer has the same effect on the growth of their antlers as on other deer, but that in Lapland the operation is usually very imperfect, and so the effect is less, and sometimes is so little, that the antler still matures, and is regularly cast off every year, while on others the operation is more complete, when the antler never matures, but is broken off near the head when it becomes frozen through, and from the stump a new antler grows the following year, as we shall presently see is the case with other deer.

It is not remarkable that facts like these should be quite overlooked by the Lapps, for to them they have no interest; and the obliging Lapp was no doubt much surprised that I should come so far to make inquiries about matters which to him were so utterly unimportant, for he could not see how they could help to fill the pot.

But even naturalists, if they have not entirely overlooked the subject, have not deemed it of sufficient importance to institute careful experiments so as to arrive at correct conclusions. While most writers on the Cervidæ have alluded to the subject, they have generally despatched it in a paragraph or two, in which they have given vague rumors, or adopted loose statements from careless observers, and so as might be expected they have arrived at contradictory or very unsatisfactory conclusions.

Dr. Owens' statements on this subject [1] accord more closely with the results which I have obtained than any others which I have met. Still they differ in some very important particulars, but they are mostly founded on experiments not made by himself; and I must say that I think it quite probable, from what is said, that there was much room for error. It is possible, indeed, that a different effect may be produced on some species of deer from that produced on others, but all analogy would render this exceedingly improbable. When it is said that the antler on a castrated specimen has been shed and renewed annually as on the perfect animal, a doubt is left whether the animal was really or at least completely castrated; such we have seen was the information given me by the Lapp as his first impression, but a careful examination showed that he was probably mistaken in his supposition, that castration had no effect on the growth of the antler on the reindeer. We may still doubt whether the operation was complete, or whether the breaking off of the antler near the head, and the growing of a new one from the stump, which as we shall presently see always occurs on the smaller species in this latitude, has not been mistaken for a shedding and renewal of the antler. Long practice and great care, as well as a full appreciation of the distinctive features to be sought for, are indispensable to qualify us to make observations which may be absolutely relied upon.

My experiments have been tried upon two species only in my own grounds, but they have been numerous, and upon individuals of almost every age, and continued through a long course of years. I proceed to results.

If a deer be castrated at any time after the antlers are so far matured that their velvet may be removed without material injury, and while they still firmly occupy their seat, they will *invariably* drop off within thirty days thereafter, though it may be months before the time when they would have been shed in the course of nature. In this case, and also when the operation is performed after the antlers are dropped naturally, in the spring following when the new antlers on the perfect buck commence their growth, the same growth commences on the mutilated animal, and progresses to all external appearance the same as on the perfect animal till they have attained nearly the same size as those which were last cast off. If the buck be a young one with a spike antler, this will be a spike also of nearly the same length.

<hr>

[1] *Comparative Anatomy and Physiology of Vertebrates*, vol. iii., p. 631.

If an old buck with five tines, these will be of nearly the same size as the former, with five tines also. These, however, never perfect their growth and never lose their velvet ; but at the time the antlers on the perfect bucks lose the velvet, those on the mutilated bucks stop their growth, but a moderate circulation is kept up in the velvet, which remains warm to the touch, and so they continue stationary till the severe weather of winter freezes the antlers through down to or very near the burr, when by the application of some accidental force they snap off within a half an inch or an inch of the burr, depending on the size of the antler. If we now examine the detached portion of an antler we shall see that its entire body is loose and spongy, more condensed at the circumference than within, but has nowhere attained the consistency of hard bone, so as to close up the blood-vessels leading into it from the periosteum. The communication has been all the while kept up between the external and the internal circulation, as was the case during the period of growth of the antler on the perfect animal.

These stumps of the antlers are carried till the next spring, when a new antler shoots out from the old stump not so large as its predecessor, and grows on in the same way and at the same rate as on the perfect animal, till those so far mature as to shed their velvet, when as before that on the mutilated animal stops its growth. In the mean time the old stump has enlarged its diameter and put out large tubercles as if supplemental to the burr, which is also considerably enlarged. The new antler thus produced is not so large as the former, and if branched has less tines. And so this process goes on year after year, each succeeding antler being less in size and perfection than its predecessor, while the enlargement at the lower end becomes an exaggerated burr. This process of growth differs very considerably in different individuals of the same species. In some, in a few years, these stumps grow to an enormous size, covered all over with large tubercles, some of them amounting to shafts two or three inches long, which may be frozen and broken off in the winter, while neither may be so conspicuous as to be recognized as a beam. The whole of this irregular mass is ever covered with the fine, soft, glossy fur. These two large masses in the place of the antlers, covered all over with these rudimentary shafts, present a very curious and interesting appearance on the head of a deer.

By far the finest specimen of this sort I ever had I presented to the Central Park, New York, in 1865. I do not know if he is still living, but if he is, and this extraordinary appendage has continued its growth in the same unique direction, it must exhibit a curious spectacle at this time and be an interesting object for study to the naturalist.

I have several castrated deer in my grounds which were there when "Billy" was sent to New York, but none of them have approached the specimen mentioned in the redundancy of this basilar growth. Still the difference is only in degree. This enlargement of the base and diminution of the shaft seems to be less and less each year as the animal grows older.

In October, 1865, I castrated my first Wapiti, or Elk, the day after he had killed Mr. Demmick, who in spite of locks and a very substantial picket fence eight feet high had managed to get into the park appropriated exclusively to the elk. That was the most terribly wicked elk I have ever seen. For a few days after the operation he seemed madder than ever. At length, however, his rage gradually subsided, and he was ever after quite an amiable brute.

As I expected, within four weeks the splendid antlers which had adorned his head had disappeared, and only the large pedicels which had supported them remained to disfigure the contour of his head. The next year new antlers grew, but smaller and with fewer branches than the old, differing in this respect materially from those observed on the smaller species castrated when fully adult. As was expected, these did not lose their velvet at the time it was shed from the antlers of the perfect bucks, but the growth was simply suspended. During December, the beam of one antler, about eighteen inches from the point, was broken off by some accident. This fragment afforded a rich field for study, but I was not satisfied with it and killed the animal during the winter, and was so enabled to establish many facts only suspected before, but to state each in detail would be too tedious.

The successor to the deposed monarch of the herd was only less wicked than the other. He was castrated on the 1st of January, 1867. The present antlers were cast and the new ones grew, and suspended their growth as in the former case, and so they have continued to the present day. These were too large to be frozen through and so were not broken off near the head, as has always been the case with the smaller species, but only an inch or two of the ends were broken. The next year's growth was to teach me something new, and I watched it with interest, rather expecting to see active growths shooting out from the broken points to unknown lengths. In this I was disappointed; the ends grew over, presenting something the appearance of the end of an amputated limb after it is healed, but only on one point was there any considerable elongation and that did not exceed three or four inches. The new growth was principally expended in the enlargement of the old remaining parts. Of these the actual diameter was appreciably increased, but the greatest volume consisted in large tubercles all over the surface, some with large bases, others attached to the parent stem by small necks. These tubercles are largest on the lower part of the antler and especially about the burr, some extending down over the pedicel, and one nearly two inches broad now extends down over the face nearly to the eye.

This animal is now carrying these antlers the eighth winter. Each year portions have been broken off from the ends by accident, so that now but tineless stubs remain scarcely eighteen inches long. These fragments have rarely been found, and I have been able to add but one to my collection. The actual diameters of these shafts have been more than doubled. Some of the old tubercles are broken off annually, and those remaining are enlarged somewhat each year, and new ones crowd their way out among the old, but the number of new ones and the growth of the old ones seem to diminish each year as the animal grows older. One of these tubercles I found hanging by the skin, which I secured. That was sufficient to show that they are composed of the same cancellous tissue as the main stem on this and the growing antler on the perfect animal. The periosteum, and the cuticle covering it in which the fine soft fur of the velvet is inserted, expand with the growth of the tubercles, so as to completely envelop them, penetrating them with the nutriment conduits, the same as described when treating of the growth of the antler on the perfect animal.

On the 15th of July I castrated a common buck four years old, when his antlers were more than three quarters grown. He soon recovered from the wound. I watched the result, comparing his antlers with those of several others of about the same age not castrated. I could detect no difference in the progress of growth till all seemed to have attained their full size. Those on the castrated animal never so far matured as to lose the velvet, while that on the perfect animal was of course rubbed off as usual. The results of my experiments seem to establish this state of facts: that the removal of the testes of the deer whose antlers are grown, at once arrests the supply of nutriment which has hitherto flowed into the antler which has lost the velvet, through its base, the same as when the lower extremity has attained its maximum density, and that the absorbent process immediately commences upon the lower surface of the articular plate, which in the course of a single month has so far proceeded as to loosen the antler at the articulation, and it drops off precisely the same as on the perfect animal when the fullness of time has arrived.

If the operation is performed before the antler has so far completed its growth, the deposit of earthy matter is arrested before the canals leading from the periosteum are filled up and the connection between the external and internal blood-vessels is cut off, when the antler never matures, but retains its vitality and becomes persistent, although it attains a higher degree of perfection in its growth than the antler which is wholly grown on the castrated buck.

Upon the return of spring the absorption within the pedicel commences in the mutilated as in the perfect animal, whereby the canals for the passage of the blood-vessels are enlarged, and an active circulation is established, and the new antler commences its growth on both alike, and is so continued, though with diminished force on the mutilated animal, till the summer wanes and the rutting season approaches. Then a certain point is attained in the growth of the antler which can never be passed on the animal from which the testes have been completely removed, while by the stimulating influence which they afford, the requisite nutriment is forced into the antlers of the unmutilated animal which enables them to grow on to complete perfection. This influence seems to be mostly excited in those blood-vessels which enter the antler at its base, upon which the internal growth of the antler depends, after the destruction of the periosteum, but the latter also is deprived of a certain portion of its energy, for it seems unable to so solidify the surface of the antler as to close the nutriment vessels which lead from it, and through which the blood which ascends through the arteries of the periosteum is returned. The greatest deprivation would seem to be in the capacity to transport and properly deposit the earthy matter by which the bone is solidified, for it is, after all, this deficiency which distinguishes the one antler from the other. It is after the rutting season is past, and the activity and excitement of the generative organs have ceased, that the absorbents commence their work at the articulation, and so loosen the antler from its seat ; but even at that time, in many cases the suspension of the circulation through the articular plate is incomplete for a time, and then the absorption on its lower surface is very gradual, if it has even commenced, and it may take months before the antler is loosened, while, as we have seen, if the testes are absolutely removed, this work is at once commenced and rapidly prosecuted, so that within a month at most the antler is thrown off. But those who have supposed that the generative organs of the male Cervidæ are entirely dormant and incapable of action from the time the antler is cast till it is again completely renewed, are mistaken in their conclusions. I have seen both the wapiti and the smaller deer copulate out of season, and after they had cast their antlers, with fruitful results, so that the old theories on this subject are not founded on facts. It is no doubt true, as a general rule, that the sexual organs are less stimulated, and the male is not maddened by desire during the time when he is deprived of this weapon of warfare, so much as he is when it is in perfect condition ; and this is a wise order of nature to prevent those combats which are excited by jealousy at a time when the growing of the antlers operates as a sure bond to keep the peace, for a single battle would utterly destroy them. No doubt a consciousness of this weakness may have a quieting effect upon their belligerent dispositions, for it does not entirely leave them with the rutting season, but is manifested, though less recklessly, so long as the weapon remains.

We may admit that one physical body can only produce a physical effect upon another body by a physical medium, and so conclude that there must be a physical medium between the testes and the antlers, *specially designed and qualified* to produce the effect observed ; but if so it is as yet not identified, and we can only hope that some more ingenious and careful observer may find it. The utmost we may safely say now is, that in some way the testes enable or stimulate the proper blood-vessels to carry into the antler a larger amount of earthy matter and there properly deposit it, than they can do after the testes are removed, presuming at the same time that the absence of the generative organs deprives these vessels of, or weakens other important functions necessary to the full maturity of the antler.

When the fact is established, that the testes exercise a potent influence over the growth of the antlers of the deer, we might expect that such growth would be entirely cut off by their removal as much as it is by nature in the female ; possibly it might be so if those organs were removed before they had exercised their influence upon the organs of nutrition upon which the antler depends for its growth. This is a question I have in vain endeavored to settle ; but I have never been able to save a fawn castrated before the first antler had grown. From the fact that the antler grown after the operation, never exceeds, or even equals in size the one previously grown, I will venture the opinion that no antler would grow on the male castrated when very young and before the antler has made an appreciable start, so that he would always resemble the doe in this regard, but in trying this experiment we must remember that the fawn is born with the rudiments of the antler already developed, and that frequently an appreciable growth may be observed during the first year of its life, if it is an early fawn. In early fawns, this growth is sometimes sufficient to perforate the skin the first season

What has been said would be a sufficient answer to Buffon's theory, that the antlers of the Cervidæ are vegetable growths on the animal body, had not all subsequent authors discarded his assumption as unworthy of the least consideration.

It is indeed remarkable that an author so renowned, and who devoted so much time and labor to the study of natural history, should have observed so superficially as to render such an error possible when a very little examination would have prevented it.

We will now consider the forms and locations and uses of the antlers of the different species of the deer. I have already alluded to the fact that these have been too much relied upon to distinguish species ; still they are by no means to be overlooked in determining classifications. True, the fawns and the females, with the exception of the reindeer, are always without this evidence, to tell of the species ; it is much if they can aid us in placing the older males. We shall see, however, that even for this they are not reliable, for some very distinct species have antlers precisely alike, while sometimes we shall find them widely variant in different localities on the same species. After all, our investigations of the natural history of these animals would be very imperfect, without a careful study of the forms, locations, and uses of the antlers, in addition to what has been said of their structure and mode of growth.

It may be proper to explain preliminarily, the terms used in the description of this appendage of the deer. It has been often, though incorrectly, called a horn. As as we have already seen, it is an external osseous member, and is as different in its components from true horn, as it is from muscle. Only in its uses as a weapon and in its location does it resemble the horn.

As a whole, the appendage is properly termed an *antler.* The main stem is called the *beam;* the larger branches from the beam are called *tines,* and the branches from these and small branches from the beam, are called *snags.* The flattened portions of either the beam or the tines are called *palms.* The irregular enlargement at the base, is called the *burr,* and the warty eminences, more usually found on the lower portion of the beam, are called *knobs, warts,* or *tubercles.* The lower anterior conspicuous branch, is called the *brow-tine,* and the next the *bez-tine,* and the third the *royal-tine ;* then the *sur-royal,* etc. These are most distinct on the antler of wapiti. Usually the first antler grown on the young buck is not branched, but con-

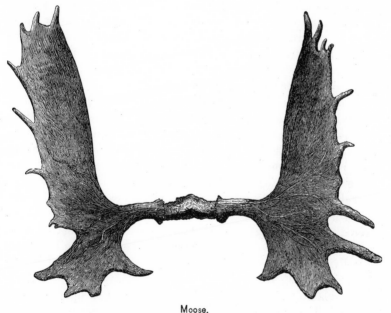

Moose.

sists of beam only, and is called a *dag* or *spike* antler, and the latter term applies to the antlers of the adults when they are not branched, which is sometimes the case. The *pedicel* is the permanent process of the skull on which the antler grows.

The most conspicuous example of palmated antlers is found on the largest of the deer family, — our Moose. It, however,

13

does not decidedly assume this character till the animal becomes nearly adult; although after the first, it begins to show a tendency to flatten at the place of bifurcation.

I have experienced much difficulty in determining the ages of the Moose, upon which were grown the different antlers which I have examined, nor have I yet arrived at a satisfactory result. Hunters, of large experience and also good observers, will disagree as to the age of a young animal judging from the antlers, some believing it to have been one year old, while others pronounce it to have been two years old. For instance, I have in my collection six sets of moose antlers, showing a regular gradation in size and development; and yet the largest was sent me from Halifax, as coming from an animal four years old, which I think is correct, while it is a disputed question, whether the smallest are from an animal one or two years old, though I believe it to be from the latter. It is almost impossible to settle these questions with certainty, except where the animal is grown in domestication; and even then, many specimens must be examined to avoid being misled, for on the other members of the family a wide difference is observed in the development of the first antlers; some being spikes, while others are bifurcated, as we shall have occasion hereafter to notice.

The character of the palm on the antlers of the Moose is an irregular, oblong sheet terminating the beam. It is thinner in the middle than at the circumference, and has snags of a greater or less length set upon the border; which snags vary very much in number and size. It is rare that more than one of these palms is found on the same antler, yet sometimes a branch, when it is nearly the size of the beam above the fork, has a well-formed palm; but in that case neither may be expected to be as large as when the beam alone bears the palm. Some specimens have been met with where the beam low down has divided into nearly equal branches with palms of nearly equal size.

An example of this is shown in the illustration upon the next page, which is from a Scandinavian elk which I met in the Royal Museum in Copenhagen. It was difficult to show both palms in the drawing. The left antler divides into nearly equal parts, the one above the other, four inches from the burr, and on each branch is a well-formed palm. In the collection of the Chicago Academy of Sciences, which was destroyed in the fire of 1871, was a fossil skull and antlers of a Moose, one of which antlers was divided near the burr, presenting good palms on each division.

The pedicels on which the Moose antlers grow are situate at
the top of the head, and are from seven to nine inches apart,
with a lateral projection.   From these the antlers grow out laterally in horizontal positions.   A few inches from their bases they
commence an upward and forward curve, so that the palm usually
occupies nearly a vertical position with an anterior inclination,
and is laterally compressed.

I know of no other living species possessing this lateral projection of the antler; but the remains of the extinct Irish elk
shows not only a lateral, but a depressed position of the antler

Double-palmed Antler from a Scandinavian Elk.

for a short distance from the head, when it takes a slightly upward curve scarcely more than sufficient to bring it to a horizontal position, which it maintains for nearly its whole length, so
that the extreme points of the antlers are about as far apart as
their enormous length will permit.   I believe there is not any
existing representative of the genus which presents this extraordinary spread of the antlers.

The palms on the antlers of the Moose are oblong, say twice
as long as they are wide, but in this they show great variations.
The tines on the borders of the palms are variant in size and
numbers on different individuals, and are stoutest and most abundant on the anterior borders, a position in which they are presented to the adversary in battle.   When the edge of the broad,
thin palm is presented with its deeply serrated blade in front, it
may bear the shock of battle with more resistance than the same

volume would do in a cylindrical form, but should the vicissi tudes of battle expose it to a lateral force, it would be less able to withstand the shock. As we shall hereafter see, the Moose, like all the others of this genus, join battle with a great rush, which must often try the strength of the antlers to the utmost, yet we have no account of the antlers being broken short off, but it frequently happens that the tines or snags are dislocated. But for the great elasticity possessed by all antlers over all other bones, owing to the larger proportion of animal matter which they contain, a single battle would serve to destroy them.

Another peculiarity of the antlers of the Moose, is that they are very considerably less in volume, just above the burr where they are cylindrical, than farther up. They increase in volume, including the tines and palms, till above the middle of the whole length of the antlers, and then diminish to their extremities.

In proportion to their volume they are much shorter than the antlers on any of the other species, very rarely reaching a length of thirty inches, although they sometimes exceed sixty pounds in weight. This limited length in proportion to bulk, of course adds greatly to the strength of the weapon.

This enormous growth is accomplished in about three months' time. The time when the antlers of the Moose are cast is quite variant, and depends much on the age of the animal. It seems to be a universal law with the Cervidæ that the younger the animal is the longer is the antler in maturing and the later is it carried.

The time when the active growth of the antler commences, depends upon the latitude, or rather on the advancement of the season. In its southern range, say in Nova Scotia, the growth usually commences late in April, or the time when the sap commences to flow in the trees. On the adults the external growth of the antler is completed by the first of September, when the velvet is rubbed off, which is the commencement of the rutting season. This lasts from forty to fifty days, as we shall have occasion to observe hereafter. It is during this season that the antler is most required as a weapon of warfare, when it is all alive with the internal growth, and is more elastic and capable of enduring a greater strain, than after it dies by the destruction of the nutrient vessels, as has been before related. On the older specimens the antler is sometimes shed in December, but by far the largest proportion are cast during January and February, while some of the younger specimens carry their antlers till

April, or even the May following. After the rutting season is past, during which the antlers are still in an effective condition as weapons or shields, there is rarely occasion for their use, as the belligerent disposition ceases with the rut.

As my experiments show that the absorbent process which loosens the antler from its seat, requires about one month to accomplish its work, during which it is an inert foreign appendage, we see that the weapon retains its vitality and efficiency for a considerable time, when its use would seem to be no longer demanded by the disposition of the animal.

The following are the observations of Mr. Morrow of Halifax, on this subject: " The old Moose shed their horns in the early part of winter, a very few in December, the greatest number in January and February. I have seen some in February, which had just lost their horns. I once shot a young bull in February, which still wore his horns firmly set on his head. The first horns I believe are carried until early spring. The Moose rub their velvet from their horns, just before and during the early part of the rutting season." Captain Hardy, in " Forest Life in Acadie," says, " The young bull moose grows his first horn (a little dag of a cylindrical form) in his second summer, *i. e.,* when one year old. Both these and the next year's growth, which are bifurcate, remain on the head throughout the winter, till April or May. The palmate horns of succeeding years are dropped earlier, in January or February, a new growth commencing in April. The full development of the horn appears to be attained when the animal is in its seventh year."

Dr. Gilpin says,[1] " In the bull calf of the first year two knobs swell out upon the forehead beneath the skin; in the second year the true horn appears, — a single prong six or eight inches long; in the third year the new horn is usually trifingered and a little flattened; and in the fourth year assumes the adult form, though small. The Indians and hunters say, they increase till the eighth year. The horn of the adult bull springs at right angles from a broad knobby base on the forehead, throws off one, two, or three brow-prongs or tines, and then rapidly flattening, reflects backwards nearly at right angles, forming a broad flattened palm, the anterior convex edge of which is subdivided into more or less numerous tines. There is some analogy between the number of these tines and the age of the owner, but

[1] In Art. iv., *On the Mammalia of Nova Scotia,* by J. Barnard Gilpin, A. B., M. D., M. R. S. C.

not accurate enough for calculation. About seven or eight tines
are the usual number. The largest pair of horns I have seen,
measured five feet and two inches from tip to tip, the heaviest
weighed about fifty pounds. . . . . They shed them in February, and I have seen the young velvet horn in April."

These quotations are from the very best authorities, — good
observers, with the very best attainable opportunities for observing. Mr. Morrow's observations, that some old specimens drop
their antlers in December, merely establishes a fact which had
not been observed by the others, but which he had himself witnessed. It is the general impression that the antlers of the
Moose attain their greatest development when the animal has
reached his full maturity ; and that when advancing age begins
to impair his vigor the antlers grow less in size and are less perfectly developed, and that this deterioration progresses as age
enfeebles the animal ; and I think the weight of the evidence is in
favor of this conclusion ; but if this be so I think it is exceptional,
for with the other members of the family, judging from my own
observations and the best evidence I can get from others, the
antlers increase in size after the animal has attained his full
development. and probably so long as he lives, in health at least.

The antlers on the young Moose are of a chestnut brown ; as
they grow older they lose the chestnut shade and become a gray
brown, and as they grow older still, they assume a lighter shade,
till finally on aged animals they become fairly white.

These observations apply equally to the Scandinavian Elk,
only as a general rule the antler on the latter is less palmated
than on our Moose, and the tines are longer and larger, although
specimens may be found from the American variety, presenting
this peculiarity to as great an extent as in Europe, and there too
antlers are found as much palmated as here, so that it is only of
the average that the remark just made is applicable if a number
are compared together. By reason of the exceptional structures
met with on both continents, it is never safe to declare the origin
of any single specimen presented, although an inspection of a
considerable number together might leave little doubt as to
whence they came. Those from America would be found to be
larger, by reason of the increased size of the animal here, as well
as more palmated, with smaller tines.

As we have already seen, bifurcated antlers with double palms
are met with in both countries, though they are very rare.

I here present an illustration of an antler of a Scandinavian

This last came from Labrador, and I think grew upon a doe. The other may be either a Nova Scotian or Newfoundland specimen. Between these two, which may be considered the ultra extremes, the variety is endless."

Another typical feature is, that almost always one, and generally both, of the brow tines, project downwards over the face, reaching with the spurs on the palms, nearly to the end of the nose, and very frequently obstructing the vision more or less. Sometimes both the brow and the bez tine descend from the same antler together, and are broadly palmated at the ends. These palms generally stand vertically, or nearly so, or are compressed laterally.

I have in my collection four sets of male caribou antlers, and in all, the antlers on each head are exceptionally alike, as will be seen in the illustrations.

The largest (Fig. 2) are three feet long each. The beams are nearly cylindrical, or rather triangular, to near their ends, where they have small palms bordered with spurs. Each brow tine which descends over the face is seventeen inches long. They are compressed laterally towards their ends to widths of three and four inches respectively, the spurs of which approach each other to within three inches, while they are apart ten inches at the beams. Each in my collection, except the smallest, throws off one or more posterior tines. These show an exceptional absence of palmation, and much more resemble the antlers of the European variety than is usually met with in this country. A glance at the illustrations of the antlers of the Reindeer of Europe and of the Woodland Caribou will show this, but that the comparison may be the better understood I will give the measurements of the antlers of the male wild Reindeer which I brought from Lapland, shown in the illustration. (Fig. 7, p. 203.) The right antler is thirty-eight inches and six lines long. On that the brow tine is twelve inches and eight lines. It has two posterior tines near the end of the beam, the first of which is eight inches and three lines in length, and the other is six inches and nine lines. There is no bez-tine on this antler. The left antler is thirty-five inches and six lines long. The brow tine is nine inches and three lines in length, and the bez-tine is thirteen inches long. While these tines are flattened they are not palmated, as is usually observed on the American variety. Although the burrs are not entirely wanting they are very insignificant, as is always the case on both continents, and the pedicels are shorter than on any other of our species. Near the upper part of the beam three posterior tines are thrown off, the longest ten and one half inches, and the shortest two inches and nine lines. As I do not find the antlers of the female Caribou elsewhere described, only as that they are smaller than on the male, I will give a particular description of a pair in my collection (Fig. 3), in addition to the illustration. They stand on conical

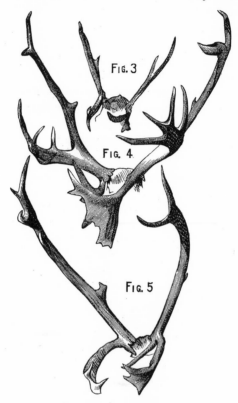

3. Female Caribou Antlers.
4 and 5. Male Caribou Antlers.

pedicels, which are nearly four inches apart, and which at their tops are one inch in their longest diameter, and nine lines in the shortest, which represents about the size and shape of the antler at the butt, where there is scarcely any burr. The pedicel is seven lines long. The entire length of the right antler is eleven and a half inches. The brow-tine is seven inches long, is thrown off one and a half inches above the butt. This tine is forked two and a half inches from the end. Six inches above the brow tine a posterior snag is thrown off, nine lines long.

The whole length of the left antler is thirteen inches; above the butt, two inches, the brow-tine is thrown off, which is six and a half inches long and not forked. Six inches above this, a posterior snag shoots off, which is two inches long. No broad palms are shown on these antlers. Both beams and tines are greatly compressed laterally, thickest in their middle and drawing quite regularly to edges each way. These are interesting for the entire absence of any palm, although the flattened form shows a strong tendency throughout to palmatation. Our authors and hunters seem to have equally overlooked the importance of a careful study of the antlers of the female and the

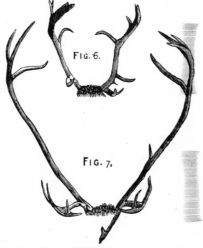

6. From Female Wild Reindeer from Lapland.
7. From Male Wild Reindeer from Lapland.

young male of this species, though the difference to me is very plain. These certainly bear a strong resemblance to the small pair in Dr. Gilpin's collection, his description of which I will repeat: " I possess another pair of very small horns with one simple brow-antler and but one tine, from a scarcely palmated horn. This last came from Labrador, and I think is a doe's." Now these are the only words of any author which I find, tending to give the least idea of the antlers of the doe, except that they are much smaller than those of the buck.

An examination of many specimens, especially from the European Reindeer, shows that the Doctor was undoubtedly correct in his conclusion that his specimen was from a female Caribou. Compare his description with the illustrations of the antlers of

the American and European female Reindeer, and any doubt remaining must be removed.

Let us now give a description and measurements of the pair of
female wild Reindeer antlers which I brought from Lapland.
(Fig. 6 on p. 203.)

The right antler is eighteen inches and five lines long, with a
brow-tine seven inches and three lines long, and two posterior
tines, the longest five inches and three lines in length. The
left antler is nineteen inches and four lines in length. The
brow-antler is six inches and seven lines in length, with a small
snag above it and then an anterior tine five and a half inches
long. There are four posterior tines or snags. There are no
palms on these antlers, though the tines are considerably flattened, especially the brow tines, which descend over the face as
is invariably the case with the antlers of the Reindeer. These
we see are considerably larger than those from the American
variety, but this is accidental, for such is not usually the case.

Ordinarily the antlers of the Caribou spring from the head in an
oblique direction, about forty-five degrees from the horizontal, or
ninety degrees from each other ; their direction is first backward
and outward for about half their length, and then forward, upward, and inward, so that the terminal points are nearer together
than the beams are at the angle of the curvature, and about as
far forward as the seats of the antlers ; many, however, depart
from these characteristics. Strangely variant as these antlers
often are from each other, even when grown on the same head
and at the same time, yet they possess features never to be
mistaken by the careful observer, who will at once recognize the
Caribou's antler, no matter what its form.

In another respect the antlers of the Caribou and also of the
European Reindeer are quite peculiar. They have by far the
least burr of any antlers grown upon any deer. Generally they
have what may be called a rudimental burr, and very few are
destitute of it, but on all it is very insignificant and on most it
is quite wanting on some part of the circumference.

A glance at the illustrations will show, while the antlers of the
Woodland Caribou and the Barren-ground Caribou are formed
on the same general plan, they present differences generally sufficient to identify the species on which they grew.

The most striking difference between the two species is in their
relative size. The Woodland Caribou is twice as large as his more
northern relative, and the antlers of the latter are twice as large

as those of the former, so that the smaller animal has antlers which are four times as large in proportion to the size of the animal as the former. As the antlers of the Woodland Caribou are as large in proportion to his size as those of any of the other species, we see that those grown on the Barren-ground Caribou are so excessive in growth as to excite our wonder. It creates the impression that he must be fairly laden down with their weight, and that the drain upon the system to supply this enormous growth of bone in a few months, must enfeeble the animal, for the time at least. This is not so, however, more than with the other species. All the other species which I have personally observed, while the antler is growing, seem to be more or less enfeebled and in poor condition, and most of all is this the case with the Virginia deer. During the same period the females are suckling their young, which would seem to be a sufficient explanation why they are poor also ; but my observations teach me that the barren does maintain a better condition of flesh during the summer than the others, though these also become quite poor in early summer.

How far the Barren-ground Caribou are an exception to this rule, I am not prepared to say. " The reindeer, " says Captain Lyon, " visits the polar regions at the latter end of May, or early part of June, and remains until late in September. On his arrival he is thin and his flesh is tasteless, but the short summer is sufficient to fatten him to two or three inches on the haunches." Richardson (p. 243) says : " When in condition there is a layer of fat deposited on the back or rump of the males to the depth of two or three inches or more immediately under the skin, which is termed *depouillé* by the Canadian voyagers ; and as an article of Indian trade it is often of more value than all the remainder of the carcass. The *depouillé* is thickest at the commencement of the rutting season; it then becomes of a red color, acquires a high flavor, and soon after disappears."

One not familiar with the habit of the deer, would be likely to understand Captain Lyon's remark as stating that the animal had been increasing in flesh during the whole time his antlers had been growing. This would be a great mistake. The fact that the deer are in the finest condition at the beginning of the rut, which is shortly after the velvet is rubbed off the antlers, is not confined to the Barren-ground Caribou, but applies to all of the family. It does not require the whole of even the shortest summer for any deer to improve from a lean condition to that of

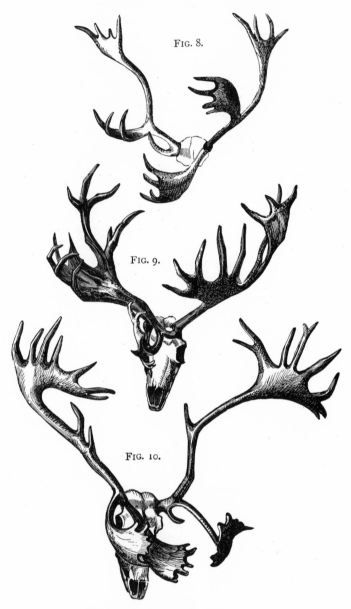

FIG. 8.

FIG. 9.

FIG. 10.

Woodland Caribou.   [Copied from Hardy.]

8. The Ordinary Canada Type.   9. Caribou Horns from Newfoundland.
10. Horns from Labrador.

Fig. 11.

Fig. 12.

Barren-ground Caribou.   [Copied from Richardson.]

a very fat one.   Our common deer, which is usually very poor
during the growth of the antlers, until they are very nearly
formed, suddenly commences to improve in condition, and in a
very short time after the velvet is rubbed off is fatter than at
any other time.   We need not doubt that a very few weeks at
the most are required to effect an equal change in this Caribou
when feeding upon an abundance of the most nutritious vegetation known to botany.

We. may safely assume that this deer is in the poorest condition at the time when the other deer are poorest, that is, when
the antlers are in their most vigorous growth; and we may well
conclude that the larger proportionate size of the antlers of this
deer must make a greater demand on the system than occurs in
the case of the others.   Hence we see that the deer is not only
poor, but as Richardson tells us, a large proportion of the elements
of nutrition are drawn from the flesh, so that it is nearly worthless as food, while the meat of the moose, whose antler is not one
sixth the relative size, is still nutritious though the animal be
poor.

Buffon thinks that the size of the deer's antler depends on the
amount of nutriment which he takes; that a well-fed deer will
have larger antlers than one even of the same species not well
nourished.   If this be so, then by applying the theory to this
species, we may find some explanation of the enormous development of the antlers, for the very nutritious lichens on which
they feed are practically unlimited within their range.

In form, too, as well as in size, there is an appreciable difference between the large and the small Caribou, although they
possess the same general characteristics which distinguish them
from those of the other Cervidæ.   As a general rule the beam
of the antler is longer in proportion to its diameter than on the
larger species; it has less tines, is less palmated, and presents
more curvature, although exceptions to this general rule are frequently met with.

In speaking of the Northern Indians, Richardson says : " Of
the caribou horns they form their fish spears and hooks, and
previous to the introduction of European iron, ice-chisels, and various other utensils were likewise made of them."   This is certainly suggestive of the solidity and tenacity of these antlers,
and shows that although so large and grown in so short a season,
their growth is quite as perfect, and they are as well matured as
the antlers of any of the other deer.

My only information is that the old bucks shed their antlers by the end of November, while the young bucks carry theirs until spring, and the females retain theirs until May or June, when they are about to drop their young.

In one respect only do the antlers of the Barren-ground Caribou resemble those of the Lapland Reindeer more than do those of the Woodland Caribou, and that is in the feature that they are less palmated in proportion to their volume. In this we observe the same distinction between the reindeer of the Old World and those of America that we see between the elk of Europe and the moose of this country. In both a larger proportion of the antler is in the palms on the American varieties than on the European, and yet we find both extremes in this regard in both countries.

With the female Caribou the dropping of the antlers seems to be intimately connected with the time of parturition, and yet we would suppose that that of all the year would be the time when she most needs weapons for the defense of her young. If, as a general economy of nature, parts are adapted to wants or ends, this would seem to be an exception ; yet I think it not improbable that a more intimate acquaintance with the subject would explain these phenomena consistently with the general rule.

The naturalist must remember that he is not required to explain the purpose of every provision in nature which he observes, or else abandon this law, at least till he is sure that he understands all its uses ; and yet so thoroughly imbued is the mind with the integrity of this law that one is often tempted to conclusions from partially observed facts when a more intimate acquaintance with the subject would instruct him that he had been too hasty in reaching conclusions, or convince him that he has not yet discovered the purposes designed by the provision. We must not understand this law as requiring that everything is designed for the benefit of the individual, for it may be designed for the benefit or protection of others. Hence some naturalists have concluded that the early shedding of the antlers of the male deer is designed to deprive him of the means of destroying the young of the species, when these are too feeble to escape his persecutions. Now this assumes that the aged males have such destructive dispositions, without, so far as I know, a single fact to warrant it, and especially does it overlook the fact that all the members of this family use the fore feet as powerful weapons, except in earnest combat, when the antlers serve as shields as well as swords. Undoubtedly were the male disposed

14

to destroy the young fawns, he would use his fore feet for the purpose instead of his antlers, even though the latter were in perfection.

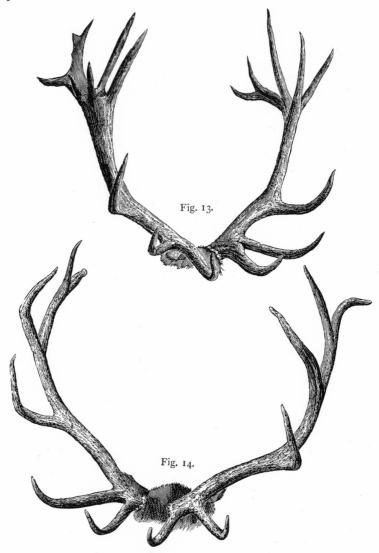

13. Crown Antler of American Elk.
14. Common Form of Antler of American Elk.

I must close this branch of my subject with the remark that further observations are necessary to enable us to fully understand this interesting feature of the economy of this animal, and if what I have said shall induce any who have the opportunity for making the necessary observations to do so, I shall feel highly gratified.

Of all known deer the male Wapiti, or American Elk, is provided with the longest, the most graceful and symmetrical antlers; and which are also most effective as both weapons and shields. Not only the beam but the tines are cylindrical in form, although on adults they are more or less flattened toward the ends, where forks with nearly equal branches occur, — a form of manifest utility.

They are grown on pedicels which rise somewhat obliquely from either side of the crown of the head to a height of four inches, more or less, and are much longer than those on any other American deer, though the barking deer of Asia (*Cervus muntjak*) far exceeds it in this respect, having a pedicel equaling in length the antler above it.

Fig. 15.

First or Dag Antlers of a Young American Elk.

The dag antler of our Elk has a form peculiar to itself. It is usually a spike from a few inches to twenty-four inches in length. It is larger at the base and for two or three inches above, in proportion to the size of the rest of the antler, than any subsequent antler grown on the same, or on any other deer. However, no one familiar with them can ever mistake one for the spike antler of any other deer. They arise from the head

with a posterior and lateral inclination, and then at half their
length they curve anteriorly and inward so that the points approach each other more or less. The lower part of the beam is
more angular or less round than the subsequent antlers. The
taper, from a few inches above the burr to the point, is very uniform and the curvature is graceful.

In several instances in my grounds, the dag antler on the
young Elk has been bifurcated. This took place near the upper
end, and the prongs were not widely different in their lengths.
This has occurred on the large specimens, though not necessarily the largest, for the largest it has happened were spikes.
These large specimens are divested of their velvet in October or
November, and are dropped in April or May ; and are only
grown on the earliest fawns dropped in May or early in June ;
later fawns have smaller antlers when they become yearlings,
and I have had some dropped late in July, whose first antlers the
next season would be but a few inches in length, and the velvet
would remain till late in the winter, and they would retain their
antlers till June, or even later, and I once had a very late fawn
whose antlers did not mature the first season of their growth,
but carried the velvet all winter, and grew on and matured the
next season. These are phenomena not likely to have been observed, except by those who have a large number in confinement,
and who have studied them for a number of years in succession ;
which may serve to explain why hunters, of even the largest experience, may sometimes disagree as to the age of the deer on
which given specimens grew. It is not sufficient to enable a person to arrive at correct conclusions to have five or six sets of
antlers grown in successive years on the same animal to judge
from, for as we have seen, even the first may be quite different
from those grown on another individual of the same age.

There is more uniformity in the second antlers grown on the
Wapiti. On all these which have been reared in my grounds, the
second antlers have both the brow and the bez tines, and sometimes a snag or tine in addition, has appeared on one or both
antlers, though I have met with specimens elsewhere, on which
the bez-tine was wanting or was merely rudimentary.

The third antlers almost uniformly have the royal-tine, and
rarely more. The fourth and the fifth year may, or may not,
produce the sur-royal on one or both antlers. Those of succeeding years may be expected to have additional tines, but their
presence one year furnishes no certain evidence that they will

appear the next ; still the four first tines and a bifurcation above them, may, with considerable confidence, be relied upon, for all after the first are forked near the ends; frequently the specimens taken from the older bucks show three tines at the upper fork.

The second and subsequent antlers present forms of the same general characteristics, though they are subject to considerable variation in detail. These antlers rise with a lateral inclination more or less pronounced, some being very spreading while others are much more vertical. They assume at first an anterior direction, and then curve backward. All the normal tines have an anterior projection, though frequently abnormal tines or snags occur which violate this law.

The burr is large and rough. The brow-tine springs from immediately above the burr, in a descending and lateral direction ; but at about one third its length from the point, it commences a graceful upward curve so that the point stands nearly vertical. The terminal point is very sharp. Immediately above the brow-tine, the bez-tine springs out in a less depressed and more lateral direction. It is nearly the same length and form as the brow-tine ; above this the beam becomes reduced in size and rises as a naked round shaft, till the royal-tine is thrown out. This is generally considerably smaller than those below, and has an upward inclination. In this it differs from the antlers on the stag of Europe, where the royal-tine is usually larger than the brow-tine. In Europe, also, on the red deer, the bez-tine is usually much smaller than the brow-tine, though I have met with specimens there, which correspond with our Elk in these particulars, and I have met with specimens grown here, having the small bez-tine and more frequently with the large royal-tine. I have in my collection a very large fossil antler, on which the royal-tine is as large proportionately as any I ever saw from the red deer.

Up to and including the royal-tine, usually both antlers are very much alike. Above this, while they generally nearly correspond in length and volume, they are quite likely to differ in the number and size of their prongs ; but we may always expect to find them near the ends, either bifurcated or trifurcated. On the red deer it is not uncommon to find the upper part of the antler greatly expanded, with a deep indentation, forming a cup of the capacity of a gill or more, from the irregular rim of which several tines, probably of unequal length, spring up. These are called crown antlers. When studying these abroad, I regarded

this indentation in the top of the enlarged antler as a modification, though an important one, of the forked extremity of the
antler of our Elk ; some of which I had seen approach it in external appearance. I have since met with a pair of Elk's antlers,
one of which has the indentation described, and is as perfect a
crown antler as is often met with from the red deer, while the
other approaches it very nearly. These are illustrated in Fig. 13,
page 210. There may be many of these antlers found on the
Wapiti deer, but this is the only one I have ever met with, having a dish at the end, with a capacity sufficient to hold a good
drink of wine. These antlers may be compared with crown antlers of the red deer by examining the illustrations.

Fig. 16.

Crown Antlers of the Red Deer or Stag of Europe.

Abnormal snags may frequently occur on any part of the beam
or the tines, more frequently on the brow-tines. These more
rarely occur on the Atlantic than on the Pacific coast. There, I
have found the brow-tine forked near the end into equal branches,
— an illustration of which I give. This I have never observed
on an eastern Elk, or on the red deer. On about five per cent.
of the antlers grown on Elk in the Rocky Mountains and east of
them, a short snag, more or less developed, appears on the upper
side and usually nearest the end of the brow-tine, and sometimes
on the bez-tine. This may be an inch long or a mere protuberance. I examined a large collection of the antlers of the red deer
in Berlin, and found the same development on these tines there
and in about the same proportion. Those from Bohemia and

Hungary were much the largest antlers, and not easily distinguished from the antlers of our Elk, of which there were a number in the collection. There were several specimens, which I was at a loss to determine whether they were grown in America or Europe. I must say that the typical indicia of the antlers of both these varieties are precisely alike.

I present upon the next page (Fig. 18) an illustration of triplet antlers on the same head, from a Red Deer, which I saw in Rosenburg Castle, Copenhagen, said to have been killed by the king several centuries ago. Each, it will be observed, has a distinct and independent pedicel. The right antler is thirty-two

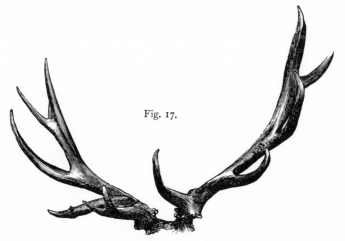

Fig. 17.

From a California Elk.

inches long. The upper left antler is twenty-nine and a half inches long, and the lower left antler is twenty-five inches in length. A similar abnormal growth occurred in this State (Illinois) some years since, on an American Elk, only the extra antler was between the other two, nearer to one than the other, and was relatively smaller than the European specimen. It had a distinct pedicel, and seemed to grow quite independently of the other antlers. The specimen was in the collection of Dr. Velay and was destroyed in the great Chicago fire in 1871. I have never heard of an instance where triplet antlers have grown upon any other species of deer.

On both our Elk and the European Stag, those antlers which spread the most are usually the longest, are the most symmetrical, and are the most admired.

Five feet is the extreme length of the antler of the Elk, of which I have any authentic account. These are now in the collection of the late Mr. W. F. Parker, of West Meriden, Conn. On the right antler the sur-royal tine is bifurcated, the two points of which are of about equal lengths. Around the burrs they are thirteen inches, between the burrs and the brow-tines the circumference of the beam is ten and one half inches. The right antler presents eight, and the left six points. These antlers are as remarkable for their symmetrical and elegant form and graceful curvatures as for their extraordinary size.

The type of the antler is established when the animal is in his third year, that is, with his second antlers. If these antlers are

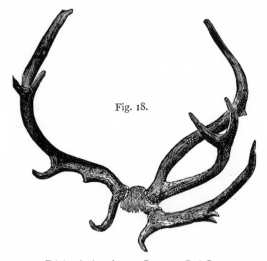

Fig. 18.

Triplet Antlers from a European Red Deer.

remarkably large, or remarkably broad or spreading or the reverse, the same characteristics may, with confidence, be expected in all the antlers subsequently grown on that animal.

With many other interesting views, Dr. Hayden, U. S. Geologist, presented me with the photograph, by Jackson, of an Elk killed on the 28th of August, 1871, at an altitude of about 10,000 feet above the sea, on the divide between the Yellowstone Lake and the head waters of the East Fork of the Yellowstone River, which is shown in the illustration. Both these antlers show remarkable imperfections in their growth, which may, no doubt, be attributed to some injury received in their early stages. This Elk was two years old, or in his third year's growth with his second set of antlers. The antlers were in the velvet, were inferior in size as well as imperfect in form. Their deficiencies in tines are manifest at a glance. They were about equal in length to the dag antler of an early fawn, but the tines show that they were second antlers.

Fig. 19. Hayden's Elk.

But the most remarkable feature of these antlers is their retarded growth, which may be attributed to the altitude of the home of the individual, for injuries to the antler when growing do not retard their maturity. With the photograph before me, I spent much time in comparing it with the growing antlers on a number of two year old Elks in my grounds. It was early apparent that these were much in advance of those on the Hayden Elk. I was from home at the time when mine reached the same stage of maturity which Dr. Hayden's had attained when it was killed; but on the 29th of July, just one month earlier than that time, I had a fine view of the whole band of Elk, with most of the two year olds together, and as near to me as I desired them for the inspection. All showed both brow and bez tines, completely formed; showing upon one or both antlers a royal-tine, all being bifurcated near the ends. So far as I could judge, these were about two weeks in advance of those on the Hayden Elk; and as that was killed a month later than the time when I made these observations, we see that from some cause the growth of the antler on the mountain Elk was retarded at least six weeks, as compared with those in my grounds, besides being very inferior in size and very deficient in members. We may not account for this marked effect by a want of food, for it was in the midst of forests and shrubbery, which is its favorite aliment; neither could it have suffered from want of grasses, for we hear no complaint that the numerous horses of a large expedition did not find plenty for their subsistence while in the same country. We may safely assume, however, that in that region vegetation was as much retarded in the spring as was the growth of these antlers in the summer; and this I think the most probable explanation of their late growth, for everywhere the commencement of the growth of the antler of the deer seems to be about the time when vegetation begins to shoot forth.

I may say here, that I think the antlers of all the deer are not as largely developed when they are confined in parks of even large extent as when running wild. This may be partly attributable to change of habit, but more probably to a want of that selection of food which they find in the wild state. They suffer most for the lack of an abundance of arboreous food, for they seem to make it their first business to kill off all the shrubbery within their reach. However, I have had some very fine antlers grown in my grounds. The antler of the Elk continues to increase in volume long after the body has attained its full size, and in many cases, probably, through life. I have heard no suggestion from any source that the antlers of the Elk decrease in size after the animal has passed its full vigor, nor have I made any observation to warrant such conclusion, as is said to be the case with the moose. The largest antlers are not necessarily from the largest animals. The largest ever grown in my grounds were on a medium sized animal, and he was always subject to the control of a larger buck with smaller antlers. Indeed, there were several in the band with antlers larger than those on this monarch. He is now a mounted specimen in the Royal Museum in Christiana, Norway.

After the first set of antlers, usually, a line drawn from the seat of the antler to the tip will be in a line with the face, so that when running through the bush with the nose thrown up so as to bring the face in a horizontal position, the butts and the tips of the antlers will be on the same level with the face. Then all the tines are curved backwards, so that they cannot become entangled in the brush. Still these immense antlers are a serious impediment to their speed through dense thickets. Hence we always find their paths avoid such places when practicable, and are made through the open glades ; though they seem to have no objection to the deep shades produced by dense foliage above. In our latitude, the velvet on the antler of the aged elk is with great uniformity discarded in August, and the antler is invariably dropped in April. The Wapiti is the only species of our deer which carries its antlers for so long a time, or so late in the spring, and is so uniform in the time of shedding them. I was for a long time disinclined to credit this exceptional uniformity, but its recurrence for many years and with every individual (and I have had large numbers to observe), compelled me to relinquish my doubt. That the times of shedding may differ in different latitudes is no doubt true, but I feel confident that the same uniformity prevails everywhere. I may remark here, that the European red deer also carries its antlers throughout the winter, and with the same uniformity drops them in the spring about the season that fresh vegetation begins to shoot forth. Such is the information given me by the director of the zoölogical gardens at Berlin, where there are a considerable number of red deer, and I found his observations corroborated by others.

Although possessing many marked specific differences, the Mule Deer and the Columbia Black-tailed Deer have antlers so nearly alike in all their features, even in their eccentricities, that I, at least, am unable to distinguish them from each other, and so shall treat of them together.

As might be expected, the first antler on the young buck is usually a spike from six to nine inches long.

The first which I had dropped in my grounds was a Columbia Deer, with a spike antler about six inches in length. The next was a Mule Deer. It was an early fawn dropped the last of May. His first antlers were eight inches long, and both were forked at the ends with tines two inches long. Another Mule fawn had spike antlers about six inches long.

The antlers of these deer start from the head in a direction inclining backward and outward ; but below the middle of the antler, commence a graceful forward curve. They present a slightly crinkled appearance and are not perfectly round.

After the dag antlers, their distinguishing characteristic is a bifurcation into pretty nearly equal parts, and on old specimens a second bifurcation, or a division of these parts into nearly equal tines ; but there is less certainly in the regularity of these divisions than in the former. These characteristics I find as constant and uniform on animals found on the east side of the Rocky Mountains as on the Pacific Coast.

The second and subsequent antlers grown on these deer usually have a very small snag an inch or two above the burr, on the upper or inner side of the beam, standing in nearly a vertical position, but sometimes curved one way or the other. This answers well to the basal snag on the antler of the Virginia deer, only it is very much smaller. The lower part of the beams of the antlers of these are covered more or less with tubercles, those near the burr being the largest and quite disappearing at the first fork, but these are mostly confined to the upper side of the beam, These tubercles also appear on the antler of the Virginia deer, even more abundant, for they are found on the lower side of the beam as well.

A medium pair of antlers in my collection and shown in the illustration (Fig. 21, p. 221), may be briefly described. They arise from the head, in a line with the face, but spread laterally. Two and a half inches above the burr, a basal snag appears on the upper side, which is two inches long. From this point the beam has a slight anterior curvature for seven and one half inches, then it divides. The anterior prong of the left antler continues with the same curve, for six inches, when it forks ; the front tine being four inches and three lines long, and the other four inches in length. The posterior prong of the first bifurcation curves posteriorly for six inches, where it forks into quite unequal tines, the front one being five inches long and the other three inches and three lines in length. The extreme length of this antler is twenty-one inches. The same description will answer for the right antler, except that the first posterior prong rises eight inches before it forks, with tines but two inches and three lines long. These antlers are from a Columbia Black-tailed Deer, and as before remarked, are of medium size. I have a much larger pair from the same species, taken near Igo, in Shasta County, California, already referred to (p. 183), and illustrated in Fig. 22, p. 221, which exhibit the abnormal diseased prong descending from the lower side of the beam of the left antler. These antlers are twenty-four inches long. They have an unusual spread at the tips. Another pair of antlers, also illustrated (Fig. 23), are from a Mule Deer from the Black Hills ; these are also twenty-four inches long, but have not so broad a spread. An abnormal descending tine is also found on the beam of the right antler of this pair. Both of these pairs of antlers show the double bifurcations characteristic of the antlers of these two species, and are here illustrated on the same plate, to show how

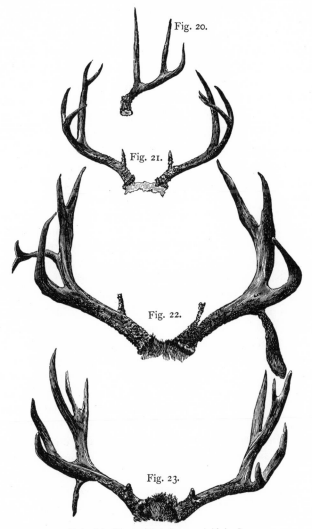

Fig. 20.

Fig. 21.

Fig. 22.

Fig. 23.

Columbia Black-tailed Deer and Mule Deer.

20. Abnormal Form of Antler from Black-tailed Deer.
21. Normal Form of Antler from Black-tailed Deer from California.
22. Normal Form of Antler from Black-tailed Deer from California, with an Abnormal Diseased Tine on the Left Antler.
23. Normal Form of Antler from Mule Deer from the Black Hills, with an Abnormal Tine on the Right Antler.

exactly alike they are in general features. I express the confident opinion that no one, no matter how long and carefully he may study the subject, can ever decide by their inspection from which species either came; while he will readily determine that they grew on no other species of deer.

There is, however, another form of antler sometimes met with on both the Columbia and the Mule deer, much more resembling the antler of the Virginia deer, and which one who had not carefully studied them might readily mistake for the antler of the latter. One of these in my collection is from a Columbia Deer, killed near the Calaveras grove of big trees, in the Sierra Nevadas, and is shown in Fig. 20, and another specimen is now on a two year old Mule Deer in my grounds; they are his second antlers, the first having been medium sized spike antlers. Those on the Mule Deer are about the same size as those from the Columbia Deer, which were probably also from a young animal. They are considerably smaller than the usual size of the antlers grown on the adult of both these species. From this we might be led to the conclusion that this exceptional form is usually grown on young animals, and it may be so, but it certainly is not always so, for there is a skeleton of a fully adult Mule Deer in the museum of the Chicago Medical College, which has this form of antler with all its peculiarities; nor do the young males always have this form of antler, for as we have seen, I had a Mule Deer with dag antlers which were forked, with tines of equal lengths; and I have seen many specimens not fully adult, with antlers of the usual form grown on these species. This exceptional form of antler for its lower part has a posterior inclination, and then curves anteriorly like the beam of the Virginia deer, but the radius of the curve is much longer than that on the latter animal; nor does the upper part of the beam ever point so directly forward. If this form of the beam is ever found on the Virginia deer it must be very exceptional, for I have never observed it. The next departure from the antler of the Virginia deer is in the basal snag, which is much smaller, corresponding in size with that on the usual bifurcated antler. The tines are all projected posteriorly from the beam, like those on the Virginia deer, but they are proportionally much longer, are not curved, and are of a different form. On the common deer if the tines are flattened at all it is at their base, where they always show their greatest diameters. On the others the lower part of the tine is always round, one quarter or one third of the way up, where it flattens out into something of a triangular form, so that it there shows a larger diameter than below. As we proceed toward the point, however, it gradually resumes the cylindrical form, so that its upper part is again round. This form is more observable on the lower tine than on those above it. On all the specimens I have met with the beam is round, while on the Virginia deer the beam is frequently flattened, having a lateral compression.

Altogether the careful observer will have little trouble in distinguishing this exceptional form of the antlers of these deer from those of the Virginia deer, although the resemblance is very strong in some of their features. Indeed, the basal snag alone would in most cases be sufficient to distinguish them beyond a doubt. To me it was an interesting fact to observe that not only the antlers of the ordinary form on these two species are indistinguishable from each other, but that on both are sometimes found this exceptional form, having the same peculiarities which distinguish it from that of the Virginia deer. This form is not by any means anomalistic, for when it occurs it conforms to those described, and so seems to obey an established law, but it is simply unusual. The Mule Deer in my grounds whose first antlers after the spikes were of this exceptional form, the next year had antlers of the same form, and had he lived we may conclude would always have had them. So we may strongly suspect it is a characteristic of the individual. I wish I knew if it is hereditary.

In comparing this unusual antler with that of the Virginia deer, I find that the tubercles found on both, for some distance above the burrs, are nearly all confined on the former to the upper side while the lower side is quite smooth, as is usually the case on those of the ordinary bifurcated form, while on the antler of the Virginia deer the tubercles are found on the lower as well as the upper side, and are larger and more abundant than on either form from the Mule Deer or the Columbia Deer.

What has been already said must give some idea of the peculiar characteristics of the antlers of *C. Virginianus,* — our Common Deer.

They are in form quite unlike those of any other of the genus, unless it be the exceptional form of the antlers of the mule and the Columbia deer, already described. Their great characteristic, which distinguishes them from the antlers of all the other Cervidæ, except as before stated, is that all the normal tines have a posterior projection. This necessitates a peculiar shape of the beam in order to present these tines to the adversary to make them efficient weapons of offense or defense in their battles.

Generally the antler of the Virginia Deer arises from the pedicel in the facial line spreading more or less to the basal snag. From that point it commences to curve upward and forward, and then downward and inward, till the extremities of the beams remotely approach each other. This enables the animal by bowing his head in battle, as is his habit, to present the tines to the adversary in front. When two meet in the shock of battle thus armed, these antlers form so complete a shield that I have never known a point to reach an adversary, as will be seen when we

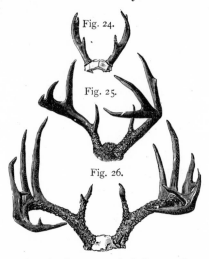

24. Acapulco Deer.   25 and 26, Common Deer.

come to describe their mode of warfare. The basal snag starts about two inches above the burr and rises to the height of from two to five inches at an angle of from fifteen to thirty degrees to the beam. This snag is usually more covered with tubercles than the tines above, and on very large specimens from aged animals is sometimes bifurcated, and sometimes flattened as in Fig. 26; sometimes a small supplemental snag occurs near the base, and I have occasionally observed one or more of the tubercles of the burr extend to snags an inch long. Usually from one to half a dozen tines occur on each antler, the lower ones being the longest and largest; on very large specimens some of these tines may produce snags, or a snag may arise from the beam at about the same point where a tine occurs. On the smaller specimens, the tines usually correspond on the two antlers on the same head, but as the animal grows older and the antlers larger this is less likely to be the case, though if one antler has an extraordinary number of points, the other is quite sure to have an unusual number also.

A very common idea has prevailed among hunters and frontiersmen that the number of tines on the antlers of the deer indicate its age, each point representing a year. This certainly is a popular error, though it approximates the truth more with young animals than with old ones. The most that can be said is, that the older the animal the more prongs are likely to occur on the antlers. In domestication, I have never seen one grown with more than five points. I have, however, in my collection two pairs of antlers of the Common Deer, both of which were killed in this vicinity (La Salle County, Ill.) in 1848, which are of nearly equal size, and the largest I ever remember to have seen. The antlers of the one which fell to my own rifle weigh five pounds and eleven ounces ; each antler has six points besides the stub of a broken prong on the left antler. The other, killed by Mr. Mackey, weigh five pounds and one ounce. The right antler has eleven points, and the left twelve. Thus we see that the largest antlers have but about half the number of points that are found on the smaller ones. On each of these antlers the basal snag is bifurcated, which only occurs on the largest specimens. One of the prongs of the basal snag of the left of the largest antlers is five inches in length. The size and positions of these basal snags would almost entitle them to the name of brow-tines, although ordinarily that term would be quite inappropriate to this member on the antlers of the Virginia, the mule, or the black-tailed deer.

Many abnormal growths of the antlers of the Common Deer are to be met with, one of which now in my collection is illustrated on p. 226, and was referred to when considering the mode of growth of antlers. In these we see there is no beam, but they consist entirely of tines and snags starting out from the circumference of the bases of the antlers. The bases of these tines constitute rims of depressions forming cups, each of which would hold a quantity of water, and so in this regard resemble the crown antler of the red deer and wapiti. Others have the appearance of two beams arising from the same pedicel with an uncommon system of snags or tines. Probably all of these cases are due to accidental injuries, either to the pedicel or to the antler in its early growth, as was no doubt the case with the spike antler on the deer in Lincoln Park, which has proved so destructive a weapon in battle, with which he killed all the other

15

bucks in the park. If the injury was to the pedicel, disarrang-
ing the nutrient vessels within it, we might expect that all subsequent antlers grown on it would be deformed. If the injury
was simply to the antler in its early growth, then it would have
no influence on that of the next year's growth.

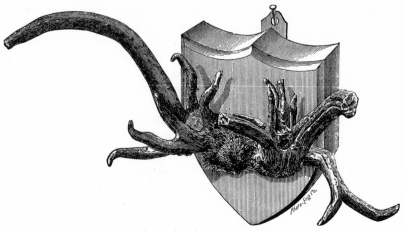

Abnormal Antlers of Common Deer.

I ought not to close this part of my subject without referring
to three fossil antlers in my collection, found in the lower drift in
the valley of the Fox River, near Ottawa, Illinois. Here has
been an upheaval which elevated the coal measures, and exposed
all to the action of the great currents which sweep southward,
and which carried away everything, down to the St. Peter's sand-
stone, except in a few places where, for a few hundred acres,
the lower vein of coal remains. Over this sometimes a portion
of the soapstone remains, and in others it is gone. Where these
fossils were found, about two feet of the soapstone remained in
place over the coal; the deep furrows on the top of which show
plainly the glacial action, or rather the plowings of the icebergs,
which drifted down with the great current and grounded two or
three miles lower down, where the extent and forms of many may
now be seen and traced, by the clusters of great bowlders which
they left when they melted away, as plainly as if marked on a
map. After this denudation there was deposited a stratum of
gravel six inches thick and above that, more than sixteen feet
first of sand and gravel, then sand, then sand and clay, then clay,
and lastly, surface loam. In this lowest stratum of gravel, which

was the first deposit after the icebergs had ceased to drift, and the denuding process was finished, these antlers were found, in positions showing beyond doubt that they were drifted in with the gravel. They were not found together but at considerable distances apart, and are from different animals. In the same vein of gravel are found a considerable variety of fossil woods; several specimens of which I have submitted to the inspection of the learned professor, Leo Lasquereaux, who, forty years ago, examined the peat-beds of Denmark, and distinguished the successive generations of trees there deposited, which had grown, flourished, decayed, and disappeared, leaving only that decayed record of their having once existed in a land where for unknown ages they have been entire strangers. These he finds to be arborescent conifers which are not now found nearer than the regions of Lake Superior, and oaks which are now flourishing here but are not growing there.

Two of these fossil antlers exhibit all the peculiar characteristics of the antlers of the Virginia Deer now inhabiting this country in the most pronounced form : one from a fully adult animal and the other about four years old. They had both been dropped in the course of nature. The other presents but about six inches of the lower part of the beam and before any of the tines had occurred, and so it may not be identified with certainty. The basal snag is rudimentary, and the beam is straighter than is usual on the Virginia Deer. And in these respects it resembles the exceptional form of the antler of the mule deer and the Columbia deer, but it is not safe to declare that it did grow on a deer of one of these species.

In the same locality and at the same depth, in a pocket of clay deposited in the lower stratum of gravel, I found nearly the entire skeleton of a female Virginia deer. With great pains I have compared these bones individually with the bones of a fully adult female Common Deer that died in my grounds, and can discover no appreciable difference in size or form. They are as nearly identical as possible throughout. These were evidently deposited at a later period than were the antlers.

We learn from those relics that our Common Deer was an inhabitant of our elevated plains or at least of a region north of us, soon after the waters left them and while this great valley from a mile and a half to two miles wide and more than one hundred feet deep was yet filled with the great current which swept down from the north and brought with it and deposited the first drift, after the more rapid current with its icebergs had swept off most of the surface material down to the bed rock, — the St. Peter's sand-stone, — and at the same time the oaks and the conifers which formed his shelter. I am not aware that we have satisfactory evidence that any other of our existing fauna lived here, even at that time. So far as the proof goes, we may pronounce our deer the oldest of our extant fauna. The late Dr. J. W. Foster carefully examined the locality with me, and he pronounced it the oldest of the valley drift which had deposited these remains, and considered the find of the highest geological interest.

The antlers of the Acapulco Deer, which is the smallest of all our North American species, are widely separated from those of either of the other species both in size and form. I have but one pair of these in my collection from an adult, though I have several from young bucks. The large ones were from an animal that died of old age in the park of Governor Latham in California, to whom I am indebted for a female of the same species.

It is unfortunate that I have not antlers from a considerable number of full grown bucks of this species so that I could feel a confident assurance that I am presenting typical characteristics. Now there is a bare possibility, that the antlers before me are exceptional in their forms. However, in describing this single pair we may provisionally assume that the peculiarities are characteristic of the species, admitting that there may be minor differences in individuals, as we observe with all the others. They are illustrated in Fig. 24, on p. 224.

These antlers spring from pedicels of unusual height for their size, which at their tops are two and one half inches apart. The extreme length of these antlers is seven inches and three lines and above the burr the circumference of each is two inches and nine lines where they are nearly round, but they very soon assume a triangular shape, and at two inches above the burrs from the inner side of the beams, the basal snags arise. That on the right antler is one inch in length and on the left it is nine lines long. Above these snags, the antlers flatten out from the triangular form into distinct palms, increasing in width and diminishing in thickness to their ends, which are notched, the right deeply and the left slightly. At the broadest part, just below the notch, the right antler is one inch and ten lines wide, and the left is one inch and seven lines wide. The beam above the notch, which is an extension of the posterior edge of the palm, extends two inches and three lines to the point on the right antler, and on the left one and one half inches. The anterior edge of the palm is thickest and it thins down gradually to the posterior edge, which is sharp for its whole length. The compression is lateral. The directions of the antlers for the lower half are outward, then they gracefully curve in slightly inward directions, when they approach each other for the upper half, so that the points are but four and one half inches apart, while at the point of widest separation they are six inches and ten lines asunder.

No tubercles appear above the burrs, but the longitudinal channels for the arteries of the periosteum are very distinct. There are no tines proper on these antlers, but the basal snags are unusually developed for the size of the antlers. The notches at the ends present distinct points, so that we may be justified in saying that each antler presents three points. These antlers are remarkably stout for their length and worn quite smooth by abrasion.

These antlers, it will be observed, are much more palmate than any of the others, except the moose and the caribou, which this deer also resembles, as we have already seen, in the absence of the metatarsal gland; and so in another important feature, also, we see these extremes meet where they widely differ from the intermediate species.

On a young buck which I have of this species, the first antlers were deformed from injuries. The second antlers are two and one half inches long, with a rudimentary basal snag, showing as yet no tendency to flatten. I have another pair from a two-year old buck much smaller than these, but with the same characteristics.

The antlers on the Ceylon buck in my grounds, which in size, form, and color, most resembles the Acapulco deer, may not be entirely neglected. Those of the first pair grown on this buck after I got him are considerably smaller than those first described; they are straighter and much more cylindrical, although they show a little disposition to flatten towards the ends.

But the most striking feature is a long brow-tine in place of the basal snag. This tine is stout and nearly half the length of the antler.

The second antlers grown on this buck in my grounds more

nearly resemble those from the Acapulco deer, while they resemble the first in most of their characteristics, except that the long tine is now reduced to a snag scarcely more than an inch long, and the left antler is more flattened at the end. These are more fully considered under the title " Analogues."

Mr. Darwin, the distinguished naturalist, when preparing his celebrated work, " The Descent of Man," for the press, asked me for my observations as to the utility to the animal of the branched forms of the antlers of the Cervidæ. This is a question certainly not easily solved, and yet the mode of warfare of these animals may serve to throw some light on the subject.

The mode of joining battle, as we shall see in another place, with all the cervine species, is with a tremendous rush together. Some species fall back and repeat the rush many times, like the ram, while others, after they thus meet continue pressing and worrying each other, maneuvering to break each other's foil. Now if the antlers on each presented but single points, death to one or both the combatants would almost surely ensue upon the first collision, and thus would the species soon become exterminated.

There was in the fall of 1875, in Lincoln Park, a Virginia buck five years old, whose left antler was a spike about ten inches long with a largely developed basal snag, while the right antler was of the ordinary form and size. The keeper informed me that this buck had killed the two others in the same enclosure, the last but the day before my visit, and that it was this sharp, straight spike which did the mischief. Always before, the antlers of this buck had been of the ordinary form and size, with which he had never injured the other deer. He thought the singular growth was due to an injury to the antler in the early stage of its growth.

The many branches with which the antler of the deer is provided, undoubtedly impair its efficiency as a weapon of attack, but they convert it into a shield which effectually foils the blow from a similar weapon, though it may not certainly ward off a blow from a single shaft. I have never yet known an instance, except in the case of the spike antler, in which either combatant received a wound in these sudden onsets. The battle is won by persistent endurance, or by some accident or want of skill or agility which exposes one to the reach of the other. If the branched antler is a disadvantage to the individual, there can be no doubt that it contributes largely to the well being, the preservation, and the improvement of the race. The most vigorous and active males are still left masters of the field and so become the progenitors of succeeding generations.

It has long been a prevalent opinion among hunters, and to some extent has been adopted by naturalists, that a race of common deer the adults of which have antlers without branches, have established themselves in the northeastern part of the United States and in Canada, whence they are driving out the prong-antlered bucks.

This is a matter of the greatest scientific importance, and I have taken pains to investigate it to my satisfaction, and am entirely convinced that it is a popular error, founded upon incomplete observations. The *spike bucks* found in the Adirondacks are all yearling bucks with their first antlers. The universal testimony, so far as I have been able to gather it, is, that they are smaller than the average of the prong-antlered bucks, and that their spikes vary in length from eight inches, or ten inches at the very utmost, down to two or three inches in length. It is only the largest of these, that any have claimed to be adults. It is very easy for a hunter to say, and even believe, that he has killed deer with spikes ten inches long, but did he actually measure them, and make a note of the fact, with time and place, describing its appearance, and take and note the measurements of the animal, or did he preserve the head, so that he could carefully examine it, after the excitement of the chase was over, or so that he could submit it to the examination of others? I have never heard of such a case; such a head and antlers would bring more than many times the value of the largest carcasses ever sent to market. It is never safe for an observer to guess at dimensions, but he should always resort to measurements, and even then he must not trust his memory. All observations should be noted down on the spot and at the time, even while the eye is upon the object, and be sure that every important fact is stated. He who waits till he gets to camp to make his notes, is sure to make them of little value. The very act of noting down our observations, leads us to notice many important things, which would otherwise be entirely overlooked. If hunters and anglers would generally provide themselves with note books and measure, and whenever they kill an interesting specimen would make careful measurements and minute notes of them, they would soon educate themselves into excellent naturalists, and would add vastly to our fund of reliable zoölogical knowledge, and I trust the time is coming when sportsmen will generally adopt this course. In this way, they will double the pleasures of the chase, and when they meet in the camp or at the club house, to recount their triumphs and compare their observations, they will enjoy an intellectual treat, far surpassing the story of the simple score or the skillful shot.

But let us return to the consideration of the spike buck. I repeat, so far as I know, we have no well authenticated, reliable observations to justify the conclusion that these spike antlers are ever grown upon adult animals. All we have on the subject is a sort of general conjecture, founded no doubt upon exceptional cases.

Continued observations upon the young deer in my parks, have enlightened me much on this subject. For several years, I really persuaded myself that I had the true spike-antlered bucks, and set myself to carefully note their peculiarities, and fondly believed that I was about to add an important chapter to scientific knowledge. But these careful and continued observations soon undeceived and disappointed me. By marking the spike buck of one year, which was as large as one feeding by his side, having two or three tines on each antler, I found the next year that his antlers were also branched, and my spike-antlered buck had become a fine specimen of the ordinary kind. And then the early fawn of the year before, dropped from a fully adult vigorous doe, which had furnished him plenty of milk, had now grown to the size of a medium adult, and had fine spike antlers, resembling in all things his older brother of the preceding year now bearing the pronged antlers. And so I anxiously pursued my observations for a number of years, ever looking in vain for a second antler without prongs. Without this certain means of knowledge, I should have believed that those large spike-antlered bucks were more than yearlings and nearly adult. It is true the dentition might have undeceived me, but this I could not ascertain while the animal was alive, and this test has probably been rarely examined and carefully studied by those hunters, who believe they have killed adult deer, with spike antlers. I feel quite sure that they had not the means of accurately determining the true ages of the wild deer which they had killed; and what I have already stated may serve to show how very liable all are to be misled in relation to a point, upon a certain knowledge of which the whole question depends.

I think the evidence satisfactory to establish the fact, that in a few instances female Virginia deer have been killed having small spike antlers, and I have noticed an account of one in California, probably a Columbia deer. One example is found in the Smithsonian collection which I have had an opportunity of studying. The antlers are on low, small pedicels. They are in the velvet, but appear to have been nearly matured. They are about six inches in length and half an inch in diameter, and have a graceful anterior curvature, and spread apart less than is usual on the spiked buck. The spike on the perfect buck is always straight, so far as my observations extend, and I have examined hundreds, I presume, so that this anterior curvature distinguishes it from the spike on the male. I have, however, noticed a similar curvature on the velvet antler of a castrated buck, where the operation was performed when he carried his spike antlers, and had I met with this specimen without information that it was from a female, I should have concluded it was from a young castrated buck. But I am willing to accept the statement that it was from a female.

Such an occurrence may be as probable as that a woman should have a full flowing beard, which we sometimes, though very rarely, see.

I have noticed many other accounts in sporting papers and in the journals of the day, of antlered does having been killed, and if mention was made of their form and condition, they were always small spike antlers and in the velvet; and the periods when the notices appeared would indicate that they were killed when the antlers on the bucks had perfected their external growth and lost their velvet. Now this has suggested to me the possibility, that when the antler is found upon the doe, it is still of an imperfect growth, like the antlers upon the castrated buck, so that it never matures so far as to lose its velvet, and that in winter it is frozen and broken off without being shed as is the antler of the perfect buck. It may not be improbable that these antlered does will always be found to be barren. My observations upon the effect of castration on the growth of the antlers of the buck, show that there is an intimate connection between the reproductive organs and the growth of antlers, and so it is not unreasonable to suppose, that the phenomenon of antlers upon a female deer may arise from some peculiarity in the ovaries, or some other of the genital organs.

I make these suggestions more with the hope that those who may have the opportunity, may be induced to make careful observations on the subject, than for any other value which they may possess.

TAILS.

The tails of the deer have been mostly described when treating of the different species separately, so that now a little repetition may become unavoidable when it becomes necessary to compare them.

As the tails of the three largest species (Figs. 8, 9, 10) most resemble each other, and are quite unlike those of any of the other species, we will treat of them first and together. The tail of the Moose is longer than that of either of the other three, and is longer and larger than that of its European congener. Audubon and Bachman give us the measurements of two, one of which was eleven and one half inches, and the other nine inches long. Should we take these for a fair average, we find them much longer than those of the Wapiti. Both are carried closely depressed, though that of the Moose is the most utilized. The tail of our Elk is never elevated, and rarely moved at all, whether standing at ease or going at their best speed. Flies or mosquitoes may annoy

1. Tail of Common Deer. 2, 3, and 4. Tails of Mule Deer at Different Ages. 5, Side View, and 6, Vertical View of Tail of Black-tailed Deer. 7. Tail of Acapulco Deer. 8. Tail of Caribou. 9. Tail of Wapiti or Elk. 10. Tail of Moose.

them never so much, still the tail remains quiet, while they may be stamping with their feet or thrashing about the head in a frantic way.

On both these animals the tails are round; on the Moose they are somewhat tapering, while on the Elk the tail is of a uniform diameter, with an abrupt termination.

The tail of the Caribou is something longer than that of the Elk. It is somewhat flattened, very broad at the base, tapering all the way to the end. It is very short for so large an animal, but is more active than on the Elk.

On the Moose the color of the tail varies from very light to dark brown.

The tail of the Caribou is of a dark shade on top, approaching a brown, and on some specimens it is decidedly so.

On all the smaller species the tail is found to be a prominent, and to some extent, a useful member. Each has a tail constructed on a plan peculiarly its own, by which it may be readily distinguished, and by this mark alone may the species be identified. While each may vary from the others in length, all are of sufficient size to harmonize with the general structure of the animal.

The largest of this group, and the one which we shall first consider, is the Mule Deer. In many respects this tail differs from all the others of the species, and its individualities are such as to identify it at once and everywhere.

In my earlier studies I was led into some erroneous conclusions as to the tail of this deer, which I have been able to correct by subsequent observations.

The most striking peculiarities and which first strike the observer, are that it is of a yellowish white color except a tuft at the lower end which is black, and for most of the way it is naked on the under side; the color of this tail is a shade the lightest on the under side bordering the naked part.

There are two varieties of the Mule Deer. The eastern or Rocky Mountain variety I shall first consider. While in color the tails of different specimens are quite alike, in form they are quite variant. Most are large at the base, tapering to small dimensions to the limit of the white hair, and then terminating with a large black tuft.

This form is most observable on the aged animals. In other specimens the white hairs are nearer of a uniform length, so that very little taper is observed. In these specimens the white hairs overlap the upper part of the black so as to hide a portion of it. This condition usually occurs in the fall of the year and on young animals not more than three or four years old. The former condition is, to some extent at least, artificial. It results from those white hairs near the lower part of the tail becoming worn off so that they are shorter. This is rendered possible from the white hairs being open, spongy, non-elastic, and brittle, so that they are readily broken off by coming in contact with objects when the tail is moved by the animal. Those hairs near the upper end of the tail are less exposed to abrasion than those lower down and near the end. The black hairs composing the switch are different. They are quite solid, firm, and elastic, like those on the tail of the horse, and so can bear a great amount of friction without being broken off. They endure the violence, while the white hairs just above them become worn down short. The two extremes and an intermediate form are shown in the illustrations. Figs. 2, 3, 4, p. 234.

Independent of this abrasion there is in most specimens a certain degree of taper resulting from the fact that on them the white hairs are shorter on the lower than on the upper part of the tail. On aged specimens these white hairs are more brittle than on younger animals, hence they are worn shorter on them and so present a much more tapering form.

Take a specimen about the first of August, when the old white hairs are nearly shed and the new ones are still short, and above the black tuft the tail is very small all the way up, while the black hairs which are constant, like those on the tail of the horse, remain conspicuous throughout the year. These black hairs are generally shorter and stand in a more radical position on the old specimens than on the young. On the young, that which is worn off of the black hairs is replaced by new growth which is more vigorous on the young than the old; on the latter the growth is tardy and does not fully repair the loss, so that on the young the black tuft appears longer and of less diameter than on the old.

I have said that the under side of the tail of the Mule Deer is naked down to near the end, like the horse's tail. This is not absolutely so, for even the on young specimens a careful inspection will reveal to the naked eyes a number of scattering very short fine hairs, more abundant towards the lower end of the naked space ; these grow somewhat larger as the animal grows older, but are always kept worn short, so that on old specimens the lower part of the naked portion exhibits a good many short stubs of hairs, of almost the diameter of the hairs on the upper side, which they are like in color and texture.

The black hairs cover from one eighth to one tenth of the vertebræ at its extremity, and as before stated are not shed with the general coat as are the white hairs on the rest of the tail. This black portion is clothed as abundantly on the lower as on the upper side. Altogether the characteristics of the tail of this deer are so peculiar that any one of the least observation can readily distinguish it in any of its forms, at any season of the year or at any age.

I have only had in domestication six specimens, taken wild, of which three were of each sex. They exhibited these several forms, but the specimens killed by hunters which I have examined showed greater extremes than those in my own grounds, especially did they show the hairs more worn off on the parts most exposed ; that is, I have found on the wild animals tails more tapering from the upper end down to the black tuft and on the oldest and largest the most so. I think the males show this more than the females.

These tails always appear to be round. Even the absence of hairs on the under side fails to give them the flat appearance always seen on the Virginia deer. By measurements, taken on a female Mule Deer four years old in my grounds, I find the diameter of the tail at the base, measuring from the ends of the hairs in their natural position, is two and one half inches, and five inches lower down I find the diameter to be one and one half inches. The diameter of the tuft of black hairs corresponds with that at the base of the tail.

Another specimen in my collection (Fig. 2), from a very large buck killed in the Black Hills, shows that the diameters are nearly half an inch less at all the points indicated, which gives the tail a much more tapering appearance than the first. The length of the vertebræ of this tail is eight and one half inches, while the black hairs extend three and one half inches further, making the tail twelve inches long. I have another specimen in which the vertebræ is five and one half inches long, while it is fully ten inches to the end of the black hairs. This was from a young animal killed early in the season. The white hairs are but little worn down, and they overlap the black hairs for more than half their length, so that the black tuft is no larger than the white hairs above it, but there is a gradual though slight taper all the way from the base to and including the black tuft in its

largest part ; thence it tapers to a point. I have in my grounds a
Mule buck in his second year, whose tail in December was almost
the counterpart of this. In the latter part of winter it was considerably diminished in size towards the lower portion of the
white, showing the tapering form down to the black tuft. In
July following, the white hairs were nearly all shed, leaving the
tail scarcely larger than one's finger, while the tuft of black hairs
maintained its original bigness. The vertebræ was six inches
long, and to the end of the tuft the tail was ten inches long.

On the California variety of this deer, the tail has nearly the
same form but averages a little longer. Its great distinction is
in the color of the tail, which alone is sufficient to declare it a
very distinct variety, were other indicia, which are plainly de-
clared, wanting. It has the naked portion on the under side the
same as the eastern variety, but instead of all being white above
the black tuft at the end, a stripe of the color of the back above
the tail, with which it unites, runs down the upper side of the
tail and unites with the terminal black tuft. On some specimens
this brown stripe grows darker towards the lower end, and on
some the tawny brown shade of the stripe invades the black tuft.

Ordinarily the tail of the Mule Deer is carried depressed, close
to the body. In running it is elevated a little but not generally
above the horizontal; but when the male is very happy and feels
very self-important he will strut about with the tail elevated to
a vertical position or inclining a little forward, reminding one of
the actions of the male goat when he feels his self-importance in
a high degree. This is peculiar to the Mule Deer, certainly among
the American species.

It is to be regretted that this deer, with more of a white tail
than any other of our deer, — with in fact a white tail tipped with
black, — is universally called by the hunters of the Rocky Mountains *the Black-tailed Deer*. As they know nothing of the true
black-tailed deer of the Pacific Slope, it creates no local incon-
venience, but whenever one's inquiries extend west of this locality confusion necessarily results. Whether this inappropriate
local name will ever be given up by those who do not extend
their observations beyond that region, I very much doubt.

The tail of the Columbia Deer is peculiar and characteristic of
the animal, and shows the appropriateness of the name given it
by Lewis and Clarke, of *Black-tailed Deer*. It is short, or about
the length of the tail of the mule deer. It is very nearly straight,

though a slight upward and then reversed curve may be observed. It is an active member that is capable of being whisked about, though it is not much used in that way. The position in which the tail is carried is in marked contrast to that of all the other deer. This position is not vertical or depressed against the body, but it stands out in a drooping or inclined position about in a line with the backbone, from the top of the hips posteriorly, or perhaps a few degrees more depressed.

In form the tail is round, terminating with a sharp but abrupt tip, the point of which is on a line with the lower side of the tail or a little depressed. It is covered all around with hairs of nearly a uniform length, giving it the form described.

On top and on the sides at the lower end for half its length the tail is black. Thence upward the ends of a part of the hairs become tipped for a quarter of an inch or more with a tawny shade. The number of these increase rapidly as we ascend in the examination, and the bodies of the hairs become lighter, especially on the lower half, until near the root of the tail the lower half of the hair becomes a light gray, then intervenes a considerably darker shade, terminating with the tawny tip which gives a reddish cast to the upper portion of the tail. The under side of the tail is white, near the root fully one half of the circumference ; but a little lower down, not more than one quarter of the circumference is white, so that we may properly say that there is a white stripe along the under side of the tail which is bordered by a russet streak on each side along the lower half more conspicuous towards the end, and as these russet hairs and even some of the white ones are longer than the black, the extreme point of the tail is a tawny white. A careful inspection shows that the hairs attached to the lower side of the last inch of the vertebræ are all black, with different degrees of intensity on their outer parts and the inner portions white or tawny, whereas above that point the white hairs maintain that color the whole length. The tail tapers slightly and has a slight upward curve, as shown in the illustration.

The above descriptions are from the only four I have, one male and three females now in my grounds, whose tails are almost exactly alike ; yet I have a number of specimens which I obtained from dried skins at Victoria, B. C., and Portland, Oregon, some of which are considerably longer and a little more pointed at the ends. Still all hold their bigness with great uniformity to very near the extreme ends, and in this respect differ very much from the Virginia deer.   In color, I cannot perceive any appreciable difference between my live specimens and those obtained at Victoria and Portland.

The white between the hams, under the tail of this deer, is wider than the tail itself, so that when looking at the deer from behind, it is seen about one inch broad on each side of the tail for its whole length.

The tail of the Virginia Deer exceeds in length that of any other of our deer.   It varies very much on different adult individuals, on some being not more than eleven or twelve inches long, while on others it is found to be sixteen or even eighteen inches in length.   In shape it is flattened, being the broadest a little posterior to its base ; thence it contracts in width gradually and quite regularly to a point at the end, giving it a lanceolate form, as shown in the illustration.

On the under side and on the edges it is always white, but on top it is very variant in color.   I have some specimens in my grounds which are jet black for the lower half, growing lighter towards the anterior or upper part by the interspersion of gray hairs with the black, which become more abundant anteriorly. These very black specimens are quite rare, but a majority have more or less black towards the extremities.   Very many, however, have no black upon them, but are of a tawny gray on top. Scarcely any two are exactly of the same shade of color, some being of an exceedingly light gray on top, and between these and the black every intermediate shade is to be found.

The blackest specimens are met with east of the Mississippi River.   In the Rocky Mountains and west of them, the lightest colored specimens are met with, and I have never met with one there with any black upon it.   Hence in that region they are called the White-tailed Deer.   In the northwest they have been called the Long-tailed Deer, not, I imagine, because the tails there are longer than on the same species east, but because they have longer tails than any other deer in that region.

When viewed posteriorly, the white of the edges shows distinctly as a border to the colored portion on top.   And when the tail is elevated and the hairs radiate in excitement, nothing but the white is seen, except from an anterior view.   The natural position of the tail is depressed or vertical.   When the animal is excited, as by seeing a dog, for instance, the tail is elevated to a horizontal position, and the hairs become radiate, while the animal is standing deliberating whether to run or not ; and so it is when the deer approaches an object in a threatening way. When it runs away in fright, it generally raises the tail to a vertical position, the hairs still spread out so as to much enlarge its appearance. This, however, is by no means universally the case. They frequently run at full speed with the tail as much depressed as when quietly standing. I have often observed a lot of a dozen or twenty when alarmed, running from one part of the park to another to escape a supposed danger, and usually have seen one, or perhaps several, with the tails depressed. Indeed, a larger proportion will have the flag elevated when running at a moderate speed than when apparently doing their best.

When a Virginia Deer is wounded, he almost invariably drops his tail and runs with it pendent, or if much hurt, he will lash it from side to side, and by this, more than any other indication, the hunter determines the extent of the injury inflicted by his shot. As the tail of the Virginia Deer is longer than that of any of the others, so it is more used or is more frequently in motion, but with all this the hairs are never perceptibly worn off as on the tail of the mule deer. All the hairs on the tail are much more solid, elastic, and enduring, than on the body.

No matter what the size or color of the tail of this deer, its flattened and lanceolate form and white borders will always declare its identity to even an indifferent observer.

As I have said, the tail of the Virginia Deer is flat and tapering to a point. The anterior part is twice as wide as it is thick. The white at the under side and the borders occupies fully two thirds of the circumference of the tail.

The tail of the Acapulco Deer more resembles that of the Virginia deer than any of the others ; yet it has its distinctive characteristics. While it is considerably flattened, it is not as much so as on the common deer, yet much more so than on any of the others. By reference to the illustration it will be seen that it does not taper regularly from the root to the point, but nearly maintains its width till near the end and then tapers rapidly to a much more blunt point.

The under side is pure white, but this does not extend around the sides or edges so it can be seen from a posterior view as on the common deer when the position of the tail is depressed, but only the colored portion which pervades the top of the tail is seen.

16

I have already stated that the color of this species is very variant on different individuals, from a dark russet gray to a russet brown; and the same is true of the color of the upper part of the tail, — some are decidedly brown, approaching a dull black, which is more pronounced on the lower part, while others are of a light tawny shade, with no part black or even brown. The length of the tail may be stated at eight inches.

The position of the tail on the Acapulco Deer is usually closely depressed, and ordinarily is but little raised from this when running, especially when pursuing the other deer to amuse itself. It is more frequently raised when fleeing from supposed danger, but not as much as is usual with the common deer. When excited the hairs are radiated as on the common deer.

I am unable to distinguish any appreciable difference between the tail of the Acapulco deer and that of the Ceylon deer.

On the tails of all the deer the hair is shed but once in the year, which process is gradual and occurs in the summer time, while, as stated, the black switch on the Mule Deer is not shed at all.

THE FOOT.

The forms of the hoofs of the different species of the deer may receive our attention for a short time. I have found them so dependent on circumstances that it is not practicable at all times to determine to which of several species a given specimen belonged. This is more particularly the case with the smaller species; that is, those less in size than the caribou, at the head of which stands the Mule Deer. If the hoofs on these smaller species differ somewhat in the proportions of length to breadth, still in general configurations they are alike, and the difference in their proportions is so slight that observers do not always agree in their conclusions.

Those inhabiting rocky or gravelly ground become worn down so as to change their size and proportions, as compared with those which live on the prairies and travel principally on the soft grass. When examining a specimen, therefore, it is necessary to inquire as the character of the country which it inhabited. This is no doubt the principal cause of disagreement among observers, as to the form and extent of the hoofs of the different species. When all are grown in the same place, as in a park for instance, then the equality of condition renders our observations of more value than when they are limited to wild animals.

The form of the foot combines with other causes elsewhere mentioned to establish a line, which separates our deer into two divisions.

The first, embracing the moose, the wapiti, and the two species of caribou, which have shorter, broader, and flatter hoofs than the second, which embraces the mule deer, the Columbia deer, the Virginia deer, and the Acapulco deer, which have higher, longer, and narrower feet.

The hoofs of the Moose are not remarkably large, considering the size of the animal, and would seem to be less than would be convenient for him in the deep snows of winter and the soft marshy grounds which he affects in summer. They are not long but broad, and convex at the outer edges. They spread only less than those of the caribou. The hoofs themselves are not rigidly attached, but have considerable involuntary motion, when the foot is lifted from the ground, especially if the animal is traveling fast, so that they strike together at every step, producing a loud clacking noise, which the hunters used to ascribe to the cracking of the joints.

The hind hoofs or dew claws, as they are often called in this country, are rather loosely attached and are far apart. The foot has more spread than any of the other species, except the caribou.

Our Elk has a neat and well shaped foot, longer and narrower than the ox in proportion to his size. It is convex at the lower outer edge. The false or hind hoofs are small and point well downward, never touching the ground unless it is very soft, so that the track is deeply impressed.

The foot of the Caribou has more remarkable characteristics than any other of the deer family, and is peculiarly adapted to sustain it in snows and in soft swampy ground. The hoof is large and very broad, maintaining its breadth well to the point. The cleft between the toes extends far up, and enables the foot to spread so as to expose a large bearing surface, so that the foot at some times appears nearly twice as large as at others, and the imprint in soft ground is so much larger than on a hard surface, as to require the eye of a practical hunter to recognize the track as made by the same animal. Each hoof is surrounded with an abundance of coarse stiff hairs extending quite down the cleft, which add to the bearing surface when the animal is traveling over soft material. The hind or accessory hoofs on this animal are of real use, which will be readily appreciated upon careful observation. These are larger than on any other quadruped of its size. Their position is more lateral than on the other species, which enables them when required by circumstances to add much to the bearing surface of the foot.

The following is Captain Hardy's description of the foot of the Woodland Caribou in the winter : " But for the Caribou I can aver that its foot is a beautiful adaptation to the snow-covered country in which it resides, and that on ice it has naturally an advantage similar to that obtained artificially by the skater. In winter time the frog is almost entirely absorbed, and the edges of the hoof, now quite concave, grow out in thin sharp ridges ; each division on the under surface presenting the appearance of a huge muscle shell. According to ' The Old Hunter,' who has kindly forwarded to me some specimens shot by him in New-foundland in the fall of 1867, for comparison with examples of my own shot in winter, the frog is absorbed by the latter end of November, when the lakes are frozen ; the shell grows with great rapidity, and the frog does not fill up again till spring, when the antlers bud out. With this singular conformation of the foot, its great lateral spread and the additional assistance afforded in maintaining a foothold on slippery surfaces by the long stiff bristles which grow downwards from the fetlock, curving upward underneath between the divisions, the Caribou is enabled to proceed over crusted snow, to cross frozen lakes, or ascend icy precipices, with an ease which places him, when in flight, beyond the reach of all enemies, except, perhaps, the nimble and untiring wolf." [1]

These judicious observations show the appreciative naturalist in the study of his subject, and should teach us not to pass by facts which appear to be unimportant as unworthy of our attention. In this case our author readily perceived their significance, and points out their importance in the economy of the animal. They show us how readily nature interposes to change structural formations to meet emergencies arising from peculiar conditions of life. We can readily understand how such a foot is required to secure safe and rapid locomotion in the winter season in the frigid zone and a rough and broken country, intersected by ice-bound lakelets and frozen streams. But these conditions only exist for a part of the year, and it is only during that season that the foot of the Caribou is made to conform to the exigencies which they impose. Upon the disappearance of the snow and ice, the sharp

[1] *Forest Life in Acadie*, pp. 129, 130.

and concave foot which these made necessary to the well-being of the animal, fills up with a more elastic substance, better adapting it to the conditions of its summer range.

If I do not quite agree with Captain Hardy that the frog of the foot of the Caribou disappears in the fall by absorption, still the fact which he first mentions, so far as I know, is none the less significant. My own observations incline me to think that the frog disappears by abrasion and detachment. By taking the foot of the Caribou with the full frog and soaking it in diluted alcohol, or even in a weak brine, we may observe that the frog is laminated or arranged in layers, and after a while it becomes almost as soft as muck, and may be all removed by the finger up to a hard horny crust, capable of resisting abrasion almost as effectually as the outside of the hoof, leaving the hoof a thin plate, senseless and elastic. My own conclusion is that this inner wall, which is less dense, and through which the blood-vessels pass during the summer, and nourish the frog during its growth and maturity, becomes more indurated towards fall, and finally gradually closes those blood-vessels, when for the want of nourishment the frog dies, and becomes a dead, inert substance, and then decay and destruction commence. This first occurs on the lower surface, where it is exposed to abrasion, and proceeds gradually till all is gone ; in the spring, when this peculiarity of the foot is no longer required, this plate, which constitutes the wall on which the frog is built, becomes softer, and allows the blood-vessels which pass through it to resume their functions, when the growth of the new frog is commenced, and proceeds rapidly till the foot is again filled with the rather soft, tough, and elastic mass, which comparative anatomists call the frog. The truth, however, can only be revealed by the microscope, and I now feel a self-reproach for leaving this undetermined. Others, I trust, will assume the task, who can perform it better than I can. These peculiarities in the feet of the Woodland Caribou I find even amplified in the Barren-ground Caribou. The hind feet are larger and broader than the fore feet. The hoofs on the hind feet of the former in my collection are two inches and six lines long at the cleft, and three inches broad, and measure five inches around the sharp edge from the point to the heel. The accessory hoof is two inches long, and one inch and six lines broad. In the accessory hoof the frog is but partially gone, but the edge is very sharp, especially at the point. The hoof of the fore foot is also two inches and six lines long, but is only two inches and three lines broad, and four inches around the outer edge. The accessory hoof on the fore foot is one inch and eleven lines long, and one inch and five lines broad. The edges are less worn or sharper on the fore feet than on the hind feet. It is evident that the hind feet are prepared for, and endure much the hardest service. On the fore feet the lower phalangeal bone, to which the accessory hoof is attached, is half an inch long above the hoof, the next, or upper phalangeal bone between the articulations, is ten lines long and six lines in diameter, and the splint, or accessory carpal bone, above the articulation, is three inches long and half an inch in diameter at the lower end, tapering to a blunt point at the upper end. This accessory carpal bone, which possesses an imperfect facet of articulation, is attached longitudinally to the carpal bone for its whole length by ligamentary tissue which admits of great vertical and lateral motion, thus facilitating the great spread of these members of the foot observed in the reindeer. All the bones connected with this accessory hoof in the reindeer, are more than ten times as large as they are in the common deer. This alone should convince us that real work is expected to be performed by this accessory hoof of the Caribou. These bones are appreciably larger and stouter in the hind foot than in the fore foot.

That we may compare the foot of the Barren-ground Caribou with that of the Woodland Caribou, I give the measurements of a fore foot of this last species in my collection. It is two inches and six lines long at the cleft, and is two inches and six lines broad ; measuring around the curved edge, it is four inches and nine lines.

When we remember that the Barren-ground is but half the size of his Woodland cousin, it will be observed that its foot is much the largest proportionally, and that the outer edge is much more convex, that is, it maintains its width towards the point much better, thus presenting more bearing surface in proportion to its length and greatest width. This peculiarity is very striking to the eye when they are viewed side by side. On the smaller animal the accessory hoof is, in fact, larger than on the other. On the specimen before me from the larger species, the accessory hoof is one inch and nine lines long, and one inch and six lines broad. This much greater bearing surface of the foot, it being about twice as large in proportion to the size of the animal, would seem to be required by the more northern and snowy region occupied by the deer. The hoofs of the hind foot of the wild reindeer from Norway, are at the cleft two inches long and are two inches and six lines broad, and measure around the curved edge three inches and six lines. The accessory hoof is one inch and nine lines long, and one inch and six lines broad. The accessory carpal bone is two inches and six lines long. This hoof corresponds in shape with that of our Woodland Caribou, with which the deer is specifically identical, and is of about the same proportionate size. I regret that I have no specimens of the Woodland Caribou from the northwest, where it reaches the frozen ocean west of the Mackenzie River, nor have I reliable information as to the size of this animal in that region.

I have already shown that there is no marked peculiarity about the forms of the feet of the other species of our deer, nor is the distinction between them very marked. I have spent much time in examining their tracks in light snows, and could generally distinguish the track of the mule deer by its being longer and slimmer than the other ; but even as to this, I was sometimes in doubt, except in the cases of fully adult specimens, the feet of which are larger than the feet of the largest Virginia deer.

When compared with that of any other quadrupeds, the track of the smaller deer is readily distinguishable. Its narrow heel and sharp points — its length in proportion to its breadth and graceful outside curvature, can never leave a doubt of the identity of the track of a deer. It can never be mistaken for the track of the sheep, the goat, or the antelope.

The white fugitive marking around the feet of the Virginia Deer, and its absence on all the others, except the caribou, has been explained in another place.

THE GLANDS.

From necessity the naturalist must ever be in search for peculiarities in organized beings which will enable him satisfactorily to separate them into divisions, orders, genera, and species, and it is not remarkable that some more than others should attach importance to peculiar characteristics.

On the 28th of June, 1836, Dr. Gray made some observations before the Zoölogical Society of London — see its proceedings of that date — " On the tufts of hair observable on the posterior legs of animals of the genus Cervus, as a characteristic of that group and a means of subdividing it into natural sections."

These tufts are found on the inside or the outside, or sometimes on both sides of the hinder legs of all the deer which Dr. Gray had had an opportunity of examining, with the exception of the muntjak, and he thought that if upon more critical examination, both were wanting on this animal, together with its having a persistent horn and some other peculiar characteristics, it would afford an additional motive for excluding it from the genus Cervus.

He says truly that these tufts are found at all ages and on both sexes, and hence their value to determine the species of hornless females, and that the horn is unreliable as being unstable and only on the males. From these tufts Dr. Gray di vides the Cervidæ into sections as follows : —

1. The first has a pencil of hairs seated on the outside of the hinder part of the metatarsus, about one third of the distance from the calcaneum, towards the hoof. In this section he includes *C. elaphus, C. Canadensis, C. axis, C. porcinus, C. hippilaphus, C. dama* and its varieties, and *C. niger*, etc.

2. In the second section, in which he includes *C. Virginianus* and its variety *C. Mexicanus*, there exists two tufts of hair, one seated on the outer side of the hinder part of the metatarsus, about two thirds of the distance from the calcaneum to the hoof, and the other on the inside of the hock or heel. In this section would also be included *C. macrotis* and *C. Columbianus*, although the outside tufts differ very widely in extent and location from *C. Virginianus*, as we shall hereafter explain.

3. The third section comprises those which have a distinct tuft inside the hock and none on the outside of the metatarsus. Dr. Gray found this on two species from Demerara and one allied species from South America. He thought he could discern the internal tuft on the reindeer in the Society's museum, but no trace of one on the outside of the metatarsus, which was covered by a very uniform thick coat of hair. In this section would be included our moose and caribou, as we shall presently see, and also my diminutive Acapulco deer.

4. Of the fourth section he speaks with doubt, but assigns to it the European elk, *Cervus alces*, on which he found distinct tufts on the inside of the hock and on the outside of the metatarsus, about one third of its length from the heel, as in the first section, but of the existence of the latter tuft he is by no means certain on account of the age and state of the specimen.

I must say that I have carefully examined the Swedish elk, and am enabled to say that there is no tuft of hair on the outside of the hind legs, and that the metatarsal gland is entirely wanting. In this regard he is precisely like our moose, so we must dispense with his fourth section.

We may briefly summarize these sections thus : *First*, where the outside tuft is present and the inside wanting, *Second*, where both are present, and *Third*, where the inside tuft is present and that on the outside wanting. This certainly divides the genus into very natural sections easily recognized.

By a careful study of these tufts of hair and the structures which they indicate and cover, I find we are enabled with equal certainty to subdivide these sections and designate the species composing them respectively. Dissection, with aid of the microscope, shows us that each of these tufts of hair indicates the place of, and covers and surrounds a cutaneous gland, a distinct organ which in the economy of the animal has its proper and peculiar functions to perform. When we find such an organ present in one class of animals, and absent in another class sufficiently resembling them to be ranked in the same genus, we are almost prepared to declare them to be specifically different, and are led at once to look for other difference to corroborate the suspicion. A distinct member, always constant in all its features, among all the individuals of a class who freely associate together, wherever such association is permitted without restraint, and who avoid the society of all other similar animals destitute of that member, — this peculiarity adds to the suspicion of a specific difference ; and so on, whenever we can find differences either in structure or habit which cannot be assigned to accidental or factitious circumstances or surroundings, such as climate, altitude, aliment, and the like, we are more and more inclined to draw the dividing line of species. But whenever we can ascribe peculiarities either of structure or habit to such accidental surroundings, we may conclude that the differences would gradually disappear on a change of circumstances ; then we may be justified in the opinion that the change is transient and we have but a variety.

I know of no feature or member of any of these animals so exactly alike, in dimensions, location, coloring, and structure, on every individual of each species of our deer, as these tufts of hair and the glands which they conceal, and yet those on the outside of the metatarsus are entirely different from each other on the different species, and this difference is so great that when one's attention is once called to them the most casual observation is sufficient to identify them, and enable us to say, with certainty, to which species they belong. We look in vain for any other mark so limited in extent which so distinctly declares the species.

Unless I exaggerate to myself the importance of these indicia, I shall be justified in describing them on each of the species of which I treat with such particularity as will enable any one to distinguish them.

The gland on the outside of the hind leg has long been designated the metatarsal gland, from its location. That on the inside of the hock, for the sake of distinction and from its location, I have called the tarsal gland. Both occupy the whole body of the skin where they are situate. I here present figures showing

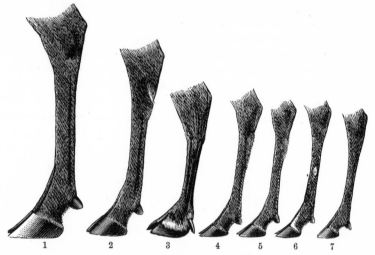

1   2   3   4   5   6   7

1. Moose.   2. Wapiti or Elk.   3. Caribou.   4. Mule Deer.   5. Black-tailed Deer.
6. Common Deer.   7. Acapulco Deer.

the outside of the hind legs of all the species of which I treat, except that of the barren-ground caribou, which would only differ from that of the woodland caribou in size and in having more white upon it. The location and extent of the metatarsal gland is shown on Figs. 2, 4, 5 and 6, while it is entirely wanting on Figs. 1, 3, and 7. These marks or their absence are shown on the full figures of the animals.

If we commence with the largest in our examination, we find that the metatarsal gland is entirely wanting on the Moose, nor is there any tuft of hair on the outside of the metatarsus. All the hairs are of an even length, and lie smooth and flat. I have been led to a more careful examination for this gland, or some tuft of hair in its place, from the fact that Dr. Gray, in "Knows-

ley Menagerie," describes this gland as present in the Swedish
elk, which I have found by careful study to be specifically identical with our moose. In his specific description of *C. alces* he
declares its presence in these words, " hind legs have the tuft of
hair rather above the middle of the metatarsus." He had previously stated to the Zoölogical Society at the meeting to which I
have referred, that he had examined the elk at the British Museum and " it appeared to have very distinct tufts on the inner
side of the hocks, and others also on the outside of the metatarsus about one third of its length from the heel," though of the
latter tufts he says he was by no means certain on account of the
age and state of the specimen.

I have been to no small pains to satisfy myself by a personal
examination, and find that there is no gland or tuft of hair on
the outside of the hind leg of the Scandinavian elk, so that it
exactly resembles our Moose in this regard. The best observer
is liable to be misled when examining mounted specimens, especially of quadrupeds.

There are some features of the tarsal gland found on the inside
of the hock, which are common to all, which may be first mentioned. All are entirely overgrown with hairs which are elevated to a greater or less angle from the skin, and more than the
surrounding coat.

Except on *C. alces*, the rise or elevation of the hairs commences at the upper and smaller end of the tuft, at which point
the hairs are longest and extend down to the large end of the
tuft, which is the highest, and terminates rather abruptly. The
skin under this tuft is occupied with the gland composed of secreting ducts, with their canals extending to the surface, now partially obliterated and nearly dormant. The skin presents to the
casual observer a spongy appearance, of twice the thickness of
the surrounding skin. A peculiar muscular and nervous arrangement enables and prompts the animal, whenever excited by fear
or hostility, to elevate the hairs of this tuft, so that they stand
out at right angles to the skin.

On our Moose and on the Swedish Elk, the tuft of hair covering the tarsal gland differs in size, position, and color from that
on any of the other species. It commences at a point at the posterior extremity of the hock: from this point a seam slightly
elevated, caused by the meeting of the short hairs which approach from above and below inclining forward, extends anteriorly on the inside of the hock for one inch and three lines.

Here this seam divides so as to embrace the tuft proper. This tuft is one inch and nine lines long, widening out from the point of commencement for one inch of its length, where it is nearly nine lines wide; thence it narrows down to its anterior extremity, where it is rounded off. From all directions the hairs on the surrounding region, — which are of a very light roan color, or dull white with red hairs sparsely scattered through them, — point to this tuft and overlap its borders. Most of the hairs in the tuft are a dull black, but a few are white and some a russet red; on many the general appearance is jet black. The contrast in color of most specimens make this a conspicuous mark, but on some the surrounding coat is much darker, and others are lighter than that from which the above description is taken, so that the con-

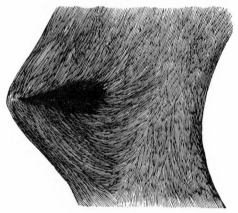

Fig. 1. Tarsal Gland of Moose and Swedish Elk.

trast may be more or less striking, but the initial radial point, the seam and the tuft itself, are found just alike on all, in position and color, only varying in extent with the size of the animal.

It will be observed that this differs from those on all the other species, in that it occupies a horizontal instead of a vertical position; is black, and is much smaller in proportion to the size of the animal. No one who has carefully studied it could ever hesitate to declare the species, from an inspection of this tuft alone. It is as certain indicia of the species, as is the metatarsal gland on the mule deer to be hereafter described. It is more individualized than is the tuft covering the tarsal gland on either of the other species.

To sum up, we may say that the glandular system on the hind leg of the Moose, which is the largest of the species, is much

nearer obliterated than on any of our other species, as not a vestige remains of the metatarsal gland, and the tarsal is the least
of all in size. As we shall hereafter see, the metatarsal gland is
wanting on three of the other species, yet on all these the tarsal
gland remains in full size or nearly so in proportion to the size of
the animal.

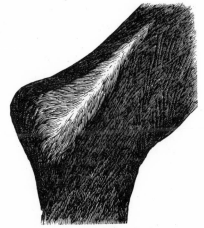

FIG. 2.

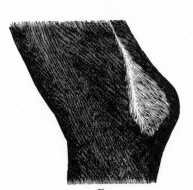

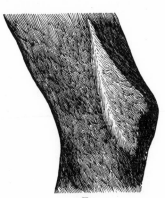

FIG. 3. FIG. 4.

2 is from the Woodland Caribou. 3 is from the Male, and 4 is from the Female Wild
Reindeer of Norway.

On the Woodland Caribou the tuft of hairs over the tarsal
gland also has its characteristics, which enable one who has
studied it to readily recognize it, though it is more variable in
size and shape than on the moose. The hairs composing the tuft
occupy a descending position. From the upper end the tuft
commences to rise up gradually, and so continues to the lower

end, where the elevation is greatest. The length of this tuft is two inches, while the breadth is one inch and three lines. The middle of this tuft is a yellowish white, for a horizontal extent of two inches, and a vertical extent of one inch and three lines. The greatest diameter of the white portion is near the lower border of the tuft. Below the white portion the tuft shades down to the olive brown of the rest of the leg. It occupies the internal cavity of the hock posterior to the central part. It is not quite so large in proportion to the size of the animal as on most of the other species, neither is it much below them in relative size. It is not so exactly alike on each individual of this species as it is on the smaller species.

A careful examination of his congener, the European Reindeer, shows that they correspond in the glandular system on the hind leg as well as in other respects. The illustrations show the tufts of hair on the inside of the hocks of both varieties of this deer. It will be seen that they correspond both in location, form, and extent. Those from the male and female wild European Reindeer, were drawn from a pair I obtained from Tromso, within the arctic circle on the west coast of Norway. It will be observed that they do not correspond exactly with each other or with that on the Caribou. Those on the female reindeer and the Caribou being more alike than those on the male and female Reindeer. They vary a little in size, that on the female being the largest as well as most irregular at the lower part of the tuft. Altogether the difference is more marked than is to be found among individuals of any of the other species, and to that extent it impairs the reliability to be placed upon this tuft as a distinguishing mark, and yet they are quite unlike those found on any of the other species. After all they have distinct characteristics which tell us their origin at once. I studied several hundred tame Reindeer in Lapland, and observed that those general characteristics prevailed, while the difference in size and form here represented was observed among them.

This tuft of hair on the inside of the hock is present on the Barren-ground Caribou, and the specimen in my collection is much more circular in form, wanting the long, sharp point at the upper end which is so observable on the Woodland Caribou.

On both species of our Caribou, as well as on the European Reindeer, the most careful scrutiny fails to disclose the least vestige of a gland or tuft of hairs on the outer side of the metatarsus, and in this respect it corresponds with its neighbor, occupying the same sub-Arctic region, the moose and the Swedish elk.

The specific identity of our Woodland Caribou with the Lapland Reindeer, *C. tarandus*, has long been a subject of discussion, if not of controversy, among naturalists; but I have studied them in vain to find any specific difference between them, and the correspondence of this mark, to say the least, harmonizes with this conclusion. In another place, I assign the reasons which incline me to think that there is a specific difference between our northern and southern Reindeer, which it is unnecessary to here anticipate, and if this conclusion be justified, it would follow that the European species could not be the same as our Barren-ground Caribou. The Woodland Caribou is undoubtedly larger than either the wild or the tame Reindeer of Europe, but there is said to be a variety of Reindeer in northeastern Asia corresponding in size to our Woodland Caribou. It was the Lapland Reindeer which I personally studied, on all of which the metatarsal gland was entirely wanting, and so I am constrained to conclude that Dr. Gray was in error, when, in his specific description of the same animal, he said: " The external metatarsal gland is above the middle of the leg." However, the same careful and intelligent observer tells us that upon an examination of the reindeer in the British Museum, he thought he could observe the internal tufts, but no trace of the external, the entire hinder edge of the metatarsus being covered with a uniform very thick coat of hair, thus corresponding with my observations of the same animal and of our Woodland Caribou. I will add that I was unable to detect the metatarsal gland or any outside tuft of hair on the mounted specimen of the European Reindeer in the Smithsonian collection, but the difficulty of making sure work with dried specimens always leaves me in doubt as to correct conclusions, and especially on this particular point. I sought long and carefully for this gland on a dried skin of a deer from South America without detecting a trace of it, but after softening the skin with a day's soaking, a very little examination plainly revealed it uncovered with hair, but with the horny scale, as on the Virginia deer or the mule deer.

On the two specimens of the Barren-ground Caribou I find the same glandular system on the hind leg as on the larger species.

Our Elk, *C. Canadensis*, is the only species of North American deer which is without the tarsal gland, and so falls into the first section of Dr. Gray's classification, as elsewhere stated, although he cites a number of other species from other countries possessing the same peculiarity.

The first and the only mention I find of this interesting fact, as connected with our Elk, is by Professor Baird in his description of the quadrupeds in Pacific Railroad Reports, but the hesitancy with which he mentions it shows how remarkable he considered it, and that he thought it possible that the specimen which he examined might be exceptional in this regard. It is also wanting on the red deer of Europe.

The metatarsal gland on the outside of the hind leg of the Wapiti, and so of the red deer, is conspicuously present, though we may with propriety say that it is more obliterated than on the others which still retain it. On this animal alone this gland is entirely overgrown with hairs. It is situated on the outside, near the back edge, and about two inches below the upper end of the cannon bone, and is covered with a tuft of long white hairs, on the outside of which there is a border of long colored hairs (see Fig. 6, p. 258). The tuft is ovate in shape, is from three to four inches long, and is one inch and six lines broad. The space occupied by the white hairs is about one inch and six lines long, and less than one inch broad. These white hairs are frequently concealed by longer surrounding hairs overlaying them, and sometimes the white hairs are much longer than the others, and become quite conspicuous, and extend themselves posteriorly as if they would embrace the back edge of the leg. When the surrounding hairs are the longest, and overlay the white, they unite in a seam which has a descending posterior direction. Surrounding the long colored hairs is a border of short cinnamon-colored hairs. This border of short hairs is of a much lighter color than those on the leg beyond it, and is about half an inch broad. From the bottom of the tuft descends a stripe of the same rufous color, nine lines broad, down the posterior edge of the leg to between the small hind toes or accessory hoofs. The structure of the gland beneath is much like that of the tarsal gland on the other members of this family. This metatarsal gland has almost become inactive on Wapiti, and presents a massive spongy appearance, making the skin appear much thicker there than on the surrounding parts; or perhaps it has not yet attained that vitality and activity which enables it to obliterate the hairs which cover it, as is observed on the other species where it is present.

In this connection it is interesting to repeat, that no remnant or rudiment of this metatarsal gland is found on the two other large species of deer — the Moose and the Caribou. The extent of the tarsal gland on the Moose is less than is the metatarsal gland on the Wapiti, while the latter is something less in relative extent than the tarsal gland on the Caribou, which is a smaller animal than our elk while the Moose is larger. We might infer from this, that with the advancement in size the demand in the animal economy for this glandular system is less urgent, and with the decrease of this demand the glands themselves are gradually disappearing, and in the process of time may finally become extinct altogether.

But here we are met with the fact that the smallest of our species as well as the largest, is also without the metatarsal gland, which is not compensated by an increased development of the tarsal gland, so that at last we may not be at liberty to attribute the disappearance of these glands to the increased size of the species. But my object is to state impartially observed and well authenticated facts, rather than to speculate upon them or to deduce or sustain theories from them.

On the other extreme of development of the metatarsal gland is the Mule Deer (Fig. 5, p. 258), which animal is next in size to the woodland caribou, on which as we have seen it is entirely wanting.

On the inside of the hock of this deer the tuft of hair covering the tarsal gland is larger than on any of the preceding, is of pear shaped form, and occupies a vertical position with the small end uppermost. Like the others it is composed of long, elevated hairs, those on the top being the longest and finding their seat at or near the upper point and descending to the abrupt lower end. In color, the tuft on the surface is of a lightish tawny yellow, but upon opening it appears black within. When examined separately the hairs are found to be from an inch and six lines to an inch and nine lines long. For one quarter of their length, at their upper ends, they are of the tawny yellow shade stated, and the lower three quarters black, less intense towards the lower ends. A few white hairs are found among them. When the animal is excited this tuft is raised up and spreads out like a fan, when the dark shade below overpowers the lighter shade of the ends, and the whole tuft appears black.

The metatarsal gland is situate on the outside and near the posterior edge of the metatarsus. The tuft of hairs covering and overlaying the gland commence just below the tarsus, and extends down the leg eight inches, and is in width about one inch

17

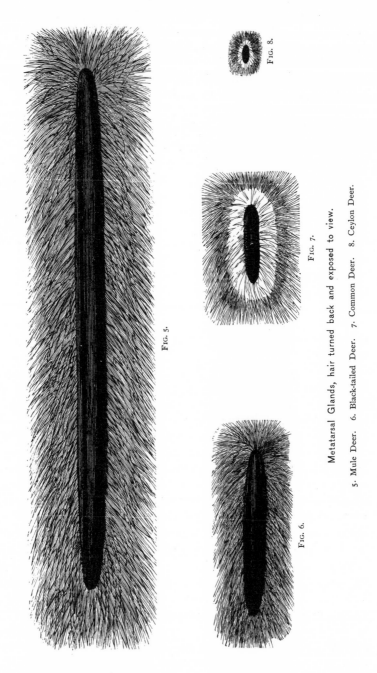

FIG. 5.

FIG. 6.

FIG. 7.

FIG. 8.

Metatarsal Glands, hair turned back and exposed to view.

5. Mule Deer.   6. Black-tailed Deer.   7. Common Deer.   8. Ceylon Deer.

and six lines at the upper end, but is narrower below the gland. About six lines below the upper end of this tuft commences the upper end of the naked space over the gland. This naked space is from five inches and one line to six inches long on very large specimens, and from four lines to half an inch broad, and is covered by a black scale of the concentrated exudation. (Fig. 5, p. 258.) The gland extends beyond the naked portion so that its borders are under the tuft of hairs, but the portion covered with hairs is much less active than the naked portion, so that the encroachment of the hairs would seem to be gradually obliterating the gland, or the advancement of the gland, by degrees displacing the hairs. The elevated hairs on either side of the gland approach each other over its centre, and then when they meet turn back and so form a sort of seam directly over the organ.

I have critically examined a great number of specimens, and have found this organ remarkably uniform in all, varying only in extent according to the size of the animal. Not a single white or black hair ever occurs in the tuft, but the whole surface is a uniform, tawny yellow of exactly the same shade as on the rest of the leg. Nor is the inside black as is the tuft on the inside of the hock just described, but the lower part of the hairs is of a lighter shade than the outer portion. I could never observe these to be disturbed by excitement as is the case with the other.

I here present illustrations of these glands of all our species on which they are found, and also on the small deer from Ceylon, with the tufts of hair which cover them, opened so as to expose the naked portions covered with the black incrustations. By seeing them thus brought together, we are the better enabled to compare them.

In this glandular system the Black-tailed deer, *C. Columbianus*, as well as in some other peculiar characteristics, is nearest allied to the mule deer, as we shall see in another place, although in other respects these species are widely divergent. The metatarsal gland commences a little lower down on the metatarsus, than on the mule deer, and its tuft of long partially reversed hairs occupies a space about four inches long and fully one inch broad. On a large specimen the naked crusted portion is two inches in length and scarcely three lines broad. The hairs of this tuft are disposed much as on the mule deer, though the central seam over the gland is not so well defined. Like the other it corresponds exactly in color with the hairs on the rest of the leg, without a single white or black hair in the region, and altogether is scarcely distinguishable from that on the mule deer, except from its diminished size. These indicia of species I have found exactly alike, whether taken from specimens captured a thousand miles apart or bred in my grounds.

The tarsal gland on this deer occupies about the same position as on the mule deer, is similarly shaped, but is a little less in extent. The tuft covering it differs from the other most strikingly in color. Instead of presenting a lightish yellow color on the surface it is a foxy red, and it presents but little change when opened, although careful inspection shows a darker shade near the skin; the hairs when individually examined are for the upper half a foxy red color, then they begin to turn a little gray, and near the lower end are a light brown. When the hairs of this tuft are spread out in excitement, no appreciable change of color is observed in the appearance of the tuft. Its individual characteristics are sufficiently pronounced to declare the species to which it belongs.

Scarcely less characteristic are these glands on the Virginia Deer, though from their wide distribution slight variations in size are found on those taken from widely different localities. Still, they possess such distinctive qualities as never to leave the least doubt as to the species to which they belong when nothing but the skin of that portion of the leg is examined.

The tuft of hairs covering the metatarsal gland on the Virginia Deer commences six lines above the middle of the cannon bone, and extends downward one inch and six lines, and is nine lines broad, the posterior line extending a little beyond the posterior edge of the leg, as in all the other species. On the fully adult the naked portion, which is covered with the same hard black scale as the others, is nine lines long, the upper end of which is as near as possible at the longitudinal middle of the leg and is about two lines wide.

The largest proportionate specimens I have found were on the coast of the Gulf of Mexico, although the animals are smaller than further north. The longest I have ever met with, on a medium sized animal, was one inch and one line long, and taken from an animal I found in the Mobile market; and on a yearling buck we killed on Negro Hummock near the mouth of Burwicks Bay, I found the naked portion nearly one inch in length. From all the specimens I have been able to examine, from near our southern border, I can scarcely doubt that this gland is appreciably larger on the Virginia Deer there than it is in this latitude, and this, beside the diminished size of the animal, is the only peculiarity I have been able to discover in the animals found in the far south. On the very large buck which I killed in Wisconsin, in 1876, the metatarsal gland was one inch and six lines long, which, however, was no larger proportionately than is observed on animals of the ordinary size. The smallest I have ever found on on adult was on a small female and was six lines long. In all, both wild and in parks, from one ocean to the other, in the middle States and north of them, I have found a wonderful uniformity in the size of this gland, varying, of course, with the size of the animal.

Immediately around the naked space is a band of white hairs, which occupies a space on the skin about two lines broad, although from their being longer than those around them they appear to occupy a greater space. Immediately outside this white band there is usually a very narrow dark border, shading down to the prevailing color of the balance of the leg, which is more generally of a fawn color, though there is great variation in the color of the leg of the Common Deer, even more than on other parts of the body. Sometimes the band surrounding the white hairs is fairly black with the outer border adjoining the rufous colored and shorter hairs well defined.

On the specimens found in the western mountainous regions and in the high northern latitudes — where they are called the white-tailed or the long-tailed deer, and have been doubtfully named *C. leucurus* — this dark border is wanting, and this is the only difference I can find in and about this gland from the common variety here. In location, formation, size, and covering, they are precisely alike, save only this small pencil of deeply colored hairs surrounding the white tuft, which would never be noticed by the casual observer, and which would be unworthy the attention of the most critical inquirer, were it not for their constant presence and exact uniformity, except as to the depth of the color on nearly every specimen found east of the Rocky Mountain slope and south of latitude forty-three degrees north.

On specimens from the far north and west, the white portions of the animal are appreciably more extensive than on specimens found here, as we have seen, when speaking of the coat and color ; and on one specimen in my collection from the far northwest, not only all the hairs in the region of this gland, but the whole leg, including the hock, is white, with a few red hairs interspersed along the lower front part. I cannot think that the

absence of the pencil of dark hairs around the white which surrounds the gland, is sufficient to justify us in setting up a new
species or retaining an old one. Many individuals from each region may be met with exactly alike in color, only this little dark
pencil of hairs is almost universally found on those native here,
and generally wanting on those grown there.

The tarsal gland and the tuft of hairs covering it on the Virginia Deer, are just alike on all the varieties. It is larger than
on any of the other species. It is pear-shaped, and is placed
with the small end upwards, from the upper end of which the
tuft gradually rises to its lower broad extremity, where it terminates abruptly. The hairs composing this tuft are white, but
are generally more or less stained, so that at first we would often
suspect them to be of another color, and very frequently the centre of the lower extremity of the tuft is stained to a deep black
color for a space the size of a dime or larger. It is, however,
only the extreme tips of the hairs that are stained sufficiently to
show when they lie compactly together. Let but a dog come
along on the outside of the fence and look in, and these tufts on
every deer near enough to notice him, will immediately rise up
and spread out, presenting the appearance of a great snow-ball
of the purest white on the inside of each hock, and not a trace
of the stains will be observed.

Lastly, we come to my little Acapulco Deer, which may be soon
disposed of, for as previously remarked, the metatarsal gland is
entirely wanting, as it is on the moose and the caribou. But the
tarsal gland is present, with the tuft of hair covering it of a good
size, considering the size of the animal. It bears the same general appearance as on all the other species, except the moose, but
is of the same color as the regions surrounding it.

The want of the metatarsal gland separates it more distinctly
from the Ceylon Deer in my grounds than any other characteristic, though it is something smaller in stature, and the antlers
differ somewhat, as we have seen, when that branch of my subject was considered. The tarsal gland is present on this Ceylon
species as well, resembling much those on the others, while the
gland on the outside of the leg is situated lower down, and is
much smaller than on any of the other species (see Fig. 8, p. 258).
A few white hairs are observed about this gland, though the tuft
is so small as to elude detection, except on a close examination.

Dr. Gray expressed the opinion when he first suggested the importance of the tufts of hairs covering these cutaneous glands as

a means of dividing the genus, that domestication or confinement tends to diminish the size of these tufts. From this suggestion I have been led to carefully look for such effect under
the conditions suggested, but I have been unable to detect any
difference in the size of these tufts, on the wild animals and
those reared in parks or kept in close confinement.

While on each of the separate species the tarsal gland and the
tuft of hairs covering it, is not so marked in its distinctive characteristics, except indeed upon the moose, yet there is quite
a plain difference between those found on any one species and
those on either of the others. The fact that they are just alike
on each individual of either species, renders these marks of great
value, and justifies a careful study of each so as to clearly appreciate differences between those found on the different species.

There is another set of glands, which, though not found on all
of the species, are constant on some, and would seem to be usual,
to say the least, on others. These are interdigital glands, and
like the others of which I have treated, are conglomerate and
dermal. They are situated between the upper phalangeal bones.
They are in the form of small sacks opening anteriorly. On
some species they are larger in diameter and in depth, proportionally, than on others, and in a given species they vary according to the size of the animal, as do the other glands treated of.
All have more or less hairs growing within the sack, and they
vary considerably in their activity. On the more active ones, at
least, when dissected out from the recently killed animal and examined on the flesh side, they seem to be literally covered with
ducts or divided into lobules readily distinguished by the naked
eye.

So far as I have been able to make a personal examination I
have found them the most extensive in the smallest species, the
little Acapulco Deer. On a fully adult doe I find the sack to
be about one inch in depth and five lines in diameter. The sack
contains a limited amount of hairs and a considerable amount of
secreted matter which has a pungent, disagreeable, musky odor.
I find it on all the feet in all the specimens I have had an opportunity to examine, and all substantially corresponding to the
above description, only on smaller specimens it is proportionally
less. About the same may be stated of the Ceylon Deer.

Of the Virginia Deer I have examined great numbers for this
gland. It is always present in all the feet. It is about the
same size in both sexes. On a medium sized animal it is fully

one inch in depth and seven lines in diameter. On very large animals I have found it fully one inch and a half in depth. Hairs, though to a limited number, are found within it. On this deer I have found this gland more active than on any of the others. It always contains a considerable amount of the secreted matter, which is about the consistency of cerumen, and a portion of it frequently assumes the form of pellets about the size of a small pea, which, however, are so soft as to be more or less flattened. This substance is of a grayish color, and emits an odor which is strong and offensive to most nostrils. I have never seen a white man smell of it who did not look and express himself disgusted.

The Columbia Deer possess this gland in each foot. While its location is the same its position seems to be a little different from that on any of the others, and it is more massive, and has the appearance of muscle attached to the inner side of the skin, though in fact it pervades the whole skin. The lobules are larger than on any others examined, being half a line in diameter, and sexangular or octangular in form, and readily distinguished by the naked eye.

The direction of the opening is more parallel with the line of the foot, the opening being found by passing the probe up the deep indentation between the phalangeal bones. The sack is about seven lines deep and five lines in diameter at the orifice, contracting toward the end. It contains a limited amount of hairs, and the amount of secreted matter within is moderately abundant. The gland is not confined to the sack, but extends down to the extreme point of division between the hoofs, the hairs overgrowing it at the bottom of the indentation, all the way down, being stained a yellowish shade by the exudation. This retains its pungent odor a long time after the death of the animal. This gland is appreciably larger, as we shall see, than is that on the mule deer, which has identically the same gait when at its best speed.

My opportunities for examining the Mule Deer have been sufficiently extensive to be satisfactory. This gland is present in all the feet, but is much less extensive than in the Virginia deer and proportionally less than on the Columbia deer. On a fully adult animal the sack is six lines deep and five lines in diameter. This sack is more abundantly lined with hairs than that on the Virginia deer. These hairs are fine, soft, and elastic, and from their confinement have assumed a curled or curved form. The secretions I found less abundant, and less pungent to the smell than in the Virginia deer or the Columbia deer.

My opportunities to examine the Barren-ground Caribou for this gland have been limited. I have but two hind feet and one fore foot of this animal, which I have carefully dissected. On the fore foot there is no appearance of the gland. On one hind foot I found it very conspicuous. It was an inch and five lines in depth and six lines in diameter, and was literally filled with coarse, stiff hairs, pointing to and even protruding from the orifice. All of the hairs within the sack were stained a tawny yellow color, deepest near the orifice, but beyond it the ends faded out to nearly white. When soaked and washed much of this coloring matter is removed, but still the hairs do not become white. This coloring matter is the exudation of the glandular ducts, which is very abundant upon and near the skin among the lower part of the hairs, and is found in detached particles adhering to the hairs for some distance up from their roots. I observed no odor from this secretion, nor should I have expected any after the specimen had been dried for a year or two. On the left hind foot as well as on the fore foot of this Caribou, this gland was entirely wanting. The fact that it was conspicuously present in the right hind foot and wanting in the left foot of the same animal, shows that in that species at least this mark is not reliable. The same thing may occur in other deer, but I have heard of no example of it unless it be in the Woodland Caribou. I have not had an opportunity to examine the feet of the Woodland Caribou, but Dr. Gilpin informs me that he finds these glands in the hind feet of this animal and not in the fore feet of the adult, though he found them distinct though very small in a fawn of this species, which suggested to him the possibility that they might be present in the fawns and become obliterated in the adult. This I understand also corresponds with the observations of Mr. Morrow of Halifax. My examination of the wild reindeer which I brought from Norway shows that they agree with the Woodland Caribou in having the interdigital glands in the hind feet and not in the fore feet.

From the many specimens examined of our Elk, I think I may safely say that this gland is entirely wanting in all of its feet; at least I have never found a vestige of it in any specimen. The cleft or indentation between the phalangeal bones is very deep, but that is all.

I have no reliable information whether this gland is present in any of the feet of the Moose or not, and so must leave that to future observations.

That the odor emitted by these glands is left upon the track of the deer may be presumed, but as the trail of other animals not provided with these organs seems to be as readily followed by the hounds, we may safely conclude that they are not the only sources of the scent left in the track. The capacity of an animal to leave a scent which may be followed by an enemy, would seem to be detrimental to its safety or well being, especially in a wild state, but it is common to most if not all terrestrial animals. There are compensating advantages, no doubt, at least to some extent, for it enables them to find companions which they might otherwise seek in vain.

Whatever may be the uses of these glands, certain it is that they are very active, constantly secreting matter; and this, in every case where I have examined the live or recently killed animal, emits a pungent odor.

I prefer rather to give the facts, than to advance or maintain doubtful theories.

The longer and the more minutely I have examined this glandular system on the hind legs of the different species of this genus, the more I have become impressed with its importance in the division into or identification of species. As Dr. Gray justly remarked, they are not transient, or exceptional, like the antlers, but are present on both sexes and at all ages, and had he studied them with care he would have added that they are as near alike as possible on each individual of each species, and that those on the outside of the legs, when present, are entirely unlike on the different species; so that upon an examination of the part of the skin containing this gland, no one familiar with the subject could hesitate to declare with certainty from which species it came. Hardly any other single mark pervading so many species is so reliable as this, and certainly none of so small dimensions. The tail of the mule deer, no doubt, will always declare itself, and so will the foot of the caribou; but still they vary in size even proportionately, while this gland is so exact that from it alone one may closely approximate the size of the animal. Should I be presented with a piece of skin, containing a gland similar to the one which I have above described, yet differing from it, I should conclude that it came from some distant country, and that other distinctions would probably be found establishing a species differing from any of ours. As, for instance, should I find one resembling that on our Virginia deer, but without the white band, or especially with a black band around it, or one otherwise corresponding to that of the mule deer or the Columbia deer, with either a white or a black band around it, I could not hesitate to declare that it belonged to neither of those species, nor yet to any of the others which I have described.

It will be observed that there is a great similarity in the color, and not a very wide difference in the extent of the tufts over the metatarsal glands on the Virginia deer and the wapiti, while they differ widely in their location, and especially in that on the latter the gland is entirely overgrown with the white hairs, while on the former the gland is covered with a horny scale and is entirely destitute of hairs, except around its outer and nearly dormant border upon which most of the white hairs grow.

In the mule and the Columbia deer they closely resemble each other, in shape and location, and differ principally in extent, and appreciably in color; and this is so marked on all the individuals of each species, as to separate them widely, and leave no difficulty in determining as to which any given specimen belonged. If from the fawn of the mule deer and so no larger than from an adult black-tailed deer, the entire absence of the horny crust, or concentrated exudation from the gland, would remove all doubt as to where it should be placed.

I now see that I have omitted to mention in the proper place, that this horny crust does not appear upon the fawn, but later, after the secretions of the gland have been emitted and concentrated, and this increases in thickness and in density with the age of the animal.

Once I had three female black-tailed deer sent me from Oregon, by Dr. Plummer. The long voyage told severely upon them, and all arrived very poor, and one sick. In defiance of the most careful attention, she continued ill for two months, when she dropped two fawns. She lived a month longer and died. The fawns were scarcely a third the natural size and were unable to stand, but when fed with warm cows' milk they were soon able to stagger about, but both died in a couple of days. On both these premature fawns, as I suspect they were, the metatarsal glands were entirely overgrown with soft, fine hairs. About a month later both the other does dropped a fawn each, which were small and emaciated, but I think mature, on which this gland was naked, in the middle at least, but appeared to be more encroached upon by fine, short hairs than on the adults. These fine hairs soon disappeared from the spaces where there are no hairs on the adults. These seemed to thrive moderately well for about four months, and till they had shed their ornamental coat, which was replaced by a full coat of bay red hairs, when they died, and their skins were added to the Smithsonian collection.

From the fact observed, as above stated, we may infer, that when the coat of hairs appears on the fœtal fawn, it pervades the whole surface of the gland, but that even before birth it ordinarily disappears, at least partially, and very soon after to the same extent as on the adult. Those acquainted with the subject will recognize that this is not an uncommon occurrence to fœtal growth ; still it seems to me not without interest in connection with the other facts I have stated, of the present condition of this glandular system on the different species of which I particularly treat.

GROUPINGS.

I HAVE already shown that there are many means which we might adopt for classifying the deer of our country, but none which would be completely satisfactory. If we make a class of those whose antlers are palmated, and another of those whose antlers are cylindrical, we should find ourselves in harmony with another mode of, classification, for on all the former, the metatarsal gland is wanting, while it is present on all those which have cylindrical antlers. In this first class, I repeat, we include the largest and the smallest of the species, that is, the moose and the Acapulco deer, and it would also embrace the reindeer. Although the palmatation is less pronounced on the smallest species, it is very distinct on the upper part of the antlers of the adult, being flattened out, almost like a knife blade.

THE GENITALS.

The genital organs afford us another and very distinct mode of classification, as will be seen by a more particular description of them. On all, the scrotum is moderately pendent, more so than that of the horse, but less so than that of the bull, the ram, or the goat, and it is much less in size than on either of these. It enlarges very decidedly during the rut.

On the Moose the theca extends up the abdomen about half way to the umbilicus and terminates with a simple orifice without a prepuce. The same description answers for the Caribou as well.

On the Elk, the theca extends up the abdomen appreciably further than on either of the others, fully two thirds of the way or more to the umbilicus, much like that of the bull, terminating also without a prepuce, but at times during the rut the limp male organ is partially exposed, which might be mistaken by a casual observer for a very conspicuous prepuce. On neither is there a tuft of long hairs at the orifice of the theca as is seen on the bull. In these characteristics, I find the European elk to correspond with our moose, the reindeer of Lapland to agree with our caribou, and the red deer of Europe to be like our wapiti.

In all the other species of our country the theca extends up the abdomen hardly at all, but is quite detached from it, and drops down vertically close to the scrotum, to a length of two inches or more. From this case, ordinarily, the penis does not entirely retreat. This is a feature which I have not elsewhere met among ruminants; nor do I remember to have observed it on any other quadruped.

Here, then, is a very distinguishing characteristic common to all the lesser species of the deer, while the three larger species resemble in this part of their organization most other ruminants.

There is nothing remarkable in the location of the female organs of any of the species, except in our Elk. In her this organ is situated much further below the anus than in the other species. It is so far down that it is not covered by the short tail of the animal, which, as we have seen, is about four inches long. In this respect, that is, in the length of the tail, the red deer differs from the Wapiti. In the former, the tail is generally sufficiently long to cover the female organ.

GAIT.

In beauty of both form and motion the Virginia Deer far surpasses either of the other species of the genus. Its slender, delicate legs, and its symmetrical proportions, make it an object of universal admiration; but it is the indescribable ease and grace of its motion which fill one with absolute delight. These I have already described on page 155, in connection with the ornamental coat of this fawn, which have always associated themselves in my mind, each seeming to add a charm to the other, It is unnecessary to repeat here what was there said of the graceful step of the fawn of the Virginia Deer. The trot, both of the fawn and the adult, frequently varies to a graceful amble when it is about to stop, but does not change to that pace when it is about to increase its speed. When startled by surprise the Virginia Deer's first gait is a canter, which it pursues for two, three, or four jumps, when it makes a high, long leap, as if to enable itself to take a broader survey of surrounding objects; then follow a few of the ordinary lower and shorter jumps, which are again succeeded by the high, long leaps, and so on till it becomes satisfied that its apprehensions are groundless, when it subsides to a trot or amble, and then stops, with head and ears erect, and looks with great earnestness at the object which startled it. If, however, it is pursued by a dog, for instance, it runs at great speed, with a low, long gallop, entirely omitting the high leaps, which but impede his progress. These are never repeated when the deer is running at speed. In a large majority of cases, in all of these paces, the Virginia Deer elevates its tail, all the hairs of which are radiated, or spread out, so as to form a very conspicuous white object as it wags from side to side, but at high speed the tail is less elevated, and the wagging motion is less observed than when at a more moderate pace, and quite often when running the tail is carried close down, and all hunters know that, when a deer is wounded, it will drop its tail and switch it from side to side when it runs away, and by this means they judge whether the game is hit or not, as has been already explained.

In addition to the gaits above specified, this deer has a slow, quiet walk, and a leisurely short trot, as for instance, when he sees corn in my hand which he is invited to come for, or falls a little behind his fellows, and wishes to overtake them. He rarely goes out of a walk when passing from one part of the grounds to another of his own volition.

There is another step taken by the Virginia Deer which displays a graceful elasticity, which must be mentioned to complete the description of its locomotion. When standing at a little distance from a passer-by, and staring with a timid look, as if suspicious, but not really alarmed, it will quickly raise one fore foot, suspend it for a moment, the foot itself pendent, and then quickly drop it to the ground with a threatening stamp, and then repeat the same motions with the other foot, again bringing it to the ground with a stamp in a threatening way, as if to try the courage of the exciting object. This motion may terminate with a stand still and an earnest gaze, or in the graceful trot above described, or he may rush away with a loud whistle or snort.

The gaits of the Acapulco Deer and of the Ceylon Deer are the same as those of the Virginia deer, only they are less graceful and agile. When they run the back assumes more of a convex curvature. They run, however, with great speed, especially the Ceylon Deer. I have no observations indicating whether they are capable of maintaining this high speed for a great length of time. Their shorter legs and shorter, thicker bodies explain the want of that graceful elasticity observed in the Virginia deer.

There is nothing graceful or attractive in any of the paces of

the Mule Deer, according to my appreciation, though less so in the
wild state than in semi-domestication. It has an awkward and
shambling walk, and its trot is still less to be admired. Mollie,
an old doe, was fond of following me around the grounds when I
was riding in a buggy, and when she had to trot to keep up, she
presented so ludicrous an object as to be quite laughable. I
never saw her or any other adult of the species in my grounds at
full speed, but I have seen the wild deer in the mountains when
fleeing from danger. Then it is that the gait exactly resembles
that of the musk deer (*Moschus moschiferus*, Linn.), of the Him-
aláyas. It is not a leap but a bound, all the feet leaving and
striking the ground at the same time. These bounds display
wonderful elasticity for a time, but after a while they seem to
become fatiguing, and the stride becomes less, and the speed
slackens. It is evident that this motion is less adapted to a long
and rapid flight than the long, leaping gait of the Virginia deer.
The fawns, when started from their concealment in my grounds,
would spring up with a high bound, alighting on all the feet at
once, and bound away with astonishing swiftness in the same way
as the adults. The walk, the gallop, the trot, and the bound, as
above described, are the only paces I have observed practiced by
the Mule Deer. The three first are always performed in a lazy,
leisurely way, and the last is resorted to only in alarm and excitement.

The same description may be given to the gait of the Columbia Black-tailed Deer, except that the walk may be a little
slower and more deliberate, and the trot is less awkward and less
frequently practiced. Notwithstanding this apparent want of
elasticity in the motions of these two species as compared with
the Virginia deer, they are much more inclined to leap fences.
Mollie would leap a fence four feet high into a yard, the gate of
which was open, as soon as go six feet further to pass through
the gate, and Albert, the Black-tailed buck, would climb up four
feet upon the hay which had been left against the fence, eight
feet high, and jump into the road, appearing as indifferent to the
drop of eight feet upon the frozen ground, as if it were but two
feet. Their strong bony legs seem to stand them well in hand
on such occasions. I have seen the Black-tailed buck at full
speed. When I was quietly standing near the edge of the bluff in
the North Park, he came rushing up the steep hill at a fearful
rate, and was about to pass me when I spoke to him. He at
once stopped his tremendous bounds, and walked up to me, not

rapidly, but in an agitated way, as if glad of my protection. Something must have greatly alarmed him, though I could not discover what it was. His tail was elevated, though not vertical, and the hairs spread out, as described on the Virginia deer, under similar circumstances. His bounds were on all the feet at once, precisely as described for the mule deer. I repeat, I think the paces of the two species, as well as the antlers, are as nearly alike as possible, and quite unlike those of any of the other species.

The Moose walks, trots, gallops, and makes long horizontal leaps. When pressed his principal gait is a long, swinging, and rapid trot. He thus passes through deep snows, over the high trunks of fallen trees, and through thick brush in a manner truly astonishing. He very rarely resorts to a running gait, unless when thrown off his balance by excitement, as when charging an adversary. His stealthy and rapid walk when he sees or smells approaching danger is well calculated to astonish the hunter. The latter gets a glimpse of the game, and supposing himself unobserved, thinks it cannot escape without his knowledge, and commences stalking it, while the animal snuffs the taint in the air and stealthily glides away almost before his eyes and at a rapid rate, without the least rustling among the leaves or the cracking of a twig, and is miles away before his escape is even suspected. All agree that the Moose will escape with great celerity and without noise over ground where an Indian with moccasoned feet could not go without being heard, unless at a very slow and cautious rate.

The gaits of the Caribou are, the walk, the trot, and the run, or gallop. When undisturbed and migrating from place to place, the gait is invariably a walk, unless one lags behind the band to pick up some choice morsel which has tempted it, when it may strike into a moderate trot to overtake its companions. When the Reindeer becomes alarmed, he will strike into a long swinging trot, which he maintains for hours, and he allows nothing to divert him, till he has fairly left the country, or at least till he has placed many miles between himself and the object which alarmed him. His ordinary traveling gait then, is a walk; when in haste he trots, but when greatly alarmed he runs with speed. When Captain Hardy missed his first Caribou, which was lying down in the snow, he says: " Up they jumped, five of them, apparently rising from all directions around us, and, after a brief stare, made off in long graceful bounds." [1] Before, on p. 230,

[1] *Forest Life in Acadie,* London ed., p. 148.

18

he says : " The pace of the Caribou when started is like that of the Moose, — a long steady trot, breaking into a brisk walk, at intervals, as the point of alarm is left behind. He sometimes gallops, or rather bounds for a short distance at first. This the Moose never does."

The paces of the Wapiti Deer are, the walk, the trot, and the gallop, or run. When moving voluntarily, not hastened by any sense of alarm, his pace is always a walk. This may be very rapid if bent on changing his feeding grounds to a distant region. This is always done in the night, and even when feeding by the way he frequently will cover an immense distance in a single night. But he is a natural trotter. This is the gait which he always adopts when fleeing from danger, unless he is thrown off his feet, when he may break into a run ; but this is so unnatural a gait for him that if he is fat it soon worries him and breaks him down. When the animal is lean, and so it is with the young animal, he is much more inclined to break his trot and adopt the running gait. He can run faster than he can trot, and if in condition to maintain that pace it increases his chances for escape, but when the fat buck is once forced into a run, he must soon come to bay.

On this subject Colonel Dodge [1] says : " Singular as it may appear, plains hunters are equally divided in opinion as to the gait of the Elk when going at his best speed. Some old hunters who have bagged their hundreds of Elk, stoutly maintain that the Elk only trots when at his best pace ; while other equally good authorities insist that he runs like a deer. The truth is, both are somewhat right and both wrong. The Elk trots with great speed, and this seems to be his easiest and most natural gait. He can, however, and does run much faster than he can trot, but it is a great effort and soon tires him out."

In my grounds the Elk have learned to come to the call, though in the summer time, when the weather is warm and the pasturage is abundant, the keeper may call till he is hoarse, before one will get up in the cool shade, but when the weather gets cooler, they will come towards him in a slow, lazy walk, but after the frost has come, and they have had a few tastes of maize (an old one will crunch an ear ten inches long, and an inch and a half in diameter, without making two bites of it), they answer with alacrity though half a mile away. The whole herd will start at first quite leisurely ; presently, one or two will strike a

[1] *The Plains of the Great West*, p. 164.

trot, when all will do so, except the young ones, which break into a run. The pace is increased by all, till they reach a bluff, or ravine, when all break into a furious run, and come thundering down the cliff like an avalanche. When you see forty or fifty Elk, more than one fourth of them having huge antlers, come rushing down towards you, you feel glad there is a good fence in front of you. Such a sight is worth going many miles to see.

When chasing a dog in the grounds, or when pursuing each other in animosity, they always run. The Elk is undoubtedly a natural trotter, and Colonel Dodge says: "I believe an Elk will trot across ordinary prairie at the rate of about a mile in three minutes thirty seconds." There is, however, about the same difference in speed among Elk as among horses.

HABIT AND DOMESTICATION.

ALL of the deer family are easily tamed. In a wild state they flee from man and all their natural enemies, and except during the rutting season they are peaceable among themselves. When stimulated and even goaded on by their passions during the rut, the males become very belligerent towards each other, but this arises from jealousy or rivalry alone, for even at this season their timidity generally restrains them from attacking other animals.

THE MOOSE.

From this general remark we may possibly except the Moose, whose great size and strength emboldens him in rare instances so as to make him voluntarily attack even men, during the rutting season. Dr. Gilpin says: " Towards the end of the rut some few bulls become infuriated, attacking the cow equally with the bull, — attacking everything." [1] Some other authors make similar statements ; but the general conclusion is that the Moose very rarely attacks the hunter in the woods unless he is both wounded and very hardly pressed, seeing no reasonable chance for escape. He does not attack from rage or for revenge but for defense. There are, however, a few cases recorded where the wounded Moose has pursued and attacked the hunter, but such cases are very exceptional. In domestication, like the other members of this family, they lose their fear of man to a certain extent, when, at particular seasons, they are inclined to attack him. Mr. Morrow writes me : " When a boy, I recollect that a Moose which was brought from the country in a semi-domesticated state and kept in a barn adjoining my father's house (I think in the latter part of the month of September), would attack any one who, while visiting it, showed any signs of fear." We may safely conclude that it is not from an innocent disposition but from a lack of courage that they do not attack the hunter in the forest. From timidity or fear they flee from him. If this is lost by intercourse with him, their naturally wicked disposition asserts itself. This timidity is much overcome, no doubt, by the stimulant of desire during the rut, but it is not destroyed. Then they are the more easily provoked and are much the most dangerous. Then they

[1] *On the Mammalia of Nova Scotia*, p. 111.

will attack an enemy or defend themselves under circumstances, when they would only think of escape at other seasons.

The female also loses her timidity sometimes, and becomes courageous and even desperate in defense of her young. Mr. Gilpin, son of Dr. Gilpin, of Halifax, once met one when hunting small game, that charged him on sight, most furiously, but he had the presence of mind to meet the charge with his fowling piece, and severed her windpipe with a charge of shot. Her fawn was too young to escape, and in her maternal solicitude she forgot her fears of even her most dreaded enemy.

These deer are less migratory than the caribou, and so confine their range to more limited areas, nor are they so easily driven away from their usual haunts by the encroachments of the white settler. Though very wary and ever on the look-out for an enemy, they will listen with complacency to the distant sound of the woodman's axe, the rumbling of the railroad train, or the sound of the whistle of the engine, without being driven to another country, or even being much disturbed.

The Moose has often been reared and tamed in this country; but I know of no systematic attempt to domesticate them, nor have I ever heard of their breeding in domestication. They have been sometimes broken to the harness and proved themselves able to draw good loads; and yet I know of no regular effort that has been made to reduce them to servitude. When tamed, they are reasonably docile, except the males during the rutting season, when, as might be suspected, they become ferocious, and should be kept in close quarters where they can do no harm. If castrated young, and early taught obedience to man, we may not doubt that they would readily submit to his dominion, and their great strength would give promise of useful beasts of draught, especially in countries where deep snows prevail, through which they pass with facility where ordinary cattle could make no progress.

Of his European brother, Louis Figuier, in " Mammalia," says : " The elk when caught young may be completely tamed without difficulty. It recognizes the person who takes care of it and will follow him like a dog, manifesting considerable joy on seeing him after a separation. It goes in harness as well as a reindeer, and can thus perform long journeys. For two or three centuries it was used for this purpose in Sweden, but the custom is now given up." If in this the learned author is not mistaken, then the Swedish Elk at that time must have been bred in domestication, else sufficient stock could not have been procured for general use. If once fairly subjected to domestication and use it may be difficult to understand why it was given up in a country so well adapted to its use. On this subject we may receive the statement of Mr. Lloyd in explanation. He says: " Formerly these animals were made use of in Sweden to draw sledges ; but owing, as it was said, to their speed frequently accelerating the escape of people who had been guilty of murders or other crimes, their use was prohibited under great penalties. Though I apprehend those ordinances, if not abrogated are obsolete, I am not aware that the elk are ever made use of in that kingdom at the present day either to draw a sledge or for other domestic purposes." [1] Again, in a subsequent and more elaborate work,[2] the same author says : " The elk can be easily domesticated. Several instances have come to my knowledge, when brought up from a tender age, have become nearly as tame as the cattle, with which they were, not unfrequently, allowed to consort and pasture. But I never heard of this animal being trained to harness as formerly was often the case in Scandinavia."

It is to be deeply regretted that some one, in a locality in this country adapted to their natural wants, has not thoroughly tried the experiment of domesticating our Moose, and determined the practicability of breeding them in domestication and of their uses. We may fear that there would be found difficulty in procuring an abundance of their favorite food, around habitations or in enclosures, but as we shall presently see that our elk is healthy and thrives well on herbaceous food almost entirely, so it might prove that the Moose can prosper on a less proportion of arboreous food than he gets in the wild state.

One of the most remarkable features of this deer, which distinguishes it from all our other species, is its monogamous habit. While seeking a companion during the rutting season the male is no doubt very much in earnest, and manifests a high state of excitement. When he finds himself accepted by an agreeable partner they retire to a deep, secluded thicket in low marshy ground, where they spend their honeymoon of three or four weeks quite contented with each other's society, never leaving the locality, the male at least scarcely taking food, living a rather quiet and respectable life, quite in contrast to the one he led while he was a roving bachelor seeking an associate. If, however, his quiet pri-

[1] *Field Sports of the North of Europe*, p. 331.
[2] *Scandinavian Adventures*, 2d edition, London, 1854, p. 102.

vacy is disturbed by a rival, his fierceness and rage are at once kindled into a fury, and he goes to meet the foe beyond the precinct of his lair. In his private retreat he paws up the soft, moist earth till he makes a considerable excavation, in which he wallows, having sprinkled it with his urine, and which becomes scented with a very powerful odor which is said to be so offensive that none but an Indian cares to encounter it. It is interesting to observe how exactly the habits of his European congener correspond with those of the Moose in this extraordinary feature. Mr. Lloyd says : " Although just prior to the rutting season the males wander greatly in search of mates, yet as soon as they have found a partner the pair retire together to a dense brake, generally consisting of fir or spruce, in the wildest recesses of the forest. Here the male forms a gross or cavity in the ground, which he very plentifully besprinkles with urine, and hence the term gross. It is said that for some three weeks, during which the rutting season continues, the pair confine themselves to the immediate vicinity of the spot, to within a space, indeed, of some few feet in diameter, which spot of their own accord, they will on no account desert ; and even should they be scared from thence by people or dogs, they will, as soon as the pursuit has ceased, return to it again. Several pair of elk are sometimes found near to the gross, the selection of which is frequently made known by the males scoring the small trees in the vicinity with their horns, or it may be in twisting them in the manner of withs." [1] Here is an exact correspondence in habit with the Moose in a very extraordinary disposition, which is something more than accidental, occurring with animals separated by a great ocean, which of itself would suggest a near relationship. We are even more surprised at the detail than at the monogamic habit itself, still this is exceedingly exceptional among quadrupeds, although quite common among birds. This habit is said to be sometimes observed among the monkey tribes, and there is one other species of deer, in which it is more marked than in *C. alces*, that is the roe-deer of Europe, where the male and female, once having made their selection, continue constant to each other through life, ever associating together, eschewing the society of all others even of their own kind, except their own offspring, to the care of which both parents devote themselves, as we have seen in another place. But to return to the Moose.

During this connubial period the male Moose becomes emaci-

[1] *Scandinavian Adventures*, by L. Lloyd, 2d London ed., 1854, vol. ii., p. 100.

ated, and at its termination retires to still deeper seclusion, where with returned appetite he tries to recruit his flesh and strength, wherewith to meet the rigors of winter; but if he be an old buck he but partially succeeds in this, and if the hunter has to depend on his flesh to supply his camp he needs sharp teeth and-a good appetite to make it tender and delicious.

The rutting season with the old animals commences in September and the fawns are dropped in May. With young animals this season is later with both sexes. In general it may be said to commence at the time the antlers of the males are divested of their velvet, and this remark is equally applicable to all of this great family of ruminants, though, as I have shown elsewhere, they are capable of procreation at any other season of the year, and when opportunities are wanting at the proper season they at least sometimes breed at other times of the year.

THE CARIBOU.

Of the disposition of our Caribou I know nothing from my own observation, and learn nothing from others, except of their fear of man and their efforts to escape his pursuit. I find no record of a manifestation of courage even in desperate circumstances, and I learn nothing from the hunters of such an occurence. Of the domesticated reindeer, in Northern Europe, which is identical in species with ours, we know that they frequently become dangerous during the rut, and even at other seasons they sometimes become unmanageable and attack their driver, but this frenzied state lasts but a short time, and they are soon induced to resume the journey. As only the castrated reindeer are worked in harness by the Lapps, this vicious disposition which thus sometimes manifests itself when at work should be considered exceptional did we not remember that the operation of emasculation is very imperfectly performed , so that the stimulating, or provoking influence is still felt, at least partially. In all of the species with which I have experimented in this direction, after complete emasculation every vestige of wickedness seems to be eradicated, and scarcely any courage, even, seems to be left; and I doubt much if the reindeer should be considered exceptional in this regard.

But few efforts have been made to domesticate either species of our Caribou. The Woodland Caribou, at least, seems to be a wild, restless animal, even during the winter ranging through wide districts of country, and often changing his home, and very suspicious and wary. An alarm, from which the moose would only flee a few miles, will send away the Caribou a whole day, at a rapid pace, which takes him quite out of the country, and defies the pursuit of the hunter. These are characteristics which do not promise well for their domestication. When raised as pets, like all the other deer, they lose their fear of man and become very tame, and systematic effort through a long course of years might, no doubt, bring them to a state of semi-domestication, which, after all, is about as much as can be said of the domesticated reindeer of Northern Europe and Asia. There is no other domestic animal which propagates its species in that condition which retains so much of its wild nature as these reindeer. This possibly may be accounted for by the frequent intermixture of wild blood among the domestic herds, which is said to be encouraged by the Lapps, as it is supposed to infuse vigor into the stock. This is not a difficult end to accomplish, as the wild deer often range the same mountains which are inhabited by the tame. The domestication of our Caribou should only be attempted in situations where the climate and food are adapted to the well being of the animal in the wild state.

In the few instances recorded, or of which I have heard, no attempt has been made to breed them in the domestic state, but they have been simply kept as pets, or for exhibition. So far as I am informed, most of the efforts to transport them to Europe have failed, they dying during the voyage. This may, possibly, have resulted from a neglect to take along the reindeer moss, which, as I have shown, is indispensable to the health of the European reindeer, whether tame or wild. It is not too late yet for a fair trial of the experiment of domesticating this deer; still it might be better to try and import those already domesticated from Lapland, and if the greater size of the Caribou be desired they could be bred to them. I am a little surprised that the Hudson's Bay Company, which has ever shown remarkable enterprise and perseverance in the conduct of its business, has never imported the reindeer for transportation purposes, wherever the proper food is found, as they would certainly be more economical than dogs for that purpose.

THE ELK, OR WAPITI DEER.

I have had a good opportunity to study the disposition of our Elk and of all the other smaller species in my own grounds. After all it is only in semi-domestication that we are enabled to sufficiently observe the animal in various circumstances and conditions, to determine his real nature.

There is not the least reason to believe that our Elk have ever shown belligerent dispositions in the wild state, except towards each other. Although very powerful animals, they are timid and wary. They do not confine themselves to a limited range, but are liable to roam over extensive districts of country : now high up the mountains, again in the deep cañons or fertile valleys, and again, far out on the plains along the borders of some watercourse.

When carefully studied in parks, they manifest dispositions not altogether lovely, nor yet desperately wicked. The males show no sense of gallantry towards the females, nor do any of them manifest a sympathy for each other. At any time the buck will drive the doe ruthlessly from any choice thing she may be eating, in his brutish selfishness, having not the least regard for anything but his own gratification. Even in the season of love, as we shall see, he rules his harem with a brutal despotism, without the least manifestation of affection. Even with the females, only the maternal instinct shows any trait of tenderness or regard for the comfort or welfare of another. Indeed, the doe is much more likely to ill treat a young member of the family, not her own, than a buck. If the latter will drive it away quietly, the former will hit it a fearful bat if it comes in her way, and if she knocks it down, she will very likely stamp it to death. I have lost two Elk, less than a year old, by being thus roughly handled. One had received a blow on the back, and it never again rose to its feet without assistance. When it was reported to me as ill, I went and examined it. Suspecting the trouble, I pressed my finger along the spinal column without its flinching, till two thirds back from the shoulders to the hips, when it fairly screamed, in so piercing a tone that it startled me, and its whole frame quivered from the pain. It must have been a fearful blow to have thus disabled the poor thing. It died in two days in spite of all I could do for it. The other I found bruised in a frightful way, indicating that it had been murdered in malicious wickedness. I am sorry to write such unkind things of pets, for which I have kindly cared for so many years, but I must tell the truth.

I think the females show more real courage than the males. I was once driving through the park, when we observed an old doe whose anxious look excited suspicion ; we hitched the horses, and commenced a search for a fawn; at last we saw it curled up in the leaves, perhaps two hundred feet from the dam, who faced us all the while. When she saw we had discovered it, and were going towards it, she uttered a succession of threatening squeals which sounded to us anything but musical, at the same time walking slowly towards us, with an air and a gleam of the eye not to be mistaken. We did not count the spots on that fawn that day, but retreated in as good order as possible with our faces to the foe. My friend, who was not used to the animal, remarked — while I was admonishing him to show no signs of fear but to retire as if it was quite voluntary — " I would give a big check to be in that buggy now ! " Had we run from her, we might not have won the race without trouble.

At another time, when alone, I came across an old doe which was very tame, and which I had very often fed from my hand. She was licking her young fawn, probably not two hours old. I spoke to her kindly, as usual, and she received me with great cordiality, and when I petted her baby, and even lifted it to its feet, she seemed pleased with my attentions, and rather proud of her offspring. She had no fear that I would hurt her darling, but rather remembered the many ears of corn I had given her, and no doubt expected some then, as usual. It evidently did not occur to her that I could hurt anything. She associated nothing of harm with my presence, while in the other case, the mother thought of nothing else, when she observed that we had found her fawn. This one was never tame like the other, and so had never received so many of my favors. But the amiable one was not always amiable, and not always to be trusted. I once came across her when walking through the park with my little daughter. I left her feeding the Elk, and walked away, perhaps to pick some wild flower, and turned round just as the brute struck at the child; fortunately, she was not quite in reach. I spoke to her in no very mild terms, and the blow was not repeated. There was manifested a disposition to strike the child simply because she knew it was unable to protect itself.

The animosity to dogs seems to be much stronger in the females, and appears to be all the same with those that have young and those that have not. If a dog gets into the park the does always lead the chase, while the bucks go lumbering along behind, as if rather to see the result than to join in the fray. While the females show the ferocity of tigers, the bucks do not seem to care very much whether the dog gets away or not. It is the females that rush at the fence to get at the dog on the opposite side, while the males stand back and treat the matter with apparent indifference. If a dog gets into the park and first meets a band of buck Elk, they will take fright and break away towards the does ; but, when he falls in with even a single doe, the white patch upon the rump rises up immediately ; her eyes flash with rage, and, without an instant's hesitation, she pitches at him, while the bucks will fall in the rear, and perhaps stop or follow up, rather than join in the chase. Indeed, I am obliged to say that the buck Elk is not only extremely selfish and tyrannical, but, as is usual with tyrants, is an arrant coward. He may be ferocious, but not courageous. Neither in the wild or the domestic state will he make an effort to protect or defend either the young or the female, but seems willing to sacrifice them all for his own safety.

Individuals differ very much in their dispositions, some being much more vicious than others, or rather some being naturally very wicked, while a large majority show no such disposition. I have had more than one hundred in my grounds altogether, and yet I never had but two that were positively wicked. These reached as near the point of total depravity during the rutting season as I think it possible for a brute to do. Both these animals I purchased with four does. They were probably raised by hand, which, as we shall see, tends to divest all the deer family of their natural fear of man, which allows their native viciousness to manifest itself, which is very apt to happen, at least with the males, during the rut. This, no doubt, tended to aggravate the innate wickedness of these Elk, but is quite insufficient to explain it all. I had previously had a very fine specimen, five years old, which had not only been brought up by hand, but kept in a show for a long time, and, although during the rut he would make ugly faces, utter the threatening squeal, and make threatening gestures, especially to strangers, he never made an assault upon any one, and not only his keeper but strangers were in the habit of going through the park at all seasons.

The fall after he was three years old, having returned home after a short absence, I went into the park and met the Elk which proved to be so wicked. During my absence, he had shed the velvet from his antlers, which were now well polished. As soon as he saw me he walked towards me in a confident and rather impudent way. I picked up a hickory club I found near, and stepped behind a small tree, which he directly straddled with his antlers, and tried to reach me, not very viciously, but still in an unpleasant way. I struck him a good blow on the head, the force of which, however, was principally spent on his antlers. The only effect was to increase his efforts to reach me. I did not much like the situation and proposed a compromise. I threw down an ear of corn a little to one side which he readily took, and another thrown still further away was accepted as a peace offering. When he had finished them he walked quietly away, and as I could not remember any other important business in the park just then I concluded to return home. I gave orders to have all the Elk turned into the North Park the next morning, the propriety of which was the more apparent when I learned that he had run every man out of the park that went into it that same evening.

In the morning he was absolutely furious, and would rush against the fence with great force, at the sight of a man on the opposite side, and would follow him along the fence, fighting it all the way, and by this means alone was he transferred from the South to the North Park, and led to the north part of it quite out of the way, while the balance of the herd were transferred to the same inclosure, the gates securely locked, and the fence examined and repaired with the utmost care. If he did not grow more vicious as the season advanced it was simply because there was no room for him to do so. He was already at the extreme point of wickedness, and so he could not go beyond it. He was truly terrible.

All visitors were of course excluded from the North Park, and every possible notice given of the danger of invading it. Within a month three men, who thought they knew best and were not afraid of anybody's Elk, scaled the fence, and quietly walked along till they met the herd of Elk, when the leader started after them in a very dignified walk. They thought they had seen enough, and commenced an orderly retreat. The Elk increased his pace, and soon treed two of the party and killed the other. One of them, a young, active, athletic man, left his tree and by running from tree to tree finally escaped, gave the alarm, raised a party who fought the Elk with pitch-forks till they finally drove him off, although at first he drove the three resolute active men, thus armed, several hundred feet before they could sufficiently break his guard to compel him to acknowledge the virtues of their sharp hay-forks. He did not charge upon them with a rush, in the ordinary mode of joining battle practiced by all the deer, but lowered his head so as to bring his face nearly parallel with the ground, presenting his great antlers to the enemy, rendering it difficult for the men to reach him with their weapons. In order to see before him he was obliged to turn his head more or less sideways when one of the antlers would reach the ground and raise the head somewhat. At length the flankers were enabled to reach him low down back of the fore leg, where the skin is thin. This caused him to give way and finally to retire, but slowly and sullenly and without flight. We may well suppose that under the circumstances, trying to drive an infuriated brute from a dying man, they struck heavy blows with their sharp forks, either one of which would no doubt have killed a horse or an ox, and yet they barely sufficed to keep this Elk a short distance away. And after the wounded man was placed in the carriage and guarded by all but the driver he followed them closely and threateningly till they passed out of the gate, and they no doubt felt relieved when the high fence was between them. After they left he seemed beside himself with rage, and towards evening, when his keeper, who had often punished him severely with the fork, was walking along the fence, he rushed at him as if he desired an opportunity to settle all scores at once, and no doubt he would have done so could he have got at him. The keeper passed down the fence, the deer following screaming with rage all the way to an opening left for the smaller deer. Through this he thrust his face, when the man struck him with all his might with a heavy hickory club with the purpose of killing him if possible. The blow staggered him, but that was all. The man quickly passed through the opening to repeat the blow before the brute could recover. The punishment was so severe that the Elk retired a little way and would retreat so long as he was pursued, but so soon as the man turned to leave the park the brute followed, though at a respectful distance.

The next morning I went with the keeper and two other active men and castrated the buck. We had no trouble to catch him, for so soon as we came in sight outside the park he rushed to the fence and tried to break through. The keeper had but to get on to the upper rail and with a strong rope throw a noose over the end of one antler below the first prong while the animal was making frantic efforts to reach him. So soon as this was done we bore willing hands and drew the antler tight against the palings. He made tremendous efforts to break loose, and I expected to see the antler give way, but it held him, although it sprung very much under the great strain, nor would he break his neck, a result which I rather desired. After he had become well worried I took a long chain and after a while succeeded in getting it secured around his neck, and fastened it firmly to a post. We then detached the rope from his antler and went inside and commenced operations to cast him. This we at last succeeded in doing and in tying all his feet firmly together, when the operation was readily performed. We then undid the chain, and then his feet, and let him up, appreciating that he was too much exhausted and subdued to attack us. Still he retired in good order, and repeatedly looked around savagely, but that was all. By evening, however, he got wicked again and tried to break the fence to reach his keeper. The next day he showed less vicious symptoms, and his wickedness seemed to abate day by day, and by the end of a week all had disappeared and he was ever after as docile as a lamb. This was soon discovered by the other buck, which was a year younger and over which he had tyrannized in a lordly way. Long before his antlers dropped off, which occurred in about four weeks, the young fellow was taking his revenge abundantly, and my sympathies were very little excited, when I saw him chasing the old tyrant through the brush at a rattling pace, whenever he ventured near the harem, the government of which the young buck assumed and exercised with the same despotism which had characterized the rule of the other. This was in September, the height of the rutting season. In a very short time this young buck developed all the wickedness of the first, but as I had no other one old enough for breeding I was obliged to endure him till a year from the first of the next January, when I castrated him also. And now for the last ten years he has been the tamest and most inoffensive Elk in the band. Even the monarch holds him in such contempt that he allows him to run with the does during the rutting season, although if he comes near him he will most likely get an admonition to keep at a respectful distance.

I have been thus particular in describing the conduct of these two animals, because it serves to convey a more correct idea of their dispositions than I could give by any general explanation. These, however, must be regarded as showing the extreme of wickedness. The one that succeeded to the rule when he was two years old, after the second was castrated, never offered to attack a person, and manifested about the same disposition as the first which I had, of which I have before spoken. He felt his courage stimulated, no doubt, during the rutting season, and was as wicked as he need be towards the younger bucks; nor did I consider it safe for a stranger to go into the park, but my own men went through it at all times in security. One fall, I sent my teams in to haul stone from the Elk Park during the rutting season. It was manifest he did not like it, but he made no attack upon them, though he would frequently place himself in the road and face them, but would allow them to quietly turn out and drive around him. Of course, they were prepared for emergencies, and were ordered to diminish the number by one if he offered to attack. The other bucks — and there were at least a dozen about as large as he was — never showed the least viciousness at any season, and so it was with the second one during the reign of the first as above described, and yet as soon as he succeeded to the rule his whole disposition seemed changed at once, and he immediately became as bad as the other. As we shall hereafter see, this was the last of my very vicious Elk.

I think that the very wicked bucks are exceptional, probably, as much so as vicious bulls among our common stock. We all know that occasionally a bull is met with which will attack any person on sight, still they are generally docile. Perhaps with some limitations, I think the same law governs the Elk, and that we shall rarely find specimens as vicious as those described. The first and finest male Elk I ever had was brought up by hand, was well halter broken, had been constantly handled, and yet he was not vicious in disposition, although he would often make demonstrations towards strangers during the rut. While they seem to have no individual attachments, and no affection for each other, and are very selfish, they are still social in their nature, and so are gregarious in their habits. It is rare to find a solitary individual, and then I think it is the result of accident rather than choice. They are easily alarmed, and when one shows signs of fear it instantly communicates itself to the whole band. The first to take alarm is most likely a buck. If they see the keeper coming towards them, and a single one fails to recognize him, and dashes away on that long trot, and with a high head indicating alarm, the chances are that all will take fright and dash away into the woods, or onto the next side-hill, and there stop and turn around to see what frightened them. A few calls and his well known voice is recognized, when they will come towards him. Since the band has got large and they have been more confined to the secluded East Park, those does which were formerly so very tame have been less petted and have become more shy, and do not come up to me with the confidence and familiarity they once manifested.

I often see the young bucks, that is, those three or four years old and younger, engaged at play with their antlers as if in sham fight, in the fall and winter. This is the only amusement I have ever seen them engaged in. I have never observed the least disposition in the young fawns or the does to play together in any way.

Our Elk is more polygamous in his habits than any other deer except his congener the Red Deer of Europe (*C. elaphus*), or even any other quadruped with whose habits I am acquainted. Although they show such a lack of affection or sympathy for each other individually, still all are generally found together throughout the year till the commencement of the rut, when the master Elk asserts his prerogative, drives from the band all the other bucks, and gathers the does around him and keeps them together as much as possible. During this time the young bucks submit with tolerable grace to this discipline, and mostly keep together by themselves in a distant part of the park, generally with a few does that have eluded the vigilance of the master. But sometimes a refractory young fellow will be seen hanging around the skirts of the band of does and gives the despot great trouble, which seems to be a real source of enjoyment to his tormentor. If he shows himself too near, his senior will rush at him with a wild ferocity and chase him, with threatening squeals, perhaps one or two hundred yards, making a terrible crash in the brush during the chase, for the pursued seeks the thickest shrubbery in his flight, and, if hard pressed, the youngster will utter a shrill scream of alarm, but always manages to save his hide, and stops short so soon as the pursuit is over, and follows back pretty close upon the heels of the old buck, who hardly gets his family well collected before his jealousy is again excited by the impertinence of his tormentor, when another rush is made and the maneuver is repeated. Where there are a dozen or more nearly as large as himself, with twenty or thirty does to watch, the old fellow has a distressing time of it, and sometimes he gets so enraged that his defiant and threatening notes may be heard at a great distance. This note so nearly resembles that of a steam whistle, when pitched on a high key, that I have sometimes mistaken the one for the other when half a mile away. This note is heard in the night much more than in the day time. This is

19

sometimes so continuous as to disturb the rest of the keeper's family, whose house is little more than a quarter of a mile from the Elk Park. This note of rage is sometimes really appalling, and, when the animal is half a mile away, sounds as if it were right under the window. In the height of the season these revels seem to be kept up nearly the whole night, during which the revelers give the master no peace of his life. Why do not two or more form an alliance and attack and whip the master? But their philosophy does not reach to that extent, and it is well ordered that it should not, for should one attack him with vigor while he is engaged with another he would be surely killed at the first charge, and if such a system were followed up the bucks would soon be reduced to two; so we see it is better as it is. Except during the rutting season, in my grounds at least, the Elk can hardly be considered a nocturnal animal, though in the wild state, and when surrounded by dangerous enemies, he will seek his food at night and ruminate in some secret place during the day.

I never see the bucks chasing the does at speed during the rutting season, as is the constant habit with the common deer, for, after all, they seem less importunate, and so the does are not driven to shun the society of the males before their proper time arrives, which is not till some time after the bucks become very ardent. If the female Elk desires to get away from the control of the master she slips off quietly while his attention is engaged in another direction, when she generally resorts to the band of younger bucks, who seem to pay scarcely more attention to her than to each other.

This continual excitement and activity reduces the flesh of the old buck so that he always commences the winter poorer than any of the others, although at the first of September he was fully up to the average in condition, as round and sleek as one could wish. During the rut, and while supreme, he is rarely seen to feed, but seems to live in a round of excitement and rage. He loses flesh pretty rapidly, looks hollow and gaunt, the fire of his eye only testifying to his continued vigor, or rather energy, for he maintains his sway for a considerable time by his undaunted mien, after his actual strength no longer entitles him to the mastery. In this condition he is sometimes attacked by another buck nearly equal to him at the best, and is driven from the harem with contumely, and sullenly takes his place on the outside among the young bucks, when the new sovereign lords it over him and his own late companions with whom, but the day before, he had grazed some secluded corner of the park in peace and friendship. His continued reign, however, is not always assured, for once, at least, I observed that the deposed monarch, after recruiting for a week or ten days, had attacked and deposed the usurper, who again retired to private life with the best grace possible. The does seem to look upon these struggles with great indifference. What matter to them whether a Bourbon or a Bonaparte rules, as it is nothing but tyranny always, at least during this exciting season?

About the commencement of the rut, the male Elks have frequent battles to settle the question not only of sovereignty but of superiority; nor are these settled by a single victory between the individuals. While it is rare that one is actually injured by these contests, they are sometimes fatal. I have lost two adult Elks in this way. In the fall of 1875, one was found badly gored, and appeared to have been dead several days, and in November, 1876, the monarch was found dead, exhibiting many wounds. Like the other deer, the Elk always join battle with a rush, when the shock is really terrific, and the clash of antlers may be heard for a great distance; they then push and worry each other for a time, till one finds himself to a disadvantage in some way, when he will quickly jump to one side and course around a little way and again face his antagonist, when another rush and collision takes place; and this may be repeated several times before one finally acknowledges defeat. In none of the battles which have been witnessed in my grounds, has either sustained injury, so that I cannot explain the incidents of those which have been accompanied with fatal results, but probably some obstacle has intervened which prevented the escape of the vanquished, which has always been effected when the contests have been observed. I have never witnessed one of these meetings myself, but several have occurred in view of my men, who had received particular instructions how to observe, and from them I have obtained what I believe to be full and reliable information.

The Wapiti is much better adapted to domestication than any of the other deer with which I have experimented. In the first place, they are much more healthy. Indeed, I never had a sick Elk in my grounds to my knowledge. They are liberal feeders, no doubt, but then they are not particular about their diet. Mildness and timidity are not so ingrained with them as with the others. The men who feed them in winter go among them, and are shunned scarcely more, by either old or young, than they would be by our common cattle, that have no more constant association with man than they have. They will not submit to be driven from one park to another through the gate, for instance, or into a yard, but so soon as they perceive the object, their suspicions seem to be aroused and they will break back and retreat to a distant part of the park. This no doubt results from want of breaking. Had we practiced driving and herding them from the beginning, I have no doubt they could have been as readily handled as our sheep or cattle. They are very easily broken, when they quietly submit. A young Elk may be caught up and put in the stable, and so soon as he appreciates that he cannot get away, that his efforts to escape avail him nothing, and that he is kindly treated and has nothing to fear, he submits to be handled and harnessed like a colt, though in this experiment I have found individuals to differ much in disposition. I have found no difficulty in completely subduing the fully adult Elk, and this must be done before it is safe to put him in a cage to send away. I once had to ship a pair to friends in California, and got a number in the yard and captured and caged the buck (he was a fine specimen, weighing eleven hundred and fifty pounds with the cage, which may have weighed three hundred pounds). We concluded, as it was getting late, to catch the doe in an easier and quicker way: so we removed a board from the side of the yard and placed the cage in front of it; she saw the opening and dashed in and was secured in a moment. I saw she made a good deal of fuss about it, but thought she would be quiet by morning, and so she was, for I found she had broken her neck during the night, when we had to catch and subdue another, and had no further difficulty. A short explanation of how this is done, taking a large buck, for example, may be interesting. For the purpose I have a Spanish lasso, the noose of which is spread upon the ground in the yard or on the feeding grounds, when we manage to get him to step into it with a hind foot; then three stout men on the outside spring it and draw him towards the fence, being sure at all times to keep the leg drawn out. That is all they are to do without drawing him home too fast. His efforts to escape are at first almost appalling. Directly he throws himself and perhaps will roll quite over and endeavor to spring up, and if too near the fence he must be allowed to do this, at least so far as to get further away, when another strong pull will bring him down, and then when he goes to rise again a good pull will prevent him, and so he is allowed to struggle till he is fairly exhausted. A man then goes in and throws the noose of a long rope over an antler. The gate is now opened quickly and he is dragged out and the gate closed on the remaining Elk. So soon as this is done the man at the rope snubs it around a post or a tree, while those at the lasso pull away till he is fairly stretched out and is perfectly helpless, when all is made fast. In this condition two men will stand upon the antler which lies upon the ground, when a cord is attached to the loose hind foot, which is drawn up and tied to the opposite fore foot. The other hind foot is now drawn up by the lasso and securely tied to the other fore foot. A stout halter is now put upon the head ; first one and then the other antler is sawed off just above the burrs. He is then rolled about to see if he can be induced to make another struggle, but never struck or hurt more than is necessarily involved in this unpleasant operation. When he has completely submitted to his fate, the open end of the cage is brought up, the fall of the halter passed through it, the head is raised and put into the cage as far as it will go, when the feet are loosened, and as he rises the men at the halter pull him in, and by the time he is fairly on his feet he is completely within his prison. The open end is now closed, the halter tied to the cage, and the job is done. After this treatment I have never known one to make a struggle, though the cage be tipped and carried about as it must necessarily be in being put into a wagon or car. In short, they are fairly subdued, acknowledge their weakness, and resign themselves to whatever may come. Generally in a few minutes after they are in the cage they will go to eating hay and corn as if nothing had happened.

Last fall I directed a female Elk to be caught and caged. The men caught her by the hind leg, as described, and when they supposed she was well worried, one went into the yard to throw a noose over her head, when, in a great struggle, the lariat which held the hind foot broke. She made no attempt to run away, but went for the man in a way that left no mistake as to her purpose. He showed unwonted agility in dodging behind the trees, and leaping to the upper rail of the fence, and so escaped.

The most prominent instinct in the young fawn, is that of deception. I have several times come across fawns evidently but a few hours old, left by the mother in supposed security. They affect death to perfection, only they forget to shut their eyes. They lay without a motion, and if you pick them up, they are as

limp as a wet rag, the head and limbs hanging down, without
the least muscular action, the bright eye fairly sparkling all the
time.   The first I met really deceived me, for I thought it had
met with some accident by which it was completely paralyzed,
and returned the next day expecting to find it dead.   It was
gone, and soon after I found it following its dam as sprightly as
possible.   Last spring I found one, picked it up, and carried it
some distance and laid it down, and watched for some time from
a distance, but not the least sign of life would it manifest, save
only in the bright eye.

The Elk's fawn follows its dam much sooner than most of the
other deer.   At most it is left in seclusion but a day or two,
when the mother takes it in immediate charge, and they mingle
with the herd.   In this regard the habit of Wapiti differs from
that of the smaller deer, who keep their young secluded for
several weeks.

The result of my experiments shows that the confinement of
this deer in parks of even considerable extent, impairs its reproductive powers.   This result, I think, is attributable to both
sexes.   On the part of the female the inclination to breed seems
much diminished, and this is especially so with the young ones.
In the wild state they breed at two years old, while in my
grounds I do not think one has ever bred till after she was four
years old, and scarcely more than half of the older females may
be expected to produce young.   This, however, may be attributed to the male.   With him the inclination to breed seems to be
unimpaired, at least it is strong enough, but the limited range
gives the monarch such an opportunity to indulge his propensity
to appropriate all the does to himself, and there is such a constant
effort required to keep them together, when the number is considerable, besides the continual worry occasioned by a dozen or fifteen other large bucks, some of which, at least, intrude upon his
privacy, and seem to take delight in teasing him, and provoking
him to paroxysms of ungovernable rage, that his vital powers
are soon impaired, and his capacity for reproduction, if not destroyed, is greatly reduced.   This was especially manifest with
the " Sultan," who reigned supreme the longest in my grounds,
and now may be seen as a mounted specimen in the Royal Museum
at Christiana, Norway.   At first his progeny were reasonably
numerous, but during the last three years'of his life they gradually diminished from a dozen down to a single fawn in 1875, with
about twenty-five females, more than half of which had pre-

viously produced fawns. It was now evident that his day of usefulness was passed, and he was translated to a very respectable position under Professor Esmark, as stated above. He was succeeded by a buck not more than a year younger, who lost, and then regained, his sway during the season. The result was that I had twelve fawns the next season, including one pair of twins, which are rare from the Elk in domestication. Such is the character of the evidence which induces the conclusion at which I have arrived as to the diminished reproductive powers of the Elk in semi-domestication. The disinclination of the female, especially the young, may be partly owing to the limited selection of food, or want of proper aliment; but as she keeps in perfect health, and in fine condition, it can hardly be attributed to this entirely. After all, I think the partial restraint to which they are subjected, which is so unnatural to them, their ancestors for untold generations having had unlimited range to go when and where they pleased, and to select such associates as they pleased, is the greatest cause of the disinclination of the females to reproduce, and no doubt has its influence upon the fertility of the male. In the wild state the female is believed to breed at two, or at most three, years old, the young females producing one fawn at a birth, and the old ones generally twins, and three are sometimes produced at a birth. The fact that in my grounds the females, never, to my knowledge, have bred before four years old, and never, I think, more than two thirds of these have bred in any one year, and that twins are of very rare occurrence, certainly shows a sad degeneracy. The last summer I saw three great fellows sucking a large doe at one time, and she bore their rough treatment with maternal resignation; but I suspect that one of them, at least, was a poacher on the others' preserves. Remember that all the deer tribe have four active mammæ. No doubt long domestication of Wapiti would produce such a change in the constitution of the race that it would so conform itself to the changed condition that its reproductive powers would be practically restored.

I have never experimented with this deer as a beast of draught, which, after all, as a question of practical utility, is one of great importance. I have a pair of castrated fawns now in the stable, which promise good results. I have seen them a few times in harness, but always too young to work. I once bought a pair of yearling does in harness, but they were only partially broken, and were overloaded with a light buggy and man in it, and so would have been two heifers or colts of the same age. I never harnessed them afterwards. They are undoubtedly as strong as a horse of the same size, and are much more natural trotters than the horse, and with training, I think, would fully equal him in speed and endurance, and would, when fully adult, probably surpass him in both. The Elk has not the weight for heavy draught, but seems well adapted for light, quick work. I confess I have too long neglected this practical question.

THE MULE DEER.

The disposition of the Mule Deer presents a study of more interest than that of any of the others. In some respects they are worse and in others better than either of the other species. The adult bucks when brought up by hand are wicked during the rutting season, and seem to take a positive delight in threatening if not in attacking their best friend, so that it is never safe to venture very near to them without a good club during the rut. The old does, too, are treacherous at all seasons, and are liable to attack children whenever they find them unprotected ; at the same time they are the greatest cowards alive. I had an old doe, almost as large as a small elk, that would even attack women if she met them alone in the park, while she would be very complacent to a man whom she thought able to defend himself ; still she was so great a coward that the smallest Virginia deer would drive her wherever it pleased. I have been vastly amused in observing the little Acapulco doe chasing an adult Mule doe around the grounds. The little thing does not appear to be actuated by malice, but does it rather for amusement. The Mule Deer would be following me through the park, and whenever it would happen to get a little way from me the little one would dash in between us and run it off, while the Mule Deer would make a circuit and as soon as possible run to me for protection, when the little tease would stop a little way off and look as if it would enjoy a hearty laugh. This was repeated many times during a single walk. The larger one is fully three times the size of her tormentor, but I have never seen it offer the least resistance to these attacks. I have often seen her chase a Mule buck, which was two years old, in the same way.

The Mule Deer is the only one I have ever seen manifest a clear and decided disposition to play. This they do something after the manner of lambs, by running courses and gamboling about and running up and down the bluffs manifestly for amusement only. I have once noticed something like this in a common deer, but at the best it was the faintest sort of a play, if indeed that was its meaning. And this pestering of the Mule Deer was the only amusement I have seen the diminutive species indulge in. But the Mule Deer not only amuses itself in the way described but loves to have me join him in a little sham fight, and if I handle him a little roughly, or try to throw him down when he rears up and places his feet on my shoulders, he will recover and jump sideways and backwards twisting himself into grotesque attitudes, though he does this in an awkward way. I have not observed this disposition to play after the animal is two or three years old, and the male seems more inclined to it than the female. I elsewhere mention that he sometimes appears to become very appreciative of his own importance, when he will strut around, his tail elevated to a vertical position, as is observed with the male goat.

Altogether there is little to admire in the disposition of the Mule Deer beyond his taste for amusement as above described. The viciousness of the adult male during the rutting season exceeds that of any of the others, in my grounds, at least, which is far from commending him as a familiar pet. This may arise from the fact that they have not the natural fear of man of the Virginia deer, for, as we shall see, when the young are raised by their dams in the park they become much more tame than the others, indeed nearly as much so as if raised by hand.

The Mule Deer manifests by far the most salacious disposition of any of the deer which I have had an opportunity of closely studying.

My efforts to domesticate the Mule Deer and the Columbia Deer have been practical failures. For the last eight years I have with great care and at considerable expense, experimented with both these species, and have brought many individuals from great distances, and have studied their wants and cared for them with unwearied pains, but now all are dead. The last died but a few weeks since. My failures, however, by no means assure us that they may not sustain the burden of domestication in countries where they live and prosper in a wild state. Both are natives of the far West. The Mule Deer I brought from Utah and Nevada, distances from fifteen hundred to two thousand miles, and the Columbia Deer from Washington Territory and Oregon, say three thousand miles away. No wild Mule Deer was ever heard of within five hundred miles of here, and no wild Columbia Deer was ever seen either in or east of the Rocky Mountains. We may well suppose that the change of climate and probably of aliment was too great for them. All have died of one disease, — diarrhea. I hope some one in a congenial locality will make a serious effort to domesticate both these species.

Of both species the first I had dropped in my grounds were twins. Those from the Mule doe lived nearly a year and a half, which gave me a good opportunity to observe the habits of the young. They grew to a fair size; and on the male grew very large antlers for his age, both of which were bifurcated. Neither of these fawns showed the least inclination to breed the summer they were a year old. The conduct of the mother as connected with these fawns, of course interested me. She hid them in separate places, and only sought them at intervals to give them nourishment, and would never go near them, if she suspected she was watched, imitating exactly in this regard the Virginia deer. When one was found and placed in a yard with a fence four feet high, she would sometimes jump the fence and visit it, but refused to allow it to suck till the other was found and placed in the same yard, when she nursed them both indifferently. I could not imagine the cause of her conduct to the first till I found she had another, for which she was evidently saving all the milk. I kept them in the yard but a couple of weeks, where they were visited frequently in order to tame them, but we made little progress in that direction; and believing they would do better at large I turned them out, when she immediately secreted them, and it was six weeks more before she allowed them to follow her, never being seen to visit them except very early in the morning, or late in the evening. I would sometimes come across one in its seclusion, when after the manner of the Virginia fawn it would crouch as low down as possible, with its chin upon the ground and great ears laid back upon its neck, and if it believed itself undiscovered would remain perfectly still, following me with its bright eyes till very near it, but as soon as it appreciated that it was discovered would bound away with the jumps before described, towards some ravine or thicket till out of sight, never stopping once to look back, as is frequently the case with the fawns of the Virginia deer. In the fall, however, they become much tamer than the Virginia fawns raised in the same grounds and under the same circumstance, except the two weeks' confinement before mentioned. By November they would cautiously venture to take corn from my hand, a familiarity never indulged in by a Virginia deer raised by its mother. Ever after they were almost as tame as the Virginia deer raised by hand, ever ready to come to my call and take food from my hand when offered, and follow me all over the grounds, being sure of getting something to encourage them, — still they would never allow me to handle them, as their dam or sire did who were raised by hand, evidently thinking it a great condescension if they allowed me to rub their faces a little. How much I am indebted for this familiarity to the short confinement when they were very young, it is impossible to say, but I think not very much, for they seemed as wild immediately after they were let out as Virginia fawns of the same age, and so continued till in the fall, when they followed their mother up and began to get feed. The Virginia fawns that follow up in the same way soon learn what shelled corn is, and in the course of the winter become so emboldened as to pick it up within ten feet of the keeper, who feeds them every day. All the deer, as well as the flock of wild turkeys, the sand-hill cranes, and the wild geese, and Southdown sheep in my grounds, soon learn what the rattling of the corn-sheller means, and it is one of the pleasantest sights I have among my pets, to see all start at this sound and make a rush for the feeding grounds where all eat together pretty harmoniously, the wildest of each always showing a little suspicion and keeping well on the outer borders.

THE BLACK–TAILED DEER.

The male of the Columbia Black-tailed Deer is only less wicked than I have reason to believe the fully adult mule deer, when he has been raised by hand. How he would behave if raised by his dam in the park I cannot say. I have never observed any vicious manifestations by the adult does, as is the case with the mule does.

The first of *C. Columbianus* which I ever had I procured on the Cowlitz River in Washington Territory, in 1870. The male was then one year old and the female two years old. They stood the journey of three thousand miles by sea and land well, and arrived in fine condition. Both had been brought up by hand, but the doe had never been subjected to the halter, and for a time gave me some trouble in transferring her from one conveyance to another, but by the time she got through she was well halter-broken.

They appeared to thrive well when turned into the parks in July, and showed no symptoms of salivation from the white clover, which was so severe upon the mule deer the year before. In the fall they were turned into the orchard and vineyard with a pair of mule deer, a year or two older than they were. Here they remained till early winter, when they were all returned to the parks. In the late winter the Columbia doe died, having in her two fawns sufficiently developed to show they were from the Columbia buck. For the next two years I only had the buck of this species. He continued as tame as any deer in my grounds, but always manifested a morose if not a vicious disposition.

At first, the doe, being a year the oldest, tyrannized over him in a very undutiful way, but so soon as his spike antlers, nearly seven inches long, were matured, the mastery was changed and he returned her attentions in kind. While in the vineyard by themselves neither of the four deer seemed inclined to associate with either of the others, but I always found them solitary, even during the rutting season, although both does became *enciente* while there by the bucks of their own species. I never saw either of these bucks make the least attempt to chase the does, which is so prominent a habit with the Virginia deer.

During the next summer and after, so long as he lived, the buck ranged the parks at will, but generally solitary. So soon as his second antlers matured he showed such signs of viciousness that I sawed them off, which reduced his threatening demonstrations, but still his conduct seemed to say that he wanted to hurt somebody. This was when he was two years old past, an age at which I have never observed a Virginia buck to show the least wickedness. He walked about the grounds, even while his antlers were growing, with a slow and measured step, with his ears laid back upon his neck, when there was nothing in sight to excite his animosity. He would come to my call to take corn from my hand, but he approached not with gladness but slowly and with that everlasting leer, as if he would prefer to strike me rather than take the corn. I think, however, that sometimes at least this expression did him injustice, for he would frequently lay his head upon my breast in an affectionate way as if to invite caresses, which he seemed to enjoy. After his antlers were sawed off he would follow a pedestrian in the road, for half a mile along the fence, as if he would be glad to get at him. A month or six weeks after his antlers were taken off, he somehow escaped from the park and went up the road half a mile, when he met a man and a boy with whom he disputed the right of way at once. The man broke up a fence board over his head, but went to grass twice in the conflict and received some bruises from his fore feet, but the fence saved him from serious injury. So soon as his escape and this feat were reported, the keeper went for him and at· tempted to put a strap around his neck and lead him home, when he knocked him down, but was satisfied with that, and quietly submitted to be led back to the park. Indeed I think he showed as much wickedness as did the mule deer at his age ; and during the entire winter he looked and acted as if troubled with bad digestion, and consequently in an ill humor with everybody and everything. However, he eat full rations and grew fat. The next year we were again obliged to remove his antlers, but towards winter he began to show symptoms of disease ; though he eat his allowance well, in the latter part of winter he failed rapidly and died in the spring.

I never knew him to take any notice of a Virginia deer, except to drive it away from some food he coveted, but he sometimes condescended to play, in a very lazy way, with the young mule buck that sported his first antlers, by rubbing their heads together, as if in mimic battle. He evidently thought the mule deer more worthy of his attention than the Virginia deer.

This was the only manifestation of a disposition to play which I have ever observed in the Columbia Deer. The Columbia Deer are not the arrant cowards which the mule deer proved to be.

I never raised a Columbia fawn. None survived more than a few days, though, as is elsewhere explained, I think this was due to accidental causes. Under more favorable circumstances, the fawns might live for a year or two, but I do not believe it practicable to bring them directly from their native haunts and propagate successfully from them here. However, we cannot tell. I have inquired for many years why the Columbia deer never comes east of the Sierras in California, or even into the western slopes of the Rocky Mountains further north. When I consider the variety of climate which he endures on the Pacific coast, and that there is no kind of food there which he could not find elsewhere, I am surprised that their range is circumscribed by an imaginary line, beyond which they cannot pass more than if the boundary were a Chinese wall.

THE COMMON DEER.

By nature the Virginia Deer is more timid than either of the above. When raised by hand the male forgets that man is its natural enemy, and so ceases to fear him, and then he is very apt during the rut to become wicked and dangerous. This disposition, however, is not manifested till he is three or four years old ; nor is it universal, for I have had some that never became vicious even during the rut, though this is exceptional. But very few can be safely kept as pets after they become adult, unless one has proper facilities for confining them. Usually sawing off the antlers will so moderate their viciousness as to render them comparatively harmless, but not always. Generally it may be said that the Virginia does never become vicious, though I have had one or two that would strike a child when feeding them, if one thought she did not get her share, or it was not given her as fast as suited her.

When raised in the park by its dam, the Virginia Deer never loses its fear of man so as to show the least disposition to attack him, or to come near enough to take food from his hand. Still there is a great difference among them in this regard, some venturing within a few feet to pick up corn from the ground, while others will always keep at a wary distance. They soon learn to come to the call of one who feeds them, and it is a pretty sight to see twenty or thirty, which were quietly lying down ruminating, at the first sound of the keeper's voice all jump to their feet like a flash, dash away without a moment's pause, flags lifted high, and course among the trees and across the ravines, as if each life depended on being first.

The great characteristic of the Virginia Deer is its natural wildness, which it never overcomes so as to lose its dread of man, unless taken when a few days old and fed by his hand and kept in constant and intimate association with him ; for if separated from him but for a single season, associating with the wilder deer he forgets the kindness he has received, and resumes, though to a less extent than the others, his wild timidity. If taken very young, like all the other deer of the same age, it seems to know no difference between its captor and its dam. Pick one up from its leafy bed, and carry it a few minutes, petting it tenderly, and then set it down, and it will follow you with the same confidence it would its own mother ; and then if this intercourse and kindness be continued, it bestows its confidence upon the hand that feeds it without stint and without restraint. If taken after a few months old, its wildness seems ineradicable. I once caught a fawn in December in the deep snow, which had become so emaciated that it could not escape, and placed it in a comfortable stall in the barn. So soon as it became warm, and recovered something of its vitality, it made frantic efforts to escape. It, however, soon commenced to eat, if no one was present, when it recovered its strength and spirit. It was kept in the same comfortable quarters during the winter, and got in fine condition, but seemed absolutely untamable, though daily efforts were made by the keeper to acquire its confidence. Whenever he would go into the stall and try to pet it, it would make strong efforts to escape by jumping against the sides, and when it found that impossible, it would turn and fight him, dealing fierce blows with its little feet; and when it was turned out in April, it seemed as wild as at the first, though it had received nothing but kindness from him during its four months of confinement. It hastened away to the flock, and was the sleekest deer of them all, and by this means it was recognized for a time, but none of them was wilder than he was so long as he could be identified.

More efforts have been made to domesticate this deer than any of our other species, and generally under more favorable circumstances than my grounds afford. Some years since I visited the plantation of General Harding, near Nashville, Tennessee, to learn the result of his experiments. I found his parks much larger than mine and the conditions much more favorable for success. Here was a large, gently rolling lawn carpeted with a heavy coat of blue grass, and scattered through it a great number of magnificent old oaks, whose broad spreading branches afforded a delightful shade everywhere. Beyond, and separated from it by a low fence which the deer could easily scale, was an inclosure of high rolling ground densely covered with a thicket of evergreen cane and several other kinds of shrubbery, of which nearly all ruminants are very fond. The grounds were well watered. Here we find every condition requisite for the well being of the deer, with little restraint and conditions nearly approaching the wild state. The deer we met with in driving through the grounds were wilder than most of mine, and yet they did not seem alarmed when we approached them but trotted away so as to keep some distance off. I learned they were reasonably fertile, though not as much so as in the wild state. At the commencement of the late war there were about eighty deer in these grounds, but the march of great armies is not favorable to the prosperity of deer in such a place, and soon all were either driven away or killed. The General was surprised and gratified to observe that after the war was over and peace and quiet once more reigned about their old home, the deer began voluntarily to return, so that in a few years the grounds were again well stocked. I thought it a fact of much interest that the deer returned voluntarily after an absence of three or four years.

I have heard of some deer parks in the upland portions of Virginia where deer were successfully entrapped as well as reared. To accomplish the former the well known habit during the rut, of the doe fleeing from the pursuit of the buck was utilized. The inclosure along a steep hillside was so prepared that the deer could easily jump into the park but could not jump out. An old doe, which had been brought up by hand and always accustomed to the place and well acquainted with this runway, was turned loose in the surrounding forest and roamed about at will, till she met with a gallant buck when the race would commence; the ardent lover would be quickly led to the runway and into the park from which there was no escape.

When I first began to gather my stock of Virginia Deer I succeeded in obtaining about sixteen individuals in the course of three years, mostly females, all but one born in a wild state. For two or three years they were moderately prolific, rarely breeding till they were three years old, and still more rarely having twins. A few died from age, but the fawns seemed reasonably vigorous, and my stock increased to about sixty, notwithstanding considerable losses from a swelling under the jaw. The fawns, however, came later and later each succeeding year; the bucks showed less inclination to pursue the does, and a less proportion of the does had fawns, showing altogether a great decrease in the vigor of the herd generally; but this was more especially manifest in the fawns, a very large proportion of which died before cold weather set in. I sometimes found two or three dead fawns in a morning's walk through the ground. A perusal of my note-book shows that at that time I absolutely began to despair of perpetuating the species in domestication; one season, particularly, I did not winter more than three out of more than twenty fawns. This, however, was the culminating point of my misfortune. The most feeble ones had been evidently eliminated from the lot, while the numbers had been reduced more than one half from the highest point, though I had taken but few of the bucks for my own table. I had observed two or three does that generally had two fawns at a birth which appeared vigorous and healthy, while the other does that survived became or always had been barren. I think I may safely express the opinion that from a few exceptional individuals that could bear domestication and who were capable of imparting similar vigor to their descendants, I have obtained a stock of Virginia Deer, which though not as prolific by any means as the wild deer, are still moderately so and have sufficient vigor to insure the success of my experiment, while the descendants of ninety per cent. of those taken from the wild state will degenerate in domestication, so that in a few generations they will become extinct. This want of vigor does not show itself so much in the first stock as in the second and third generation, while but very few will reach the fourth generation. I am now passing the fifth winter with what I may call vigorous fawns, none of which have died from an apparent want of vigor, as was the case before, so that my stock has actually increased, while I have supplied my table abundantly with venison from the bucks. A majority of the does are still barren, but this I deem fortunate, for they are not giving me enfeebled descendants to perpetuate for a time a stock which cannot bear domestication. However, a part of the barrenness of one year may probably be attributed to my attempt to force a cross between the Virginia does and the black-tailed buck, to effect which I kept quite a number of the does in one of the parks with that buck alone, but none of them had fawns, and my experiment was a failure. Indeed, the buck paid no more attention to the does, so far as we could observe, than did the Southdown ram in the same inclosure. Each would drive a doe from coveted food with equal rudeness.

The want of vigor and reproductive powers in the deer are probably due, to some extent at least, to the want of arboreous food, of which the Virginia Deer have to a large extent been deprived. However, a want of proper food is not the sole cause of the deterioration produced by domestication. The confinement which prevents them from roaming abroad, the want of exercise, and the absence of that constant vigilance, prompted by the instinct of self preservation to avoid enemies, no doubt, have a large influence to produce the result I have observed. But we may not be able to wholly explain why it is that a considerable proportion of the Common Deer taken from the wild state and subjected to the influence of domestication, so deteriorate as to become

20

either wholly or partially barren, and their progeny in a few generations become so enfeebled as to die out altogether. But we have seen that a few do apparently retain much of their native vigor, and reproductive powers, which they transmit in a large degree to their descendants. "Gipsy," a favorite doe now ten years old, taken in the wild state when a fawn, did, for several years at least, produce healthy vigorous twins, although she rarely got arboreous food, except what was broken from the trees by storms, or fell in the course of nature, — for in the North and South Parks the deer have killed off all the shrubbery, which was there originally, and while the deterioration in vigor and reproductive powers was not observable, was very abundant. I do not despair of finally producing a race of deer that will be both healthy and prolific in domestication, and that, too, when confined entirely to herbaceous food. To accomplish this, I have no doubt much weakness must be eliminated from the stock, but nature is doing that, and if but some survive the test then is the experiment a success. Could we go far enough back in history to learn of the particulars of the domestication of many of our domestic animals, which now breed and thrive well in our hands, we should probably find some such experience as I have related. However, if this be generally true of the quadrupeds, it is scarcely so of all the feathered tribes. My experiments with the wild turkey show that the wild birds reared in domestication are remarkably vigorous and healthy, much more so than the common domestic turkey, while they are equally prolific, though in many instances both the male and female are a year later in breeding than the domestic bird. Probably, as a general rule, the reproductive powers of birds are less impaired by domestication than are those of quadrupeds.

The young bucks seem to quite forget their dams after they are one year old. The habits of the wild deer are not very much modified by partial domestication, although after the rutting season is over they seem to be more gregarious in a wild state than in the parks; yet solitary deer are frequently met with in the prairies and in the forests.

There is no recognized monarch among the bucks, though where they meet frequently a superiority is soon settled which, for the time, is respected; but if separated for some months a new contest is required to determine which is the *better* deer.

The passage between the North and East Park was closed during the last summer, and there was a large buck in each of about equal age and size. In September, after their antlers had become hard, they occasionally saw each other on opposite sides of the fence, when they would make faces at each other, with various threatening demonstrations, showing that both were ready for the fray. I directed the passage to be opened ; and when the one in the East Park came into the North Park he soon met his antagonist, when a terrific battle ensued. The battle was joined by a rush together like rams, their faces bowed down nearly to a level with the ground, when the clash of horns could have been heard at a great distance ; but they did not again fall back to repeat the shock, as is usual with rams, but the battle was continued by pushing, guarding, and attempting to break each other's guard, and goading whenever a chance could be got, which was very rare. It was a trial of strength and endurance, assisted by skill in fencing and activity. The contest lasted for two hours without the animals being once separated, during which they fought over perhaps half an acre of ground. Almost from the beginning, both fought with their mouths open, for they do not protrude the tongue prominently, like the ox, when breathing through the mouth. So evenly matched were they that both were nearly exhausted, when one at last suddenly turned tail to and fled ; his adversary pursued him but a little way. I could not detect a scratch upon either sufficient to scrape off the hair, and the only punishment suffered was fatigue and a consciousness of defeat by the vanquished. I may remark that the victor was the intruder from the East Park, where he had lived with perhaps a dozen companions, almost as wild as in a state of nature, for it is mostly appropriated to the elk, where visitors are not allowed. There they can be as secluded as they please. It contains sixty-five acres, is broken with several broad ravines, and is covered with a young forest with many dense thickets of shrubs, and is a real paradise for the Virginia Deer whose timidity prompts him to seek seclusion.

The pursuit of the doe by the buck commences before her season has arrived, and hence for two or three weeks she remains as secluded as possible. He follows her track with his nose to the ground, and when started from her bed the race is very spirited ; but she manages to elude the pursuit by mingling with the other deer and again slipping away. No attempt is made by a buck to herd the does, as is the custom of the elk, and but few of these deer are found associating together during the rutting season ; but after it is passed they assemble in larger herds than at any other season.

The fawns are weaned by the time they are four months old, but they follow the dam,— the males for one year, and the females for two years. After the fawns are weaned, the does improve very rapidly in flesh. Indeed it is astonishing to see how rapidly a buck or a doe will improve so soon as the acorns begin to fall. Ten days are sufficient to change a poor deer to a fat one, at the time when the summer coat is discarded and the glossy winter dress appears.

THE ACAPULCO DEER.[1]

While I cannot charge the Acapulco Deer with having a wicked disposition, it certainly has more courage and combativeness than any of our other deer, and corresponds in these respects with the Ceylon deer. This is apparent from what has been already incidentally mentioned in several places in this work. They do not hesitate to attack deer of the other species three times their size and strength, and beat them by mere force of courage and will. I shall not now repeat examples to illustrate this.

They seem to be hardy in domestication, but whether they would continue so and would be prolific through succeeding generations, are questions yet to be proved. So far both they and the Ceylon deer have proved hardy and prolific, but so it was with the Virginia deer at first, and it was not till the third or fourth generation, that the great want of vigor and reproductive

---

[1] While this work is going through the press, I find in the Museum of Comparative Zoölogy of Harvard College a mounted specimen of this Acapulco Deer marked " *Cervus Mexicanus* " and referring to " Hassler Expedition," and giving Acapulco as its location. *Cervus Mexicanus* of the naturalists is much larger than this deer, and has all the indicia of *C. Virginianus*, only it is smaller than the same species farther north. I have found the best representatives of *C. Mexicanus* in the gardens of the London Zoölogical Society. Without again going into the detail of the indicia observed, I may say that the metatarsal gland is present on *C. Mexicanus*, and is in all respects case marked precisely as on the common deer ; while this gland is entirely wanting on *C. Acapulcensis*, and so it is on the mounted specimen referred to. It is not remarkable that one who has not made a special study of the deer, should confound the two, and so give the smaller and more southern species the name of the other, actually believing them to be identical. Had not the name *Cervus Mexicanus* been long appropriated to a variety of the Virginia deer, I should have selected it for the name of this small species, which, so far as I know, I have for the first time accurately described, but to have given it that most appropriate name would have ever confounded it with the variety of the common deer to which the name has been so long attached. Hence I was compelled to give it another name in order to preserve the proper distinction. If travelers, and even naturalists, have hitherto supposed these two species of small Mexican deer to be identical, I trust hereafter they will have no trouble in distinguishing and identifying a specimen of either whenever met with.

powers were so fatally manifest. The second generation of the Ceylon deer are good breeders, but I think are not as hardy as the first. At least I have lost two the past summer, one in yeaning, and the other when I was absent, and from an unknown cause. The fact that they never saw snow till they came into my grounds, when they were fully adult, and have borne three winters, the two first very severe, without injury, except the loss of small portions of the ears, would indicate that they have hardy constitutions, naturally; but that two of the second generation of the Ceylon deer have had the swelling under the head indicates a tendency to weakness; but the fact again, that both recovered without treatment, while the disease, if left to take its course, has always proved fatal to the common deer, encourages the belief that they possess a large amount of vitality. Certain it is that they have been much more healthy in domestication than either the mule deer or the Columbia deer, although much further removed from their native habitat, and from the torrid zone to a rigorous climate, where they have endured a temperature at times forty or fifty degrees below the freezing point of water, while the home of the latter is at least as cold as it is here. It is safe to say then, that they are capable of enduring greater changes in the conditions of life than the larger species, which are sure to die in a few years, upon being brought from the Pacific coast, or even the Rocky Mountains, to the east of the Mississippi River.

HYBRIDITY OF THE CERVIDÆ.

As has been already several times intimated, nature seems to have established a law of sexual aversion not only among the genera, but even among the species of animals and plants, which is more or less intense as the dividing line which separates the species is more or less pronounced. This aversion is more potent with the female than the male, and is more commanding in the wild state than when they are brought together in confinement, and partial or complete domestication. This aversion is sufficient to prevent the commingling of blood of species very nearly allied when unrestrained in the wild state, though inhabiting abundantly the same wild range, and perhaps this law of sexual aversion may furnish as safe a rule as any to distinguish species from varieties. Varieties are never constant and distinguishable in the same district of country, for the simple reason that there is no sexual restraint, which absolutely prevents the maintenance of hereditary distinctions which distinguish varieties, and so would it happen among species, were there no natural restraint to keep them asunder. When such restraint exists which amounts to practical prohibition, nature itself declares a purpose to maintain a specific distinction.

If we recognize the law of evolution, then the lines of separa- ration of divergent families from an original stock, have become so widely separated as to interpose this law of sexual aversion between them, and we shall be sure to find permanent physical characteristics dependent not upon factitious circumstances, but solely on hereditary influences, which, uniting with the law of sexual aversion, satisfactorily declares distinct species, where, a long time before, when the lines of divergence were less sep- arated, they were but varieties, with scarcely impaired sexual inclinations for each other.

We may admit that sexual intercourse sometimes occurs be- tween individuals of different species in the wild state, just as we see unnatural impulses manifested sometimes in both man and brute, but they are so exceedingly rare as to be entitled to no influence in the general discussion, and we may if you choose agree with those who contend that when such intercourse does take place it is more apt to be fertile, than when the individuals are in confinement or semi-domestication. Indeed we should anticipate such a result, for as I show elsewhere, nearly all wild animals are less fertile in confinement than in the wild state, and this arises not so much because of less inclination to sexual intercourse, but because such intercourse when it does occur is less fruitful.

But it is not my purpose to go far back of the present and grope my way in intricate paths which at best must be but imperfectly lighted up, and discuss subjects not embraced in my present inquiry, and which I am less qualified to examine than others who can bring to their elucidation a much broader inquiry and much more abundant facts than are at my command. My ambition rather is to bring new facts arising within the limited sphere of my observations, which will serve as a single brick to be placed by other and more competent hands in the great structure of ultimate truth, the construction of which is already commenced in the world of science. He who shall furnish the most accurately observed facts, will provide the most acceptable material for the hands of the architect, and an exhaustive inquiry as to facts even within a very narrow sphere will have only done that which must be done in reference to all other subjects before the skillful generalizer will be provided with the necessary material for his great work.

A very common error has prevailed, even to some extent in scientific quarters, that hybrids, or the issue of parents of different species, are necessarily unfertile; in other words, if a supposed hybrid is capable of propagation it is conclusive evidence that the parents were of the same species.

The fact that hybrids are less likely to be productive or are less fertile than the progeny of parents of the same species is undoubtedly true, and a fertile offspring goes a very long way to prove that the parents were of the same species; but there are many well anthenticated cases of fertile hybrids.

The most common and familiar hybrid is the cross between the ass and the mare, which as a general rule is incapable of propagation, either among themselves or with either parent, and this no doubt has had a large influence in creating the general belief referred to; still there are many cases where the mule has bred from the horse; and Dr. Morton says that this is very common in Spain. In his essay on hybridity, published in the "American Journal of Arts and Sciences," 1847, page 212, Dr. Morton has collected together many facts on this subject, tending to show the fertility of many hybrids produced from very distinct species, and some from distinct genera. Although many of the cases cited are of doubtful authority and may have been pressed into the service to support a favorite theory, enough is left to convince us that hybrids from some distinct species are uniformly fertile and in others they are exceptionally fertile. At any rate we may consider it too well settled to admit of successful controversy that fertility of offspring is not conclusive evidence that the parents were of the same species, although in the investigation of that question it should by no means be overlooked.

Indeed it is not improbable that some of our well established species, of quadrupeds, birds, fishes, and plants, may have had their origin in hybrid ancestors, although, as a general rule, we may expect that they would gradually revert to one or the other of the original parents.

A hundred years ago Count de Buffon examined this subject with great industry, and collected many facts tending to throw light upon it; and I can do no better than to quote his conclusions as recorded in Smellie's translation, London edition of 1812, vol. iv., p. 29. He says: "However this matter stands, it is certain from what is above remarked, that mules in general which have uniformly been accused of sterility are neither really or universally barren; and that this sterility is particularly apparent only in the mule which proceeds from the ass and horse, for the mule produced by the he-goat and the ewe is equally fertile as its parents; and most of the mules produced by different species of birds are not barren. It is therefore in the particular nature of the horse and ass that we must search for the cause of the sterility of the mules which proceed from their union; and instead of supposing barrenness to be a general and necessary defect common to all mules it should be limited to the mule produced by the ass and horse; and even this limitation ought to be restricted, as these same mules in certain circumstances become fertile, particularly when brought a degree nearer their original species."

I have for many years sought to produce hybrids from the various species of deer in my grounds, but have succeeded in but four cases. The first of these was a cross between a male Columbia deer and a female mule deer, the second was between the Ceylon buck and the doe from Acapulco. The third was between a Virginia buck and a Ceylon doe, and the fourth was between the Virginia buck and the Acapulco doe. In the first case the male was three years old, in full health and vigor, and the female was two years old, in fine condition. During that season there was no buck of her own species about the place old enough for service. She did not receive the Columbia buck, with which she had been long acquainted, till six weeks after the usual season. Before the fawn was dropped she had become sickly and both the mother and offspring died within four months after.

I had previously kept the same male with an older female mule deer confined together in a small inclosure for some months during the proper season, but she refused all his advances persistently, nor did he manifest much ardor in the pursuit. The year before I had kept this same female mule deer with a male of the same species, and a female Columbia deer with this same male of that species in the vineyard, and each doe produced a pair of fawns true to their species, although the male of *C. macrotis* was older and stronger than that of *C. Columbianus*, and always manifested a hostile disposition towards him, so that it was clearly the choice of the female which determined the paternity.

In the second case, both male and female were in fine condition ; had been brought from California in the same cage, and for a time at least after their arrival associated much together ; and I had no male deer of the same species with the female, and still they passed by the ordinary season without coupling, and the union only took place six months later, and the offspring when produced was still-born, or at least was dead when found.

The next fall the Ceylon buck met with an accident and died before the rut. In his absence the Ceylon does associated, probably reluctantly, with a Virginia buck, from which the oldest produced two hybrids, and the youngest one. These were born after the usual season, but have always been healthy and vigorous, and partake largely of the qualities of the sire. They are nearly as large as the Virginia fawns of the same age, and the tuft of hair over the metatarsal gland is so conspicuous that it may be seen nearly as far as on the Virginia deer, while on their mothers it can only be seen on very close inspection. All the Ceylon does have freely bred to the Virginia buck ever since.

The Acapulco doe which had reluctantly bred to the Ceylon buck six months after the usual time, after his death refused the advances of the Virginia buck for the first season, but finally submitted, and produced two fine hybrids, which, by November, were nearly as large as the mother. On these, the tuft of hair over the metatarsal gland is plainly seen, while, as I have stated, the hybrids from the Ceylon buck, on which this gland is exceedingly small, showed no vestige of the gland, the absence of which they inherited from the mother. The hybrids from the Virginia buck, on which the gland is conspicuous, inherited it from the sire.

The readiness with which the Ceylon does bred to the Virginia bucks would point to the conclusion that they are specifically more nearly allied than are the Ceylon and the Acapulco deer, although in the former case one is more than twice as large as the other; besides, they differ very much in form, color, and habit, for the Virginia deer are very gregarious, while the Ceylon deer are quite solitary in their habits, never associating together, except the doe with her fawns. In the other case, where I found so much reluctance to inter-breeding, there is very little difference in size, and scarcely an appreciable difference in form, and in color they are very much alike; and, as I have in another place stated, no one would suspect a difference of species, were it not for the presence of the gland in the one and its absence in the other, to which must be added the sexual aversion already noted. None of these hybrids have as yet bred, though I shall be disappointed if they do not prove reasonably fertile. In every instance where I have succeeded in procuring hybrids the females have not had access to males of their own species. Wherever there has been such opportunity, they have always bred true to the species. Now that I have procured an Acapulco buck, it will be interesting to know whether the female of that species will forsake her unnatural associations with the Virginia buck. During the summer, these Acapulco deer seemed to take no notice of each other, but in September I generally found them in the vicinity of each other; but the doe, which was fully one third larger than the young buck, showed herself a vicious termagant, and chased him about fearfully, especially if she saw me feeding him. By November he began to resent this, and would turn upon her and exchange a few passes, and by the first of December he succeeded in conquering her, and now seems to lead a more peaceable domestic life. I never saw him appear to pay the least attention to any other doe in the park, though I was very anxious to see him with the Ceylon does. Still I have my apprehensions that both the Ceylon and Acapulco does will again breed to the common bucks, for my observations have convinced me that when a female has once bred to a male of another species she becomes debauched and so demoralized that she is inclined to receive anything that comes along, no matter how repulsive he may have been at first. Had not this Acapulco doe first allowed herself to be seduced by the Ceylon buck, which so much resembled her in size, form, and color, and with whom she was so well acquainted, I very much doubt whether she would ever have received the attentions of the Virginia buck, nearly three times her size, and differing from her in so many important particulars. But once having submitted to the Ceylon buck, she coquetted a while with the larger species, and finally submitted. Still I hope she has virtue enough left to return to her own species, now that she has an opportunity.

While it is undoubtedly true that the sexes of the same species will, as a general rule, associate together when they can, and manifest no inclination to interbreed with a nearly allied species, yet we sometimes see unnatural attachments between opposite sexes of different genera even, in domestication at least, which seem to overcome the natural repugnance which ordinarily prevails.

A remarkable instance of this once occurred in my grounds. When I had but one male elk, with several females, a strong attachment grew up between the buck and a two-year old Durham heifer, so that he abandoned the society of the female elk, as the heifer did that of the cows in the same inclosure with which she had been reared, and they devoted themselves exclusively to each other. When they laid down in the shade to ruminate, they were always found close together, and when one got up to feed, the other would immediately follow. They kept away by themselves, always avoiding the society of all the other animals. Whenever the heifer was in season, which occurred quite regularly every month, she accepted the embraces of the elk, without showing an inclination to seek the other cattle; nor did this seem to be the result of any constraint. This intercourse continued throughout the summer, during the entire growth of the antlers of the elk, but unfortunately he was killed before the rut commenced with the female elk. It is hardly necessary to state that no impregnation ever occurred from her intercourse with the elk, and so far as this instance may go to establish it, we may conclude that the constitutional differences of the elk and the cow are so great that they cannot successfully interbreed.

Probably no intelligent naturalist of the present day would

give the least credence to the stories of the ancients of a hybrid from the bull and the mare, which the French called *jumar*. Although they are less unlike each other than the wolf and the sheep, still the boundary between them is far too broad to render interbreeding in the remotest degree probable. Still less dissimilar are the Cervidæ and the Bos, for their digestive and generative organs are on the same general plan, but in other respects they are so very dissimilar in their organization and economy, that we should require the most conclusive proof before we could believe that their union could ever prove fertile. The most conspicuous, or at least obvious distinction is, that one has a hollow, permanent horn, while that of the other is solid and temporary. A much closer alliance, or at least similitude, is found between the goat, the sheep, and the antelope, and yet all naturalists have agreed in placing them in separate genera; but for all this, I know not how to reject the evidence that the sheep and the goat have sometimes propagated together, and that their hybrid offspring have proved permanently fertile. How much more readily, then, may we admit the interbreeding of closely allied species — as all the deer certainly are, — and that their hybrids should sometimes be capable of reproduction, although the repugnance is so great that when unconstrained they do not approach each other. The wapiti deer is so much larger than any of the other species in my grounds, that I have never conceived the possibility of hybridizing them; and indeed the moose is the only member of the family on this continent, with which we might expect no great difficulty in an attempt to breed them together, although the size of the woodland caribou is not so inferior as to render the attempt absolutely unpromising.

The red deer of Europe (*C. elaphus*), resembles most our elk or wapiti deer, and I state my reasons in another place, for considering them if not absolutely identical in species, at least very nearly allied, and that probably they have descended from the same ancestors. I have been so much interested with the following account of hybridizing the wapiti and the red deer, — if that be the true term, — from " Land and Water," that I cannot do better than to copy it : —

" The Prince Pless, who has large possessions in Silesia, has succeeded, after repeated trials, in obtaining a cross between the Wapiti (*Cervus Canadensis*), and the common red deer.

" In 1862 the Prince bought fourteen Wapitis from Count Arco, a Bavarian gentleman, who had reared these from four brought from Canada six years previously. They had thriven and bred well in the bleak mountain climate of the Berchtesgaden.

"Out of the fourteen, seven were hinds far gone with calf. The keeper who had charge of them entered at the time of the purchase into the service of the Prince. It took three days to transport the animals by rail to Pless, where they were provided on their arrival with accommodation similar in every respect to that which they had enjoyed in Berchtesgaden. At the end of a week two died, and a few days later seven more, after an illness of some hours. Three more were attacked, but saved by the use of proper remedies. The disease was a distemper brought on by feeding on the sour-forest grass, and is called in German 'Anthraxkrankheit,' of which there are different phrases, Milzbrand, Lungenbrand, Karbuncles Euche.

"The survivors were removed to higher and healthier ground. Another fell a victim to the distemper, and four now remained, which multiplied rapidly. Every hind dropped her calf regularly. The deer were unaffected by cold; for in a temperature of fifteen degrees to twenty-three degrees below zero (Reaumur), they lay out in an exposed windy spot. Still the distemper renewed its attacks every year, and sometimes with deadly result, so that the stock fluctuated in numbers between two and fourteen.

"The breeding of the pure Wapiti appearing to be a failure, it was decided to try a cross with the native red deer, although zoölogists had pronounced this to be an impossibility, or at least had predicted that the offspring would be sterile.

"Fifteen hinds of the common red deer breed were taken and enclosed in the neighborhood of the Wapitis; and in the rutting season a three-year old Wapiti stag was admitted to them. A two-year old Wapiti stag got five calves. Half-breed hinds, when three years old, bore calves, and thus the fecundity of the hybrids was a *fait accompli* in spite of the zoölogists. As the supply of two-year old Wapiti stags failed they were replaced by yearlings, which, however, invariably died. The two-year old stags of half breed were enclosed and separated from the hinds. A two-year old Wapiti stag admitted to the half bred hinds was replaced by one of mixed breed. The produce of the hinds proved that the cross of the Wapiti stag with half breeds was a success.

"Early in 1868 all the pure Wapitis except one had died, and there remained twenty-eight head of half breeds, of which three or four had been twice and some once, crossed with pure Wapiti. The breeding with the half blooded stock is to be continued, and they are to be let into the open forest when the present space becomes too small.

"The half breed deer is of colossal size, little inferior to a Wapiti in bulk and antlers. Its roar is less sonorous than that of the red deer. A four-year old half breed, twice crossed, carries large antlers with fourteen points. In general appearance it resembles the red deer but is larger."

Let me again repeat that I am strongly inclined to the opinion, however, that this is not a real case of hybridity, but that the European stag and our wapiti should be ranked as specifically the same, having descended originally from the same progenitors, though for a long time they have been separated by impassable physical barriers, and so have descended in separate lines, during which permanent changes have taken place in each, many of them diverging, or opposite, while in other and more permanent characteristics, no change has taken place. But this question I consider elsewhere. I regret that similar experiments have not to my knowledge been tried with our moose and the European elk, and our caribou and the Lapland reindeer. I doubt not that they would breed freely together, with a fertile progeny.

ALIMENT.

So much has been said in other places, of the food upon which the various species of our deer subsist, that we need devote but little space to this branch of our subject now.

All the Cervidæ are strictly vegetarians; generally, they consume more arboreous food than most other ruminants, but none depend upon it exclusively. The Moose alone habitually eats the leaves and twigs of the conifers. In the winter, particularly, they subsist largely upon these, and, indeed, they take them at all seasons when met with. Mr. Morrill says, that this is so much the case that their droppings emit a very pungent odor, derived from their evergreen food, which, like musk, is very agreeable to some people, while to others it is very offensive. They consume largely, also, the leaves, twigs, and bark of the deciduous trees, to obtain which they bend down large saplings; and in their winter yards they denude the large trees of their bark as high up as they can reach. To do this they place the extremity of the upper jaw, which is furnished with a sort of pad, against the tree, and scrape upwards with their powerful incisors, tearing off the thick, rough bark with astonishing force and facility. But they partake of herbaceous food as well, though they cannot conveniently graze like other ruminants, but they can crop the ends of long grass, which is often found in the marshy grounds which they frequent in the summer time. At this season, also, they depend largely on aquatic vegetation, found in lakes and rivers. The long grasses and lily pads, which grow along the borders of the lakes, are favorite articles of food for the Moose, which they readily reach by wading into the water; and after the appetite is satisfied they submerge themselves all but a part of the head in the deeper water to escape the flies and mosquitoes.

The Wapiti Deer selects his food from the trees and shrubs, the grasses and the weeds, though he is not so fond of the latter as some of the others. Like several of the other species he prefers the bitter and the astringent, like the hickory and the oak, to the hazel and the maple. He may be often seen standing erect on his hind feet, stretching his neck to the utmost to get a bunch of leaves nearly beyond his reach. In the winter, he

frequently pulls down the twigs bearing the dry oak leaves, and
eats them with apparent relish, though he is rarely seen to pick
up those which have fallen after maturity. If deprived of arboreous food he will keep healthy and fat on grass alone. In
winter he will scrape away deep snow with his feet to obtain the
grass beneath it, and by some unexplained means seems always
to select the best places.

I feed my herd of Elk in winter almost exclusively on corn
(maize) stalks, and they will keep fat upon them if only they get
enough, though they be compelled to eat all the stalks not larger
than one's finger. They are promiscuous consumers, though great
feeders, requiring as much to keep them as the same number of
our black cattle ; but they will eat greedily damaged hay, which
the cattle or horses would reject. After we commence feeding
them in winter they stop foraging for themselves, until their
rations are stopped, and they are forced to it by two or three
days' fasting. They make no attempt in the winter to strip the
bark from even the wild apple or the poplar, although they do
this sometimes, though rarely, in summer. In a very few years
they killed out all the shrubbery in their park, and keep the
trees thoroughly trimmed as far as they can reach. I am not
aware that they ever eat the leaves or twigs of evergreens, nor
have I ever known them to eat the parasitic lichens which frequently grow upon the trees, or the mosses found on decaying
logs. They are very fond of all sorts of grain, and it is astonishing to see what an enormous ear of maize they will take and
crunch up at once. Even the cob, after the corn has all been
removed, I have never known them to reject. They soon learn
to come to the call of one who feeds them, in the latter part of
the season, but in the summer, when the grass is sweet and tender, they are more indifferent, and may refuse to answer.

Both species of Caribou live largely upon a variety of lichens
found in their respective ranges, and indeed these seem indispensable to their well-being. At least it is so with the European
reindeer, for wherever they are kept in gardens or menageries
the mosses from their native ranges have to be imported for
them. This, however, is not their only food. They, too, feed
upon the trees and shrubbery, and upon the grasses, wherever
they find them. The experienced hunter follows them through
the bush with great facility by noticing where they have cropped
the twigs or stripped the moss from the trees in passing, and by
careful inspection will judge something of their number, and

how recently they have passed. This cropping is done by the
animal without stopping to feed, but as it walks along. They
take the various kinds of grasses found in their range freely,
though I lack the evidence to show that they are as fond of
aquatic vegetation as is the moose. After all, their great resource is the reindeer moss, which, in many places, burdens the
ground to great depths, sometimes even two or three feet, where
scarcely any other vegetation can survive.

Of the Woodland Caribou, Captain Hardy says : " The
Caribou feeds principally on the *Cladonia rangiferina*, with
which barrens and all permanent clearings in the fir forests are
thickly carpeted, and which appears to grow more luxuriantly in
the sub-arctic regions than in more temperate latitudes. Mr.
Hind, in ' Explorations in Labrador,' describes the beauty and
luxuriance of this moss in the Laurentian country, ' with admiration for which,' he says, ' the traveler is inspired, as well as
for its wonderful adaptation to the climate, and its value as a
source of food to the mainstay of the Indian, and consequently
of the fur trade in these regions, — the Caribou.[1] The recently
announced discovery by a French chemist, who has succeeded in
extracting alcohol in large quantities from lichens, and especially
from the reindeer moss (identical in Europe with that of America), is interesting, and readily suggests the value of this primitive vegetation, in supporting animal life in that boreal climate,
as a heat-producing food. Besides the above, which appears to be
its staple food, the Caribou partakes of the *tripe de roche* (*Sticta
pulmonaria*), and other parasitic lichens growing on the bark of
trees, and is exceedingly fond of the *Usnea* which grows on the
boughs (especially affecting the tops) of the black spruce, in
long pendent hanks. In the forests on the Cumberland Hills, in
Nova Scotia, I have observed the snow quite trodden down during
the night by the Caribou, which had resorted to feed on the ' old
men's beards ' in the tops of the spruces, felled by the lumberers
on the day previous. In the same locality, I have observed such
frequent scratchings in the first light snows of the season at the
foot of the trees in beech groves, that I am convinced that the
animal, like the bear, is partial to the rich food afforded by the
moss. I am not aware that the favorite item of the diet of the
Norwegian reindeer (*Ranunculus glacialis*) is found in America,
and the Woodland Caribou has no chance of exhibiting the

---

[1] Mr. Hind describes the reindeer moss as covering the broken, rocky surface to
a great depth, and which, when burned off, they found almost impassable on foot.

strange but well authenticated taste of the former animal by devouring the lemming;[1] otherwise the habits of the two varieties are perfectly similar as regards food."

Speaking of the Barren-ground Caribou, Sir John Richardson says: "The lichens on which the Caribou feed whilst on the barren grounds are the *Cornicularia tristis, divergens,* and *ochrileuca,* the *Cetraria nivalis, cucullata,* and *Islandica,* and the *Cononyce rangiferina.*"

In the southern part of their range, to which they retire in the winter season, these deer find forests bordering the barren grounds, and no doubt here they partake more or less of arboreous food.

Of the four other species of deer it may be said in general that they all affect the same kinds of food. The leaves and twigs of trees and shrubs, all the finer kinds of grasses, at least a great variety of weeds, especially the bitter sorts, the seeds of grasses, the fruits of trees, as the wild apples, and plums, and cherries, acorns, and all sorts of berries and rose apples, and all sorts of grain and seeds to which they have access, are freely taken by them. The Virginia Deer alone seems capable of masticating the hickory nut, and it is with difficulty that the Mule Deer and the Acapulco Deer can masticate the well dried grains of the maize, but they soon learn to swallow them whole, and after they have been well softened in the stomach they are ruminated with great apparent satisfaction.

In my grounds, they will only eat the blades and heads of the coarser hay, like timothy and clover, and I find it best to provide a good supply of fine rowen hay for their use, or better yet, a fodder consisting mostly of weeds, no matter how large and coarse, well cured. This they will pick over with great satisfaction. A good coat of blue grass under the snow is the best provision for a winter supply for them. This they reach with great facility by scraping away the snow; but with all this, no matter how abundant, they do not consider themselves well used without a ration of corn every day in the winter. I have never seen any of the deer ruminating, except when lying down. All are fond of salt, and they should have that condiment always accessible, and even then the want of an abundance of arboreous food seems to impair their health and vigor.

---

[1] I frequently meet with the statement, even in respectable works on natural history, that the Lapland reindeer are in the habit of devouring the lemming, but I do not remember to have met the statement by any one that he has actually seen it done, so that I do not really know how authentic the statement is.

CONGENERS.

OUR study of the American Deer would be quite incomplete, were we to omit a comparison of them with European species and see whether we there find their analogies. I have pursued this inquiry with some industry, and find nothing there, bearing such a similitude to our mule deer, our black-tailed deer, our Virginia deer, or our Acapulco deer, as to suggest a common origin, at least in modern times, even in a geological sense. In the form of the antlers there is nothing which suggests a near relationship, although all are composed of the same material, and are grown in the same way, and all are more or less branched, characteristics which distinguish the Cervidæ from all other ruminants.

In other parts of the world we find many species of deer with important peculiarities, which are entirely wanting in all our species. We have others, however, which are so nearly like European species that we feel constrained to declare that there is no specific difference between them.

THE MOOSE AND THE ELK.

The first of these which demand our attention are the American Moose and the European Elk. These are not alike absolutely, nor are the individuals composing the distinct varieties in each country; but the distinctions, whatever they are, must be determined by the average of large numbers in each country, when, we may fairly conclude, they arise from the different conditions in which they have lived, during the many ages they have been separated by impassable physical barriers. I present an illustration of the Scandinavian Elk, and the reader can readily compare with him the Moose at page 68.

The American Moose is larger in size and darker in color than the European Elk. These distinctions have been recognized ever since the American variety was first discovered by those familiar with the other variety. This is only ascertained by observing a large number, for individuals may be found which, if considered by themselves, would contradict the conclusion. There is, no

doubt, more variation in color as well as in size observed among
our Moose than among the Eastern Elk. Some attain to enormous size, larger than any individuals found in the north of
Europe, and some are black to a degree never met with among
the others, while other smaller and lighter specimens are met
with here not essentially differing from the average of those
found in Europe.

Scandinavian Elk.

There is, too, an observable difference in the antlers, although
in both the general characteristics are the same. The antlers are
not much smaller on the Elk than on the Moose, in proportion to
the size of the animal, but they are less palmated, that is, a less
proportion of the volume of the antler is spread out in the
palm, and a greater proportion devoted to the cylindrical parts.
Besides the palms being less, relatively, the tines, set upon their
borders, are larger and longer than on our variety. While this
is true as a general rule, it is by no means universally so. I have

seen specimens of the Moose antlers, where the tines upon the palms were quite as stout and as long as on any from the European variety, and the examiner would be inclined to assign to them an eastern origin, though the large size might make him hesitate, while I met with no specimens in the east where it would be little exaggeration to say that the whole antler was one great palm, as in the Halifax specimen shown in the illustration (*ante*, p. 193). I think all careful observers who have examined large numbers of both varieties, will agree with me that the antlers of the Moose are, as a general rule, more palmated, and have less conspicuous tines than those of the Swedish Elk. While I have selected those for illustration, which I believed would give a fair idea of the average form of the Elk's antlers, I met with none of those extreme cases sometimes met with here, and none showing larger relative palms and less tines than some of these illustrated (see *ante*, pp. 195, 199). I may say the same of the illustrations of the American variety, though the specimen from the Halifax museum should, undoubtedly, be considered as bor-. dering on the extreme.

The difference, then, consists in the size and color of the animals, and in the form of the antler, though in the latter the same general characteristics prevail in both. While these differences occur in a majority of cases, they are by no means universal, nor are entire similitudes in these regards extremely rare, or even uncommon.

Some comparative anatomists or osteologists have supposed they could discover a difference in the forms of the crania, which others could not see. While the form of the skull in each of the species of this genus is very constant, and so of great value in this investigation, a slight, and at most a doubtful, difference cannot be allowed a controlling influence. For myself I have been unable to find the supposed difference, and am by no means prepared to admit its actual existence. The most that has been claimed is, that one is a little broader than the other, which, however, I repeat, is not an accepted fact. Were the difference really appreciable, it would be universally recognized, for it is open to the inspection of all.

In all other respects these animals are precisely alike, at least I can detect no other differences, and I know of no one who has pretended to do so.

I will refer to a few of the similitudes, some of which are peculiar to this animal.

They occupy the northern portions of both continents, being only exceeded in their northern range by the reindeer. They must live in a wooded country. They affect the same kinds of food, and are the only deer which we find habitually browsing upon conifers. The whole form of the animal presents many peculiar characteristics, entirely wanting in all other animals; among which I cannot overlook, that peculiar tuft of black hair on the inside of the hock, which is exactly alike on every individual of both varieties, so far as it has been possible to examine, while never a gland or tuft of hair is found on the outside of the hind leg, although this is exceptional in the genus.

Perhaps the most remarkable feature of all is, both are monogamous in their habits, with strange peculiarities, which are particularly described on p. 278, *et seq.*, where I also show that with the exception of one other species of deer (*C. capreolus*), found in Europe, and some of the monkey tribe, so far as I recollect, I have never seen this habit ascribed to any other quadruped. At any rate it is exceedingly rare, and so has the more value in the catalogue of similitudes when comparing these animals. How strikingly in every detail this peculiar habit is practiced by the Elk in Europe as it is by the Moose in America, is there shown. One could write a book almost, without exhausting the similitudes between these animals, many of which are peculiar to them, while their few and slight differences are specified in a few words, every one of which may be found in individuals on either continent.

THE CARIBOU AND THE REINDEER.

That the Reindeer and our Woodland Caribou are specifically identical, I think equally clear. The divergence which has resulted from long separation under somewhat different conditions of life is even less, if possible, than that which has occurred with the two varieties of *Alces*. Their differences are easily enumerated.

The first to be noticed with them is in the antlers. The general configuration is the same in both. With a long and slender beam, first retreating and spreading, and then curving forward and inward, they present fundamental peculiarities observed in none others of the genus, except that which is closely allied to them, to say the least, namely, the Barren-ground Caribou. Both have brow-tines exceedingly variant on individuals, and even in different antlers on the same animal, with the universal characteristic, however, that they spring from the beam in front just above the burr in a descending direction nearly in the facial line one or both of which usually extend nearly the length of the face and is palmated at the end, presenting numerous snags curving inward. Above, the antler is more or less palmated. The antlers on both varieties are of about the same magnitude proportioned to the size of the animal.

As with the moose and the elk, the difference in these consists principally in the extent of the palmatation. This feature is even more marked in *Tarandus* than in *Alces*. They are also less branched in the European variety than in the American. These differences will be better understood by an examination of the illustrations than they could be by verbal descriptions. Those copied from Captain Hardy's " Forest Life in Acadie," [1] present nearly the extreme of palmatation in the American variety, and for that very reason are valuable as showing to what extent this feature sometimes occurs in this country, — an extent which I have nowhere found paralleled in the European variety, either in life, in collections, or illustrations. I have met with a few fancy sketches greatly exaggerating the extent and number of branches on the European variety, which were evidently designed to impress those who saw them rather than instruct the student of natural history. These should not mislead us. The illustrations of the antlers of the Woodland Caribou (*ante*, pp. 200, 202) are carefully drawn copies of specimens in my own collection, and are selected to give the fair ordinary form of the Caribou's antlers, that is, the average form. One of these, from the Caribou, shows as little palmatation as that from the European Reindeer and may be considered the other extreme in this regard, and should be set opposite those from Hardy, while the mean between them may be considered the truth. It will be observed, that the nearly palmless antlers of the Caribou are very much stouter than those from the European Reindeer.

If we take mounted specimens, to be met with in public collections, they would generally be found more palmated, for the simple reason that we are apt to select the best, that is, the largest, the most branching, or most palmated specimens for mounting; and indeed the hunter is more apt to save these than inferior or ordinary specimens, for the reason that they will bring him a higher price. These are matters ever to be borne in mind by him who would study or illustrate nature as it actually exists.

[1] *Ante*, p. 206.

One set of the illustrations of antlers on the European Reindeer, are from a living pair in the Zoölogical Gardens at Berlin, and the others are faithful copies of the antlers of a male and female wild Reindeer, which I brought from Arctic Norway, procured in Tromsöe (see *ante*, p. 203, and *post*, 329, 330). I have not illustrated any extreme cases of palmatation of the European variety, for the simple reason that I have not met with them, though I have examined many collections in Europe ; still I have no doubt they exist, though far short of those copied from Captain Hardy's valuable work. Those presented I believe fairly illustrate the average antler of the European variety, and by comparison the reader will readily appreciate the difference in structure which my investigations teach me exists.

There are two other peculiarities common to these varieties and not observed on the antlers of the other deer. The first is the exceedingly small burr, which frequently in some portions of the circumference is quite wanting, and in no part is ever prominent ; and the other is that the beam is never round, but its surface presents rounded angles and partially flat spaces between them, approaching nearer to a triangular form than any other figure.

In size the European Reindeer, whether wild or tame, is appreciably smaller than our Woodland Caribou, though much larger than the Barren-ground Caribou. There is as great a difference in size between the American and the European varieties of the Reindeer as there is between the moose and the elk, the difference in both cases being in favor of the American varieties. Thus we see that in the American varieties we have the most palmated antlers and the largest size.

The Woodland Caribou in exceptional cases attain to a very large size ; and from the best examination I have been able to give the subject, I think it safe to say that they average one quarter to one third larger than the wild Reindeer in Europe. Captain Hardy supposed that they attain their best development and perfection on the Atlantic side of the continent ; but further investigations I think tend strongly to show that they are quite as large on the western side of the continent.

In Northeastern Asia the Reindeer are represented, as we have elsewhere seen, as attaining an extraordinary size in domestication ; and as the experiments in Western Europe do not show that man's direct care and dominion over them have tended to increase their development, we may fairly presume that the same improvement in size may be met among the wild specimens in that far eastern country. The difference in size, therefore, between the eastern and the western varieties is not universal, but is only observed when ours is compared with those of the North of Europe.

In form, also, there is an appreciable difference between the American and European varieties of this deer. This will be readily appreciated by comparing the illustrations here presented

Wild European Reindeer, Male.

of a pair of wild Reindeer in the Zoölogical Gardens at Berlin, which were drawn by a skillful artist there under the supervision of Prof. William Peters, expressly for this work, and the illustrations of the Woodland Caribou (see pp. 85, 88). The former has more the form of a prize bullock than of a deer. Ours is a little more graceful in form, but still lacks those symmetrical proportions, which would suggest those agile movements of which they are certainly capable. We must remember, however, that the animals are represented when standing perfectly at ease ruminating. When excited they present an animated appearance, and would hardly be taken for the same animals. The extraordinarily broad foot is common to both, though more conspicuous on the European than the American variety. Altogether these animals are so strikingly alike, even in their exceptional forms, as to at once suggest a relationship. I have had no more interesting study during my investigations than comparing these animals.

Wild European Reindeer, Female.

In color, also, there is a marked difference between the wild deer of Norway and our Caribou, but unlike the larger species, in which the Swedish elk is lighter than the moose, we find the Norwegian Reindeer in the wild state are very appreciably darker than ours and much more uniform in shade on the different individuals, and especially with less white about the neck. A study of the domesticated Reindeer in Lapland of course can teach us nothing on this point, for as with other domesticated animals their color has become unstable to a very considerable extent, although even with them a large proportion retain the dark brown chocolate shade which is quite uniform on the wild deer, in that region, especially in early winter coat.

In all else I have been unable to detect any difference in these two varieties of reindeer; and unless we are very ambitious to multiply species, it seems to me that we cannot be justified in declaring that these slight and comparatively unimportant distinctions, which are also quite common among individuals of each variety, constitute specific differences. If any one of these distinctions were found to be strictly uniform on each individual of the respective varieties, we might well pause before concluding that the difference was owing to factitious causes. If, for instance, we had found that the antlers on each individual of the Caribou were formed exactly alike, and on each individual of the Eastern Reindeer the antlers were found invariably of a precise pattern, but sensibly differing from the others, we might be led to suspect a fundamental cause for the variation.

In all else the similitudes are perfect, so far as I have been able to discover, in habits, structure, and markings. Many of these are peculiar to this species, and very remarkable.

What more can I, or need I, say in vindication of those zoölogists, who have concluded that the Reindeer of Europe and America are of the same species?

THE WAPITI AND THE RED DEER.

We now come to the third and last species in which strong analogies are found between the specimens found on the two continents. These are the American Elk (*C. Canadensis*), and the Red Deer, or Stag of Europe (*C. elaphus*). That there are more discrepancies and fewer analogies between these than between the species just considered, is very plain to the careful observer, especially if he only examines the specimens of the present day. It is necessary, however, if we would fully understand their natural history, to study them in the light of the past as well as of the present, for the important inquiry is as to a common origin, even in remote antiquity. If in this we can trace two separate lines constantly diverging, though it may be but little, we may rationally conclude that, could we trace them back far enough while they are constantly approaching each other, we should at last find them uniting at some point whence they commenced their departure.

If originally from the same stock, long ages must have elapsed since their final separation by the interposition of a physical barrier which could not be overstepped, during which they have grown on independently with no possibility of intermingling, to bring them back to greater similitude to the common parent, during which their different conditions of life must have established physical peculiarities in each, which would finally become hereditary, and these peculiarities must have become multiplied and magnified in each with the continuance of time and generation, and so the diverging lines would become continually more and more separated. It is a divine law stamped on all matter, that nothing is stationary; change, perpetual and unceasing change must ever occur, else the work of the Supreme Architect would be at last finished, and when finished, his supervising care would be no longer required. Such a time, we think, can never come, even as to the minutest particle of matter, else it would at last arrive as to all things. If the law of change is ever active; if destruction and reconstruction are always at work, observation tells us that every reconstruction differs in some respect, however minute, from all that had been before ; the long aggregation of minute changes must in time become very great, how great no one may venture to define. The extraction of single drops of water would at length dry the bed of the ocean ; the removal of single grains of sand would displace a desert in the course of time. If change is ever continuous, who shall fix limits to transformations which may at length occur. These are considerations which may be well remembered when we approach the present inquiry.

We all know that there are certain features in the animal economy which are comparatively transitory, and so are easily obliterated or changed, while others are more persistent, and maintain their integrity to a greater or less degree under almost all circumstances or conditions. The nearer alike these peculiarities are found to be on all the individuals of a species, we may reasonably conclude the more persistent they are and the less change they have undergone during the course of time.

How long the physical condition of the earth has rendered it impossible for these two varieties to intermingle, and so keep up an absolute identity, of course it is impossible to conjecture; but, at the shortest, it must have been a very long time. At least the generations must be counted by very many thousands.

During that time we first notice that a great change has taken place in the size : the western has become much larger than the eastern. That one may have increased in size on the western continent, while the other has grown smaller on the eastern, attributable to physical causes, as aliment, climate, or the like, may be supposed, although we may be unable to recognize these causes with certainty.

The most remarkable difference, besides the size, is in the longer tail of the Stag, the partial obliteration of the white section on the rump on many of the individuals, and on others the presence of a line of spots along the flanks on either side of the dorsal line, similar to those which I have mentioned as sometimes

Red Deer or Stag of Europe.

observed on the common deer, though more distinct and more persistent. I observed these spots only on a very few of the Red Deer.

In size the antlers vary much on different individuals of both species, but I judge they would average about the same in proportion to the size of the animals. There are some characteristics of the antlers of the Red Deer in which a difference may be observed from those of our Elk, but the more the subject is studied the more these differences disappear.

On page 333 I present the figure of a Red Deer in the Zoölogical Gardens in Berlin, drawn from life, by the same artist who drew the reindeer. By comparing it with the Wapiti (*ante*, p. 76), their likeness will be seen; and by comparing its antlers and the antlers of the Red Deer (*ante*, pp. 214, 332), with the common and crown antlers of our Elk (*ante*, p. 210), it will be readily seen how peculiar and yet how alike they are. While the general figures of these antlers are quite unlike those of any other member of the family, they are strictly alike in design, though in detail there are some differences, which are frequent though not universal. The first to be noticed is that the bez-tine is much shorter than the brow or the royal tine on the Red Deer, while on our Elk it is usually about the same length as the brow-tine, and the royal is usually shorter than either; still this is not universally the case, and formerly these peculiarities were less observable in both than now. This is manifest from an examination of a great number of fossil antlers found in both countries. And this is true of another characteristic as well. It is now exceedingly rare to find the snag on the upper side of the brow-antler of the Red Deer. Of all that I examined in Europe, I found it well developed only on one pair of antlers of the present day, and they were from Bohemia, and would have been taken at once by any naturalist to have come from America, and yet we have seen that this snag is developed in about five per cent. in this country.

The crown antler, which is shown in the illustrations, is very common in Europe, but is very rare in this country; and until quite lately I had no evidence of its existence here; but I am now enabled to illustrate a pair of antlers from an American Elk from the Rocky Mountains, both of which are crown antlers, as well developed as is often met with in Europe (*ante*, p. 210).

The fossil antlers found in Europe show a much larger proportion with the snag on the brow-antler, and a less proportion of crown antlers than are grown there at the present day, while these antlers are much larger and about the size of our Elk antlers.

If we should take all the fossil antlers of this animal which I have examined in Europe and America, and arrange them together promiscuously, I at least should have difficulty in correctly classifying them, while I would make few mistakes in classifying those of the present day.

The finest collection of both together which I have ever seen was in Berlin, where they were kept for sale, and where I had an excellent opportunity of studying them, to which I have already referred in the chapter on antlers. Those from Northern Europe were easily distinguished from those from America, but those from Silesia, Bohemia, and Hungary were much larger, and in all things much more like those from the American Elk, and in many of the specimens I was at a loss to declare on which continent they grew.

Judging from the antlers alone, upon all the evidence I have been able to accumulate, I could hardly hesitate to say that the Stag of Europe is a degenerate descendant of the same parents to which our Elk owe their origin, and that this degeneracy is most marked in those of the most northern countries. I have elsewhere remarked that our own Elk grow larger in the southern ranges, than in the northern, while the reverse is the case with most if not all of the other species of the family.

Another exceptional feature as connected with the antler, may not be without significance. In no case does the Wapiti or American Elk shed its antlers in the winter, but always carries them till spring opens, if the animal be in health. All the other members of the family drop their antlers at irregular intervals, from November till spring, except the female caribou, as is more fully explained in the article on the antlers. In this very remarkable habit the Red Deer corresponds with our Elk. On this point Professor William Peters of Berlin writes me: " Concerning the shedding of the horns of our *Cervus elaphus*, I can give you for Germany the following data : generally, they drop the horns in March ; very strong stags sometimes already in February, and younger ones carry them often till the month of May." This is a confirmation of the information which I have received in answer to all the inquiries I had made in Europe of those whose opportunities enabled them to observe the occurrence and whose observations would be considered valuable. Of the Red Deer, Cuvier says : " The antlers are shed in spring, the old ones losing them first." How exactly this corresponds with the habit of our Elk may be seen by turning to what is said of them in the article on the antlers. The absence of the tarsal gland in both, which is entirely exceptional in this country, and the exact similitude of the metatarsal gland in all its minute characteristics, when we consider its extraordinary constancy in all the species, speaks very much in favor of their common origin. In both, this gland is located in the same place, in both it is entirely covered with white hairs, which are surrounded by a tuft of darker hairs; this again is surrounded by a border of tawny color, which unites below the tuft, the tawny shade continuing down the posterior edge of the leg to the foot, and in both the tuft is of the same relative size. While these are so exactly alike on all the individuals of both these varieties, on none of the other members of the genus, in this country, at least, is this gland overgrown with hair, a very remarkable coincidence if they are not relatives.

There is a difference in the color of these animals which seems to have become permanent and characteristic. The general color of the body of the Wapiti is a yellowish gray on the back and sides, with a darker shade on the belly, neck, and legs. The Stag shows a reddish gray, instead of the yellowish gray, also with a darker shade below as on the American variety, but the difference in color is no greater than on the two other species whose analogies we have already considered. The white border around the eye, a mark observed on most though not all of the deer family, though varying greatly in extent on different individuals, is still generally present on the Stag, is more faded on Wapiti, and on some individuals seems wanting.

After all, the greatest distinction I have been able to discover is in the tail, that on the Red Deer being appreciably longer in proportion to the size of the animal than on our Elk, it having more of a rufous shade of color and terminating less abruptly, or being more pointed. On our Elk the tail is so short that it does not cover the genital organ of the female, while this is completely hidden on the Red Deer. Of all the differences which I have been able to discover between these two animals, this to me has seemed the most important and has made me hesitate longest in making up my mind as to the identity of the species.

The difference in size of the animals, though very great, say more than one half, has very little significance in determining the question. Very great differences exist among individuals on both sides. I have seen some Red Deer as large as some of my smallest Elk, although this is no doubt of rare occurrence.

But we have still greater differences in size among some of our undoubted species. The average of the Virginia deer is twice as large in the north as when found in its most southern range, while in all other respects they exactly correspond, and no rational doubt should exist of their specific identity. The mule deer in the Rocky Mountains is four times as large as in Lower California, which difference is also supplemented by the fact that the change in the antler is quite as great, for on all of the small variety the antler has ceased to be bifurcated, but presents a spike like that of the yearling deer of the north ; or if ever bifurcated that feature is as rare as on the first antlers of the better developed variety of the north, and yet I do not hesitate to rank them in the same species from their exact similitude in all other respects, according to the reliable information I have received of them. With the same propriety might we deny that the Fuegian and the Patagonian are of the same species.

In considering this question of specific identity we should by no means forget that these animals freely interbreed whenever they have opportunity, and their progeny proves as fertile as either of the parents, as has been shown in the article on Hybridity. While this should not be considered as conclusive evidence of specific identity, it is important cumulative evidence in that direction. If in the wild state in the forest it were found that the sexes showed the same inclination for each other which they show for the opposite sex of their own varieties, this would add vastly to the weight of the evidence and would make out a very strong *primâ facie* case at least ; for, as is shown in another place, the sexes of separate species have a natural sexual aversion for each other which is more marked in the female, and although this no doubt may be sometimes overcome in the wild state and without constraint, and so hybrids produced voluntarily, probably if the truth could be known we should find that the female received the embraces of the male only when she could not find a male of her own species. After years of experimenting with as great facilities as are likely to be often enjoyed, I at least have been unable to obtain a hybrid under other conditions, and even when no proper male has been on any part of the grounds success has very rarely attended my efforts, as is more fully shown in another place.

After the best investigation and consideration I have been able to give the subject — and my opportunities have not been stinted, — I am inclined to fall back into the ranks of those naturalists who first compared the two animals, who failed to find sufficient differences to justify the erection of a new species to accommodate the new variety found on this continent, and I

22

should have been well justified in dropping the specific name of *Cervus Canadensis* and returning to that of *Cervus elaphus.*

THE ACAPULCO DEER AND THE CEYLON DEER.

The similarity in size, form, color, and habits of our little Aca-pulco Deer and the Ceylon Deer in my grounds, is so great, that no naturalist would be inclined to declare them specifically differ-ent, .but for the absence of the metatarsal gland in the one, while it is very distinctly present in the other (see illustration, *ante*, p. 258). Even the antlers have a striking similarity, although I have but one set grown on the adult Acapulco Deer, and two sets grown on the Ceylon buck in my grounds, and those grown in 1874 differ in an important particular from those grown on the same animal in 1873, in that the latter showed a very long anterior prong in proportion to the length of the beam, while on the former it is but a snag, although still longer than the snag on the Acapulco deer. In both there is a decided tendency to flatten towards the end of the beam, but the foreign deer has the longest and slimmest beam. Still it would be necessary to com-pare a much larger number than I have been able to do, before we can pronounce definitely as to positive distinctions, if there really be any.

At last we are brought face to face with the question whether the entire absence of the metatarsal gland on one, and its distinct presence on the other, is sufficient to establish a specific differ-ence. For myself I am prepared to recognize such difference. I am undoubtedly strengthened in this conclusion from the fact that they come from places separated by ten thousand miles of ocean, and one from an isolated island in the ocean, presenting insuperable obstacles to a common origin within an immense dis-tance of time, to say the least.

Lest there might be some mistake as to the habitat of this Ceylon Deer, which after a careful study showed so great a sim-ilarity to the deer from Mexico, I wrote to Governor Latham, who presented me with the buck, inquiring if it were not pos-sible that there was a mistake as to its origin ; to which he answered that there could be no mistake, for he took it from a sailing vessel which had just arrived at San Francisco from Cey-·lon, which had not touched at any intermediate port. The other arrived at San Francisco while I was there, on a Pacific mail steamer, from Panama, which touched at Acapulco, where the deer was taken on board. On the question of the habitat of these animals, I have deemed it important to be very particular, and the result is that I cannot doubt that their nativities are as stated.

Had both been found in the same range, I confess I should have long hesitated before concluding that the absence of the metatarsal gland in one, and its presence in the other, would alone justify us in declaring a specific difference; nor would it in any case, but from the fact that an examination of a great number of individuals of most of the species, and a considerable number of all, enable us to say that it is the most constant and uniform of all the indicia to be found on any of them. Where it is wanting on one individual of a species, it is wanting on all, and where it is present on one, it is present on all, and is precisely alike on all of the same species, and entirely unlike that found on either of the other species; so that no two of different species at all resemble each other in this regard, while in no two of the same species can any difference be detected. If other naturalists have attached less importance, or even no importance, to this than I do, I must be pardoned for saying that I think it is because they have studied it less.

Had I found this gland present or absent in both, and so been unable to point out any substantial difference between them although coming from so widely separated localities, what should I say then as to their specific identity; when it is certain that the races must have been separated for an immense period of time, to say the least? He who will answer the following question will answer that. When races or animals are alike, but in nowise related to each other, are they of the same species? In connection with this subject, I repeat, that under the most favorable circumstances I found these deer to interbreed very reluctantly, and months after the proper season, but then the union was fully fertile, for the doe produced twins; however, these were still-born, or died very soon after birth. Not the least indication of the metatarsal gland can be found on either of these fawns, which, of course, are added to my collection. I do not know but hybrids are as liable to be twins as others. Mares very rarely have twins, and yet I have heard of one well authenticated instance of twin mules in my own neighborhood.

Altogether I think it very clear that there is a sexual aversion observed in these deer which is usually observed between individuals of different species, which augments the evidence of specific

difference very much.   In this we have. the testimony of the animals themselves, which is scarcely less satisfactory than manifest
physical differences ; nay, I am not prepared to say that this
sexual aversion, which is so clearly manifest, is not more conclusive than very considerable variations of physical structure.
Should we bring together two parties of deer, of several individuals, brought from distant localities, different physically in what
we might consider important features, and find them associating and interbreeding without the least restraint or reluctance,
we should regard it as conclusive of specific identity, notwithstanding the physical differences.   A white crow is recognized by
his black brethren as a good crow, notwithstanding his degenerate color, and the albino deer is regarded by the others as
good a deer as the best of them.   The doe in my collection was
shot when standing by the side of a buck of the ordinary color.
The social standing and sexual inclination manifested must be
allowed to overcome serious difficulties in establishing relationship, and so on the other hand where aversion exists instead of
inclination, it assures us of a radical difference though we may
be unable to detect it on mere inspection.   In this case the sexual aversion adds much to the significance of the absence of the
gland on the hind leg, and leads us to expect that the comparative anatomist will surely find other differences which we cannot
now detect.   It is an additional evidence of the importance of
this gland in classifying the deer.

DISEASES OF THE DEER.

IT is only when the deer are in confinement that we can study the diseases to which they are subject and their mode of treatment. That they are liable to distempers in the wild state either epidemic or contagious, which sometimes carry off great numbers, we may not doubt, as we sometimes receive pretty well authenticated accounts of such calamities. Such accounts as I have noticed have, however, been confined to the Virginia Deer. If the moose or the caribou are in the wild state subject to distempers I do not know it, and yet it is not improbable that such calamities may sometimes befall them but have not been observed.

The Wapiti are undoubtedly very healthy and hardy, and capable of enduring great vicissitudes. I have for many years had large numbers, and am not aware that one was ever sick. If only they get enough to eat, it scarcely matters what, they remain healthy and in good condition.

With me the Mule Deer have not proved healthy. The first pair I procured, I turned into the park where a considerable growth of white clover had established itself among the blue grass. In about a month I observed them drooling, and examination showed that both were badly salivated. This I attributed to the white clover, and I immediately turned them into the flower garden where they could not find the clover, but a great variety of other food. All the deer are very fond of flowers and flowering plants and shrubs. The female, which was the oldest and not so badly affected as the other, recovered in a few weeks, but the buck was too far gone ; his teeth finally dropped out and he died. The doe was never again afflicted in the same way, — nor for that matter any other deer, — though she ran in the same grounds for several years thereafter.

The next Mule buck I procured seemed quite healthy for several years; when at last, in the month of May, I found him in the East Park with hoofs grown to fully four inches in length, so that he could only walk with great difficulty and on his heels. I sawed about an inch from each toe, which enabled him to walk more comfortably, and turned him into the orchard. Although he seemed to eat and ruminate pretty well, still he grew worse, and died within a month. His liver was greatly enlarged and gorged with bile. In both the East Park and in the orchard this deer had found a plenty of arboreous food.

When the Mule fawns were about a year old, they both showed the same symptoms, — elongation of the hoofs. I immediately took them up and put them on dry feed, and gave them small doses of *podophyllum*, and tonics, as ginseng, quassia, quinine, and the like, giving them daily a small supply of the foliage and twigs of the wild cherry. Their hoofs immediately stopped the abnormal growth, and in ten days they commenced ruminating again, and in a month they were turned out quite well. These are all the cases of this distemper I have ever had. In the fall both these fawns were attacked with a diarrhea when they were again put in hospital and treated as before, with promising results. The disease was checked, and returned several times, but before winter the female died. The buck struggled with it for two months, till finally he seemed quite recovered and did finely till spring. The disease then returned and he succumbed when two years old. In short this is the history of all the Mule Deer I have had except the two first, and the one which died having the elongated hoof. This disease has proved fatal to all the Mule Deer after remaining healthy for one or two or three years, and most of the Columbia deer have died of the same disease. I have had a pretty extensive practice with these deer, and have often been able to afford relief, but this disease was sure to return, perhaps, on some slight provocation. The last I had was when the acorns were ripe, which I gathered and fed to her. For a day this seemed but to aggravate the distemper, but being persisted in she got much better, but my hopes were again disappointed, and she died in November. Only these two species have been afflicted with diarrhea.

I have lost many Virginia Deer with a swelling under the lower jaw. It commences two or three inches back of the chin, and finally swells out so as to involve the whole head below the eyes; sometimes it gathers in a sac of half an ounce of pus-like matter, one of which I opened, but the deer died. I never knew one to break itself. When the tame deer are attacked with this distemper, and it is observed in time, I have never failed to cure it. If when it first appears it is examined, a small hard kernel is found just under the skin. If this is then cut out the deer gets well at once. Later, the lump seems to be dissipated, but if the swelling has not extended above the lower jaw, though it may be three inches long, and the protuberance an inch thick, and really has an alarming appearance, a deep central incision an inch or more long has always proved effectual. But as only the tame deer, which can be caught, can be treated, all the wild Virginia Deer which have been attacked, so far as I know, have died. In the early part of my experiments, this disease was much more prevalent than in later years, and so I conclude that those more remotely descended from the wild stock are the least liable to it. It only attacks the adults, or those more than two years old.

Two of the Ceylon adult does have been attacked with it, both of which were dropped in my ground. They were too wild to be taken and treated, but to my surprise both recovered, which has I think never happened with the Virginia Deer. I have no account that this disease has ever been observed among the wild deer of the forests; certainly, I have never seen one afflicted with it.

I have never observed any symptoms of it either among the Elk, the Mule deer, the Columbia deer, or the Acapulco deer.

THE CHASE.

No saint in the calendar has had more devoted or more pains-taking disciples than Saint Hubert. In savage life, the pursuit of wild beasts or the capture of fish has always been a necessity, and in all ages, and in all civilized countries, many persons have found their most exquisite enjoyments in the same pursuit. As a general rule, these persons are lovers of nature unmarred by the hand of man. They love to hear the rushing of mighty waters, and they love the soft cadence of the murmuring brook. They love the deep shade of the primeval forest, and they love the broad expanse of the wild prairie, with its green, grassy carpet, gemmed all over with brilliant wild flowers whose fragrance they inhale with a new delight. They love the rocky cañon and the mountain crag, where the throes of nature have upheaved the earth's deep crust and thrown all into a wild confusion, as if in anger an Almighty hand had there dashed the debris of another world. They love to sleep beneath the old pine tree, and listen to the sighing of the wind as it softly creeps through its long and slender leaves, or upon the soft grass by the side of the sweet spring of water under the broad spreading oak, the rustling of whose leaves soothes to quiet repose. They love to listen to the raging storm, and see its wild work all around them; and so they love the soothing influence of the quiet calm, when nature seems in profound repose, and all is still as the infant's sleep. At the break of day upon the mountain side they love to count the stars, and witness the waking of animated nature, when the birds fly forth to sing, and the beasts leave their lairs to seek their food while yet the dew softens the herbage which they love the best. They love to catch the sun's first rays as they dart from beneath the distant horizon, feeling new life and vigor as they shine upon them, and with swelling heart they watch him rise, as if from a bed of rest, and cast his smile upon the new-born day. Oh, it is a glorious joy to be where the defacing hand of man has never marred the harmonious beauty which pervades Nature's handiworks. There we look with reverence and awe upon what God has done, and what God alone could do, and re-joice, even in our insignificance, that we are permitted there to contemplate such sublime display. Far away from ever-restless city life, and its surging crowd and its tainted air, we love to breathe the air of freedom sweet and uncontaminated, where every breath revives the spirits, stimulates the circulation, awakens the dormant energies, and inspires new life within us. If this be savage life, then am I a savage still. If these be traits of character inherited from remote barbaric ancestors, I rejoice that civilization has failed to strangle what in them was purest and most elevating.

But the sportsman of the present day is admitted to a higher pleasure than those of ancient times could ever know. For this he is indebted to our civilization, which while it could not eradicate in him a love of nature, has enabled him to understand nature,— to become a naturalist; to know about that nature which surrounds him, and which he loves so well; to appreciate the characteristics and the peculiarities of those objects whose chase and capture fills him with such a thrill of pleasure. When he has shot a bird, captured a quadruped, or taken a fish, he takes it up and examines it as he would a book full of knowledge, and is enabled to see its peculiarities, and discover its many points of beauty and harmony, which those who simply kill to eat, or perhaps from a love of blood and slaughter, can never see, or seeing could not appreciate, and so enjoy.

The cougar seeks his prey to satisfy his hunger, the sportsman that he may study nature in her various phases and understand her harmonies; the better he is qualified to do these, the higher will be his sense of pleasure at his captures. I am gratified to observe among modern sportsmen a more elevated tone, a higher culture, by which they the better understand the natural history of the various objects which they pursue. Of all men they have the greatest opportunities to observe the characteristics of the animals which they meet with in the chase, and the better they learn how to observe, the more will they observe and compare, and note down, and through them may we soon hope to gather a fund of scientific observations, which will leave far behind all that has been written or known of many of our most familiar animals. Even now he takes with him to his camp in the forest works on natural history, treating of those animals which he proposes to pursue, and critically compares his captures with the observations of the authors, and corrects or confirms their statements. To the pot hunter, who kills the game to sell as a butcher does a sheep, pursues it not because he is a lover of nature, and takes no more pleasure in it than he would in weeding a bed of onions, of course a study of the animals he kills would afford him no pleasure, but to the cultivated mind capable of understanding and appreciating the works of the Divine hand, the pleasures of the pursuit are immeasurably enhanced by a capacity to understand the object taken.

No other genus of quadrupeds is distributed over so large a portion of the earth's surface as the Cervidæ, no other has so largely contributed to the sustenance of uncivilized man, and the flesh of no other is so generally admired as food. From the fact that it has contributed more than any other quadruped to the support of savage life, it has been more the object of pursuit than any other by uncivilized races.

In the border settlements of our own country, the deer has been an important source of food supply to our frontier settlers, who might justly be called a race of hunters; very few indeed have made it a constant business, but nearly all have made it an occasional and incidental pursuit.

From the earliest times to the present, the deer has occupied the first rank as a game animal, affording exercise and excitement to the sportsman. In Africa alone the deer are not abundant, but the antelope, the buffalo, and the elephant, are there the principal objects of pursuit by the savage and the civilized.

In a very limited area in our own country, the bison is, or was, more important than the deer, but the district is so small where the bison is or was found in plenty, that it loses all comparison with the deer, which are abundant, in mountain and valley, in forest and prairie, from the Atlantic to the Pacific, and from Cape Horn to the frozen islands in the Arctic Sea.

In savage life, without the means furnished by civilization, the capture of the deer and other game was accomplished to a considerable extent by bows and arrows, but chiefly by means of traps or inclosures of various kinds, and the promptings of want developed contrivances which insured a large measure of success. These are all based upon the capabilities of the animals, developed by their habits, which were a life study of the Indian hunter, and were comprehended by him in a remarkable degree.

The principal of these, or at least the most important, are the defect of vision and the acuteness of the senses of smell and of hearing. These are characteristics which are common to all deer, and must never be forgotten by the savage hunter or the civilized sportsman. All have recognized the acute senses of smell an hearing, and so they have acted upon the defective vision, sometimes without clearly comprehending why it was that they were required so to act in order to insure success.

THE MOOSE.

We have reason to believe that the Indian was not particularly successful in the capture of the Moose with the bow and the arrow. The great size, strength, and endurance of the animal rendered it difficult to bring him down with that weapon, unless at very close range, and his ability to detect the least sound, and to notice the least taint in the air, rendered a close approach very difficult. In summer time he was more frequently captured in the water. At that season he affects marshy grounds, where lakes and lakelets abound, and into these he plunges to escape the torments of the flies and mosquitoes, deeply immersing himself much of the time, generally with only his nose above water. In this position he could be successfully attacked by the Indians in their canoes, at sufficiently close quarters to make their arrows effective, or they could even disable him with blows before he could escape. This was often dangerous sport or business, whichever you please to call it, for a single blow from the antlers or the foot of a moose was sufficient to demolish or sink a canoe, when the hunter would be fortunate if he escaped with his life. This mode of pursuit was, however, generally successful, and much meat was obtained in that way by the natives.

The Moose, and so of the other deer, have their favorite paths or highways in the forests where they abound, and in these they were frequently captured. For this purpose a lasso was cut from the green hide of the Moose, by following round it, cutting wider at the thinner portions, till the desired length was attained. The hair was then closely shaved off, the thong twisted to the proper degree, and then stretched to the utmost, and in this position dried. After this it was made pliable to a certain degree, by working or use, retaining, however, sufficient rigidity for the purpose. This was suspended across a convenient limb, with a running noose at one end, which was suspended directly over the path, abundantly large for the head and antlers of the largest Moose to pass through, but sufficiently high from the ground to obstruct the passage of the feet. To the other end a heavy weight, usually a log of wood, was attached. This was held suspended high above the ground by a trip, properly arranged, which was to spring by the least strain from the loop of the thong. Through this the Moose would unsuspectingly pass, till his breast, or fore legs should touch the lower line of the noose, when the trip would spring, the weight would drop, and the line would be drawn tightly around the neck of the animal. The attachment to the limb not being rigid, the animal could go some distance by drawing the log up to the limb, but by the time this was done, the animal would be nearly choked down, the drag of the weight always maintaining the severe tension. A few minutes rearing and struggling must always end in the death of the animal. In this mode the Indians captured many moose, elk, and other animals, before they obtained fire-arms; and even since, it has been sometimes resorted to with success.

Whymper describes the mode practiced by the Indians in Alaska, of pursuing the Moose in the summer time. He says: " One was killed in the water by the knife of the Indian. The natives do not always waste powder and shot over them, but get near the moose, maneuvering round in their birch-bark canoes till the animal is fatigued, and then stealthily approach and stab it in the heart or loins." [1]

All agree that they take to the water readily, and are good swimmers, though they swim higher than the common deer. In the summer they are usually hunted about the lakes and rivers which they frequent, and probably more are killed in the water and on the islands than on the main land. The author above quoted, in a note, says: " In some cases, the Indians in numbers surround an island known to have moose or reindeer on it, when a regular *battue* ensues."

The greatest slaughter of the Moose by the natives — and so it has been by the white men since — took place in the winter, when the country was covered over with deep snow. With the aid of snow-shoes, the Indians could pursue them at a rapid pace, while the Moose had to struggle through the snow, into which he would sink his whole depth at every step. No endurance could sustain him a long time with such labor, and his prodigious strength must at last succumb, while the Indian was rapidly pursuing him on the surface of the light snow on his broad snowshoes. Later in the season, when the surface of the snow was softened or melted by the sun during the day, and became frozen

[1] *Travels in Alaska and on the Yukon*, p. 246.

hard during the night, a crust would be formed sufficient to bear a man or a dog, but incapable of sustaining the Moose. When a Moose was found under such conditions, he was quite at the mercy of his pursuers. For a short distance he could force his way through the treacherous snow, into which he would sink at every step, but in rising from it the sharp edges of the icy crust would cut and bruise his legs in a cruel way, and he would soon be overtaken and dispatched.

This cruel mode of pursuing the deer has not been confined to the northern regions, where alone the Moose are met with, nor yet to the aborigines, who hunted for the necessaries of life, and whose greatest resource was the deer, but whenever the conditions permitted, great numbers of the Virginia deer were thus pursued and slaughtered, not only by the aborigines, but by our frontier settlers as well. Fortunately, in the lower latitudes, where the Virginia deer are most abundant, deep snows covered with this strong crust have been of rare occurrence.

In these conditions the deer are more helpless than any other quadruped, by reason of the small, sharp foot, which cuts through the crust, while most other animals would be supported upon it. The reindeer or caribou, whose foot presents a much broader surface for support, has been less persecuted in this way than the other members of the family.

Both the Moose and the caribou, during the winter, when deep snows are frequent in the forests which they inhabit, collect together in small bands and form what are called *yards*, generally the females and young by themselves. Some of these are more complete than others, and it is only the most perfect which have been usually described by authors and hunters. In these the deer tramp the snow down to a hard floor throughout the yard, leaving it surrounded by a vertical wall of the untrodden snow. The places selected for these yards are dense thickets, affording the greatest abundance of shrubbery, yielding their favorite food, which is arboreous. This they utterly destroy within their yard, by consuming the twigs and stripping off the bark. Even the large trees which they cannot bend down to reach the tops, they denude of the bark so far as they can reach. If they do not relish this coarse, dry bark of the large trees, they consume it all to satisfy their hunger. When all the food within the yard, — which sometimes becomes considerably extended to reach the shrubbery, — is consumed, they break their way to another location where a fresh supply may be found, and form a new yard.

It is rare, however, that these yards have all the surface compactly trodden down. They make paths from the radial points to reach the trees or shrubbery in the neighborhood, so that the area of their habitation is much extended by streets or paths, well packed down, between which the deep snow remains undisturbed, and frequently this system of paths constitutes the yard, with but a very limited central area, quite trodden down. When the snow is deep and covered with a hard crust, the deer are sought in these yards, but not exclusively.

The reindeer are much less accustomed to yard in winter than the Moose, and it is a habit rarely observed in any other of the deer family, so far as I have information.

Since the appearance of civilized man with firearms, and the introduction of those weapons among the savages, a change has necessarily been made in the chase of the deer, as well as other game, or at least the old modes are less relied upon, and the new weapon has become the principal dependence. The mode of hunting this deer now is, in general, the same with the civilized and the savage hunter, especially on the frontiers and with the larger species, which are only found in the wilderness beyond the borders of the white settlements.

More endurance and sagacity are required in the chase of the Moose Deer than any of the others, for they are more suspicious and cautious, and seem to possess the senses of smell and hearing in a higher degree than the smaller species. Indeed, it seems to be a general rule that the older and the larger specimens of a given species are more difficult to capture than the smaller, as well as that the larger species are more cautious than the smaller.

A life-long experience and study of the habits of the animal and of wood craft, seem to have endowed the Indian with greater skill than the white man, especially in the pursuit of the Moose and the Caribou ; hence the white hunter generally secures the services of an Indian when he goes in pursuit of this noble game.

The proper season for hunting the Moose is at the commencement of the rut, say in September, when his antlers have perfected their growth, the velvet has been rubbed off, and they have become finely polished against the trees. Then it is, that he is in the best condition and the venison is the choicest ; then it is, that his desires have stimulated his courage and deprived him of a portion of that caution which makes his capture so difficult. Then it is, that he may be met with, rashly roaming through the forest hunting for a mate, at the same time seeking combats with his own species and sex. After he has found the mate he desires, and they have retired to the secluded place selected for their home where they are to pass the honey moon — I have already stated that they are monogamic — they give up this roving habit and remain quietly at home, till the season is passed, unless disturbed by the hunter or the male is divorced and expelled by some powerful rival. When his domestic relations are thus broken up he again starts on his travels more maddened and fierce than before, and although he may be an ugly brute to meet and provoke, the lack of his customary caution makes him fall a more easy prey to the cautious hunter.

Two modes of hunting the Moose at this season are chiefly relied upon, and in both of these the skill of the Indian is quite indispensable. The first is the still hunt, in which the track of the animal is followed over the most difficult ground in profound silence and with the greatest caution, till the game is seen before he suspects the presence of his pursuer, and is then approached with still greater labor and care, till within rifle range, or is discovered in his secluded lair, and is crept upon by the cautious hunter, till he can be reached by the leaden missile which is to crown the hopes of the hunter and reward him for all his pains. The other is the *call*, in which the Indian imitates the voice of the Moose either male or female in all its variations, and by this means induces the deluded animal to approach the concealed hunter, till he comes within shooting distance. The former must be pursued in the day-time, while the night or partial darkness are generally deemed necessary to insure success in the other. Long experience and a close habit of observation alone can qualify one to detect the foot-prints of the animal pursued, over the barren rocks or the yielding and elastic moss, where the unpracticed eye can detect no sign that the animal has ever been there; and an intimate knowledge of the habits of the animal is necessary to determine the course he has taken when the track is finally lost, and to determine the places where he would be most likely to stop to feed and rest, or the covert where he would be most likely to take up his abode during the conjugal relation. The call can only be successfully resorted to by those who after infinite practice are enabled at will to imitate to perfection all the notes uttered by the Moose of both sexes, and all ages, and under all circumstances, from the feeble call of the young calf, the anxious call of the solicitous mother, the amorous note of the female seeking a mate, or the masculine response of the male, to the fierce and defiant challenge of the bull when a rival is suspected to be near. Each of these, on occasion, must be perfectly expressed, or the counterfeit will be detected and the suspicious game will instantly disappear.

I can best illustrate the first mode of hunting the Moose by an extract from that ardent and experienced sportsman and admirable writer, Captain Campbell Hardy, in "Forest Life in Acadie," p. 91. I have no fear that my extract will be too long, for it is instructive as well as interesting : —

"Presently the canoe was signaled, and going down to the water's edge I embarked, and in a few minutes stood before Joe's castle. It was a substantial farm-house, evidently built by some settler who had a notion of making his fortune by the aid of a small stream, which flowed into the lake close by, and over which stood a saw-mill. An old barn was attached, and from its rafters hung moose-hides of all ages and in all stages of decomposition ; horns, legs, and hoofs ; porcupines deprived of their quills, which are used for ornamental work by the women ; and in fact a very similar collection, only on a grander scale, to that which is often displayed on the outside of a gamekeeper's barn in England.

"A rush of lean, hungry looking curs was made through the door as Joe opened it to welcome me. 'Walk in Capten — ah, you brute of dog, *Koogimook!* Mrs. Cope from home visiting some friends in Windsor. Perhaps you take some dinner along with me and Jim before we start up lake.'

"'All right, Joe ; I'll smoke a pipe till you and Jim are ready,' I replied, not much relishing the appearance of the parboiled moose-meat, which Jim was fishing out of the pot. 'No chance of calling to-night, I'm afraid, Joe ; we shall have a wet night.'

"'I never see such weather for time of year, Capten ; everything in woods so wet — can't hardly make fire ; but grand time for creeping, oh, grand! everything you see, so soft, don't make no noise. What sort of moccasin you got ?'

"'A good pair of moose-shanks, you sold me last winter, Joe ; they are the best sort for keeping out the wet, and they are so thick and warm.'

"The moose-shank moccasin is cut from the hind leg of the Moose ; it is in shape like an angle-boot, and is sewn up tightly at the toe, and with this exception being without seam, is nearly water tight. The interior of Cope's castle was not very sweet, nor were its contents arranged in a very orderly manner — this latter fact to be accounted for, perhaps by the absence of the lady. Portions of moose were strewn everywhere; potatoes were heaped in various corners, and nothing seemed to have any certain place allotted to it; smoke-dried eels were suspended from the rafters in company with strings of moose-fat and dried cakes of concrete blueberries and apples. Joe had, however, some idea of the ornamental, for parts of the 'Illustrated News' and 'Punch' divided the walls with a number of gaudy pictures of saints and martyrs.

" The repast being over, the Indians strided out, replete, with lighted pipes, and paddles in hand, to the beach. Some fresh moose meat was placed in the canoe, with a basket of Joe's 'taters,' which Jim said, ' 't was hardly any use boiling; they were so good, they fell to pieces.' A little waterproof canvas camp was spread over the rolls of blankets, guns, camp-kettles, and bags containing the grub, which was strewed at the bottom ; and, having seated myself beside them, the Indians stepped lightly into the canoe and pushed it off, when, propelled by the long sweeping strokes of their paddles, we glided rapidly up the lake.

" Indian lake is a beautiful sheet of water, nearly ten miles in length, and, proportionately, very narrow — perhaps half a mile in its general breadth. Rolling hills, steep and covered with heavy fir and hemlock wood, bound its western shore ; those on the opposite side showing a dreary, burnt country. The maple bushes skirting the water were tinged with their brightest autumnal glow ; and in the calm water in coves and nooks on the windward side of the lake, the reflections were very beautiful. I longed for a cessation of the rain, and a gleam of sunshine across the hill-tops, if only to enjoy the scenery as we passed. And certainly a seat in a canoe is a very pleasant position from which to observe the beauties of lake and river scenery, the spectator being comfortably seated on a blanket, or bunch of elastic boughs in the bottom of the canoe, — legs stretched out in front, back well supported by rolls of blankets, and elbows resting on the gunwale on either side.

" 'Ah! here is the half-way rock, what the old Indians call the Grandmother,' said Joe, steering the canoe so as to pass close alongside a line of rocks which stood out in fantastic outlines from the water close to the western shore of the lake. ' Here is the

23

Grandmother, — we must give her something, or we have no luck.'

" To the rocks in question are attached a superstitious attribute of having the power of influencing the good or bad fortune of the hunter. They are supposed to be the enchanted form of some genius of the forest ; and few Indians, on a hunting mission up the lake, care to pass them without first propitiating the spirit of the rocks, by depositing a small offering of a piece of money, to-bacco, or biscuit.

" ' That will do, Capten ; anything a'most will do ; ' said Joe, as one cut off a small piece of tobacco, and another threw a small piece of biscuit or potato to the rock. ' Now you would n't b'lieve, Capten, that when you come back you find that all gone. I give you my word that 's true ; we always find what we leave gone.' Whereupon Joe commenced a series of illustrative yarns, showing the dangers of omitting to visit the ' Grandmother,' and how Indians who had passed her had shot themselves in the woods, or had broken their legs between rocks, or had violent pains attack them shortly after passing the rocks, and on return-ing and making the presents had immediately recovered.

" ' It looks as if it were going to be calm to-night, Joe,' said I, as we neared the head of the lake. ' Which side are we to camp on ? Those long, mossy swamps which run back into the woods on the western side look likely resorts for Moose.'

" ' No place handy for camp on that side," said Joe; ' grand place for Moose though. Guess if no luck to-morrow mornin' we cross there ; I got notion of trying this side first.' And so having beached the canoe, turned her over, and thrown her into the bushes secure from observation, we made up our bundles, apportioning the loads, and followed Joe into the forest, now darkened by the rapidly closing shades of evening. In a very short time the dripping branches discharging their heavy showers upon us as we brushed against them, and the saturated moss and rank fern made us most uncomfortably wet ; and as the difficul-ties of traveling increased as the daylight receded, and the tight, wet moccasin is not much guard to the feet coming in painful contact with unseen stump or rock, we were not sorry when the weary tramp up the long, wooded slope was ended, and a faint light through the trees in the front showed that we had arrived at the edge of the barrens. ' It 's no use trying to make call to-night, that sartin,' said Joe ; ' could n't see Moose if he come. Oh, dear me, I sorry for this weather. Come, Jem, we try make camp right away.' It was a cheerless prospect as we threw off our bundles on the wet ground; it was quite dark, and, though nearly calm, the drizzling rain still fell and pattered in large drops, falling heavily from the tree-tops to the ground beneath. First we must get a good fire, — no easy thing to an unpracticed hand in the woods, saturated with a week's rain. However it can be done, so seek we for some old stump of rotten wood, easily knocked over and rent asunder, for we may, perhaps, find some dry stuff in the heart. Joe has found one, and, with two or three efforts, over it falls with a heavy thud into the moss, and splits into a hundred fragments. The centre is dry, and we return to the spot fixed upon with as much as we can carry. The moss is scraped away, and a little carefully composed pile of the deadwood being raised, a match is applied and a cheerful tongue of flame shoots up and illuminates the dark woods, enabling us to see our way with ease. Now is the anxious time on which depends the success of the fire, a hasty gathering of more dry wood is dexterously piled on, some dead hardwood trees are felled and split with the axe into convenient sticks, and in a few minutes we have a rousing fire which will maintain itself, and greedily consume anything that is heaped upon it, in spite of the adverse element. A few young saplings are then cut and placed slantingly, which rest in the forks of two upright supports; the canvas is unrolled and stretched over the primitive frame and our camp has started into existence. The branches of the young balsam firs, which form its poles, are well shaken over the fire and disposed in layers beneath to form the bed; blankets are unrolled and stretched over the boughs, and I find to my joy that the rain had not reached the change of clothes packed in my bundle. I presently recline at full length under the sheltering camp, in front of a roaring fire which is rapidly vaporizing the moisture contained in my recent garments, suspended from the top of the camp in front. Joe is still abroad, providing a further stock of firewood for the night, while his son is squatting over the fire with a well filled frying-pan, and its hissing sounds drown the pattering of the rain-drops.

" After our comfortable meal, followed the fragrant weed, of course, and a discussion of what we should do on the morrow. The barrens we had come to were of great extent, and of a very bad nature for traveling, the ground being most intricately strewed with dead trees of the forest which once covered it; and the briars and bushes overgrowing and concealing their sharp, broken limbs and rough granite rocks often cause a severe bruise or fall to the hunter. It was, as Joe said, a grand place' for calling the Moose, as in some spots the country could be scanned for miles around, whilst the numerous small bushes and rock bowlders would afford a ready concealment from the quick sight of this animal. However, time would show. If calling could not be attempted next morning, it would most likely be suitable for creeping; so, hoping for a calm morning and a clear sky, or, at all events for a cessation of the rain, we stretched ourselves for repose; and the pattering drops and the crackling and snapping of the logs on the fire, and the hooting of the owls in the distant· forest, became less and less heeded or heard, till sleep translated us to the land of dreams.

" To our disgust, it still rained when we awoke next morning; the wind was in the same direction, and the same gloomy sky promised no better things for us that day. The old Indian, how-ever, drew on his mocasins, and started off to the barren by himself, to take a survey of the country whilst the breakfast was preparing, and I gloomily threw myself back on the blanket for another snooze. After an hour or so's absence, Joe returned and sat down to his breakfast (we had finished our's and were smok-ing), looking very wet and excited. ' Two Moose pass round close to camp last night,' said he. ' I find their tracks on bar-ren. They gone down the little valley towards the lake, and I see their tracks again in the woods quite fresh. You get ready, Capten; I have notion we see Moose to-day. I see some more tracks on the barren going southward; however, we try the tracks near camp first, — may be we find them, if not started by the smell of the fire.'

" We were soon at it; and left our camp with hopeful hearts, and in Indian file, stepping lightly in each other's tracks over the elastic moss. Everything was in first-rate order for creeping on the Moose; the fallen leaves did not rustle on the ground, and even dead sticks bent without snapping, and we progressed rap-idly and noiselessly as cats towards the lake. Presently we came on the tracks, here and there deeply impressed on a bare spot of soil, but on the moss hardly discernible, except to the Indian's keen vision. They were going down the valley; a little brook coursed through it towards the lake, and from the mossy banks sprung graceful bushes of moose-wood and maple, on the young shoots of which the Moose had been feeding as they passed. The tracks showed that they were a young bull and a cow, those of the latter being much larger and more pointed. Presently we came to an opening in the forest, where the brook discharged itself into a large circular swamp, densely grown up with alder bushes and swamp maple, with a thick undergrowth of gigantic ferns. Joe whispered, as we stood on the brow of the hill over-looking it, ' May be they are in there lying down; if not they are started;' and putting to his lips the conical bark trumpet which he carried, he gave a short, plaintive call — an imitation of a young bull approaching and wishing to join the others. No answer or sound of movement came from the swamp. 'Ah, I afraid so,' said Joe, as we passed around and examined the ground on the other side. 'I most all the time fear they started; they smell our fire this morning, while Jem was making the breakfast.' Long striding tracks, deeply plowing up the moss, showed they had gone off in alarm, and at a swinging trot, their course being for the barrens above. It was useless to follow them, so we went off to another part of the barren in search of other tracks. The walking in the open barren was very fatiguing after the luxury of the mossy carpeting of the forest, slipping con-stantly on the wet, smooth rocks, or slimy surfaces of decayed trees; forever climbing over masses of prostrate trunks, and for-cing our way through tangled brakes, and plunging into the ooz-ing moss on newly-inundated swamps, we spent a long morning without seeing Moose, though our spirits were prevented from flagging by constantly following fresh tracks. The Moose were exceedingly ' yary,' as Joe termed it, and we started two or three pairs without either hearing or seeing them, until some ex-clamation of disappointment from the Indian proclaimed the un-welcome fact. At length we reached the most elevated part of the barren. We could see the wooded hills of the opposite shore of the lake looming darkly through the mist, and here and there a portion of its dark waters. The country was very open; nothing but moss and stunted huckleberry bushes, about a foot and a half in height, covered it, save here and there a clump of dwarf maples, with a few scarlet leaves still clinging to them. The forms of prostrate trunks, blackened by fire, lying across the bleached rocks often gave me a start, as, seen at a distance, through the dark, misty air, they resembled the forms of our long-sought game — particularly so, when surmounted by twisted roots up-heaved in their fall, which appeared to crown them with antlers.

" ' Stop, Capten ! not a move ;' suddenly whispered old Joe, who was crossing the barren a few yards to my left ; ' don't

move one bit!' he half hissed and half said through his teeth.
'Down! sink down — slow, like me!' and we all gradually
subsided in the wet bushes.

" I had not seen him ; I knew it was a Moose, though I dared
not ask Joe ; but quietly awaited further directions. Presently,
on Joe's invitation, I slowly dragged my body through the
bushes to him. 'Now you see him, Capten; there — there!
My sakes, what a bull! What a pity we not a little nearer —
such open country!'

" There he stood — a gigantic fellow — black as night, moving
his head which was surmounted by massive white-looking horns,
slowly from side to side, as he scanned the country around. He
evidently had not seen us, and was not alarmed, so we all
breathed freely. This success on our part was partly attributable to the suddenness and caution with which we stopped and
dropped, when the quick eye of the Indian detected him, and
partly to the haziness of the atmosphere. His distance was
about five hundred yards, and he was standing directly facing us,
the wind blowing from him to us. After a little deliberation,
Joe applied the call to his lips and gave out a most masterly imitation of the lowing of the cow-moose to allure him towards us.
He heard it and moved his head rapidly as he scanned the horizon for a glimpse of the stranger. He did not answer, however ;
and Joe said, as afterwards proved correct, that he must have a
cow with him, somewhere close at hand. Presently, to our great
satisfaction, he quietly lay down in the bushes. 'Now we have
him,' thought I; 'but how to approach him?' The Moose lay
facing us, but partly concealed in bushes, and a long swampy
gully, filled up with alders, crossed the country obliquely between
us and the game. We have lots of time, for the Moose generally
rests for a couple of hours at a time. Slowly we worm along
towards the edge of the alder swamp; the bushes are provok-
ingly short, but the mist, and the dull gray of our homespun
dresses favor us. Gently lowering ourselves down into the
swamp, we creep noiselessly through the dense bushes, their thick
foliage closing over our heads. Now is an anxious moment — the
slightest snap of a bough, the knocking of a gun-barrel against a
stem, and the game is off.

" ' Must go back,' whispered Joe close in my ear, ' can't get
near enough this side — too open,' and the difficult task is again
undertaken and performed without disturbing the Moose. What
a relief on regaining our old ground, to see his great ears flap-

ping backwards and forwards above the bushes. Another half
hour passes in creeping like snakes through the wet bushes,
which we can scarcely hope will conceal us much longer. It
seems an age, and often, and anxiously, I look at the cap of my
single-barrel rifle. I am ahead, and at length judging one hundred and twenty yards to be the distance, I can stand it no
longer, but resolve to decide matters by a shot, and fire through
an opening in the bushes of the swamp. Joe understands my
glance, and placing the call to his lips, utters the challenge of the
bull-moose. Slowly and majestically, the great animal rises,
directly facing me, and gazes upon me for a moment. A headlong stagger follows the report, and he wheels around behind a
clump of bushes.

"'Bravo! you hit him, you hit sure enough,' shouts Joe, level-
ing and firing at the cow-moose, which had unknown to us been
lying close beside the bull. 'Come along,' and we all plunge
headlong into the swamp. Dreadful cramps attacked my legs,
and almost prevented me from getting through, — the result of
sudden violent motion, after the restrained movement, in the
cold, wet moss, and huckleberry bushes. A few paces on the
other side, and the great bull suddenly rose in front of us, and
strided on into thick covert. Another shot and he sinks lifeless
at our feet. The first ball had entered the very centre of his
breast, and cut the lower portion of the heart.

"Late that night our canoe glided through the dark waters of
the lake towards the settlement. The massive head and antlers
were with us.

"'Ah, Grandmother,' said Joe, as we passed the indistinct outlines of the spirit rocks, 'you very good to us this time, anyhow;
very much we thank you, Grandmother!'

"'It's a pity, Joe,' I observed, 'that we have not time to see
whether the offerings of yesterday are gone or not; but mind,
you go up the lake again to-morrow to bring out the meat,
and don't forget your Grandmother, for I really think she has
been most kind to us.'"

All the essential elements for still-hunting the Moose are manifested in this single narrative.

A thorough knowledge of the habits of the animal must teach
the hunter where to look for him at certain seasons of the year,
or at particular times of the day, in fair or in stormy weather.
The superior vision of man over that of the Moose, is more than
compensated to the latter by the advantage of his position, being

generally still himself, while the hunter is in motion, which helps out his defective sight, and enables him to identify the moving object. But few animals have a more correct vision than man. It enables him to identify objects at a great distance, without the aid of motion, but for successful Moose hunting — and the same remark is generally true of other game as well — the vision must be cultivated by long practice and careful study. This the Indian has succeeded in doing to a greater extent than the cultivated man. The reason of this is obvious. The mind of the Indian is occupied with few and simple thoughts, and to these he can devote all the energies of whatever intellect he has, and hence we might expect great proficiency in the few pursuits to which he devotes a life-time. But few white men make a life-long business of hunting, and even these few have learned to think of more subjects than the Indian, and those subjects will intrude themselves, more or less, upon the cultivated mind, when not under the strong excitement arising from the immediate presence of game, and so he does not cultivate those senses, the highest order of which are indispensable to meet the sharpened instincts of the larger game whose constant apprehension makes them ever on the alert. The improved vision of the Indian hunter, — and that is the occupation of nearly all Indians, from childhood to old age, — and that class of observations which enables him to draw correct conclusions from slight evidence which would escape the notice, or not arrest the attention, of the ordinary white man, has been noticed by all who have hunted much with the aborigines, and has been recorded by all who have written of their experience. The instance just narrated, when the Indian recognized the moose, when he was not moving, the instant he came within the line of vision, and before the moose observed the hunter, although in motion, is not singular, or even exceptional.

But the hunters knew they had keener senses to deal with than the dull eye of their game. His quick ear would detect the least noise, and his acute sense of smell would detect the least taint in the air, which would tell him of the presence of his enemies, when the game would be lost. How these embarrassments were overcome, is well explained, and they are always to be met with in still-hunting the deer, and so indeed in many other modes of his pursuit.

While the still hunt may be followed at all seasons of the year, and is available for all the species of the deer, the *call* hunting is peculiar to the pursuit of the Moose, and is substantially confined to the amorous season, although the call is available, as we have seen, as auxiliary to other modes of hunting, and at other seasons.

In general the deer is a very silent animal, and the use of the voice is almost entirely confined to the two largest species, the Moose and the wapiti. The Moose, most of all, expresses his passions or his sensibilities by uttering sounds expressive of different passions and sensibilities, which are intelligible not only to his own kind, but are understood by the hunter as well. To imitate these, sometimes an instrument, made of bark or a hollow horn, is used as an aid, while others succeed well by muffling the mouth with the hands ; some possess this faculty of imitation in a much higher degree than others, and some even can never acquire it.

During the rutting season, as has been said, the male Moose especially, impelled by the ardor of his passions, loses a part of that timidity and caution by which he is governed at other seasons. They become not only ardent, but courageous and combative. Until mated with a female, they crush through the forests and swamps in a half frenzied condition, seeking the desired object, and apparently aching for a fight. Now it is that the hunter seeks to take advantage of his temperament, by imitating such calls of his kind as are most likely to allure him to love or to combat. In the call hunt the hunter has comparatively little to fear from the sight of the Moose, but from the senses of smell and hearing he has everything to apprehend. The time chosen is either night or early morning. He must make his camp a sufficient distance from the ground selected for the hunt, to prevent its giving notice to the game of his presence in the neighborhood. There must be no wind to carry the odor of the hunter in any direction, else the sagacious and suspicious animal will be sure to take advantage of it, to approach the hunter from the leeward, and so detect the fraud at once, when the hunt is spoiled. A full moon is required to enable the hunter to see the game when it approaches, and to shoot with accuracy when in range.

On a still night in September or October, with a good moon, after the antlers of the Moose have become nicely polished by being rubbed against the tree-stems, the experienced hunter repairs to the well-known resort of the Moose, selecting an elevated position in a country as open as may be found, and conceals him self behind some prostrate tree or great rock in a dark shadow, where he remains for a time in perfect quiet, listening for the well-known call of the cow or the bull Moose seeking for a mate. If heard, a fitting answer is imitated, and the game is allured within fatal range of the deadly rifle. No matter how perfect the imitation, a doubt seems to rest in the mind, especially of an old bull, and his approach is slow and cautious, frequently passing quite around the place where the hunter is concealed, snuffing the air to catch the scent of an enemy, if he has been deceived, or of a mate, if his hopes are to be realized, and if the least breath of air is stirring to carry the scent, he is sure to catch it, and beats a retreat so quietly that not a twig snaps beneath his feet, while before the cracking noise of his great antlers thrashing among the dry limbs, could be heard at a great distance. When suspicion is thus confirmed, the retreat of the Moose is so quiet, the hunter will strain his eyes to get a glimpse of the game where he last heard him, when he is rapidly retreating a long distance away. If no suspicious scent or noise confirms the fears of the Moose, he gradually approaches the spot where the call was heard, which he readily locates with unerring certainty, till at last his great form looms up against the horizon, and then it is the fault of the hunter if Moose steaks are not over the camp-fire the next morning.

The bull Moose is the principal object of pursuit in call hunting, the cow being rarely enticed by the call.

Although this is no doubt exciting sport at times, for it is difficult to conceive of a feeling more intense than that inspired by the crashing tread of the advancing bull or the rolling of his great antlers among the dry limbs, as he thrashes them about in defiance of a supposed adversary, whose challenge he thinks he has heard, and with whom he is ambitious to do battle, yet this is not in general a successful mode of hunting the Moose, and failures are many, while successes are few.

In Scandinavia, Mr. Lloyd tells us that the elk is successfully hunted with dogs held in leash. He cautiously follows in the track till the game is approached, when the dog is tied to a tree and the hunter stalks the quarry alone. This mode only meets with qualified success there. I have no information that this mode of hunting the Moose has ever been practiced here.

THE WOODLAND CARIBOU.

The endowments of this animal render its pursuit a work of care and labor in those regions where it has been much hunted, and so the excitement of the chase is enhanced in a corresponding degree. Indeed none other of the deer family abhors civilization so much as this, and none so quickly desert a country upon its approach. While it occupies the range jointly with the moose, they are by no means social neighbors, and the Caribou hastens away, whenever it finds itself in close contact with its larger cousin.

Except in unfrequented regions it is only found in timbered lands or in the bushy barrens, where it can find safe covert from its pursuers. If once alarmed by the hunter, it flees away in continued alarm, nor stops to rest or feed, till it has gone so great a distance that pursuit is quite out of the question. If the experienced hunter wounds the Caribou, he makes no attempt to follow him, unless he believes him so disabled that he lacks the physical strength to escape to any great distance, for he knows he will never stop till compelled by absolute exhaustion, or a perfectly safe distance has been attained.

If, like the other deer, it does not readily recognize objects by sight alone, its senses of hearing and smell are acute and discriminating, and this must be ever borne in mind by the successful hunter. The habits of this deer vary very much in different localities, so they must be specially studied under varying circumstances. The mode of pursuit which may be very successful, in remote seclusion, where it is rarely alarmed, might be quite fruitless where it is frequently pursued, and so has become ever watchful and vigilant.

Although the Caribou is nearly voiceless, yet it is not wholly so. During the love season the male expresses his desires, and invites a mate, by a short deep note, something approaching a bellow, but the Indians, of the present day at least, do not attempt to imitate it and so attempt to *call* the deer within range of the rifle, as we have seen they do the moose, though they claim that in former times this was successfully practiced by their ancestors. Stalking or creeping is the only resource left to the sportsman in regions at all accessible to him, where the deer have been rendered cautious and wary by pursuit. In the interior of Newfoundland and the sterile regions of Labrador, where the country has not been harried by the white man, the case is quite different. I may here repeat, what I have intimated in another place, that the Indian, even since he has acquired the use of fire-arms, does not ordinarily drive game from a country, as the white settler or even the white hunter is quite likely to do. His quiet, stealthy mode of proceeding does not create that permanent im-pression of alarm, which results from the boisterous and careless proceedings too often indulged in or practiced by the white man. If he kills his game, it is done so quietly and everything is so quiet afterwards, that those escaping are hardly able to appre-ciate what enemy has thinned their ranks.

In what may be termed the alarmed districts, nothing short of the skill of the Indian can successfully pursue the Caribou, and so it is indispensable to the sportsman who would hunt him, to secure the services of a native hunter, whose life-long training alone could qualify him for the difficult task. The sport is de-ferred till early winter sets in, when the ground is covered with snow, which reveals the tracks of the deer, and finds more or less lodgment in the boughs and on the bark of the trees, making everything so nearly correspond with the color of the Caribou, that nothing short of the quick eye of the Indian can detect him, till he bounds away forever.

Many expert Indians have for many years almost made it a profession to assist the sportsman in the pursuit of the moose and the Caribou, in those few districts where these deer are found and are still accessible to the sportsman. These Indians are not only skillful hunters, but are often amusing companions and use-ful camp servants: making camp, supplying the fires, cleaning the guns and cooking the meals, and bringing in the game.

It is in the damp and fresh fallen snow that the Caribou is most successfully stalked. Then it is that the foot, clad in the moccasin, made from the skin of the hock of the moose, returns no sound to the hunter's step, and he is enabled to glide through the dark forest or the bleak barren as noiselessly as a cat upon a carpet.

The Caribou, like the moose, frequently crops the parasitic mosses or the twigs of bushes while he is traveling, and by this means the experienced hunter is assisted in following his trail when his tracks are indistinct; and from the freshness of these signs he judges how recently the animal has passed.

In districts where the Caribou is not hunted except by the Indians, as in the interior of Newfoundland and Labrador, they are less suspicious, and less difficult to approach. There they have their regular trails and runways, which they pursue in their regular migrations, always crossing the streams at favorite fords. In these migrations the deer march in small bands, in single file, generally several feet apart, in well beaten paths. Their march is leisurely made, and rather slow, frequently picking the lichens as they pass, unless they observe something to excite their suspicions. This is the time for the natives to make their harvest of meat. The greatest opportunity is at the ford of a broad stream.

Dr. Richardson, in treating of the Woodland Caribou, says: " Mr. Hutchins mentions that he has seen eighty carcasses of this kind of deer brought into York Factory in one day, and many others were refused for the want of salt to preserve them. These were killed when in the act of crossing Hays River, and the natives continued to destroy them, for the sake of the skins, long after they had stored up more meat than they required. I have been informed by several of the residents of York Factory that the herds are sometimes so large as to require several hours to cross the river in a crowded phalanx."

On the island of Newfoundland, this deer is equally migratory; but necessarily its migrations are more limited territorially, except in the few instances when they cross the broad waters which separate the island from Labrador, in the winter on the ice; but this rather facilitates than impedes this mode of capture by the natives, for it compels them to pursue their travels within more defined routes, and so they are the more easily waylaid and destroyed.

In the interior of Labrador this deer, especially in the winter season, contributes largely to the sustenance of the natives, who still pursue it with the bow and arrow with some degree of success. Hind, standing on the divide between the waters of the Miosie and the Ashwanipi, listened to the story of the Indian, Michel, the theatre of which lay before them, and gives it thus: " He had been watching for some hours with his companion when they heard the clatter of hoofs over the rocks. Looking in a direction from which they least expected Caribou would come, they saw two Caribou, pursued by a small band of wolves, making directly for the spot where they were lying. They were not more than three hundred yards away, and coming with tremendous bounds, and fast increasing the distance between themselves and the wolves, who had evidently surprised them only a short time before. Neither Michel nor his companion had fire-

arms, but each was provided with his bow and arrows. The
deer came on ; the Indians lay in the snow, ready to shoot. The
unsuspecting animals darted past the hunters like the wind, but
each received an arrow, and one dropped. Instantly taking a
fresh arrow, they waited for the wolves. With a long and steady
gallop, these ravenous creatures followed their prey, but when
they came within ten yards of the Indians, the latter suddenly
rose, each discharged an arrow at the amazed brutes, and succeeded in transfixing one with a second arrow before it could get
out of reach. Leaving the wolves, they hastened after the
Caribou. There," said Louis (the interpreter), " quite close to
that steep rock, the Caribou which Michel had shot was dead ;
he had shot it in the eye, and it could not go far. Michel
stopped to guard his Caribou, as the wolves were about; one of
his cousins went after the deer he had hit; the other went back
after the wolves which had been wounded. The wolf cousin had
not gone far back when he heard a loud yelling and howling.
He knew what the wolves were at : they had turned upon their
wounded companion, and were quarreling over the meal. The
Indian ran on and came quite close to the wolves, who made so
much noise, and were so greedily devouring the first he had shot,
that he approached quite close to them and shot another, killing
it at once. The Caribou cousin had to go a long distance before
he got his deer."

THE BARREN-GROUND CARIBOU.

The Barren-ground Caribou is never an object of pursuit by the
mere sportsman. His habitat is so remote from civilization, and
so inaccessible, that he is sought only as a matter of business and
not of pleasure. Only the Indian and the fur trader frequent his
haunts, and they hunt him for his meat and his pelt.

In its southern range, this deer finds forest lands which it inhabits during the winter season, making excursions into the
mossy plains for food, but in its northern migration in the summer, it goes beyond the forest regions, and dwells upon the barren grounds exclusively, where it finds an abundance of lichens,
which are its favorite food.

Dr. Richardson says :[1] " The Chepewyans, the Copper Indians,
the Dog-ribs and Hare Indians of Great Bear Lake, would be
totally unable to inhabit their barren lands, were it not for the
immense herds of this deer that exist there."

[1] *Fauna Boreali Americana*, p. 244.

On the next page, the same learned author says : " The Caribou travel in herds, varying from eight or ten to two or three hundred, and their daily excursions are generally towards the quarter from whence the wind blows. The Indians kill them with the bow and arrow or gun, take them in snares, or spear them in crossing rivers or lakes. The Esquimaux also take them in traps, ingeniously formed of ice or snow. Of all the deer of North America they are the most easy of approach, and are slaughtered in the greatest numbers. A single family of Indians will sometimes destroy two or three hundred in a few weeks, and in many cases they are killed for the sake of their tongues alone."

The Esquimaux trap these deer, using the reindeer moss for bait. The trap is constructed of frozen snow or ice, inclosing a room of sufficient dimensions to hold several deer, and over this is laid a thin slab of ice, supported on wooden axles forward of the centre of gravity. The top of this is only accessible by a way prepared for the purpose, and beyond the tempting moss is laid. In reaching it, the deer passes over the treacherous slab of ice, which is tilted by the weight of the deer, and he is precipitated into the room below, when the top, relieved of the weight, resumes its horizontal position, and is ready set for another victim.

They are snared with thongs made of the skin of the animal, by placing the noose in positions where the head will pass through it, something in the manner described in snaring the moose, and if they do not find a tree convenient to which the line may be attached, they will hitch it to the middle of a loose pole, which soon becomes entangled in the bushes and among the rocks, so that the animal cannot escape to any great distance.

Great numbers are captured by the Indians by driving them into pens or inclosures made of bushes, and placed in the course of some well beaten path, where a narrow gateway is left, from either side of which a diverging line of bushes or piles of stone, perhaps one hundred feet apart, are placed. These may extend a mile or two, and at their extremities be far apart. A watch is kept from some high point of observation, and when a herd of deer is observed approaching, the whole family, men, women, and children, quietly skulk around them, and drive them within the converging lines of objects which, in their stupidity and defective eyesight, they regard as impassable barriers, and so rush straight forward upon the path into the inclosure, in which is a labyrinth

of ways made by rows of bushes, where the deer become fairly
dazed, and are slaughtered with spears, and even clubs, the
women and children in the meantime guarding the outside of the
inclosure to prevent the escape of any. The number slaughtered
in this way is very great, and furnishes the natives with provision
in great abundance.

We have many facts related of the Barren-ground Caribou
which serve to inform us of the degree and accuracy of their
powers of vision, and from these I think we may safely conclude
that if their sense of sight is quick it is not reliable. Indeed
we are led to the conclusion that they identify objects with less
certainty than any of the other deer. As we have just seen,
rows of bushes or piles of stone placed at considerable distances
apart serve to prevent them from passing the lines, and guide
them to the pound into which they are driven. This shows that
they do not identify the objects which guide them, nor do they
in their confusion even individualize those objects, but to them
they are so confused that they appear to form continuous lines
on either side, else they would pass out between them. This
defect of vision is further illustrated by what Captain Franklin
says of this deer, as quoted by Richardson : " The Reindeer has
a quick eye, but the hunter, by keeping to the windward of
them, and using a little caution, may approach very near, their
apprehensions being much more easily aroused by the smell than
the sight of any unusual object. Indeed, their curiosity often
causes them to come close up to and wheel round the hunter,
thus affording him a good opportunity of singling out the fattest
of the herd ; and upon these occasions they become so confused
by the shouts and gestures of their enemy that they run backwards and forwards with great rapidity, but without the power
of making their escape. The Copper Indians find 'by experience
that a white dress attracts them most readily, and they often
succeed in bringing them within shot by kneeling and vibrating
the gun from side to side in imitation of the motion of the deer's
horns, when he is in the act of rubbing his head against a
stone. The Dog-rib Indians have a way of killing these animals which, though simple, is very successful. It is thus described by Mr. Wentzell, who resided long amongst that people.
The hunters go in pairs, the foremost man carrying in one hand
the horns and part of the skin of the head of a deer, and in the
other a small bunch of twigs, against which he, from time to
time, rubs the horns, imitating the gestures peculiar to the animal.

His comrade follows, treading exactly in his footsteps and holding the guns of both in a horizontal position, so that the muzzles
project under the arms of him who carries the head. Both
hunters have a fillet of white skin around their foreheads, and
the foremost has a strip of the same around his waist. They
approach the herd by degrees, raising their legs very slowly but
setting them down somewhat suddenly, after the manner of a
deer, and always taking care to lift right or left feet simultaneously. If any of the herd leaves off feeding to gaze upon this
extraordinary phenomenon it instantly stops, and the head begins
to play its part by licking its shoulders and performing other
necessary movements. In this way the hunters attain the very
centre of the herd without exciting suspicion, and have leisure to
single out the fattest. The hindmost man then pushes forward
his comrade's gun, the head is dropped, and they both fire nearly
at the same instant. The deer scamper off, the hunters trot after
them. In a short time the poor animals halt to ascertain the
cause of their terror; their foes stop at the same moment, and,
having loaded as they run, greet the gazers with a second fatal
discharge. The consternation of the deer increase; they run to
and fro in the utmost confusion, and sometimes a great part of
the herd is destroyed within the space of a few hundred yards."

This long extract is fully justified by the amount of real information which it contains as to the habits of the Barren-ground
Caribou. From the facts stated I arrived at a different conclusion from that stated by Captain Franklin. He says the Reindeer " has a quick eye; " but his conduct shows that he has the
dullest eye of the genus. Any of the others with whose habits
we are well acquainted would have detected the counterfeit, especially when one hunter was following the other, long before
they reached the herd. The facts related demonstrate that the
sense of smell is not so reliable as has been often stated, else the
hunters, under no circumstances, could have reached the middle
of the herd without creating alarm.

As further illustrating the habits of this animal, I must quote
from what Captain Lyon says of the mode of hunting it by the
Esquimaux. " The Reindeer visits the Polar regions at the latter end of May, or early part of June, and remains till September. On his first arrival he is thin and his flesh is tasteless, but
the short summer is sufficient to fatten him to two or three
inches on the haunches. When feeding on the level ground an
Esquimau makes no attempt to approach him, but should a few

24

rocks be near, the wary hunter makes sure of his prey. Behind
one of these he cautiously creeps and having laid himself very
close, with his bow and arrow before him, imitates the bellow of
the deer when calling each other ; sometimes for more complete
deception the hunter wears his deer-skin coat and hood so drawn
over his head, as to resemble in a great measure the unsuspecting
animals he is enticing. Though the bellow proves considerable
attraction, yet if a man has great patience he may do without it
and may be equally certain that his prey will ultimately come to
examine him ; the Reindeer being an inquisitive animal and at
the same time so silly that if he sees any suspicious object which
is not actually chasing him he will gradually and after many ca-
perings and forming repeated circles approach nearer and nearer to
it. The Esquimaux rarely shoot till the creature is within twelve
paces, and I have been frequently told of their being killed at a
much shorter distance. It is to be observed that the hunters
never appear openly, but employ stratagem for their purpose ;
thus by patience and ingenuity rendering their rudely formed
bows, and still worse arrows, as effective as the rifles of the Eu-
ropeans. Where two men hunt in company they sometimes pur-
posely show themselves to the deer, one before the other. The
deer follows and when the hunters arrive near a stone the foremost drops behind it and prepares his bow, while his companion
continues walking steadily forward. This latter the deer still
follows unsuspectingly, who thus passes near the concealed man
who takes deliberate aim and kills the animal. When the deer
assemble in herds there are particular passes which they invariably take, and on being driven to them are killed by arrows by
the men, while the women with shouts drive them to the water.
Here they swim with the ease and activity of water-dogs, the
people in hayaks chasing and easily spearing them. The carcasses float and the hunter then presses forward and kills as many
as he finds in his track. No springs or traps are used in the
capture of these animals, as is practiced to the southward, in consequence of the total absence of standing wood."

We nowhere else find in the same space so much valuable information concerning this animal as in this extract.

It tells us of the great curiosity of this deer, which so often
leads it to destruction, in which it most resembles our antelope,
but it conclusively proves as well that the vision is so defective
that even with the aid of motion it cannot identify objects. The
facts stated also show that this deer has not the acute sense of

smell which is possessed by the other deer, or else when following up the track of the hunters their presence would have been detected. Add to these infirmities their stupidity, and the fact that they are easily distracted so that they are incapable of escape even in the open plain, and we have the picture of an animal which is very useful to the natives who have to depend on the rudest and most imperfect weapons to procure subsistence, but it should hardly be called game more than a flock of sheep. Another remarkable fact is mentioned in this extract, and that is that the deer floated after being killed. This I am very sure is quite exceptional. From my own experience, and from all the information I have been able to obtain from others, the other species of deer sink so soon as they are killed if in the water, and this is the case of those without antlers as well as those that have antlers. The fact stated is the more remarkable, because of the immense antlers which the males have, which as we have seen are much larger in proportion to their size than those of any other deer. " The carcasses float." No exception is made in the case of the bucks. The winter coats on the bodies of all deer consists of hollow cylinders which are, to be sure, very buoyant, but this coat must be enormous to sustain so great a weight in the water, but then undoubtedly they require a very warm coat to protect them in that arctic region.

From all the accounts we have of the mode of taking this little arctic Reindeer and its capabilities for self-protection, its pursuit could never become an object of interest to the sportsman. Indeed, it is too stupid an animal for its capture to create an interest in any but a hungry man or a butcher. The pleasure of the sportsman in the chase is measured by the intelligence of the game and its capacity to elude pursuit, and in the labor and even the danger involved in the capture.

The sportsman is better rewarded by the capture of a single woodland caribou, which has required all his skill with infinite pains and labor and exposure and privation, than to participate in the slaughter of a thousand of his stupid cousins of the north, which he would look upon with indifference rather than with pleasurable excitement. Among the former it is a contest with sharp wits where satisfaction is mingled with admiration for the object overcome. With the latter it must be — nothing ! The difference in the endowments for self preservation of these two species of deer, if not the most marked of those which declare them of different species, is still very remarkable and interesting.

THE ELK.

The American Elk, or Wapiti Deer, is noble game, and its pursuit affords exciting sport to the hunter. His range is much more diversified than that of the moose, for he ranges the prairies and the plains, as well as the forests and the mountains. If he does not make his home on the barren plains of the far west, he ranges across them from one belt of timber to another, which are usually found along the streams which intersect them; and before the white man had driven him from the fertile prairies of the Mississippi valley they were extensively grazed by the Elk.

Almost the only mode of hunting the Elk, either by the Indian or the white man, is by stalking, or the still hunt, or sometimes by pursuit on horseback. Being social and gregarious in their habits, they are usually found in bands of greater or less numbers, although it is by no means uncommon to find solitary individuals scattered through the country, — usually young males. They are less suspicious than the moose, and their senses of smell and hearing are less acute, while few other animals excel them in these regards. But, as the hunters express it, they have less *sense* than the moose, or, indeed, most of the smaller deer, but they are by no means so simple as to destroy one's interest in them, or make their capture an easy matter.

When sought for in prairie countries, the hunter expects to find them along the creek or river bottoms, where the grasses are more abundant and sweeter, and where they find arboreous food, which they crave to mix with the herbaceous. Here, too, they find the shade in which they delight. Thus occupying lower ground than the surrounding country, the hunter from elevated positions may overlook the valley, till the game is discovered either grazing in security below, or quietly ruminating in the shade of the trees. He has already studied the course of the wind, so as to be always to the leeward of the game. A careful study of the ground then ensues, and objects sought which may be made to cover the approach to within range. This is not so difficult as the approach to the moose, still it is indispensable to study the course of the wind, for if the wind wafts to him the least taint from his enemy, the Elk detects it in an instant, and is off. He is not sent away by the snapping of a twig, or the rustle of a leaf, if he cannot see the cause, still the hunter must observe great caution in his approach, and especially not to allow the game to get a glimpse of him when in motion. In stalking the Elk, the hunter must be particularly cautious not to stumble upon a deer, while his attention is intently devoted to another ; many are lost in this way. A thick bunch of willows, or tall bottom grass, may be selected as the object to cover his approach. Such is a most likely place for an Elk to make his bed, and he may spring up before you not ten feet away, when a single bound may take him beyond view, even if you see him at all. If it is an old buck a loud whistle of alarm may be sounded, but without this, his flight will alarm the whole band, and your sport is probably up for the day.

When started, the Elk does not, like the moose and the caribou, push right away, without a pause and swiftly ; but most likely after running a few hundred yards, the whole band will stop on some commanding elevation to see what is the matter. If he does not see his enemy, as he probably will not, still he is not quite happy, and will not delay till he has placed many miles between him and the hunter. If a lone animal is thus started from his bed of willows or high grass, before he sees the pursuer, he is very likely to stop for a moment or two after making a few leaps, and that momentary pause has been the opportunity for many a fatal shot, which has laid low the head which bore magnificent antlers.

The Elk is often found among the foot hills of the mountains, and in very broken, rocky ground. This is the most killing ground, I mean for the hunter to pursue him in, for you must leave your horse below and clamber through on foot, when you are liable to come upon a lone Elk suddenly, and close before you, when a quick shot settles the matter ; or if you see one on considerably higher or lower ground, one hundred yards or more away, with a favorable wind, he may stand several shots, if your bad shooting allows it, before he will take serious alarm and make off.

It is not easy to determine the highest altitude of the range of the Elk, but it is probable that they go to the utmost of the timber line. I have found their tracks more than ten thousand feet above the sea level, on the Sierra Madre Mountains. Whether those that frequent these high altitudes ever visit the plains, or abide permanently in the mountains, I have no means of determining. When the severe winter sets in they descend into the basins and cañons, where the mountain streams have their sources, and where they find grass beneath the snow, and in these pockets in the mountains the hunter seeks them, keeping on the higher ground which surrounds them. Instances are related where bands of Elk have been thus observed from high, overlooking points, when a gale of wind was blowing, whence the hunter has shot down a considerable number before the balance would take the alarm. They would look upon the struggles of the dying in amazement, but without suspecting it was the work of an enemy.

There is no doubt that our Elk has less tenacity of life than any other American member of the family. I have inflicted a wound upon an Elk through the head, quite below the brain, and without cutting an artery, and without occasioning much hemorrhage, which a common deer would have carried fifty miles, and found the Elk dead in half an hour after, and within half a mile of the place where he was shot. My own observations have been confirmed by the testimony of old hunters of vastly more experience than I can claim, and if my recollection rightly serves me, the observations of Lewis and Clarke were to the same effect.

I have seen a few accounts of their being pursued with grey-hounds on the western plains, by army officers stationed at frontier posts, but, from the accounts, I judge they are not as gamy as the common deer, — though they may equal in endurance the European stags, — and they undoubtedly lack the endurance of the moose or the caribou. When pursued on horseback the Elk makes for broken and rocky ground, if any be accessible, where the pursuit usually terminates, but if away on the plains, the chase is an exciting and an interesting one. The Elk leads away in a rapid trot, which if not broken he holds for a long distance, but when forced from this into a run, if the animal be fat, he soon breaks down, but if lean he endures it well, and leads a fine chase before he is run into.

None other of our deer fatten so kindly or get so fat as the Elk, and possibly this may account for their lack of *bottom* in the chase.

THE MULE DEER.

The pursuit of the Mule Deer is almost entirely confined to stalking or still hunting. They are found in the high mountains as well as in the valleys of the creeks and rivers in the plains. Where they are much pursued they are wary, and tax the skill of the hunter to approach them. They are fond of browsing on the young cottonwoods, which grow along the streams and in marshy places up the mountains. Here they are found at the first dawn of day, and before this time the hunter should secrete himself in a favorable location, which his experience and knowledge of the animal's habits will enable him to select, when he may hope to get a shot. They are not as gregarious as the Elk or the common deer, so he may expect to find but few together, if more than a single individual is met with in a place. They leave their favorite feeding grounds early in the morning, and if in hilly or mountainous regions, are sure to go to higher grounds to repose and ruminate. Here they are sought by the experienced hunter, who rarely sees them in their lairs but relies upon a snap shot when they jump up ; and, as they cannot be depended upon to stop after making a few leaps, he never waits for such an opportunity, but fires at the first sight as the best probable opportunity he will get.

In remote mountain districts, where the Mule Deer are seldom hunted, they are not remarkably shy, and the careful stalker may meet one at any time of the day feeding on favorite grounds, which one familiar with their tastes and habits has no difficulty in recognizing.

Lieutenant W. L. Carpenter, U. S. A., with whom I have had the pleasure of climbing the mountains in the pursuit of the deer, a sportsman of very large experience, especially in the mountain regions, writes me : —

" I have never seen or heard of any other deer in the Rocky Mountain region than the elk (*C. Canadensis*), the black-tailed deer (*C. macrotis*), and the white-tailed deer (*C. leucurus*).

" I have found the black-tailed deer most abundant in Northern Colorado, and the white-tailed deer on the Upper Missouri. Both species are found abundant on the treeless plains, and it is my opinion that a great many of them never see the mountains. The Republican, the South Platte, the North Platte, the White River, and the Upper Missouri, have both species in common, hundreds of miles from the Rocky Mountains. But the black-tailed deer *always* prefer the high bluffs and deep ravines near the rivers, while the white-tailed deer selects the thickest brush in the river bottoms that he can find, and will often allow you to walk within a few feet of him without moving ; he is seldom found far from cover.

" I think that 10,500 feet may be safely set down as the limit of elevation for the white-tailed deer. I have never heard of one being seen anywhere near timber line. Several times this season, in climbing the mountains in North New Mexico, I have found white-tailed deer from the foot hills up the mountain side to about 10,000 feet, and then seen no more deer till an elevation of about 12,000 feet was reached, when the black-tailed deer appeared, and were often seen above timber line. This was in the summer. On the approach of winter, both species range lower."

Altogether the Mule Deer does not afford as varied and exciting sport as some of the other deer, still they are well worthy the pursuit of the sportsman, who is inspired by that peculiar spirit which shrinks at no labor or fatigue, and finds a rich reward for all hardships and discomforts in the excitement of the chase, and the ecstasy which he experiences, when he sees such noble game answering discharges of his rifle by falling in his tracks if standing, or by turning a high somersault and then tumbling to the ground with a fearful crash, if on the run. There is a thrill of joy at such a moment, only known to the sportsman, which permeates every nerve of the human system, and which is in excitement far beyond the experiences of the sordid man, who spends his time and thoughts, and labors day and night, to win more gold or add a few more acres to his estate. I cannot explain it. It is not that brutal, sanguinary joy which gladdens at the pain it may inflict, or takes pleasure in the death of innocence; for the true sportsman will never take life for the mere pleasure of killing, if he must leave his victim to rot upon the ground. He must associate his triumph with the consideration of utility to some one, no matter whom. It may as well be a total stranger or a band of savages in whom he feels no interest beyond that of common humanity. Immaterial to him who may be the beneficiary, so that his capture may be utilized, he enjoys his success scarcely less when his own camp is well supplied than when the gnawings of hunger stimulate his effort.

There are those no doubt who will slaughter for the mere love of slaying and leave a multitude of carcasses to fester on the plains; but these are not sportsmen; they are mere butchers, and their proper place is in the abattoir, where they may satiate their desire for blood without useless destruction and to a useful purpose.

CERVUS COLUMBIANUS.

Although the range of the Columbia Black-tailed Deer is limited, its pursuit affords exciting sport. This deer avoids the open country more than any of the other species, excepting the moose and the woodland caribou. It is fond of the broken foot-hills and rocky mountain sides, as well as the deep seclusion of the dense forests of the lowlands. In California it is more fre-quently found in such localities as first described ; while in Oregon and Washington territory, it finds a welcome home in the deep shades of the vast forest regions which there abound, preferring localities not too remote from the broken rocky country, to which it can retreat in case of danger. In the southern part of their range, or as far south as San Francisco, along the coast, they fre-quently occupy the ground which they inhabit, to the almost en-tire exclusion of the other species of deer, while in the neighbor-hood of the Columbia River, they are associated with a variety of *C. Virginianus*, called the white-tailed or long-tailed deer, which in many localities outnumber them. Further north again, and on the islands of Puget's Sound they assert their numerical supe-riority.

In the mountainous regions, the common mode of pursuing this animal is by the still-hunt or stalking. As the animal is an early riser, the still hunter must be astir betimes, and by the first dawn of the morning must be far beyond the influence of his camp upon ground previously selected, and there, in profound stillness, he must attentively listen for the least sound which may advise him of the approach of the game ; and as the increased light enables him to survey a wider region from some command-ing position he may have taken, he scans the valley beneath and the mountain side, among the rocks and the bushy thickets. If at last no sound or sign from these is heard or seen, he cau-tiously moves along the ridge, if in the wet season, in search of a track, and when that is found, the course of the wind in refer-ence to the direction taken by the deer is first considered, and a direct pursuit or a detour is made, as his judgment may dictate. A rapid pursuit is not so important, as the extremest caution. The whole field of observation must be constantly and carefully scanned. Every step must be taken, as if in close proximity to the game. Not a stick must be broken under the feet, not a stone dislodged to go thrashing down the cliff, no bush shaken, which may give warning of his presence. The silent solitude must remain unbroken, while the closest attention must be given, to catch even the faintest sound from any quarter. True, the game may be miles away, but then, again, the hunter may be close upon it. If he relaxes his caution, it may be at the critical moment when the prize is just within his grasp, and his only chance will be lost. This the experienced hunter will never do, for well he knows that care will in the end be rewarded with success. He only expects to find a solitary individual, for these deer are less gregarious than the others, and seldom wander far in company. He may, as he cautiously peeps over the ridge or from behind the rock, first sight the game within close range cropping the leaves from the shrubbery, or the grass from the valley, or the wild oats from the whitened field, or he may see him half a mile away, clambering up the opposite mountain side among the broken and scattered rocks. In the first case a single deliberate shot ends the chase ; in the other, success is scarcely less assured, for now that he sees the object of his pursuit, the hunter watches his movements, according to which he lays his plans and makes his approach with continued caution, which in the end will surely bring him within range of the buck, whose first notice of the presence of an enemy will be the fatal bullet crashing through his frame, when he will leap high and fall among the rocks, and in his dying struggles will roll far down into the valley below. Sometimes the pursuit is ended while it is yet early morning, and sometimes it lasts until the evening has come, when the hunter will make a fire beside a broken rock, cut out a steak and broil it, eat his supper, smoke his inevitable pipe, and then lay himself down beside his trophy and count the stars till he goes to sleep, all the time having his trusty rifle within his reach.

Such was the history of the chase and capture of the last Black-tailed Deer which I helped to eat. He was a noble buck with magnificent twice bifurcated antlers, which no doubt still lie bleaching high up a cañon of the Coast Range, about fifteen miles from the Geyser Springs of California. It took the captor half of the next day to bring out the meat to where he could reach it with a mule, when he became too fatigued to go back for the head and antlers, exceptional as they were in size. I do not believe there is any more fatiguing sport than this ; yet for all that it is the more keenly relished, since sport without fatigue is often too cheap to have a relish, is too insipid to have a flavor.

Another favorite mode of chasing this deer is with hounds, much after the manner of chasing the Virginia deer, notably in Old Virginia, only it is generally done upon more level ground and in heavier forests, though sometimes among the foot-hills and even in the mountains. Even here the deer have their runways, which the sportsmen of the neighborhood soon learn, where they station themselves listening for the coming of the pack to indicate who is to be favored with the presence of the deer which may be looked for far in advance of the hounds.

When the watchers are warned by the hounds that the game is afoot, in those regions where both abound, to determine whether it is a black-tailed or a white-tailed deer is very desirable. If the former is approaching, probably but one has been started; if the latter, there may be two or more. If the former, he may run in a large circle, and if in the lowland forest and hard pressed, will make for the mountains or rocky broken ground, where he can the more readily throw the dogs off the scent and elude pursuit, and only when all other resources fail him will he make for the water if lake or river be in reach; if the latter, they may be expected to scatter if there be more than one, but all will probably be found making their way to a river or lake if one can be found within any reasonable distance. To determine the course of the deer, therefore, it is important to know which species has been started.

Some hunters claim to be able to determine this fact at an early stage of the run, from the course the hounds may pursue and from other sagacious observations. From the dense covert in which these deer are found in the lowlands, when their pursuit is practicable by the hounds, the shot is usually at very close range, and must be made on the instant or the deer is again lost to view, hence a heavy fowling-piece with buck-shot is generally preferred to the rifle.

When they are hunted with hounds in the vicinity of large bodies of water, as the Columbia River, or on islands in the Sound, when hard pressed they take to the water and swim with scarcely less dexterity than the other species, crossing the river to escape their pursuers or making for another island, but if the distance be too great for them to undertake, they return to shore sooner than the common deer. When they take to the water they may be pursued in a boat if one be convenient, with which they may be readily overtaken, seized by the antlers and drowned, if the pursuer chooses, or is obliged to despatch them in that way.

The still hunt is quite practicable in the forest of the lowlands, and throughout the country; ten are killed in this way, where one is taken before the hounds. In the still hunt in the forests they are more generally *jumped up*, as the hunters express it, when they must be shot on the instant, or they will make good their escape. The hunter, therefore, must be ever on the alert, and has no business to be studying mathematics when he is still-hunting the Columbia Black-tailed Deer.

THE COMMON DEER.

The Virginia Deer is not only the most abundant, and hence the most useful of all the American species, but its capture affords the most varied and the most exciting exercise to the sportsman. Its sight is fully equal if not superior to that of any of the other species, while its senses of hearing and smell are only inferior to those of the moose. It has an intelligence which enables it to resort to expedients to baffle its pursuer, and it possesses a vitality which enables it to escape with wounds, which would prostrate some other species at once. If its actual endurance is inferior to some others, in fleetness it surpasses all of them.

In all the territory now occupied by the United States and Northern Mexico at least, the Common Deer was a large resource for food to the aborigines, and hence the pursuit of them was a life study with the Indian. His principal weapon of destruction was the bow and arrow; to make this effective, it was necessary to approach the game within very short range, and to accomplish this his ingenuity was taxed to the utmost. To be successful he must be familiar with the habits, the tastes, the instincts, and the capabilities of the animal. Taking advantage of the wind he waylaid him on his known routes from one place to another, he secreted himself in trees near the salt licks, to which the deer paid nocturnal visits. At other times he would assume the skin with the head and antlers of the deer, and thus disguised, cautiously approach his game to within shooting distance. He would sometimes imitate the call of the young fawn, and thus allure the mother within his reach. In deep snows, he pursued the deer on snow-shoes, and soon exhausted the strength of the latter in the unequal chase, or followed him on the crust, through which the struggling animal would sink and lacerate his legs in his efforts to escape.

The early settlers of this country, depended largely upon this deer for their provisions, and their mode of pursuing it was generally the still-hunt. When the deer were abundant in all the forests the new comers had little trouble in securing an abundant supply of venison, without even much effort or the loss of much time. In the winter, when they cut down trees to browse their

cattle for the want of hay, it was not an uncommon thing in the
early morning, to see several deer among their stock nipping off
the buds from the lately fallen trees, and they rarely failed to
stalk them successfully. The use of oxen was often resorted to
for the accomplishment of this purpose. The oxen were yoked
and hitched to a sled, with hay or straw, or other cover placed
upon it, beneath which the farmers would be concealed, when, if
the wind should favor they would make their way into the midst
of the herd of browsing cattle, without alarming the deer ; and
then if the farmer made a close shot the venison would soon
hang in his larder.

In those districts, where the first settlers had to clear off the
heavy forest to make room for crops, they cut down an abundance of trees in order to feed their stock, during winter, which
they cleared away in summer, and for the first few years these
clearings would be close by the log cabin; and when I was a boy
those who did this laborious work in the eastern States, were still
in active and vigorous life. If they seemed to me then to be old
men, as I estimate age now, they were scarcely past the prime of
life. They never wearied of relating their early experiences of
perhaps thirty years before, and surely I never wearied of listening to them. Their hunting experiences, when deer, bear, and
wild turkeys were so abundant as to be almost nuisances, fairly
transported me to the wild woods and wild scenes, and the exciting chase which they so graphically described ; and I longed
for the time to come, when I should be old enough to carry a
rifle, and when I might wend my way to a new country such as
they described, where I too might revel among game which had
scarcely ever been alarmed by civilized man.

It might not be difficult to remember enough of these narra-
tives to fill a book. One shall suffice, as it illustrates a fact not
generally recognized. A settler had made a deep excavation for
a cellar, with a narrow sloping way leading to it. A deep, light
snow had fallen, which the wind had blown into the excavation
until it was even with the surrounding surface. The settler's
cattle were browsing in sight of his door, when he saw among
them a deer. He seized his rifle and made a circuit so as to
approach the game behind a convenient shelter, which was just
on the opposite side. By the time he reached the covert a slight
breeze had sprung up and admonished the deer of his approach,
when it started directly away from the danger which it snuffed,
and made almost directly for the cabin, in the door of which the

good housewife was anxiously watching the result. But when she saw the game gracefully bounding away, her hopes of venison nearly died out. Soon the deer passed close by the house, when in her excitement, she started after it as if she intended to run it down in a fair field. As she was a large, fat body, though young, healthy, and powerful, this to the average hunter might have seemed a desperate undertaking, and probably the act itself was solely one of impulse. However fortune kindly favored her, for in a few leaps, the deer plunged into the excavation just described, which had a vertical wall on the opposite side, which the deer failed to scale, and fell back. The excited woman comprehended her chance at a glance, and rushed down the inclined way, seized the deer by the hind legs and held it, till the husband, hastened by her outcry, ran up and ended the scuffle with his hunting knife. This great feat made the woman a heroine, the cause of which she could long years after relate to her grandchildren.

Now this was looked upon by those old, experienced hunters as scarcely less than a miracle, for with the attributes they had always ascribed to the deer, it should have kicked her to death, or at least freed itself from her in an instant; and so it would have done, had she seized but one of the hind legs, for with either hind foot loose it would have made bloody work with the adversary. My own experience shows that a man can readily hold a deer if he can seize both hind legs at once; but if he grasps but one, he must let it go immediately, or he will be sure to suffer. When the hind legs are well stretched out, and not allowed to touch the ground, the animal is almost powerless. He is always urging himself forward as much as possible with his fore legs, and unless the man holding him is so light that he can draw him up, he has no purchase with his hind legs, and cannot kick at all. It is the rapidity of the muscular action of the deer that makes it appear so strong. Its motions are so very quick, that it is the most unmanageable animal of its actual strength I have ever encountered, if it can but get a chance to act. I have seen two men try to force a pet yearling deer into a park from which it had escaped, by their carelessly leaving the gate open, when their clothes would fly off in shreds. Two strong men, with a strap around the deer's neck, can do it; but they have no leisure to do anything else at the same time. Either one of them could have walked right away with it by the hind legs. I have found this the easiest way to handle the Common Deer when castrating.

The opportunities first described afforded but one mode adopted by the early settlers for supplying their families with venison. In the winter time, they followed the deer through the snow, and seldom failed of success. They soon learned their habits, their favorite ranges and feeding grounds, and early learned where to look for them ; and could judge with great accuracy as to their destination, when they had followed a track but a short distance, and could so anticipate their arrival at a given point.

In the fall of the year, when the deer are in the finest condition, many made a business of hunting them, to lay in a store of provisions. The still-hunt was their favorite mode. They silently threaded their way through the quiet forest, frequently with a trusty dog, well trained, close behind them, seeking those places which their observations had taught them were most frequented by the deer, either for shelter or food. Oak or chestnut or beech groves always invited the deer, which sought in them their favorite food. But above all, hazel thickets, where they abound, are the favorite resort of the deer, not only for the nuts which are here found, but for the dense covert which these thickets afford.

The dog was seldom used, in those early times, until the deer had been wounded. The instant the gun was fired, the hunter, unless satisfied he had missed altogether, instantly started the dog, which followed by sight, and so soon as he came up with the wounded deer, brought him to bay, rarely attacking, if the deer stopped to fight him, but detained him with loud baying till his master should come up and with another shot secure the prize. If the deer dropped to the first shot, the dog was slipped, for the chances were that the deer would soon get up and be off, and though mortally wounded, would give the hunter a long chase before he would finally capture him. But few animals will go so far and so fast, after receiving a mortal wound, as a Virginia deer ; although, if not pursued, he will go but little ways after he is out of sight, before he will lie down, and, if not disturbed, may never rise again. The best deer dog I have ever seen, for service in the still-hunt, was a cross between the greyhound and a bull-dog. He was fleet, sagacious, and very powerful. If his master did not soon arrive after he had brought the wounded deer to bay, he was sure to take him down and kill him, and then seek his master and lead him to the spot. This might be miles away, for if the wound is not very severe a strong deer will lead the best dog a long chase through the forest before he is overtaken. The best dog I ever owned for the still-hunt was a pointer. Though not so fleet or so powerful as the other, his fine nose and great sagacity compensated for all else. He would take the track of the deer and follow it by the scent just us fast or slow as directed, and as still as a cat. When he brought a wounded deer to bay, he would give tongue as furiously as one could desire, and hold him at bay with great pertinacity ; but of course he never seized the animal.

Those early settlers often hunted the deer on horseback, and may have thought the game was more easily approached thus than on foot ; but my own experience has led me to a different conclusion. The deer when thus hunted soon learned that the mounted hunter was as dangerous as if on foot, while concealment was almost impossible. On the prairies the horse was preferable, for concealment was difficult in either case.

The mounted hunter in the event of success had the means of taking home his game when captured. If the deer was too large for him to lift to the horse's back, with a cord or the bough of a tree he might be attached to the horse's tail, and thus drawn home, and this was the usual practice of some who insisted that a horse could draw the largest deer in that way, without the least appearance of distress.

When the pedestrian hunter killed his deer, he bled him and removed the viscera, and then hung him in a tree beyond the reach of the wolves, until he could come for him with the means to remove him. This might seem a difficult matter with a heavy deer, but it is not so. Of course a long cord should be carried in the pocket for the purpose. If the deer is too heavy to be sustained by a sapling which the hunter is able to bend down, he selects the largest he can manage near to a larger tree. The sapling is bent down and fastened in that position. To it, ten or twelve feet from the ground, the deer is attached by the heels. The sapling is then allowed to spring back with the cord attached near the top. This cord is then passed over a limb of the larger tree, when a moderate pull will assist the small tree to assume a vertical position and your deer is safely suspended. Of course you must go as far from under the limb as possible to save friction. In this way a man of moderate strength can hang the largest deer quite beyond danger.

Let me say here to the honor of frontiersmen, as well as sportsmen, that I never knew a deer thus left in the woods to be stolen. I really believe a man who would not hesitate to steal a horse would revolt at the thought of stealing the hunter's prize.

These same frontiersmen in time became country gentlemen with improved farms and plantations. In the level or even hilly country the deer mostly disappeared before the march of civilization, while in the mountainous regions they remained and still remain in considerable numbers. The whilom hunters for meat became sportsmen for the excitement of the chase, or where the old stock have passed away, the new generation allowed the long, faithful rifle which had done sanguinary service in the early settlement of the country, to repose on the rack, and pursued the deer more for the sport than the saddle ; more for the prize than the real profit. The silent and sagacious deer dog was no longer prized but gave place to the slow, and boisterous, and I may add stupid, hound. The sublime stillness of silent nature in the solitude of the dark forest is broken by the noisy bay of great packs of hounds, and the timid deer goes rushing through the woods frightened out of his native gracefulness.

It is where the country is divided into ranges of wood-clad mountains, or high hills divided by valleys, down which rivers or creeks run, or in which lakelets are situated, that the proper theatre is found for running the deer with hounds. For this purpose packs of greater or less numbers are kept as in different countries of Europe. In such localities different runways are adopted by the deer, where they pass the watercourses in going from one elevation to another, or where they approach the little lake for bathing. Several sportsmen engage in the hunt. Early in a still, frosty morning they repair to the ground, generally on horseback, when one, and sometimes two, are stationed at each of the well-known runways, when their horses are concealed and the hunters secretly station themselves so as to command the crossing place and its approach. The hounds, in leash, are sent on to the mountains, and at a likely place they are slipped, and the hunt commences. So soon as the deer is started, the hounds give tongue. This is the signal anxiously listened for by the watchers at the several runways. Far away in the distant mountain, at first like a faint murmur, the sound is heard, uncertain whether it is the baying of the dogs or the whisper of an insect. The note soon becomes more distinct, and it is certain that the game is afoot. Anxiety now increases to determine who occupies the favored location. All along the line the attention of **each** watcher is strained to the utmost tension, to detect by the

25

sound the course selected by the deer. Rifles are cocked, not a whisper is breathed, not a twig is broken, not a leaf is stirred. Every wandering thought is summoned back and absorbed in the excitement of the moment. The course of the hounds may be traced by their voices, each listener calculating the chances of their arriving at his stand.

This is the moment when the inexperienced hunter is liable to make his greatest mistake. He forgets that the deer is not with the dogs, but may be a mile or more ahead of them. He listens to the dogs, and his eyes are in the direction whence the sound comes. If they seem to approach him, he forgets that the game may be already upon him. When he least expects it, there is a rushing noise, a crackling of the brush, and the deer emerges from the thicket, and with an elastic bound is already at the ford, and with a few lofty leaps is across the creek, and like a flash disappears in the dark covert beyond before the startled watcher, quaking from head to foot with the *buck-fever*, could more than bring his gun to his face and fire a random shot, when all is still again, save the tumultuous beating of his own heart.

Less fortunate is the deer if he makes the runway occupied by the experienced sportsman. Only thinking of the danger behind him, and confident of his powers to far outstrip the baying pack, he bounds through the forest, proudly throwing aloft his great branching antlers, as if in derision ; bidding defiance to his pursuers, nor dreaming of danger before, he fearlessly rushes to the little opening on the bank of the stream, where he is accustomed to make the crossing, whether at his leisure or when pursued. This is just what the watcher is hoping and expecting. While he hears the distant baying of the pack, he is intently listening for the least noise in the near forest which could indicate the approach of the game. And now he hears the breaking of a dry limb, or the heavy tramp among the rustling leaves. If his pulse quickens a little, as it surely will, still no tremor or agitation is felt, but only tension and firmness are established in every nerve and in every muscle. The trusty rifle is quickly brought to the cheek, and the next instant, with a lofty bound, the magnificent but graceful form of the stately stag bursts from the border of the covert, his face in a horizontal line, his antlers thrown back upon his shoulders, so that every branch and vine must easily glance from the backward-pointing tines, his scut erect, and his bright eye glistening in the excitement of the moment, when instantly and while he is yet in mid-air, a sharp report is heard, when, to use a hunter's expression, " he lets go all holds," his hind feet, propelled by the great momentum, are thrown high in the air as if his very hoofs would be snapped off, and he falls " *all in a heap*," or turns a complete somersault, and then rolls upon the ground pierced through the heart, or with both fore shoulders smashed ; or if the deer was descending in his leap, perhaps the shot was higher than was intended, and a stitch is dropped in the spinal column. In either case, the monarch of the forest is laid low, never to rise again. It is a glorious moment, and unsurpassed by human experience. I have been there, and know how it is myself, and so I speak from knowledge. Had the deer been standing, and with a full inspiration, he might have made a few bounds before he fell, but in the position described he could never rise again.

When the fatal shot has been fired by the successful sportsman, he winds his horn as a signal of his triumph, and to call his companions at the other stations, and the congratulatory meeting takes place over the prone form of the noble game. All admire his great antlers, which are lifted and dropped by each in turn. All admire his glossy coat which glistens in the bright sunshine like a silk robe, and all feel of the thick coat upon the ribs, and with watering mouths — remember they have been fasting since daylight — think longingly of the rich venison steaks in a chafing-dish for each, dusted with capsicum, seasoned with salt, laved in butter ; or, better still, lubricated with some slices of hard, fat pork, and flavored with a dash of good old port. Around the board so furnished, the sportsmen, after the fatigues of the day, with appetites sharpened by long abstinence as well, — selecting for the feast a saddle which has hung a few days to ripen and flavor, — while the venison slowly simmers in the rich compound, recount their experiences, their hazards, their exposures, their fatigues, and their triumphs. Then it is that the old settler, whose hair is white as snow, but who is yet hale and hearty, and is able to mount his horse and to ride him, too, with the best of them, is a most welcome companion. Seated at the head of the table, he is apt to monopolize the conversation, especially after a time, and may even become a little garrulous too, still all listen to him with anxious attention and deepest respect. He has been there from the beginning. He can tell when all was forest, when the first cabin was built, and who made the first clearing. He remembers when the whole country was full of game, when a slice of pork was a welcome change from venison, bear meat, or

wild turkey. Then it was he learned to use the rifle, and commenced the study of the habits of the various animals he hunted,
as much for sustenance as for the sport. He learned all their
hiding places and runways, and grew cunning in every mode of
their pursuit, and has watched the changes which new conditions have introduced in the mode of hunting the different game.
These were frequently men of marked intellect and culture, and
their observations with tongue and pen have contributed materially to the cause of science.

The mode of hunting the deer upon the prairies, or rather in
the prairie countries, is in many respects different from those
practiced in mountainous and timbered countries. Where prairies
predominate, as in Illinois, for instance, they are frequently dotted
with isolated groves, and are intersected by skirts of timber along
the borders of nearly all the water-courses which traverse the prairies, so soon as the streams become large enough to arrest a prairie
fire. These groves are of various sizes, from a few acres to many
miles, and the belts of timber along the streams vary from a few
rods to miles in width.

The real home of the deer is always in the timber, but he is
fond of visiting the prairies, and indeed at favorable seasons
spends much of his time there during the day at least, though
as a general rule he repairs to the timber to pass the night, unless indeed he is prowling about in the farmer's maize or wheat
fields, which he very much affects. Very often the deer may be
seen leaving the forests for the prairies in the gray of the morning and returning again in the dusk of the evening. During the
day, too, they are often seen passing from one forest to another,
whether the intervening prairie be one mile or ten miles wide,
though generally where there are long stretches, they will stop
and rest on the way. They find much of their aliment in the
prairie grasses, but they will have their arboreous food if any be
accessible, and this they usually take in the timber in the night
time. Indeed they spend most of the day in repose, well secreted in the high slough-grass, or if the flies and mosquitoes are
troublesome they resort to the high prairies where the pests
are likely to be kept down by a smart breeze ; and there conceal
themselves in a clump of tall grass which may afford a partial
shade and there enjoy their quiet siesta. All these conditions
and habits the experienced sportsman has well and carefully
studied, and having observed the time of the day, the season of
the year, the state of the weather, the topography of the coun-

try, and the relative position of the timber and the prairie, and acting upon the combined suggestion of all these, he regulates his course.

A very enjoyable mode of hunting the deer in the prairie country is for a party of four or six to make the hunt in company. The time selected should be in the autumn, say October. The outfit should consist of two or three tents, with the necessary utensils and provisions, a cook, a teamster, and one servant, besides a good pair of horses and large wagon to transport the impedimenta, a well trained strong horse, who should be a good goer, and a good deer-dog for each man. A double-barreled gun, — one barrel a rifle and the other for buckshot, — a few extra guns, ammunition, and a kit of fine tools, blankets, robes, etc.

Having arrived on the ground, make your camp in some grove or belt of timber near a spring of water, where good grass may be found for the spanceled horses.

The hunt commences with daylight, and may be around the borders of the timber, each one pursuing his own course, depending on his judgment of the ground. The question is at what points the deer will be likely to make their exit into the prairie. Here the hunters place themselves sometimes on horseback and sometimes on foot. The sportsman being secreted in a commanding position favored by the wind, by the time the first rays of light stream up from the east he listens with the deepest attention for the rustle of a leaf, the cracking of a twig or other slight noise, to indicate that the game is astir, and to determine the course it is pursuing, and if a change of position is necessary to intercept it. If he has not scented his enemy, the deer emerges from the thicket to the prairie in a leisurely walk, and becomes an easy mark for the rifle, if within a reasonable range. If there should be several deer, as is apt to be the case, and the distance not too great, the buckshot are first discharged and the rifle used at the longer range, or if they are in close range a deadly shot is made with the rifle and the other barrel used for the running shot.

After the morning hunt the party assemble at camp, where the cook has prepared breakfast, which each one takes as he comes in, if all do not arrive together. The team is sent to bring in the game, and its return is expected by the time breakfast is over, and the pipes smoked. Preparations are now made for the day's hunt in the prairie. Each one takes in his pocket a lunch (they always use the abbreviated word) of bread or crackers and cold venison steak. The course for the day is agreed upon, and the wagon is taken along and the teamster is directed to keep upon the most elevated ground and to observe as well as he can the position of the several hunters, to listen for the reports of shots, and to look out for signals, which he is to answer, and to take the game on board.

The horsemen separate, according to the nature of the ground, generally following the sloughs where the long grass is usually left standing, even when the high ground has been burned over. Here they usually expect to find the deer concealed in their lairs. The dog is taught to follow close to the heels of the horse, and on no account to leave that position till he is commanded to go, and if he is properly trained he will keep his position, no matter how many deer get up around him, or how many shots are fired. The horse is kept upon a slow walk through the tall grass, while the elevated position of the horseman enables him to command the entire view. The bridle-reins usually lay on the pommel of the saddle, across which, also, the rifle is carried, or in the angle of the left arm, usually cocked, but not always so. For myself, I never cock the gun till the game is up, whether it be bird or quadruped, always carrying it with my thumb on the hammer, at half-cock, and finger on the trigger, and if I have a double shot I lower the breech and cock the other lock, and I have always found I could shoot right and left as quickly as those who carry their guns cocked. I have never hunted with but one man whose habit was the same, though I presume there are many others. It is all a matter of practice, and, if commenced young, the act becomes automatic, and is performed as unconsciously as I now form my letters, and more unerringly. It has always seemed to me the safest way, though others may think differently.

The deer usually lay till the horseman gets nearly upon them. If there be more than one, which is usually the case, they will be found lying within a few rods or even feet of each other, but never actually together. At the least, a considerable belt of the tall grass will be found separating their beds. Usually the nearest will be the first to rise, and the first bound he makes will arouse all the others. The second bound the deer jumps high, as if to survey the situation, and this is the best for the shot, for it will likely be within ten or twenty yards. When a double shot is offered the hunter it is frequently advisable to take the longest shot first, and his own practice will suggest whether to open with the ball or the buckshot.

He must never expect the deer to stop after a few bounds, as he usually will when aroused by some object which he does not see. Here he sees you at a glance, and has no occasion to stop for a more minute survey. Indeed, he is likely to lie quiet for some time after he hears your approach, in the hope, probably, that you will pass him unperceived, and many deer are thus passed unnoticed in broad swales. If the dog is well up to his work he may scent the deer as you pass him, and by a low whining noise he may arrest your attention, and by his actions indicate the direction of the game.

After the shot is fired it is a question to be decided on the instant, whether to send off the dog or not. If the deer is badly wounded, and is not hotly pursued, he is sure to lie down soon, where he can conceal himself; while if pressed by the dog or horse, he would run for miles. If the ground is such as to give you a good view, it may be best to let him go off quietly and lay himself down where you can readily find him, and settle matters by another shot, though you must not expect him to lay as close the second time as he did at the first. The wounded deer is not so readily brought to bay in the prairie by the dog, as he is in timber; probably because he can see the mounted hunter at a greater distance; so he will keep on until he is actually in danger of being pulled down by the dog, before he will stop to fight him.

When the game has been secured and bled, and the viscera removed, the hunter rides away to the high ground to signal the wagon to come and take it on board. To accomplish this he may have to go several miles, and unless he is well up to prairie craft, he may never be able to find his deer again. He must not fail to mark well the immediate surroundings, and all landmarks which he passes on the way. This the experienced hunter does almost involuntarily, and will return to the same place without an effort; while a stranger to the prairies must give his undivided attention to marking the localities, and as objects look very differently when passing one way from what they do when going the other, he must frequently look back and mark the general topography of the prairie as well as the minuter objects. By consulting his pocket compass he will find his task very much simplified, though the old hunter rarely has occasion to do this, unless a dense fog comes on, which sometimes happens late in the fall, when the compass is indispensable. I was once caught in such a fog without a compass. I went six miles with unerring certainty and struck an object within two miles of camp, which I knew was on the way, and then I spent two hours or more circling round on a section of land; every half hour or so I would pass close by the object, with the same bearing and distance as the first time. Though I was perfectly familiar with every object on this portion of the prairie, nothing at this time looked natural except the stake stuck in a little mound or ant-hill, with that everlasting owl sitting upon it. That looked natural, and I knew I could leave it in the proper direction for camp, but before long the inevitable owl on the stake would again appear not a hundred feet away on my right. At length I detected the faint trail of the wagon, which I knew had gone out over the same ground that morning. I dismounted, carefully examined for prints of the horse's feet; and when found, I discovered I was headed the same way they had gone. No one who has not tried it, can appreciate how difficult it is to make the inclination yield to the judgment. I *felt* that I was headed directly for camp. I *knew*, from the evidence before me, that I was faced the other way. Judgment prevailed, and I carefully followed the faint back trail, and in half an hour I reached camp just before dark. Then and not till then did familiar objects look natural. I had been lost. The mental faculties had become bewildered. Why people in this condition should incline to wander in a circle, it is not my place now to inquire, but such is frequently though probably not always the case. Nor does it seem to make much difference whether one is lost in the woods or on the prairie, the same system or the want of it in bewilderment seems to prevail. It comes on when one is not suspecting it, or looking out for it, else by watchfulness it might be guarded against.

Frequently in this kind of prairie hunting, one hunter may drive the deer upon another. The instant, therefore, a shot is heard, the hunter should stop and remain perfectly still. If he does not move, the deer may come directly upon him if he is in their selected course, without recognizing him, and he may get a shot as it passes, or what is much more likely, he may trace its course at a distance, and watch it to a new bed.

" I was returning towards camp one evening," said my friend, who was an expert at this mode of hunting the deer, and enjoyed it more than any other, " slowly walking my horse along a high ridge in the prairie, when I discovered a large buck on the opposite ridge, half a mile away. He was evidently intently watching me. He stood in a narrow belt of grass which had been left by the prairie fire. I did not halt, and gave no sign that I saw him, but slowly pursued my way, bearing, however, to the left, so as to get more between the deer and the timber. The position of the deer commanded a view of the intervening valley. Presently he laid down in a bunch of high grass. I continued to walk my horse slowly across the valley, gradually drawing more in the direction of the deer, he believing he was entirely concealed, and evidently thought he had not been discovered. I approached the buck in a direction which would pass him not more than thirty yards distant. I kept whistling a low tune all the way, and assumed as careless an attitude and action as I could, appearing always to look in another direction, though now and then a quick glance showed the great antlers, which looked like a rocking chair, through the dried grass. I had for the last hundred yards or more been changing the position of my gun, sometimes to my shoulder, sometimes to my left arm, and sometimes to the pommel of my saddle. When I got opposite him I could see the outline of his head laying flat on the ground, but the body was concealed. At the proper moment I checked my horse by a word, turned in the saddle, raised the gun and fired the rifle, before the deer had fully made up his mind that he was discovered, reserving the buckshot for a fairer mark in case the ball missed, and he should jump up. But he did not. He straightened himself out, and gave up the struggle with a few spasmodic kicks. That was the largest deer killed by the party during the hunt, and was a satisfactory conclusion of a fine day's sport. An old buck is as cunning as a fox, but if you understand his ways, it is possible to circumvent him, and to do so is the very essence of sport. My companions were returning with the wagon half a mile away, and had been watching my movements for some time, but having seen no deer, supposed I had fired to bring them that way rather than go out of my way to join them, and so were reluctant to answer my signal to come. But they came at last, duly admired my trophy, assisted to put him on the wagon, when we all returned to camp together with as fine a load as I have ever seen brought in from the prairie in a single day. We were tired and hungry, no doubt, but all bore a hand to hang up the deer, and in a few minutes the trees around that camp were festooned in a way to make a hunter's heart rejoice. After bathing the face and hands in the cool spring water which burst from beneath the bank below, we gathered around our venison stew, which was our favorite dish in camp, and it seemed as if each one was determined to spoil more of it than another. At first ravenous, then moderate, then delicate, picking over the savory mess to get a sweet morsel."

The supper in camp is not a hasty meal, towards the end at least, and is usually accompanied by full accounts of the incidents of the day and of former sporting experiences, which are continued long after the pipes have been lighted and the weary hunter is stretched out upon his robe at the mouth of the tent, enjoying the soothing influence of the burned herb, without which camp life would lose half its charms.

Perhaps the most exhilarating mode of chasing the deer, is in the prairie with the greyhound. The broad, unbroken prairie presents a field for this sport unsurpassed. After the prairie fires have left most of the elevated portions of the great plain quite naked, and the dry seasons which generally prevail in the fall of the year leave the sloughs sufficiently hard for the free passage of the horse, while the tall grass which covers them and has been by moisture kept too green to feed the fire, which consumed that which had matured and withered on the dry upland, the proper conditions for this unparalleled sport exist.

The dogs should be well trained to the sport, should be strong and enduring, and the more experience they have had the better. The horse as well as the dog soon learns to enter eagerly into the spirit and the excitement of the chase, and evidently enjoys it as much as his master. It takes a smart greyhound to come up to the average deer on the prairies, and only one that has learned his lesson severely can handle the deer after he is overtaken. Much of this he must learn by experience aided by his own sagacity. His master is rarely up at the first encounter, and the neophyte is sure to be cut by the feet and antlers of the deer, which the latter knows how to use with great dexterity. These wounds are the chastening lessons of the tyro, and if intelligent, he soon learns how to avoid them. But the experienced dog appreciates help, and will prolong the chase in order to secure it, if it is in prospect, either from the hunter or the rest of the pack, and will only close when he sees that he alone can overtake the quarry. The expert greyhound will not attempt to pull down his game by main force, but will take advantage of his momentum to throw him, when the fall must be severe; and I have seen this done repeatedly before closing. In this way he greatly exhausts the deer by these repeated hard falls, and gives time for the slower dogs to come up, or his master to arrive to assist at the death.

When the party is made up, the ground agreed upon, and the time fixed, the dogs should be well fed over night, but they must not be allowed to take food in the morning, which will require much time for digestion. An early start should be made and the party proceed to the field at a smart walk. The dogs should follow on foot for two or three miles, when they should be taken into a wagon, in which they should ride the balance of the way. The deer, it will be found, have long since left the timber to seek repose through the day in the high grass, and generally will be found in the sloughs, but in unburned prairie, sometimes in patches on the high ground. In the fall of the year, or in the winter, of course the deer can remain in the low ground undisturbed by the flies and mosquitoes.

Arrived upon the ground, the hunters should arrange themselves abreast across the slough, so separated as to beat the whole. The progress is up the slough from the timber and towards the wide open prairie, so as to enable the flankers to cut off the deer from the timber and drive them into the field, for if they once reach the timber they are safe from the pursuit of the greyhound. Being thus arranged, the hunters proceed up the slough through the high grass, the pack remaining near the centre of the line with their master. When a deer is started a shout is raised, and a rush is made in the direction of the game. This is instantly understood by the pack, and they spring forward in the direction thus indicated, jumping high to get a sight of the game. Their observation and progress are obstructed by the tall grass, so that by the time they reach the open ground the deer has attained a considerable start. Now the real chase commences. The dogs and horses, stimulated by excitement and the loud shouts of the hunters, lay down to their work beautifully. The deer shapes his course for the nearest point of timber. With long and rapid strides he skims the ground almost like a bird on the wing, never spending his strength by high bounds, but running low and rapidly he passes over the ground with great swiftness. But if the ground is well chosen there will be miles of naked prairie before him, and he soon feels the pressure of his great exertions. He improves his chances by taking advantage of the inequality of the ground or tall grass, which may hide him from the sight of the dogs ; but the experienced hunter anticipates these movements and turns them to the disadvantage of the pursued by making a shorter cut when the deer makes a circuit, or gains upon him when he is obliged to slacken his pace in the denser covert. The elevated and dispersed positions of the horsemen enable them to always keep the chase in sight, and so the well trained hound is kept upon his course without loss, though the game may frequently be lost to view. It is a glorious sight when the horsemen and the hounds draw near the game, when evasion or concealment is no longer possible, and it becomes a mere question of muscle and endurance ; when the shouts of the riders stimulate both the horses and the hounds, and madden the frightened deer to the last possible effort of every sinew. The pack is strung out in a long and scattered line and so are the horsemen, each striving to the utmost to gain on the quarry, to keep the lead or to make up the lost distance. To be the foremost in such a chase, to keep even with the leading hound, and see that each stride lessens the intervening space between the pursuers and the pursued, is the culmination of excitement only known to the ardent sportsman.

At each stride the leading hound draws nearer to the deer that is straining every muscle to maintain his distance, his wild eye protruding from its socket, his mouth wide open, and his tail occasionally lashed between his legs, as evidence that he is pressed beyond his strength, and is already distressed with his great efforts. At length as he sees his pursuers are gaining upon him, and the friendly thicket is yet far distant, fear comes and increases the embarrassment of fatigue, and he begins to jump wildly, which retards his flight. The horseman, meantime, urges his steed to the utmost to keep up with the hound, which, however, he fails to do ; but, as he sees the race is soon to terminate, he strives to keep as near as possible. Now the leader of the pack is up with the game. He seizes him a little inside the thigh just as the hind feet leave the ground, and by a side jerk throws him heavily to the ground, letting go as the quarry falls. If an experienced dog, and sure of speedy support, he will wait till the deer gets up and resumes his flight, when he will again throw him in the same way, and so repeatedly till others of the pack come up, when all will close in upon the exhausted animal and usually make short work of it. But great vitality remains in an old buck. If an inexperienced dog exposes himself to the blow of a wounded buck he may be knocked ten feet away by either foot, or he may be impaled by a single dash of the sharp antlers. One severe lesson, aided by the example of the older dogs, is generally enough to make the beginner cautious even in the midst of the excitement. One or two dogs at the throat laying upon the shoulders and neck, and one or more behind can, in an incredibly short time, dispatch a large buck; but before this is accomplished the huntsmen are generally up, when the hunting-knife puts an end to the struggle.

The most successful dog I ever followed always threw his deer in the way described, and I never knew him once to fail; but I have known other dogs to seize the deer in the lower flank and throw him by so doing.

A short time gathers the horsemen around the prostrate buck, when each may have something to relate. A horse or two may have stumbled in the chase, whose riders have been dashed to the ground; possibly a broken limb, but probably a few bruises would sum up the casualties; and after the panting horses have taken breath, and the wounded have been cared for, another start is made and the scene again repeated.

It often happens that several deer are started at the same time which run in different directions, whereupon the party and the pack divide, and may be seen scouring over the prairie, pursuing the flying game, and at the conclusion of the run are separated by many miles; sometimes, indeed, so far that they are not again united the same day, unless at the dinner-table, when the incidents of the day are recounted, with such extravagant embellishments as may be necessary to enable each to outdo the others.

Of all the modes of chasing the deer, its pursuit over the prairie with horse and hound is by far the most exciting and exhilarating; and, I may add, the most expensive, also, especially to the inexperienced rider; for, if he returns with a sound horse and a sound body, he may consider himself fortunate. Practice is required in this as well as in other modes of pursuit, though in none can the neophyte in deer hunting take so active a part as in this.

There is as great a difference in speed and endurance among deer as among horses. Some may be taken almost immediately, while others can only be captured by the best dogs and best horses, after a chase of many miles, when half the party may have been left quite out of sight. Take a long-legged, lean buck, in the prime of life, and he is a marvel of speed and endurance, and will satisfy the most ambitious sportsman before he is run into.

Another mode of hunting the deer is called the *Fire Hunt.* As I have never tried it, I am unable to describe it from my own observations. It is not much favored by sportsmen, but is rather considered as befitting what are called *pot-hunters*.

The deer is largely a nocturnal animal, especially in the neighborhood of settlements, or in regions much hunted. For this mode of hunting a still, dark night is selected. The place chosen is where indications are abundant that the deer make their nocturnal visits, and where the covert is not so thick as to obstruct the artificial light too much. It may be in the farmers' grain fields, around salt licks, or along the margins of rivers.

Generally, two go together in this sort of hunt. They are provided with an artificial light, usually made of pitch-pine knots, or the loose outside bark of the hickory tree, which contains an inflammable oil, and makes an admirable torch. This is so arranged, and carried in such a position, that none of the rays of light fall upon the hunters, one of whom either precedes or follows close behind the other, who carries the torch above his head or in front of him, higher than his head. A supply of material to renew the torch, is taken along and used as occasion requires. The hunters of course proceed with care and watchfulness and without noise.

The deer sees the light slowly approaching and is rather fascinated than alarmed by it, and so he faces and starts at it in wonderment, when his eyes act as mirrors and reflect back the light, and appear to the hunters like two great stars, or as they sometimes express it, like two balls of fire set in nothing but darkness; but neither of these expressions give a correct idea of the appearance of the light reflected by the eye. The radiation of the star is not seen, and the light is white instead of the red light of fire. Nothing else of the deer is seen. The advance should be made with extreme caution, for the least noise would be sure to scare away the game. The shot, if low, should be fatal; yet it is, I am told, very frequently not so. It has sometimes happened when several deer have been thus found together that those not hit have seemed to be so fascinated with the light, that after a few bounds away they stopped to gaze upon it, and were prevented from going further. This sort of hunting can never be safely practiced in the neighborhood of settlements where cattle are running at large, or the hunter may have to pay for a colt or a cow.

Nearly allied to this is the jack-hunting, or night hunting upon the water, of which I cannot plead entire innocence. When thick underbrush obscures the view, and not a breath of air stirs a leaf upon the trees, when everything is dry, and every leaf will rustle, and every twig will snap under the lightest step, and day after day of diligent toil has failed of a single sight of game; when the larder is low, and you are thrown back upon your reserved stores of pork or bacon, even if any of this be left, then you are ready to go jack-hunting. This is done upon a river or a lakelet. Along the margins of these in shallow waters grasses grow (*vallisneria* — deer grass, tape grass), of which the deer are very fond, for which they make nocturnal visits to favorite places. By previous examination these localities are easily discovered. This must be done by water, for the footsteps of men along the shore would be detected by the keen-scented animal, when he would leave in haste. A light boat or canoe, which must be paddled, not rowed, and an expert Indian at the paddle, is much to be desired. A light is carried upon the head. Various devices have been invented for this light, called *jacks,* but a watchman's lamp, attached to the front of a fireman's leather hat, answers the purpose well. The light should be covered by a leather shield, or cap, which can be removed and replaced instantly and without the least noise. This must be so adjusted that the light falls upon the gun barrel for its whole length when the aim is being taken, and at all times when not covered throws a strong light ahead. A dark, still night is desirable for this sport.

The hunter is seated near the prow of the canoe, and the paddler in the stern. If in a river it should be where the current is gentle, and unless it is a large river the canoe is allowed to float down in mid-channel; if in a lake the canoe is gently paddled along within from one to two hundred yards of the shore. Everything is profoundly still, both listening, to hear the deer come into the water at their favorite places. In a still night this may be detected by the quick ear of the Indian two or three hundred yards away. When the step of the deer in the water is heard the Indian quickly turns the canoe to the point whence the sound is heard, and the hunter removes the cap from his light, if it has been concealed, and instantly a strong column of light is thrown ahead till it is lost in the gloom beyond. Presently, two balls of light are seen. These are the eyes of the deer reflecting back the light of the lamp. The deer seems to take no notice of the rapidly approaching light, but the head is alternately elevated and depressed in the act of feeding, though I have been at a loss to conceive how we could get the full reflection from the eyes when the head was depressed to the very water, gathering the aquatic grass, but no matter what the position is, the reflection seems always equally bright as if looking directly towards you, and it is only by the movements that you know that they are not, and that the animal is feeding unconcernedly. When sufficiently near, deliberate aim should be taken, not between the eyes, but about four inches below them. Unless one is much accustomed to this kind of shooting, he is almost sure to over-shoot, and if the face of the deer is nearly horizontal, as it will be if he is looking at you, one inch too high will miss the deer, while if you shoot too low, a shot in the neck is as fatal as if in the head. The great excitement in this mode of hunting is, when the Indian is rapidly paddling you toward the splashing in the water, while the paddle dips so softly that it gives out no sound, and all you can hear of your own advance is a gentle murmur at the bow as it swiftly divides the waters. You are then earnestly looking into the still gloom, and when the orbs of light ahead are seen moving up and down and from side to side, while you are yet too far away to shoot, but with the gun to your face waiting for the Indian to say *shoot*, if you do not breathe rapidly, and your heart does not thump as if it would break your ribs, or appear to get into your throat and half choke you, then you have become a *hardened* hunter, and lost a part of that nervous sensibility, which affords such exquisite pleasure, if not too painful, for the line between these sensations I know to be very thin. With the light upon your head you cannot so well judge of distance as the Indian in the stern, so leave that to him.

The last time I was in such a place, — and it is not many months since, — there broke out from the darkness four balls of light, both deer evidently feeding a little way apart. The Indian pulled first for the one on my right, and he dropped with a shot in the neck close to the head. Immediately I cocked the other lock for the one on the left, but when the gun came to the face I could see nothing for the smoke, but the Indian understood his work, and shot me out of the cloud of smoke in a fraction of a second, and before the big doe could turn half round to jump the bank, presenting the left hip, a shot in the loin, ranging far forward, dropped her on the spot, and it took two men to pull her out of the water and up that bank. They were a pretty pair as they lay side by side, and the loud whoop of the Indian showed that he thought it a well executed right and left.

Sometimes the deer are disturbed by the night hunter, in deeper water where they can submerge themselves to escape the flies and mosquitoes, but I have never seen it.

Not the least exciting of the different modes of pursuing the deer is in the water with a light boat or canoe. A single incident of this mode will serve for illustration. Opportunities for this sport occur when deer are driven either into a lake or river, or when they take to the water voluntarily, for the purpose of swimming across.

We had made camp near the foot of the lower of two small lakes on the head waters of Pike River in Wisconsin, which were connected by a narrow strait only navigable by canoes.[1] Night hunting had developed the fact that the waters swarmed with black bass, which were continually breaking water with loud splashes, sometimes within two feet of the canoe, and frequently with such energy as to fairly startle those within it. They had been tried with fly and spoon, but were too far back in the wild country to have received the proper education to appreciate these allurements. One of my companions had induced his Indian to secure a good lot of dace from five to seven inches long, and invited me to join him to try and ascertain what kind of fish they were which made such an uproar during the whole night. So we started with a couple of eight-ounce trout rods. Stockton was in the bow of the canoe, while I occupied the middle, and his Indian, John Komoska, took the paddle. S. placed his rifle beside me, and said we might see a deer, when he should depend on me for the venison, although the camp was well supplied with fresh meat, but Lucius wanted a chowder. (His great weakness and his greatest strength is a chowder in camp.) We passed through the lower lake and half way through the upper lake without a bite, and came to a pause at the border of the lily pads (*N. advena*), opposite the mouth of a little creek. John said we would get them there if anywhere. We exhausted all our skill in all the ways we knew for luring bass, and only took a few small ones. At length in disgust I threw my hook, with a large bait upon it, into the water, and let it sink to the bottom, perhaps twelve feet, and there let it rest. After half a minute I attempted to move it, and then the sport commenced. I had hooked a five-pound bass. Fortunately, the first dash was into the lake and the reel sung a merry tune. John was well up to

[1] A rare sensibility on my part prevents me from giving the name of these twin lakelets, since they were named for the writer !

the business and run the canoe into the lake, to keep him beyond the lily stems, for if he had got among them, my tackle would have been no more than a cob-web there. So soon as I got sea room I was sure of him, for the line was long though small. He bit as lazily as a sucker, but after that there was not a lazy muscle in him. He fought like a tiger, or rather like a salmon; several times running away and then running in, repeatedly throwing himself out of water and trying to shake the hook from his mouth, but I managed not to give him an inch of slack. After a long and gallant struggle, he surrendered and rolled over on his side, when I floated him up to the bow of the canoe and Stockton lifted him in without a struggle. He had fought till he was completely exhausted. He was as black as night, excepting on the belly, which was partly gray. He was hump-shouldered and thick meated, and altogether the finest bass I had ever seen. It proved to be *Micropterus ingrecans*, Baird.

The secret was now out. At almost every cast we took a fish, but never felt a bite. More than half of the time we were struggling with a big fish simultaneously. If it was exciting sport it was hard work. After we had each smashed a tip, we took time to look at the pile in the canoe, and concluded there was enough for that chowder. There were seventeen fish weighing seventy-five pounds. The largest was over six pounds. When we got to camp, Stockton laid him on a piece of paper, and cut out his profile. It is twenty inches and three lines long and six inches deep, and he was very thick. That was a nice chowder we had, and when the fish was fried with pork it made a hungry man amiable to eat it.

We reeled in our lines, and John headed the canoe for camp. As we were passing through the strait, we heard a pack of wolves far away in the woods, but they seemed to be approaching, and when about in the middle of the lower lake nearly ahead of us we saw a large buck dash from the thicket into the shallow water, which was covered with lily-pads, and rush through it, slacking his speed, however, as the water deepened. When he reached the edge of the lily-pads, and the deep clear water was right before him, he stopped short, threw high his head, displaying to the best advantage his great branching antlers, and looked back and listened at the yelping of his pursuers. The Indian had stopped paddling, not a breath of air was stirring, and the water was as smooth as a mirror, while the bright declining sun cast the shade of the tall pines on shore far out upon the lake. " There," said Stockton, " is the first full realization I have ever seen of Landseer's glorious picture, ' The Monarch of the Glen.' " And so it was. The ideal of the great artist stood before us in all his magnificence, an actual verity. There stood the monarch of the forest in the border of the quiet lake, where the deep solitude is rarely broken by invading man, not dreaming there were enemies before him more dangerous than those behind, of escape from which he now felt assured. " *Hist*," said the Indian, and the word fairly hissed between his teeth, " he come here straight," and at the same instant the deer plumped into the deep water and swam directly towards us. No one moved, but if truth must be told, there was hard breathing in that canoe as the deer rapidly approached us. When he was within fifty yards or less, the Indian rose to his feet, gave a loud whoop, and dashed his paddle into the water. At the same instant the deer turned for shore, and swam like a race-horse. That Indian was too economical to allow the deer to be killed without a race. The canoe fairly flew through the water, not directly after the deer, but around him, so as to cut off his retreat, and in a time too short to be reckoned in the excitement of the moment, the deer was again turned into the lake. The race was short. I had picked up the rifle the instant the Indian whooped, and held it ready. The deer swam high, the top of his hips and part of his neck always out of water; still he constantly rose and settled in the water as he progressed. When within about twenty-five yards of the deer, the Indian turned the bow of the canoe out of the line of the chase, and said, " Shoot." I needed no second bidding. I aimed to strike him in the head, just back of the antlers, but as I pulled, the head settled, — we must always find an excuse for a bad miss, — and the ball passed between the antlers, very close, of course, and struck the water just ahead of him. Thanks to the Springfield breech-loader, the reprieve was short. The next time I held for the neck, and the ball crashed through it, and came out just so as to miss the under jaw. The deer dove, as you have often seen a muskrat dive, throwing the hind parts considerably out of water, owing to the momentum. Still the Indian was well up to his work. With a great exertion he shot the canoe to the spot before the deer had sunk below the reach of his paddle, which he dipped beneath the antlers, and raised him up so I could reach them. The Indian was master of the situation, for so long as he followed the deer directly, my friend was always in the way, so I could not shoot, but if the

gun had been in unexperienced hands, I would not have been in
Stockton's place, and I was impatient with the Indian that he
would not give me a shot before we got so near, but I now saw
if we had been ten yards farther off the carcass would have sunk
out of reach. When the trophy was secured, the Indian gave a
whoop, such as only an Indian can give, though I must confess
there were some brave attempts to imitate it right then and
there. At the death, we were scarcely a quarter of a mile from
the landing, and in full hearing of the camp, and it was a sight
worth seeing to see our two companions and the three Indians,
all of whom were in camp when the shots were fired, come rushing down to the beach to see what it all meant. It was slow
towing the deer through the lily pads, which extended out for fifty
yards or more. Before we landed, the three Indians on shore
rushed into the water, seized and dragged the deer to the bank.
He must have been a great warrior, for all the points on his
antlers were broken off. He was a big deer, and a beautiful
sight as he lay there upon the green grass. But I have spoken
of his remarkable size in another and more appropriate place.

That was one of those fortunate but unexpected chances which,
however, often occur, and which the discreet hunter will be
always prepared for. It would be difficult to recall a finer after-
noon's sport, or one with more satisfactory results.

VENISON.

SINCE the quality of the flesh depends very much upon the condition of the animal when killed, we might expect to find differences of opinion as to the quality of the venison obtained from the different species of deer, especially when these opinions are expressed by those whose opportunities to judge have not been very great.

All agree that the flesh of the Moose possesses one excellence over all other venison, in this, that the external fat which is connected with the muscle is soft, and retains its fluidity at a low temperature, while the internal fat is very hard, like the fat of all other deer. It is coarse grained, no doubt, but for all that, it is sweet and juicy, even though not in the best of order. When from an old animal it is tough, but still it is always nourishing, and for that reason it is ever esteemed where food is a desideratum. Richardson says : " The flesh of the Moose is more relished by the Indians and residents in the fur countries than that of any other animal, and principally, I believe, on account of its soft fat." The flesh of the young fat moose is always highly prized, even by epicures, whether in the camp or in the dining-room. This, like all the other deer, is in the finest condition at the commencement of the rutting season, when the flesh of even the old males is considered rich and delicious. Captain Hardy had killed a very large male Moose which John, his Indian, had called up. The next morning — " Come on, Capten," said John ; " come on and eat some Moose. This Moose be very tender ; little later in the fall not so good though ; soon get tough and black."

The flesh of this animal has always been highly esteemed in countries where it is found in Northern Europe, and at times it has contributed largely to the supply of food. It is the only venison well adapted to preservation in the barrel, with pickle or brine. In this mode it is said to be as well preserved as beef, while the flesh of all the other deer must be preserved by a drying process.

Of the quality of the venison of the larger Reindeer there is a diversity of opinion ; but the weight of authority is in favor of its excellency when it is in good order in the proper season. Captain Hardy, speaking of the Woodland Caribou, says : " Every pound of meat pays for packing it out of the woods, being, in my opinion, far finer wild meat than any other venison I have tasted." On the other hand, Richardson says of this deer : " It is much larger than the Barren-ground Caribou ; has smaller horns, and is much inferior as an article of food." However, as this is but a comparison, and, as we shall presently see, he speaks in high terms of the flesh of the smaller species, the tastes of these two observers might not be irreconcilable, at last. After all, tastes so widely differ, especially as to game food, men may well disagree as to the quality of this meat. From other sources I learn that this venison is generally very highly esteemed. I have nowhere seen a comparison made between the flesh of our Caribou and that of the European Reindeer or between that of the tame and the wild Reindeer there.

Richardson is almost our only authority that speaks directly to the quality of the venison of the Barren-ground Caribou. " The flesh of the Caribou is very tender, and its flavor when in season is, in my opinion, superior to the finest English venison ; but when the animal is lean it is very insipid ; the difference being greater between well-fed and lean Caribou than any one can conceive who has not had an opportunity of judging. The lean meat fills the stomach, but never satisfies the appetite, and scarcely serves to recruit the strength when exhausted by labor. The flesh of the moose deer and buffalo, on the other hand, is tough when lean, but is never so utterly tasteless and devoid of nourishment as that of the Caribou in poor condition." All flesh from poor animals has a larger proportion of water, and is of poorer flavor, and is less nourishing than from fat animals, even the muscle ; but we may believe from this statement of so good an observer, and having such abundant opportunities to form an opinion, that the flesh of the Barren-ground Caribou is exceptional in this regard. Whether this is a constitutional peculiarity, or results from peculiarity of food, we may not safely say. Certain it is that, in the spring or summer time, when, if they are like all the other deer, they are in the poorest condition, they get no arboreous food, being dependent entirely on the lichens of the barren grounds, only finding tree food in their southern range in the fall and winter. But then that is their principal food at all times, and is generally accredited as being very nourishing. The other species, too, depend very largely on mosses for their sustenance, although they are rarely if ever entirely dependent upon them. That the flesh of this Caribou is exceptionally tender we must believe, for even in its poorest condition nothing is said about its being tough, but only that it is tasteless or insipid, and not nourishing. I think we must admit that when it is in good condition it differs from, and is decidedly superior to all other venison.

Of the venison of our Elk I should be able to speak understandingly both of the wild animals and those raised in my grounds. The tallow of this deer, that is, the internal fat, is harder than that of any of the other deer, and almost as hard as beeswax or stearine. A temperature of 90° Fahr. seems scarcely to soften the surface appreciably. The external fat is also harder than that of any other deer, though it is not so hard as the internal fat. I think, however, after careful observation, that I may safely say that both the internal and external fat are harder in the wild Elk than in those always confined in inclosures. The greater activity and larger amount of exercise which the wild Elk gets may reasonably explain this difference. But in both the external fat is so hard as to make special precautions necessary to prepare this venison for the table in order to appreciate its full excellence. It must be served hot and kept hot, or else if there be much fat in it one will find a thin scale of the fat coating the roof of the mouth, which to most persons is very disagreeable, and for which but an indifferent compensation is found in the richest flavor and the most nutritive properties.

Ordinarily it is not so tender as the venison of the smaller deer, but it is more nutritious than any other flesh with which I am acquainted. While I have no analysis with which to make the comparison, I have found, by actual use on many occasions and with many people, that about one half the amount of Elk meat will satisfy hunger and sustain the system which would be required of good beef.

Another peculiarity is that this is the most difficult of all to preserve. The difficulty of curing Elk meat, is first mentioned by Lewis and Clarke, at their winter camp near the mouth of the Columbia River, about Christmas in 1805. They say, " Our Elk meat is spoiling in consequence of the warmth of the weather — though we have kept a constant smoke under it." Again, " The whole stock of meat being now completely spoiled our pounded fish became again our chief dependence." Elk was their only meat. I lost several lots of Elk meat, which I prepared for drying in the same way I would beef for that purpose. When cut into thinner pieces it is perfectly practicable to cure and dry it. The drying should be pretty rapid and thorough, when the prepared meat will remain sweet for an indefinite time if kept dry.

The marrow-bones of the Elk are very rich, and second only to those of the bison, and the same is true of the tongue.

I have been unable to discover any appreciable difference in the quality of the venison of the Mule Deer, the Black-tailed Deer, and the Virginia Deer. Lewis and Clarke found the venison of the Columbia Black-tailed Deer dry and hard, and condemned it as the poorest of all; but it is evident that the specimens they procured must have been in bad condition, for all since speak of it in favorable terms; it commands as high a price in the markets as any other venison, and is as much approved by epicures. For myself, I may say whenever I have had an opportunity of tasting it I have always had to resort to collateral evidence to determine what deer it was from.

The venison of the Mule Deer I have, with few exceptions, only eaten in camp; and it must be admitted that a hard day's tramp in the mountains makes any dish that is really good taste very good, and has a tendency to destroy that nice discrimination which would enable one to detect the flavor of the mule's hoof in the mushroom soup, when the vegetable had been crushed by the tread of that animal. Still I doubt if any one can distinguish the flesh of the Mule Deer from that of the common deer.

Almost every one, in America at least, is familiar with the venison of the Virginia Deer. While a few persons cannot eat it, and others dislike it, to say the least, a majority of mankind admire it as food, and others esteem it above all other flesh. It is dark colored, is fine grained, and has a flavor peculiarly its own. When cooked without accessories it is dryer than beef, but is tenderer, *ceteris paribus.* This venison is tender and nourishing, and of good flavor, even in the summer time when the animal is always poor, though of course far inferior to the luscious feast afforded by the fat buck just at the commencement of the rut, when he fairly swells out with new made fat and flesh, which he has taken on in an incredibly short time. At this time I think the buck in the prime of life affords the best and most substantial venison, but at no time will the same quantity nourish the system as much as beef of the same quality, and so is vastly inferior in this respect to the venison of the Elk.

It is not admired when corned like beef or the flesh of the Moose, but when dried it is extremely delicate and nice, and inexpressibly superior to dried beef. Indeed, it is only when you cut into the dried ham of the deer that you can fully appreciate its delicate, tender texture, and its rich flavor. It is very readily cured by drying. Take the venison ham, hang it up by the shank, even in the ordinary kitchen, divide the muscles just above the hock and insert a handful of dry salt, and it will then cure to absolute perfection. It keeps a long time without curing, before it becomes tainted, and, of course, improves in tenderness and flavor all the time.

When the Indians jerk it they cut it into thin strips or sheets, and hang it upon poles over a slow fire, not sufficiently strong to absolutely cook it, and yet it does become partially cooked, as well as smoked and dried, and, if thoroughly done, it becomes as dry as a chip, and will break short off, like a biscuit, unless the strip is pretty thick. Still, it retains its flavor and sustenance, and makes an excellent soup, for which it should be pounded pretty fine. It is very good *au naturel*, and is a convenient lunch to take into the woods.

I can only conjecture as to the quality of the venison of the Acapulco Deer. To do this is unnecessary.

THE SKINS.

In texture, the skins of all the deer are alike. They consist of a mass of felted fibres, and are soft, spongy, and elastic, from which the epidermis is easily separated. These properties admirably adapt them to supply the place of cloth in the clothing of the natives, and so constitute their principal material for dress. The principal articles used by the Indians in tanning these skins are brains and smoke, though the latter is frequently omitted, especially by the western tribes. In the cold countries the skins are usually tanned with the hair on, which is sometimes worn inside, and sometimes outside. In the temperate and tropical climates the hair is removed from the skin before it is tanned, unless it is designed to be used as a robe.

Whenever the skin is thick and heavy it is chipped away on the flesh side till it is so reduced as to make it even and pliable, and convenient for use. In this way they reject the weakest part of the skin.

The skin of the Moose is thick and heavy, and always requires to be reduced to fit it for use as clothing, or even for robes. Although coarse-grained it is strong and serviceable. Here is what Richardson says, speaking of the Moose Deer: "Their skins, when properly dressed, make a soft, thick, pliable leather, excellently adapted for moccasins, or other articles of winter clothing. The Dog-ribs excel in the art of dressing the skins, which is done in the following manner : They are first scraped to an equal thickness throughout, and the hair taken off by a scraper made of the shin-bone of the deer, split longitudinally ; they are then repeatedly moistened and rubbed, after being smeared with the brains of the animal until they acquire a soft, spongy feel ; and, lastly, they are suspended over a fire, made of rotten wood, until they are well impregnated with the smoke. This last mentioned process imparts a peculiar odor to the leather, and has the effect of preventing it from becoming so hard, after being wet, as it would otherwise do." In fact, this describes the mode of tanning the skins of all the deer, by the different Indian tribes, who depend so largely upon them for their clothing, except that the hair is frequently allowed to remain, especially on the skins of the reindeer. The same author says, when treating of the Barren-ground Caribou : " The hide dressed with the fur is, as has been already mentioned, excellent for winter clothing, and supplies the place of both blanket and feather-bed, to the inhabitants of the Arctic wilds. When subjected to the process described in the article on the Moose Deer it forms a soft and pliable leather, adapted for moccasins and summer clothing, or, when sixty or seventy skins are sewed together, they make a tent sufficient for the residence of a large family." " The undressed hide, after the hair is taken off, is cut into thongs of various thickness, which are twisted into deer-snares, bow-strings, net-lines, and, in fact, supply all the purposes of rope. The finer thongs are used in the manufacture of fishing-nets, or in making snow-shoes ; while the tendons of the dorsal muscles are split into fine and excellent sewing-thread."

The portion of the skin of the Moose most prized for moccasins is that about the hock, which is peeled down without being cut open, is properly tanned with the hair on, and sewed up at the lower end, and is found to be well shaped by nature for the foot. The skin from the leg is firmer, and is more impervious to the water than that of the body, and the hair there is shorter, firmer, and more enduring than on other parts.

The skin of the Wapiti Deer is less tenacious and less enduring than that of any other of the species. This fact was discovered by Lewis and Clarke, much to their cost. To cover their iron-framed boat above the falls of the Missouri, they selected Elk skins in preference to the skins of the buffalo, because they supposed they were " more strong and durable," but when it was too late they discovered their error, and the boat had to be abandoned.

But my own experiments have been conclusive as to the comparative worthlessness of the skin of the Elk. I have had them tanned by various processes and into various kinds of leather. I had a prime buck skin tanned into harness leather. It was soft and pliable, but had very little strength and endurance. Hitching-straps made from it seemed very nice, but their tensile strength was very low, and they actually wore out by a few weeks' use. Several skins from young Elk less than a year old, tanned into shoe leather, appear all that could be desired for shoes or soft boots, but they have so little strength that they can be torn in two by the hands like a piece of muslin, while I find all the skins of the other species of deer which I have in confinement, tanned in the same way, as strong as if tanned by the

Indian process, and this, too, when the skins are from animals of all ages. Even the skins of those which died in the grounds, and very poor, although very thin and light, are as strong in proportion to their thickness as those from animals in prime condition, and prové wonderfully enduring when worn as slippers. The grain takes a good polish, though it is easily broken by rough usage. This shows that the mode of tanning did not destroy the tenacity or durability of the Elk skins.

I have had many Elk skins tanned for robes, when the skin proves sufficiently enduring to wear out the hair, which is so fragile that it is soon worn off if used as cushions or beds, though the under-fur still remains. But the loss of the ends of the long hair gives it an unsightly appearance, and it becomes of little value. If used carefully as a lap robe or covering, it endures for a long time, and is very warm and comfortable, though if the animal was in full winter coat, the burden of hair is so heavy as to make its use rather inconvenient.

What has been already said sufficiently explains the value and the uses of the skins of the common deer, the mule deer, and the Columbia deer. These are indistinguishable when tanned in any known mode. The skins of all our deer, then, when properly tanned, make fine, soft, and enduring leather, except that of the Elk, which, though pliable, is comparatively of little value where strength and endurance are desirable. It would be interesting to know whether the skin of the red deer of Europe, an animal which possesses all the other peculiarities of Wapiti, resembles it in this particular also.

It is no doubt remarkable that this exceptional quality of the Elk skin has been so rarely alluded to by those who have had extensive opportunities to observe it. It must be well known among the Indians and the fur traders, and yet I find them nowhere complaining that the Elk skin is valueless, though I nowhere learn that it is purchased by the traders like the skins of the other deer. Even Richardson, who so rarely overlooks anything of interest, makes no mention of it, though he says the skin of the antelope is considered nearly valueless by the Indians and traders, and yet a string cut from the skin of the Elk fifteen times as heavy as that cut from the antelope skin, is not as strong, and probably would not have a hundredth part the endurance when used as a string about a pack-saddle, for instance.

APPENDIX.

——♦——

At the last moment, I am enabled to present in this form the following abstract of a paper by Mr. Robert Morrow, read before the Institute of Natural Science, Halifax, N. S., April 9, 1877, deeply regretting that I was not enabled to present its important facts in the text. Mr. Morrow's examination and description of the cyst in the neck of the Caribou, first mentioned by Hutchins, and his comparison of it with that found by Mr. Camper in the Reindeer, are of especial value. His observations are made with an intelligent care, and described with a particularity, which enable us to understand the subject almost as if we had made the examination ourselves.

The examination of the interdigital glands or tubes between the toes of the Caribou and the Moose, by himself and Drs. Gilpin and Sommers, are of very great importance, and were evidently made with great care and intelligence. In the text I have suggested the probability that these members would be found wanting in the Moose, as I had found them wanting in the wapiti deer. This paper of Mr. Morrow settles that matter, and shows that they exist in the Moose to about the extent they are found in the Caribou. With this new and important information before us, I may here repeat, that these glands, which are found in the feet of deer, and are wanting in the feet of all other ruminants, so far as I am informed, lack the constancy, and hence reliability of the other glandular members peculiar to the Cervidæ.

Mr. Morrow deserves our thanks for this valuable contribution to zoölogical science. He informs me that a similar abstract has been furnished to "Forest and Stream," in which it will shortly appear.

Abstract of a Paper, read April 9, 1877, before the Institute of Natural Science, Halifax, N. S., by R. Morrow, entitled "Notes on the Caribou."

Mr. Morrow said, that the paper owed its origin to the following quotation from Sir John Richardson's "Fauna Boreali-Americana," pages 250 and 251. Mr. Hutchins "mentions that the buck (Caribou) has a peculiar bag or cist on the lower part of the neck, about the bigness of a crown piece, and filled with fine flaxen hair, neatly curled round to the thickness of an inch. There is an opening through the skin, near the head, leading to the cist, but Mr. Hutchins does not offer a conjecture as to its uses in the economy of the animal. Camper found a membranous cist on the Reindeer above the thyroid cartilage, and opening into the larynx, but I have met with no account of a cist with a duct opening externally like that described by Mr. Hutchins, and, unfortunately, I was not aware of his remarks until the means of ascertaining whether such a sac exists in the Barren-ground Caribou were beyond my reach."

Mr. Morrow had several times looked for the cyst without success, but always forgot to do so for the sac; and, in order to obtain some information on both points, he went to the woods in December last, and succeeded in killing a large buck, the result of the examination of which, and dissection of others, male and female, made since, he would place before the Institute. But first, he thought it necessary to give Camper's description of the membranous sac from a Reindeer "four years old." Camper says,[1] " that as he did not know the Reindeer, and as the imperfect account which Valentyn gave of Stenons's dissection in 1672, did not give him much light, he was forced to proceed with caution (date, June, 1771). He had often observed in the bucks, that when these animals swallowed, all the larynx rose and fell in a peculiar manner, and seemed to indicate something singular in this part. He then removed the skin of the neck with much care. The muscles being raised in the same way, he found a membranous sac, which had its origin between the os hyoides and the thyroid cartilage. He then discovered two muscles, which take their origin from the lower part of the os hyoides, exactly where the base of the os graniform and the cornua meet. These muscles were flat and thin at their beginning, but widened towards their junction with the sac, and certainly served to support it as well as to expel the air from it at the will of the animal. After he had opened the œsophagus from behind, he found under the base of the epiglottis a large orifice which admitted his finger very easily. This orifice spread, and formed a membranous canal, which passed between the two muscles already mentioned, terminating in the membranous sac. Consequently the air driven from the lungs into the larynx fell into this sac, and necessarily caused a considerable swelling."

Mr. Morrow said that when he shot the buck alluded to, he had not seen the account by Camper of the sac, and his specimen is not therefore so perfect as it might otherwise have been. Examining the outside of the throat of the animal the cyst of Mr. Hutchins, with " an opening through the skin," does not exist; but immediately under the skin, there was a roundish sub-triangular cyst or valve of cellular membrane of the " bigness of a crown piece," and on cutting through the cellular membrane, this " valve " is found to be a closed sac having a peculiar lining membrane, and closely packed with what may be called loose hairs of a flaxen color, in a considerable quantity of sebaceous matter; at the same time, however, the lining membrane is covered by hairs of the same quality growing from and rather lightly attached to it. Camper in his account has described this valve as if it were the sac, and his drawing gives only the valve, which the larynx exhibited by Mr. Morrow plainly shows. The muscles which Camper describes as connecting the sac with the os hyoides, in Mr. Morrow's specimen do not exist, but their representatives are probably the muscles found in the larynx of the young buck by Dr. Sommers, as will later appear. The valve is connected with the omo-hyoid muscles as they pass to-

---

[1] Camper, vol. i., chap. vi., page 338, Paris, 1803, where reference is made by letters to a plate, which cannot be done here.

wards their insertion in the hyoid bone. The valve which Camper has evidently taken to be the sac lies outside of the mucous sac, but is incorporated with its anterior walls; the inner wall of the true sac surrounds and is attached to the larynx extending longitudinally from the hyoid bone to the base of the thyroid cartilage, how much further it may extend cannot, from the imperfect state of the specimen already mentioned, be determined, and at present the writer would only call it an organ of voice. The slit or orifice exists as Camper describes, but opens into the laryngeal sac, which lies above the valve that is next the larynx. The dimensions of this larynx are as follows: —

Length of larynx from base of epiglottis to base of thyroid cartilage . . . . 0.5 inches.
Circumference of larynx . . . . 0.11 inches.
Inside diameter of larynx . . . . 0.2 inches.

The age of the reindeer which Camper dissected, he said was " four years," but " it had not attained its full growth." It is therefore possible that the sac was not fully developed. The muscles described by him taken in connection with those found in the young buck make this very probable.

Mr. Morrow said that he had made every exertion to obtain a more perfect specimen of the larynx from an old buck, but without success. A small buck eight months old was sent to him and dissected by Dr. Sommers, Dr. Gilpin, and himself on the 27th January; and a female calf nine months old and an adult doe was put at his disposal by Mr. T. J. Egan, and dissected February 19. Mr. Morrow gave an account of the dissection of these three animals taken from the notes of Dr. Sommers; with reference to the larynx, very much abridged, it was as follows : In the young buck the organ existed as described in the adult animal, but in an immature state; it would probably be developed with the growth of the animal; the muscles were not found as in the adult animal, but arising apparently from the base of the epiglottis on either side, possibly continuous with the thyro-epiglottidean and aryteno-epiglottidean muscles, are two bands of muscular fibres passing over on either side of a body which probably would develop and form the valve in the adult, and are connected with it by fibrous adhesions; extending forwards they unite at its upper border, forming a single muscular band which becomes inserted into the upper and inner edge of the hyoid bone. These fibres have no analogues in man. Under the microscope the structure forming this body (which was about the size of a small horse-bean) was found to consist mostly of fatty tissue with a moderate proportion of granular cells. This body, which would form the valve, was absent in the doe and very rudimentary in the female fawn.

Camper pointed out that the female reindeer is without this organ in the larynx, and also that it is not present in the male fallow deer, and from a specimen exhibited it was seen that it was not in the Virginia deer.

Inside of the hock of the Caribou there is a patch of hair of a lighter color and somewhat longer than that which covers the skin in its immediate neighborhood, and the skin under this patch is slightly thicker than that immediately around it. This spot is usually called a " gland." It is caused by an enlargement of the hair follicles, has a very strong smell, and in the Caribou is a scent " gland." The matter producing this scent is entirely different from that contained in the tubes; it appears to be a highly volatile oil, and resists salt for a long time after the rest of the skin has become saturated; when dry it collects on the outside of the skin in the form of very small scales, such as would be left by minute portions of varnish. Although Mr. Morrow did not see the animal use this so called " gland," yet his Indian hunter saw a doe Caribou use it in this way: when she had finished urinating (she squats in the act almost exactly like a sheep) she rubbed these glands together, leaving true scent behind her for a short distance. When creeping moose or Caribou, this scent floating in the air had often been with him a subject of inquiry, and he had very little doubt but that this was at least one way in which these glands are used, and in confirmation he mentioned that the dogs, at one time openly used for hunting moose, did not often take the scent of that animal from the snow, but by standing upon their hind legs as if it had been rubbed from glands as described. The point was merely mentioned in the hope that some gentleman present would be able to throw some light upon it, or keep it in mind when an opportunity offered for observation, confirmatory or otherwise.

A little further down the leg, on the outside at the hair parting, he showed the "metatarsal gland," which had been looked for during a long period by Dr. Gilpin, Mr. T. J. Egan, and himself in answer to an inquiry from the Honorable Judge Caton. This was the first they had ever seen. and may probably be taken as a mark of adult age. It was afterwards found in the old doe, but not so perfectly marked, possibly because the doe was killed in February, the buck in December.

Attention was also drawn to the tubes in the feet of the Caribou, which first attracted the notice of Dr. Gilpin from inquiries made by Judge Caton. Dr. Gilpin as well as others thought that they were only to be found in the hind feet, and the discovery of them in the fore feet of the Caribou is due entirely to Dr. Sommers.

Camper says, speaking of these tubes: "In addition to the peculiarities of the reindeer of which I have just spoken, I have discovered besides something very singular in the hind feet of this animal, that is to say, a deep sheath between the skin at the place where the dew-claws are united together, of the size of the barrel of a quill, running deeply as far as the point where the dew-claws are articulated with the bone of the metatarsus. These sheaths were filled internally with long hairs, and a yellow oleaginous matter proceeded from them, the odor of which was not very agreeable. I have not found these sheaths in the fore feet. It was not possible for me to discover the use of them, inasmuch as the heat of the summer obliged me to remove the flesh from the skeleton." And further on he says that in another reindeer he found no tube in the hind foot, but one very apparent in the fore foot, and again, he found tubes in the hind feet, but none in the fore feet. " So that I am not able to determine anything very exactly on this subject."

In the skin of one of the hind legs of the old buck, the bones of which had been removed for the purpose, the tube was shown (the tube of the other foot had been used in experiments), and also a number of other specimens of tubes from the Caribou, one from the Virginia deer, and the hind foot of a moose, containing a tube. In the skin of the fore feet of the old buck Caribou, also exhibited, there was no appearance of the tubes, they had been absorbed. By many, Mr. Morrow said, these tubes were considered to be scent "glands." Camper evidently did not think them so, although he mentions that the skin of the hind as well as the fore feet " were sprinkled with glandules which probably·

give out an oleaginous matter intended to protect the hoof against the snow." Prior to December last, Mr. Morrow said that he had paid very little attention to these tubes, and had the question been asked him, Were they scent glands ? the answer might have been affirmative, but after a careful examination of the animal while warm, he had come to the conclusion that these tubes are not "glands," properly so called. His first view, that the tubes were for the purpose of strengthening the bones of the feet of this animal in its spring, from further examination of a number of fresh tubes, and from the observations of Dr. Sommers, does not now appear to be tenable, and for his own part he had to adopt Camper's statement, and could not say what was their use; but they are not scent "glands," if they were it seemed scarcely probable that as the buck comes to maturity he would be deprived of the means of leaving scent from his fore feet at the time when he most required it, without taking into consideration the fact that the tube only exists in the fore feet of the male (up to an unknown age) or in the female in a rudimentary state.

The waxy matter is contained in the tubes of the hind feet of the Caribou, and in all the tubes in the feet of the Virginia deer, owing to their shape, and the disagreeable smell ascribed to this matter is due to the quantity of it retained in a narrow compass. The tubes of the Caribou are rather wider in the mouth and of more equal diameter to their lower end than those of the Virginia deer, which at their opening are somewhat narrow and widen towards their centre. The Moose, contrary to preconceived ideas (and this shows how little our animals are studied), also has tubes on its feet, fully developed in the hind, rudimentary in the fore feet, but of a very different shape from those of the Caribou and Virginia deer, being in the hind feet very wide at the mouth and gradually tapering towards their lower extremities; these from their shape can retain but little if any waxy matter.

In general terms, the buck Caribou when young has the tubes in the fore feet in a rudimentary form, which instead of passing upward and backward to the skin close to the dew-claws, as in the developed tube of the hind feet, lie between and nearly parallel with the bones of the feet, and they are gradually absorbed until certainly in the adult male they entirely disappear ; the doe has them also perfectly developed in the hind and rudimentary in the fore feet, and it is a question which is yet to be decided whether these tubes ever entirely fade out of the feet of the doe. In the old doe the tubes although small are still plainly to be seen. A young moose, in possession of Mr. J. W. Stairs, has the tubes in all its feet, those in the hind feet are perfectly developed, and pass, as in the Caribou, between the phalanges; in the fore feet they are, as in the Caribou of the same age, only rudimentary, but at what time of life they disappear on this animal, or whether in male or female, or both, cannot, owing to our prohibitory law, at present, be decided.

Mr. Morrow said that it had been shown that the Caribou and moose have the tubes developed in the hind and rudimentary in the fore feet. An examination of a Wapiti or Elk (*Cervus Canadensis*) skin with feet attached, in Mr. Egan's collection, presented the fact, confirmed by Judge Caton, that this animal has no tube in any foot, and that its feet are of a different shape from those of the Moose, Caribou, or Virginia deer, and that the phalanges are very much shorter in proportion to the size of the animal in the specimen referred to than in the Caribou or Virginia deer ; from the metacarpo-phalangeal articulation to the point of the hoof they measure seven inches, while those of the

27

young buck Caribou measured $7\frac{1}{4}$ inches, of the old doe $7\frac{1}{2}$ inches, and of the old buck 9 inches. The gentleman already referred to informed him that the Wapiti is a natural trotter, [1] " he, however, can and does run much faster than he can trot, but it is a labored effort and soon tires him out." " His run is an awkward, lumbering, rolling gallop. A few hundred yards of this gait tells. It is said that an elk will trot at an equal speed without stopping or even flagging, for twenty miles." The Virginia deer has a tube in each foot fully developed, which led him to inquire the gait of this animal, his impression that it would prove to be a running deer being confirmed. The inference he wished to draw was this, that the number of tubes in the feet of the different species of deer will point out the gait of the animal, those which have a tube fully developed in each foot should be bounders or runners, while those wanting the tubes, or having them partially developed in the fore and fully in the hind feet should be trotters. This point, as far as he was aware, had never been touched upon by any naturalist, and as it could not be pursued here, he mentioned it in the hope that it may be examined into by those who have access to a number of different species of deer.

Returning to the tubes, Mr. Morrow stated that as his notes upon them were only those of a hunter and therefore of very little scientific value, he would use those of Dr. Sommers, as follows : —

In the observations here annexed I have endeavored to furnish an accurate description of the so-called " interdigital glands," which exist in the feet of the Caribou, by subjecting them to very careful anatomical and microscopical inspection. The conclusion at which I arrive relative to their structure and functions is that they are not glandular in the correct meaning of that term, an opinion which coincides with that which you previously expressed.

This organ presents the appearance of a fleshy tube with thick walls and a rounded blind extremity like that of a small test tube flattened on its posterior or under side, convex on its upper or anterior side; that from the young buck being about one and a half inches in length below, somewhat shorter above; its circumference about three quarters of an inch; it tapers slightly towards its termination; when viewed in position it bears a striking resemblance to the human "uvula." The surface exposed by dissection exhibits a structure consisting of rounded or slightly polygonal spaces resembling very large cells; these are convex, of a deep red color, and united by paler interspaces. The whole organ has the appearance of a body constituted of immense cells united by their thin cell walls; this, however, is deceptive, these spaces are the rounded terminations or bases of the bulbs or follicles from which the hairs inside of the sac grow; the resemblance to cellular interspaces arises from the pressure of a very delicate layer of true skin upon which they rest, and which has been pushed into these interspaces by the growth of the hair follicles; the same structure can be observed in other parts of the skin by dissecting off the true skin which is underneath from the epithelial layer which covers it and gives origin to the hairs; but here the spaces observed are much smaller, since the hairs and their bulbs are more crowded, the space occupied by each bulb being less than in the cul-de-sac, or organ under notice.

The organ in the fore, differs from that in the hind feet by being very shallow, measuring not over a quarter of an inch in depth; when dissected from the surrounding tissue, it presents all the characteristics of the organ in the

[1] *Plains of the Great West,* by Col. Dodge, pages 164 and 166.

hind feet, yet it differs in position relative to the phalangeal bones, lying on the same plane as that of the anterior wall of the web, its own anterior wall being incorporated with the under surface of the skin and thereby shortened to about one quarter of an inch in length; the posterior wall, however, remains distinct and measures from the blind extremity to its termination somewhat over an inch.

The microscopic examination of this organ proved it to be of epidermic origin. Sections through the thickness of its walls showed an external layer of flattened prismoidal cells with small nuclei, and a deeper or internal layer, in which the cells were more rounded and filled with protoplasm. This difference in the uppermost and lowermost layer was brought out by the staining process, and it is in these only that we find the line of demarcation, the intervening layers merging gradually one into the other. Other structures observed were the hairs and hair follicles with their accompanying tissues and some fibres, representing no doubt the true skin, which is not developed in these organs to any considerable extent.

The two layers of cells correspond to the same parts in man, namely, a horny layer external, but of course internal in the cul-de-sac, a mucous layer external when the sac is dissected from its surroundings, the changed position of these layers is owing to the circumstance of the sac's being an invagination of the epidermic layer into the true skin.

Regarding the functions of this structure various and contradictory opinions are expressed, that of its being glandular being most prevalent ; again it is said to have no existence in the wapiti and moose and in the fore feet of the adult Caribou. The fact of its existence in fore and hind feet of the Virginia deer being well understood, its presence in the animal is said to be for the purpose of leaving a trace or scent on the ground, and in this way serving the union of the sexes at certain seasons ; but if this is the case, we may ask why should it not exist in the wapiti, and be fully developed in the Caribou and moose, since it must be obvious to us that the fulfillment of the conditions which obtain in the Virginia deer, are required also in the wapiti. More than this, we know that a true scent organ in the Caribou is situated on the inside of the heels or gambrils.

On the occasion of my first dissection of this structure in the Caribou buck fawn, I expressed the opinion that it would be found also in the fore feet of the adult animal, though perhaps more rudimentary, and a subsequent examination of an adult doe has fully confirmed this opinion, since I found this structure as well developed as in the young animal. I now feel more than ever convinced that it exists in all our deer tribe, not excluding the wapiti, although it may be larger in some than in others; an immature living moose, in possession of Mr. J. W. Stairs, being provided with it.

The following summary of its histological relations will aid in arriving at correct conclusions relative to its importance : —

1st. It is a growth or offset from the epidermic layer of the skin invaginated between the phalangeal bones, containing the malpighian and horny layers of the epidermis, and carrying with it a very thin layer of the true skin.

2d. Hair follicles, and hairs grow from its internal walls, and emerge through its opening, these being also epidermic, or of epithelial origin.

3d. The absence of glandular tissue, excepting the sebaceous follicles which accompany the hair follicles or bulbs over the whole integument of the animal, "this excèption is made for obvious anatomical reasons," nevertheless the sebaceous follicles were not observed in the specimens examined with the microscope.

4th. The examination of the matter filling the tubes in the Virginia deer, and present in much smaller proportion in the Caribou, showed it to consist in principal part of desquamated epidermic scales and oil globules. Microscopically it resembled smegma from the skin of man, or perhaps closer still, the " vernix caseosa " from that of a recently delivered infant ; remembering that the epidermis in man and in all animals is a non-vascular tissue, that, unlike our other tissue, it is shelled off from the surface, we can readily account for these desquamated scales being retained here in a narrow pocket, from which they could not be easily discharged. Retrograde changes in these cells, secretions from sebaceous and sweat glands in adjacent parts, will account not only for the oily matter seen, the viscidity of the substance, but also for the odor which it possesses, the latter being no greater than that of the general integument, and arises from the same cause, namely, the perspiration ; but in this respect they are not in any degree comparable with the glandular collection at the hocks before mentioned, which will retain the peculiar odor of the animal for a long period after the removal of the skin.

In presence of these facts we must conclude that this organ is only rudimentary, having no function which is obvious to us; it is not a secreting organ, since it lacks glandular tissue; the opening in the dorsum instead of the sole of the foot, would point also in this way ; it does not serve to give strength or firmness to the foot, having none of the toughness and elasticity of the skin in other parts, without comparison with the tendons, etc., which are provided for this purpose (some instances of organs without uses were also given). From an individual point of view, taking in all the circumstances referred to, there appear to be only two ways of accounting for this structure ; it is either an aborted "ungual follicle," or otherwise it is a cul-de-sac, representing the suture formed by coalescence of the skin from side to side in the fœtus. Its structure would convince one of the first conclusion if the animal had rudimentary toe bones in the same position, indicative of a three-toed ancestor ; but all observations relative to the morphology of the foot are opposed to this view, since the outer bones and their appendages are aborted in all animals of this kind; we are therefore compelled to adopt the other view, which can only be settled satisfactorily by examination of the part in the fœtus. Nevertheless, knowing the difficulty of substantiating any theory connected with its supposed origin and use, still more the difficulty of ridding one's mind of a theory once entertained, my faith in either of these is held very loosely.

The paper concluded with some general observations by Mr. Morrow, and a conversation in which a number of the members of the Institute took part.

INDEX.

NATURAL SCIENCES IN AMERICA

An Arno Press Collection

Allen, J[oel] A[saph]. **The American Bisons,** Living and Extinct. 1876

Allen, Joel Asaph. **History of the North American Pinnipeds:** A Monograph of the Walruses, Sea-Lions, Sea-Bears and Seals of North America. 1880

American Natural History Studies: The Bairdian Period. 1974

American Ornithological Bibliography. 1974

Anker, Jean. **Bird Books and Bird Art.** 1938

Audubon, John James and John Bachman. **The Quadrupeds of North America.** Three vols. 1854

Baird, Spencer F[ullerton]. **Mammals of North America.** 1859

Baird, S[pencer] F[ullerton], T[homas] M. Brewer and R[obert] Ridgway. **A History of North American Birds:** Land Birds. Three vols., 1874

Baird, Spencer F[ullerton], John Cassin and George N. Lawrence. **The Birds of North America.** 1860. Two vols. in one.

Baird, S[pencer] F[ullerton], T[homas] M. Brewer, and R[obert] Ridgway. **The Water Birds of North America.** 1884. Two vols. in one.

Barton, Benjamin Smith. **Notes on the Animals of North America.** Edited, with an Introduction by Keir B. Sterling. 1792

Bendire, Charles [Emil]. **Life Histories of North American Birds** With Special Reference to Their Breeding Habits and Eggs. 1892/1895. Two vols. in one.

Bonaparte, Charles Lucian [Jules Laurent]. **American Ornithology:** Or The Natural History of Birds Inhabiting the United States, Not Given by Wilson. 1825/1828/1833. Four vols. in one.

Cameron, Jenks. **The Bureau of Biological Survey:** Its History, Activities, and Organization. 1929

Caton, John Dean. **The Antelope and Deer of America:** A Comprehensive Scientific Treatise Upon the Natural History, Including the Characteristics, Habits, Affinities, and Capacity for Domestication of the Antilocapra and Cervidae of North America. 1877

Contributions to American Systematics. 1974

Contributions to the Bibliographical Literature of American Mammals. 1974

Contributions to the History of American Natural History. 1974

Contributions to the History of American Ornithology. 1974

Cooper, J[ames] G[raham].   **Ornithology.** Volume I, Land Birds. 1870

Cope, E[dward] D[rinker].   **The Origin of the Fittest:** Essays on Evolution and **The Primary Factors of Organic Evolution.** 1887/1896. Two vols. in one.

Coues, Elliott.   **Birds of the Colorado Valley.** 1878

Coues, Elliott.   **Birds of the Northwest.** 1874

Coues, Elliott.   **Key To North American Birds.** Two vols. 1903

Early Nineteenth-Century Studies and Surveys. 1974

Emmons, Ebenezer.   **American Geology:** Containing a Statement of the Principles of the Science. 1855. Two vols. in one.

Fauna Americana. 1825-1826

Fisher, A[lbert] K[enrick].   **The Hawks and Owls of the United States in Their Relation to Agriculture.** 1893

Godman, John D.   **American Natural History:** Part I — Mastology and **Rambles of a Naturalist.** 1826-28/1833. Three vols. in one.

Gregory, William King.   **Evolution Emerging:** A Survey of Changing Patterns from Primeval Life to Man. Two vols. 1951

Hay, Oliver Perry.   **Bibliography and Catalogue of the Fossil Vertebrata of North America.** 1902

Heilprin, Angelo.   **The Geographical and Geological Distribution of Animals.** 1887

Hitchcock, Edward.   **A Report on the Sandstone of the Connecticut Valley,** Especially Its Fossil Footmarks. 1858

Hubbs, Carl L., editor.   **Zoogeography.** 1958

[Kessel, Edward L., editor].   **A Century of Progress in the Natural Sciences:** 1853-1953. 1955

Leidy, Joseph.   **The Extinct Mammalian Fauna of Dakota and Nebraska,** Including an Account of Some Allied Forms from Other Localities, Together with a Synopsis of the Mammalian Remains of North America. 1869

Lyon, Marcus Ward, Jr.   **Mammals of Indiana.** 1936

Matthew, W[illiam] D[iller].   **Climate and Evolution.** 1915

Mayr, Ernst, editor.   **The Species Problem.** 1957

Mearns, Edgar Alexander.   **Mammals of the Mexican Boundary of the United States.** Part I: Families Didelphiidae to Muridae. 1907

Merriam, Clinton Hart. **The Mammals of the Adirondack Region,** Northeastern New York. 1884

Nuttall, Thomas. **A Manual of the Ornithology of the United States and of Canada.** Two vols. 1832-1834

Nuttall Ornithological Club. **Bulletin of the Nuttall Ornithological Club:** A Quarterly Journal of Ornithology. 1876-1883. Eight vols. in three.

[Pennant, Thomas]. **Arctic Zoology. 1784-1787.** Two vols. in one.

Richardson, John. **Fauna Boreali-Americana;** Or the Zoology of the Northern Parts of British America, Containing Descriptions of the Objects of Natural History Collected on the Late Northern Land Expeditions Under Command of Captain Sir John Franklin, R. N. Part I: Quadrupeds. 1829

Richardson, John and William Swainson. **Fauna Boreali-Americana:** Or the Zoology of the Northern Parts of British America, Containing Descriptions of the Objects of Natural History Collected by the Late Northern Land Expeditions Under Command of Captain Sir John Franklin, R. N. Part II: The Birds. 1831

Ridgway, Robert. **Ornithology.** 1877

Selected Works By Eighteenth-Century Naturalists and Travellers. 1974

Selected Works in Nineteenth-Century North American Paleontology. 1974

Selected Works of Clinton Hart Merriam. 1974

Selected Works of Joel Asaph Allen. 1974

Selections From the Literature of American Biogeography. 1974

Seton, Ernest Thompson. **Life-Histories of Northern Animals: An Account of the Mammals of Manitoba.** Two vols. 1909

Sterling, Keir Brooks. **Last of the Naturalists:** The Career of C. Hart Merriam. 1974

Vieillot, L. P. **Histoire Naturelle Des Oiseaux de L'Amerique Septentrionale,** Contenant Un Grand Nombre D'Especes Decrites ou Figurees Pour La Premiere Fois. 1807. Two vols. in one.

Wilson, Scott B., assisted by A. H. Evans. **Aves Hawaiienses:** The Birds of the Sandwich Islands. 1890-99

Wood, Casey A., editor. **An Introduction to the Literature of Vertebrate Zoology.** 1931

Zimmer, John Todd. **Catalogue of the Edward E. Ayer Ornithological Library.** 1926